THE LEADERS WE DESERVED

(AND A FEW WE DIDN'T)

THE LEADERS
WE DESERVED

(AND A FEW WE DIDN'T)

Rethinking the Presidential Rating Game

ALVIN S. FELZENBERG

A Member of the Perseus Books Group
New York

To my friend, Robert P. O'Quinn,
who patiently tries to teach me economics.

Published by Basic Books,
A Member of the Perseus Books Group

Books published by Basic Books are available at special discounts for bulk purchases in the
United States by corporations, institutions, and other organizations. For more information,
please contact the Special Markets Department at the Perseus Books Group, 2300 Chestnut
Street, Suite 200, Philadelphia, PA 19103, or call
(800) 810-4145, ext. 5000, or e-mail special.markets@perseusbooks.com.

Designed by Linda Harper

Library of Congress Cataloging-in-Publication Data

Felzenberg, Alvin S.
The leaders we deserved (and a few we didn't) : rethinking the presidential rating game
/ Alvin S. Felzenberg.
    p. cm.
Includes bibliographical references and index.
ISBN 978-0-465-00291-7 (alk. paper)
 1. Presidents—United States—Biography.   2. Presidents—United States—History.
 3. Presidents—Rating of—United States.   4. Political leadership—United States—
Case studies.   5. United States—Politics and government—Case studies.   I. Title.

E176.1.F43 2008
973.09'9—dc22

                                                                            2008005058

PB ISBN: 978-0-465-018901

10 9 8 7 6 5 4 3 2 1

Contents

PREFACE

What makes a president a great president? Since the presidency was established in 1789, Americans have asked themselves that question. In order to help answer it, historians and other experts have surveyed their peers. Most of these assessments say more about what evaluators thought of the nation's presidents than about the criteria they used in forming their conclusions.

Most of these surveys place the nation's presidents into one of six categories: great, near great, high average, low average, below average, and failure.

These surveys suffer from a number of weaknesses. For example, their results often reflect the ideological predilections of the evaluators. While this flaw can easily be remedied by assuring greater balance in the choice of participants, other problems inherent in this process cannot. Failure to set forth precise criteria has been already noted. Equally troubling has been the tendency of some jurors to reflect the findings of past surveys. Being too far out of step with the prevailing consensus among one's peers may call one's status as an expert into question.

In the dozen or more surveys since Arthur M. Schlesinger Sr. commenced what this book calls "the presidential rating game" in 1948, only two presidents have seen their ratings substantially change. Because scholars' interpretation of the Reconstruction era began to change during the civil rights revolution of the 1960s, Andrew Johnson, once considered an average president, is now rated a failure. The opening of Dwight D. Eisenhower's papers a decade or so after he left office shed new light on his managerial style and administrative competence. Consequently, survey participants have moved Ike from the ranks of low average into the company of the near greats. In most other cases, the uniformity of presidential rankings in most surveys bears a closer resemblance to an echo chamber than to a serious attempt to interpret history and impart knowledge. Even the briefest perusal of presidential biographies suggests that very few presidents performed equally well or equally poorly in all areas. Those ranked among the near greats sometimes failed, while many average or worse presidents performed some tasks admirably. These are seldom reflected in their ratings.

Woodrow Wilson, for instance, traditionally rated as near great, set back the cause of equal opportunity for African Americans considerably during his eight years in the White House. This has not had a discernible effect upon his rating. Yet, lowering Wilson several notches, as has been done with Andrew Johnson, would obscure Wilson's extraordinary successes in bringing about badly needed economic reforms, such as the creation of the Federal Reserve System. Likewise, viewing Wilson exclusively through the lens of his refusal to make the compromises necessary to assure American participation in the League of Nations would fail to do justice to his superior administrative capabilities, including his successful management of American participation in a world war and the extraordinary legislative achievements he attained, especially during his first term. All this argues for assessing Wilson according to several criteria, rather than just one.

At the same time, Ulysses S. Grant, who repeatedly ranks as a failure, often acted decisively and out of his empathy for the victims of racial persecution, sometimes at great cost to his popularity. His actions in this area have largely been lost to readers of history. Grant's successes and failures, like Wilson's, should be judged according to more than one standard. Such an approach would demonstrate that Grant was far from the incompetent he is so often made out to be. As president, he achieved almost all he set out to do and most of his objectives were high-minded.

Andrew Jackson, who usually ranks among the nation's top half-dozen presidents, is even more problematic. Jackson, too, succeeded at all he attempted and strengthened the institutional powers of his office. Yet in some instances, especially in his approach to human rights and the nation's finances, Jackson's policy successes brought disastrous results. But the existing surveys make no allowance for such distinctions. Historians who participate in them do acknowledge the problems inherent in evaluating Lyndon B. Johnson. How can his spectacular domestic achievements, especially in civil rights, be weighed against one of the greatest foreign policy failures in American history, his decision to engage the United States in a war in Vietnam, and the incompetent manner in which he waged it? Surveys tend to average the totality of Johnson's achievements and failures. No one who has studied LBJ, however, would regard his performance in anything as average.

Instead of assigning presidents a single score, the chapters that follow will evaluate the nation's presidents according to six criteria I have developed. The first three are internal attributes: character, vision, and competence. These often determine how a president approached the next three important policy realms in which all presidents engage: economic policy, the preservation and extension of liberty, and national security and defense. This approach will inevitably lead to a shift in the fundamental question from "What makes a president great?" to "At what did a particular president perform well and at what did he fare poorly?" In this survey, some presidents, like Abraham Lincoln, received the highest score in every category, while others, such as James Buchanan, came in at the bottom in every category—just where conventional surveys place them. Most of the others, like most other mortals, varied considerably from category to category.

Readers need not subscribe to all of this book's conclusions to find its approach useful in evaluating past, present, and future presidents. Hopefully, this will prove one of its strengths. In assessing the actions of their leaders, each citizen brings to the task his or her own view of what a particular president should have done. Greatness, like failure, often lies in the eyes of the beholder. How we judge political actors often says as much about us as it does about them. So let the game begin.

1

THE
RATING GAME

$\mathscr{T}$his book's origins go back to a cold, dreary December day in 1996. As I sat down to breakfast with the *New York Times Magazine*, its cover story caught my attention. The article, "The Ultimate Approval Rating," by Arthur M. Schlesinger Jr., contained the results of a survey he conducted, in which he asked leading historians to evaluate U.S. presidents.[1] Its appearance was most timely. Bill Clinton's second inauguration was a few weeks away. The media focused extensively on what Clinton might do in a second term, as the president openly speculated about his place in history.[2]

Schlesinger Jr.'s survey replicated and updated those that his father, Arthur M. Schlesinger Sr., conducted in 1948 and 1962. Both men asked their fellow historians to place each of the nation's presidents into one of five categories: great, near great, average, below average, and failure.[3] Neither of the Schlesingers suggested what criteria historians might use in filling out their ballots. Long before the elder Schlesinger introduced the "presidential rating game," perhaps even before Richard Henry Lee eulogized George Washington as "first in war, first in peace, and first in the hearts of his countrymen," Americans had spoken of great presidents and poor presidents, good presidents and bad presidents.[4]

The popularization of Schlesinger-style surveys, however, freed journalists, political commentators, museum curators, and students of all ages from having to offer *evidence* in support of their opinions. All they had to do was to cite the collective assessment of the "experts." Writers of textbooks and encyclopedias were only too happy to oblige, rushing results from the latest survey into print, often without interpretation. Slowly, the air of authority that these surveys conveyed replaced serious argument among many of their readers—save for those who happened to be specialists in one or more presidencies.

What student, other than the odd contrarian, would confidently develop a case for lowering or raising a certain chief executive's ranking after being told repeatedly that the consensus of experts, as reported in surveys, was such and such? Debate—so vital a component to a functioning democracy—had frozen.

At the same time, confusion has sometimes arisen between "expert" opinions and "public" perceptions of presidents. One modern myth, which President George W. Bush and his advisers have helped to perpetuate, perhaps inadvertently, is that historians belatedly came to appreciate Harry S Truman's contributions as president. In the 1962 Schlesinger Sr. survey—the first poll among historians to include him—Truman placed among the near greats. He has remained in that category in every subsequent survey.[5] What changed over time was less the view of historians but the impression the general public had of Truman. During his last year in office, Truman's approval rating in a Gallup Poll stood at 22 percent.[6] In a 2007 *USA Today*/Gallup survey, the public had Truman in seventh place.[7] Given that the overwhelming majority of Americans that *USA Today* and Gallup surveyed in 2007 had no personal memory of Truman's presidency, his newfound popularity resulted, in part, from the periodic publicity that surveys of presidential greatness have received. (The publication of three best-selling books—Merle Miller's *Plain Speaking* in 1972; Margaret Truman's biography of her father, also published in 1972; and David McCullough's magisterial biography, *Truman*, which appeared twenty years later—didn't hurt either.)

In addition to freezing debate and, at times, reducing rigorous assessment to a mere beauty contest, an over-reliance on surveys in the study of past presidents may lead curriculum builders to focus primarily on the so-called best and worst of leaders. It may accelerate the dumbing-down of textbooks and college lectures. This assumes, of course, that, in an era that puts a premium on inclusiveness, presidents will continue to receive much attentive coverage at all. (As of this writing, all have been white males. All were Christians. And all but a few are dead.)

More critically, with the U.S. presidency occupying a preeminent place in American life and in world affairs, the trivializing of the challenges past presidents have faced, as surveys and ratings inherently do, may impede the emergence of a clear understanding of the office, its possibilities, and its limitations. Likenesses of United States senators, members of Congress, and Supreme Court Justices do not adorn our currency. Holidays are not set aside to honor them. Their collective visages do not appear on souvenir rulers, neckties, or lunchboxes sold in gift shops in Washington, D.C. Commuters hurrying past newsstands do not encounter headlines shouting out, "Henry Clay Proclaimed Nation's Greatest House Speaker"; "Rayburn Rated Near Great"; "Historians Divided over Gingrich and Pelosi." While surveys assessing greatness among jurists, cabinet members, mayors, and governors have been made, none have acquired the cachet those purporting to assess presidents have.

An enduring limitation to the usefulness of presidential surveys has been bias on the part of the evaluators. As Calvin Coolidge, who usually pulls a low rating in such polls, once put it, "Unfortunately, not all experts are entirely disinterested. Not all specialists are without guile."[8] The below average ranking Ronald Reagan received in Schlesinger Jr.'s 1996 survey bears this out.[9] Reagan wound up in the low average group, one notch above Chester A. Arthur. Ironically, Reagan appeared in almost the same spot Eisenhower occupied Schlesinger Sr.'s 1962 survey. (Ike placed one notch *behind* Arthur!)

Schlesinger Jr. admitted that several of his thirty-two panelists espoused what may be properly termed "liberal Democratic" positions. Some served as advisers to past Democratic presidential candidates and presidents. Many signed a paid advertisement in which, citing their professional credentials as historians, they affirmed that impeaching Bill Clinton or removing him from office would be contrary to the intentions of the framers of the Constitution.[10] Among Schlesinger Jr.'s jurors were two former Democratic elected office-holders, former New York governor Mario Cuomo and former Illinois senator Paul Simon. The presumed justification for including these two was their standing as amateur historians and Lincoln enthusiasts.[11]

No self-identified conservatives appeared on Schlesinger Jr.'s list, except for historian Forrest McDonald. Absent too were Republican former officials who might have been included for purposes of philosophical balance. Several come to mind whose academic credentials and strengths as commentators were equal, if not superior, to those who did participate. Among these absentees were William J. Bennett, Jeane Kirkpatrick, Newt Gingrich, George F. Will, George P. Schultz, and Milton Friedman—all holders of Ph.D.s and all respected commentators. Richard Nixon was at least partially correct when he said that while history would treat him fairly, historians never would because they were mostly to the left.[12] (As will be shown in subsequent chapters, Nixon failed to anticipate that liberals would praise his domestic policies while conservatives would criticize his domestic and his foreign policies.)

In his analysis of the results of his 1996 survey, Schlesinger Jr. detected commonality among the nine men who placed at the top of both his poll and the one his father conducted in 1962. The greats and near greats in both surveys were Washington, Jefferson, Jackson, Polk, Lincoln, Wilson, the two Roosevelts, and Truman. All of them, Schlesinger Jr. assured his readers, articulated a sense of the ideal America and set their administrations on a path toward achieving it. Those who remember Reagan's likening of this nation to a city on a hill might find his omission from such a group puzzling. That the majority of those surveyed failed to include him underscores reader concerns about bias.

To have scored highly in this particular poll, presidents had to possess a certain kind of vision. According to most of the jurors, great or near-great presidents expanded the role of the federal government in domestic—and especially in economic—affairs at the expense of state and local government and the private sector. The jurors forged less of a consensus on what role the United States should play in the world. Viewed through this prism, Reagan never had much of a chance. After all, that city on a hill included lower tax rates, fewer regulations, a strategic defense against missile attack, and an aggressive foreign policy aimed at rendering the world bereft of an "evil empire."

Schlesinger Jr. volunteered that Reagan did receive seven near great votes. Some of these votes, he wrote, were cast by "liberal scholars impressed by [Reagan's] success in restoring the prestige of the presidency, in negotiating the last phases of the cold war, and in imposing his priorities on the country." Schlesinger Jr. recorded nine below average votes for Reagan, and four failures, from other jurors who opposed his tax policies, attacks upon government programs, and tolerance for budget deficits. (One wishes Schlesinger Jr. had explained why they thought better of John F. Kennedy's strategie embrace of deficits than they did of Reagan's mere "tolerance" of them. This discussion will be picked up on in chapter 4.) If the plethora of recent scholarly and popular works that have steadily appeared on Reagan since he left office are any guide, Reagan will not have to wait as long as Ike did to break into the top tier of presidents. In some subsequent surveys, particularly those in which care was taken to provide ideological balance, he already has.[13]

Yet once the bias of the evaluators has been addressed, an even more serious problem inherent in most surveys—their failure to distinguish *policy* from *process* in their assessments of presidents—remains. Schlesinger Jr. recognized at least part of this problem when he turned his attention to presidents his jury rated as failures. He rightly questioned whether the corruption that transpired under Ulysses S. Grant and Warren G. Harding inflicted as much harm on the country as had policies of James Buchanan or Andrew Johnson or the constitutional transgressions of Nixon. (By those lights, should Grant and Harding receive higher grades, or should Truman, whose administration was also beset by scandal, have his lowered?) Asking evaluators to put presidents into fixed categories, without affording them the opportunity to make distinctions within them, leads to difficulties in interpretation of precisely this kind.

Toward the end of the article that accompanied his survey, Schlesinger dropped any and all pretense to objectivity when he presumed to advise the recently re-elected Bill Clinton on how he might raise his grade in subsequent surveys. He recommended that the president cut free from "polls and focus groups" and abandon the very "middle of the road" policies that had helped him win re-election.[14] According to Schlesinger, Clinton no longer needed to act like the "New Democrat" that he professed to be. Schlesinger urged the president to return to old-time Democratic liberal activism. Only then could he make it into the vaunted club of the greats and near greats. Whether Clinton would have succeeded had he followed this advice, with Republicans in control of both houses of Congress, and in the face of polls showing that the public liked Clinton just the way he was, the historian did not say. "Only boldness and creativity, even if at times foiled and frustrated," Schlesinger mused, would earn Clinton "a place among the immortals."[15]

Whatever else might be said about the wisdom and effectiveness of what Clinton's successor attempted as president, George W. Bush's willingness to wage preventive wars, his undertakings to spread democracy in the Middle East, and his readiness to act unilaterally on the international stage were certainly "bold" and "creative," even if they were at times "foiled" and "frustrated." To date, these measures have not won him acclaim from Schlesinger's jurors. One wrote a cover story for a popular magazine, declaring Bush the worst president in history.[16] Others seconded this opinion in other forums. Again, it would seem that presidential greatness lies in the ideological eyes of their evaluators.

The most confounding limitation in expert surveys may be a tendency, as Fred I. Greenstein has pointed out, to divert attention from the "full range of presidential experience."[17] Great presidents can and have made serious mistakes. Franklin Delano Roosevelt made several. Presidents who placed way down the list of past surveys, such as Grant and Harding, sometimes performed noble deeds. Yet the ballots jurors complete too often make no allowance for such distinctions. Such surveys fail to capture what political scientist Walter Dean Burnham has termed the "dichotomous" nature of too many presidencies.[18] Those assessing Lyndon B. Johnson, for instance, might want to award him an "A" for civil rights and an "F" for Vietnam. Nixon might receive an "A" for his China policy and an "F" for Watergate. Surveys, as presidential biographer James MacGregor Burns noted, fuel a tendency to average these disparate grades.[19] Such an approach, however, would capture the essence of neither of their presidencies.

Lastly, through its emphasis on process, often at the expense of policy, the rating game discourages those who play it from taking into account the degree to which what a president achieved was actually good for the country. Since 1948, Andrew Jackson has consistently ranked among the near-great presidents. But would he have received such a rating if his evaluators examined the *consequences* of his far-reaching maneuvers? Jackson's unprecedented use of the veto certainly carved out for future presidents an enhanced role in the legislative process. Yet, his veto of the bill to renew the charter of the Second Bank of the United States plunged the country into the worst economic contraction it would experience until the Great Depression. Similarly, while historians now take a more sympathetic view of Radical Reconstruction than they once did, Grant's ratings have not risen, in spite of his success in destroying the first Ku Klux Klan and his efforts to enforce the Fourteenth and Fifteenth Amendments.

The chapters that follow are an attempt to compensate for failings such as these. They suggest ways in which scholars, commentators, and the general public might distinguish among past presidents. At the same time, they provide voters a way to discern among presidential contenders. The first three chapters assess the nation's presidents according to three traits they carry into office with them: character, vision, and competence. The next three consider how presidents performed in three policy areas: economic policy, the protection and expansion of liberty, and defense and foreign policies. In each chapter, an opinion is offered as to whether specific presidents left the nation they led better or worse off than they found it. Those familiar with recent surveys will encounter some surprise verdicts.

Taken together, these six components provide readers with a thorough and consistent standard against which to measure presidential performance. At some point in their lives, all presidents have had their characters tested. The manner in which they responded to these challenges helped make or break both their presidencies and their standing in history.[20] While George H. W. Bush may have belittled the "vision thing," the vision presidents carried into office set the direction their presidencies took. Those who failed to articulate a coherent vision found themselves tossed about by events. Presidents who charted a firm course for their administrations to follow were able to mobilize public and congressional opinion behind them. (Such were the stories of the Kennedy and Reagan presidencies.)

A president's level of competence determines whether he succeeds. Some noble characters failed (Herbert Hoover and Jimmy Carter come to mind), while some with less exemplary ones (Franklin Delano Roosevelt) did not. In a president, competence can take many forms. Usually it is the ability to persuade others to follow one's lead. As Richard E. Neustadt shrewdly observed, the American government is comprised not of "separated powers," but of "separate institutions *sharing* powers."[21] Unlike the head of a large corporation, presidents cannot lead by command. (In reality, few corporate leaders can either.) For a president to succeed, he must persuade others, whom he cannot dismiss or replace, to go along with him. The other actors and potential rivals he must win over, circumvent, or defeat in order to succeed are many. They include Congress, the courts, the media, the private sector, interest groups, foreign governments, and the general public. A friend of mine, a politically astute businessman, once remarked, "Imagine becoming president of a Fortune 500 company only to discover that all your major competitors are on your board of directors."

A president unable to persuade, if not inspire, has little chance of moving the nation. "I sit here all day trying to persuade people to do things they ought to have the sense to do without my persuading them," commented Harry Truman.[22] In addition to proving a master salesman, a competent president must know how to process and use information to his advantage. He must possess the ability to assemble a team able to carry out his directives. Finally, he must be able to anticipate and respond to the unexpected. Few presidents, even the best, have demonstrated competence in each of the areas in which the demands of their office compelled them to operate. Some, like Woodrow Wilson, demonstrated extraordinary competence in some circumstances and great incompetence in others.

The second set of three chapters addresses how presidents handled three types of policy issues. With regard to the economy, two questions arise: Did he put in place policies that led to long-term prosperity? Did he expand economic opportunities for ordinary Americans? On the matter of extending and preserving liberty, presidents need to be examined on how well they acted in accordance with the nation's founding mission statement. Did a president enable more people to enjoy the full liberties promised to all Americans in the nation's founding documents? Did he use the influence of the United States to expand the human rights, which those documents proclaim to be universal, to other parts of the world? On foreign and defense concerns, did a president advance American interests abroad? How well did a he function as commander in chief? When he left office, was the nation more secure than when he entered?

As the stories that follow will make clear, presidents, even the greatest of them, did not start out as carefully carved faces, staring down from the side of a mountain in South Dakota. Much went into their making. Given the capacity they have to affect the lives of so many, American presidents cannot be studied enough. The remaining chapters offer a way for historians and citizens alike to get at the essence of sound leadership in ways that shortcuts such as surveys and rating games inevitably miss.

2

CHARACTER

$\mathcal{H}$eraclitus declared two millennia ago that a "man's character is his fate." While good character does not assure presidential greatness, it can be a precursor. Character has been a running theme in presidential biographies, beginning, perhaps, with Parson Weems's mythologized account of George Washington's chopping down a cherry tree and confessing his offense to his father. Under the category of "character" fall all the traditional concepts parents have tried to instill in their young throughout the centuries: honesty (doing what one said one would do, or explaining why unforeseen circumstances necessitated a different course); courage (meeting adversity head on, often at political or personal risk); and integrity (placing the interests of one's office and one's country ahead of personal convenience or interests, or those of one's associates).

This chapter focuses on five presidents who demonstrated exemplary personal character before and during their time in office: George Washington, Abraham Lincoln, Theodore Roosevelt, Gerald Ford, and Ronald Reagan. It also examines five presidents whose characters proved less than praiseworthy: Thomas Jefferson, Franklin Pierce, James Buchanan, Woodrow Wilson, and Richard Nixon. Assessing the characters of public leaders is admittedly a subjective enterprise. Yet when presidents are compared, one can see that those who contemporaries and historians alike deemed to have possessed exemplary characters shared some characteristics. So too did several who were found wanting in this area. The United States has had significantly more presidents with exemplary character than presidents whose characters were less stellar.

Seventeen presidents had the highest character possible in a president (a score of 5). Only four warrant the lowest possible score (that of 1). Most of the others, while falling between, placed closer to the top than to the bottom. (W. H. Harrison and J. A. Garfield, who died early in their presidencies, and G. W. Bush, the incumbent president as of this writing, were not evaluated.)

THOSE WITH THE HIGHEST SCORE, IN CHRONOLOGICAL ORDER:

George Washington
John Adams
James Madison
John Quincy Adams
Zachary Taylor
Abraham Lincoln
Grover Cleveland
Benjamin Harrison
William McKinley
William H. Taft
Calvin Coolidge
Harry S Truman
Dwight D. Eisenhower
Gerald Ford
Jimmy Carter
Ronald Reagan
George H.W. Bush

THOSE WHO RECEIVED A GRADE OF 4 WERE:

Ulysses S. Grant
Theodore Roosevelt
Herbert Hoover

EIGHT PRESIDENTS RECEIVED A GRADE OF 3:

Thomas Jefferson
James Monroe
Andrew Jackson
Rutherford B. Hayes
Chester A. Arthur
Woodrow Wilson
Franklin D. Roosevelt
John F. Kennedy

SEVEN PRESIDENTS RECEIVED A GRADE OF 2:

Martin Van Buren
John Tyler
Millard Fillmore
Andrew Johnson
Warren G. Harding
Lyndon B. Johnson
Bill Clinton

FOUR PRESIDENTS RECEIVED A GRADE OF 1:

James K. Polk
Franklin Pierce
James Buchanan
Richard Nixon

Of the seventeen presidents who earned a score of 5, the five discussed in the first half of this chapter drew upon the strengths of their character to guide the United States through some of the most challenging periods of its history. All put their country's interests ahead of their own. All were confident in their ability to move the nation in the direction that they thought was best. All had the courage to risk public displeasure and even political defeat by adhering to the course that they had set. None were known to have harbored grudges or to have allowed their personal piques and prejudices to determine how they related to allies and adversaries. While none were strangers to failure and all had occasional moments of self-doubt, all remained optimistic that they would succeed in office and that the nation would be better for their efforts. While all were pragmatists, none lost the spirit of idealism that they had exhibited during their youth. None displayed the slightest sign of having grown cynical during their years of service.

The presidents examined in the second half of this chapter—those whose character left something to be desired—also demonstrated common character traits. All aspired to political careers at an early age. Each made ethical or professional compromises to further their ambitions. All harbored personal grudges and carried them into the political arena. All surrounded themselves with like-minded subordinates who acted, with a few exceptions, more as implementers than as advisers. All exuded signs of pessimism about how their policies might turn out. All were prone to more than occasional moments of self-pity, often publicly expressed. All regarded themselves as master strategists and adept politicians, who knew all the angles. Most were cynical about the motives of others. All wound up checkmating themselves.

George Washington: The Founder

Of all who have served as president, none possessed a more exemplary character or used it more effectively to achieve his goals than George Washington. His character so readily lent itself to myth creation that most Americans are probably more familiar with long-discredited legends about him than they are with the character traits that gave rise to them. Few may know that Washington consciously sought to attain his celebrated character. That he succeeded remains among his most enduring legacies.

From his early manhood practically until the end of his days, Washington strove to improve the quality of his character. Throughout his life, Washington's character remained a work in progress. One can observe its development by comparing the dour and dignified expression Washington wears on his portrait on the dollar bill to what we know of Washington when he was a young military officer. The youthful Washington was an ambitious hothead, eager to attain fame and glory. On May 28, 1754, Washington, then a twenty-one-year-old lieutenant colonel in the Virginia militia, allowed Seneca chief Tanaghrisson (also known as Half-King) to manipulate him into firing upon a French diplomatic party to which Washington had been sent to deliver an ultimatum that the French vacate the Ohio River Valley, which the British claimed as their own. After Washington's party had taken the French survivors as prisoners, Tanaghrisson assassinated their leader, Joseph Coulon de Villiers de Jumonville.

Whether through impetuosity, inexperience, or inability or disinclination to control his Seneca allies, Washington had helped spark a world war between France and Great Britain. It became known as the "French and Indian War" in North America and the "Seven Years War" elsewhere. Because of his brash actions, Washington became one of the few colonials whose name the British sovereign knew. By the time he reached middle age, however, Washington was winning accolades not for grasping for power and position but for eschewing them. "He will be the greatest man in the world," George III purportedly said upon learning of Washington's intention to return to private life after the United States had won its independence.[1]

Visitors to Mount Vernon today behold a sprawling mansion suitable for one of the most prominent and successful men of his age. Upon close inspection, they discern that two wings had been added to the original house. Above the three sections rests a single pediment that diverts attention away from the asymmetrical patchwork beneath it. Visitors may also see that Mount Vernon's exterior wooden walls were carved and painted to create the impression that the house was made of stone. Washington designed and decreed these architectural changes. In every sense, the image Washington exuded of himself was as much a conscious act of creation as the design of his home.

The eldest son of a second marriage, Washington had not expected to inherit his father's sizable holdings. When young George showed a knack for mathematics, his older half-brother Lawrence brought him into the orbit of Thomas Lord Fairfax. Lord Fairfax retained George to survey the sizable Fairfax properties and introduced him to the colony's leaders. Aspiring to join the ranks of the Virginia gentry, Washington decided upon military service as the best route. He soon determined that gaining acceptance into the highest rank of Virginia society depended on how closely one personified the gentry's ideal of what a gentleman had to be. Thus, Washington began what would become a lifelong struggle to restrain his passions.

At the age of sixteen, he began copying in his own hand the 110 signposts contained in *Rules of Civility and Decent Behavior in Company and in Conversation*. Often used as an exercise in penmanship, this work by French Jesuits was first translated into English in 1640. Its maxims served as a guide to proper etiquette in colonial Virginia and at the British Court. Washington incorporated them into his natural way of behaving. Over time, his fellow officers in the militia noticed that changes had taken place in his overall temperament. "Method and exactness are the forte of his character," one observed.[2] Washington also sought to emulate characters in theatrical plays that displayed personal qualities he deemed admirable. His favorite play was Joseph Addison's *Cato*, in which a young Roman noble committed suicide rather than submit to Caesar's tyranny. In the company in which Washington aspired to move, one's "character" was readily discernible through certain actions and patterns of speech and dress. By the time he became president, he had invented a new role, that of "Washington," from which he never deviated.

Between his earliest years and his presidency, Washington underwent two transformative experiences. The first occurred on July 9, 1755, in the Battle of Monongahela River. After British General Edward Braddock was mortally wounded, Washington assumed command. He had two horses shot out from under him and several bullets pierce his coat while he rallied the British force against a French ambush. "See the wonders of Providence!" he wrote of his travails, "The uncertainty of human things!"[3] Perhaps he concluded that he had been spared for a purpose. Washington's bravery in the war he had helped start was celebrated on both sides of the Atlantic. He discovered, however, that, demonstrated valor notwithstanding, there were limits to how high a colonial could rise in the British army. Denied a commission, Washington began to regard himself more as a Virginian or as an American and less as a British subject. Meritocracy had reared its head at Mount Vernon.

Washington resigned from the militia and became a planter, managing the property that he inherited from Lawrence. Befitting his new station, he won election to the House of Burgesses and took his seat just as tensions were beginning to rise over Parliament's power to levy direct taxes on the king's American subjects. Lacking the formal education of colleagues such as Peyton Randolph, George Wythe, or the young Thomas Jefferson, Washington formed his political opinions more from personal observation and from what he had read. "Parliament hath no more right to put their hands into my pocket without my consent than I have to put my hands into yours for money," he told a friend.[4] He arrived at the Continental Congress wearing a uniform he had designed, telegraphing his availability as Commander of the Continental Army. When he took to the field, Washington enhanced his reputation primarily through his patience, persistence, and the organizational skills through which he had built and held together the Continental Army. An officer who served under him said that Washington "brought order out of confusion, animated his troops, and led them to success."[5]

Every time his countrymen called him back into service Washington performed a well-rehearsed ritual. He weighed the prospects that his presence would tilt the scales in the direction he wanted his country to follow against the potential harm that his absence might inflict upon his reputation. As his close friends came to understand, the best way to entice Washington to take the reigns (of state) was to play upon his fears that his fellow citizens would think less of him if they came to suspect that he placed his private comforts ahead of his public duty.[6] Washington used his avowed reticence to assume power as a means of persuading others to go along with policies he wished to implement. Whenever he withdrew from public life, Washington would issue a "farewell address," in which he advised his countrymen to follow a certain course of action. (He used these farewells to make political points in the same way that more recent presidents, beginning with Theodore Roosevelt, used the presidential office as a "bully pulpit" from which to preach.)

Well before he became president, Washington used the power inherent in his person to his strategic advantage. In 1783, after the British surrendered at Yorktown but before British forces evacuated New York City, Washington averted a military coup (the "Newburg Conspiracy") against the Continental Congress by playing this special card. Upon learning of his officers' plans, Washington called them together to inform them that he considered what they contemplated to be a repudiation of the principles upon which the war was being waged and of his leadership.[7] Eyewitnesses recorded that Washington had carried the day even before he delivered his speech. As he fumbled with his papers while putting on his reading glasses, Washington announced that he had "grown not only gray, but almost blind" in the service to his country.[8] Moved by this sight, his underlings shelved their plans.

"His influence carried the government," James Monroe said of Washington's support for the proposed constitution as he presided over the convention that produced it.[9] When Pennsylvania farmers took up arms to protest an excise tax on whiskey in 1794, President Washington returned to the field to assert the authority of a freely elected government and the principle of the rule of law. The insurrection suppressed, Washington pardoned its perpetrators. "Curse his virtues, they've undone his country," an exasperated Jefferson cried out in 1795 after Washington's personal intervention thwarted Jeffersonian attempts to defeat the Jay Treaty, which Washington wanted ratified.[10]

Washington most famously drew upon his carefully cultivated prestige as he prepared to relinquish the presidency. Out of "solicitude" for the welfare of the citizens he had led, Washington offered in his farewell address for their "solemn contemplation" "sentiments" he hoped that, if followed, would make their "felicity as a people" permanent. Washington underscored his previously offered assertion that civic virtue was the precondition of liberty and that liberty could not survive without the citizenry's dedication to religious principles.

He advocated fealty to a strong national union. He urged the young country to "observe good faith and justice toward all nations" and cautioned against forming "permanent alliances." "The nation which indulges towards another a habitual hatred or a habitual fondness is in some degree a slave," Washington declared. "It is a slave to its animosity or to its affection." Either, he said, was "sufficient to lead it astray from its duty and interest."[11]

While he favored extending commercial relations to the rest of the world, Washington discouraged his countrymen from using trade as a means of advancing political or military objectives. Unlike Jefferson, James Madison, and other successors, Washington eschewed the use of economic sanctions as a means of influencing the behavior of other nations. As he prepared to leave office, the first president advised against American intrusion into the internal affairs of other nations. Even more importantly, he warned against allowing foreign agents to become involved in domestic political controversies within the United States. The long-standing influence of this address can be seen in the intensity of debates waged in and outside of Congress, at least until the United States entered into World War I, over whether the United States dared reject Washington's counsel.

Those who thought that his farewell address constituted the last public lesson Washington would offer his fellow citizens proved wrong. Even before his retirement, Washington contemplated how he would dispose of Mount Vernon and the rest of his holdings upon his death and that of his wife. He knew that his will, a public document, would attract attention. In preparing it, Washington, through a private action he had long contemplated, chipped away at a public institution he had come to abhor, but found impossible either to eradicate or to extricate himself from while he lived. That institution was, of course, slavery.

While Washington used the word "slavery" to describe the relationship between colonies and their mother country or alliances based on animosity or affection, he always referred to the human beings he owned as "servants" or "laborers." To his private secretary, Washington wrote of "a certain species of property" that he possessed "very repugnantly."[12] Of the nearly one dozen slaveholders who served as president, Washington was the only one who freed his slaves. From his youth into early middle age, Washington harbored few, if any, qualms about the practice of buying and selling humans. Eventually he came to doubt both the economic utility of the slave system and the morality of slavery itself. He resolved not to break up families whenever he sold slaves. By the 1770s, he had made it his practice not to sell slaves without their consent. Not surprisingly, the slave population at Mount Vernon grew considerably. Washington even tried (and failed) to find a way to run his plantation profitably while paying slaves wages in exchange for their labors.

Yet, if Washington could not or would not sever his ties to this institution while he lived, he made certain that the chains that bound his human chattel and their progeny to him would not pass unbroken to his heirs after he died. The explicit instructions he left in this regard suggested that he recognized the radical break he was making with the social conventions of his time and that he fully expected those, whose inheritance he had diminished, to seek to circumvent his decree. In setting his slaves free, Washington established a fund to teach children to read and write so that they "be brought up to some useful occupation."[13] He set aside funds to provide for the aged and the young. He ordered that no slave he freed be sold "under any pretext whatsoever." Were that not sufficient, Washington instructed his executors to see that every aspect of this section of his will "be religiously fulfilled" and "without evasion, neglect, or delay."[14] In short, he had left his executors "no wiggle room."

In the end, the man who began public life as a hothead, grasping for fame and glory, and who had ample reason to believe the deck had been stacked against him by the circumstances of his birth, won all that he had sought by appearing to push it away. He used whatever power he attained to establish and extend the principles of self-government and to instruct others on how best to preserve them. In the words of Gordon Wood, Washington was an "extraordinary man, who made it possible for ordinary men to rule."[15]

Abraham Lincoln: The Savior

"There have been men who proposed to me to return to slavery the black warriors. . . . I should be damned in time [and] in eternity for so doing. The world shall know that I will keep my faith to friends and enemies, come what will," Abraham Lincoln wrote toward the end of the Civil War.[16] He penned these words to a prominent northern Democrat who had been willing to wage war to preserve the Union but not to free the slaves. Contemporaries who had followed Lincoln's career could not have predicted that the man they knew as a moderate or even a conservative on the slavery question—and who was prone to find the middle ground on so many issues—would take such a firm stand.

Lincoln's position had been long in coming. He stood by it because he had become convinced that a policy that he had long favored, but did not think attainable under other circumstances, had became the only means through which he could achieve an even more immediate and important objective, the preservation of the Union. Lincoln had unknowingly spent all of his entire life preparing for this moment. When it came, he was quick to seize it.

Lincoln's ambition, which his last law partner, William Herndon, likened to a "little engine that knew no rest," was discernible long before he developed either the principles or the skills for which he became known.[17] Born in Hardin County, Kentucky, on February 12, 1809, in a one-room log cabin with a dirt floor, Lincoln moved with his family to southern Indiana at the age of seven. Though his biographers attribute the move to a disputed title to the family's farm, years later, Lincoln attributed his family's eagerness to leave Kentucky to his father's opposition to slavery. If this was so, an aversion to slavery constituted the only characteristic Lincoln shared with his father other than a gift for storytelling.

When Lincoln was nine, he watched his mother, Nancy Hanks Lincoln, die an agonizing death. A decade later, his older sister, who had been his constant companion during his youth, died in childbirth. The deaths of his mother and sister during his formative years, along with his family's periodic moves, may account for Lincoln's perhaps excessive self-reliance, his tendency not to confide in or depend on others, and his reluctance to form many permanent attachments. David Davis, a future political ally, found Lincoln the most "secretive and reticent" man he had ever encountered.[18]

Perhaps the sole source of succor Lincoln found while growing up was his stepmother, Sarah Bush Lincoln, whom his father married one year after

Nancy's death. Preferring Abraham to her own children, Sarah found him a "bright, witty, and sensitive boy" of "uncommon talents."[19] Sarah suspected that Lincoln sensed that he possessed intellectual gifts that would enable him to rise above his humble beginnings.[20] Under her watchful eye and steady encouragement, Lincoln's self-confidence grew. Sarah arranged for what limited formal education Lincoln received. He estimated its total to have been no longer than one year's duration. She encouraged Lincoln's nascent love of reading, a pastime his father regarded as a sign of laziness and a means of circumventing work. When his father ordered him to quit school and hired him out to neighbors as a day laborer, Lincoln—now a teenager—grew resentful.[21] His father's retention of Lincoln's earnings compounded his sense of injury.[22] After assisting his family with yet another move, this time to Illinois, Lincoln set out on his own.

Lincoln witnessed slavery firsthand when he helped a neighbor transport produce to New Orleans and saw slaves sold at market. His cousin Dennis Hanks, who accompanied him, recalled thirty-five years later that Lincoln vowed that if he ever got the chance, he would "hit slavery and hit it hard."[23] Lincoln confessed to Joshua Speed, one of his few close friends and a slaveholder, the "continued torrent" of anger he experienced every time he approached the border of a slave state after having witnessed "slaves shackled together in irons."[24] Whether such sentiments resulted from Lincoln's growing sense of empathy or simply from identification with others who, like him, to some degree, in his youth, had no control of their destinies cannot be known.

On what was to have been another trip to the Crescent City, Lincoln and two kinsmen managed to get their boat stuck on a milldam at the hamlet of New Salem, Illinois. Their attempts to free the boat became a source of entertainment for locals. Lincoln liked the town and decided to remain. By his own account, Lincoln took up residence in New Salem as a "friendless, uneducated, penniless boy."[25] When he departed six years later, he was both a politician of promise and a successful attorney.

While in New Salem, Lincoln became a store clerk and performed odd jobs. He won over most men in the town when he accepted a challenge from and bested a local ruffian, Jack Armstrong, in a wrestling match. Six months after settling in the town, Lincoln audaciously announced his candidacy for the state legislature. In a rare confession of his true aspirations, Lincoln all but admitted in his declaration of candidacy that his reasons for running were not entirely rooted in policy concerns. "Every man is said to have his peculiar ambition," he wrote. "I can say for one that I have no other so great as that of being truly esteemed of my fellow men, by rendering myself worthy of their esteem."[26]

Lincoln reminded his would-be constituents that he was "young and unknown" and that he had "no wealthy or popular relations" to recommend him.[27] He saw politics as a means of increasing his social status and attaining recognition. Yet in contrast to other young men of his generation who sought early entry into elective politics (such as Franklin Pierce and James Buchanan), Lincoln did not merely seek to rise up the political ladder through a series of public offices. To him, public offices were not ends in themselves but means to achieve great things. He confided to Speed that his goal as a state legislator would be to become Illinois's DeWitt Clinton (the governor who had transformed New York by building the Erie Canal).[28] During a bout of depression years after he had won several elections, Lincoln, his ambition still unfulfilled, told Speed that he would be "willing to die" except that he had done nothing to make any human being remember that he had lived.[29]

For a man who harbored such ambitions, New Salem was a good place to act on them. In a new community that lacked an established social hierarchy, Lincoln made his move before other similarly situated young men could get ahead of him. Years later, he would advise young men "not to wait to be brought forward by the older men."[30] Lincoln campaigned hard, proved an effective speaker, and enjoyed taking to the stump. In an era when voters regarded politics as a form of entertainment, Lincoln proved a master at backwoods humor, ridicule, and self-deprecation. Although he lost his first election, Lincoln carried his precinct, taking 277 of the 300 votes cast.[31] He emerged from the contest having established his bona fides as a leading citizen in his adopted hometown.

Determined to try again, Lincoln spent the next two years raising his name recognition throughout the district. He joined multiple organizations, performed tedious party chores for the Whig Party, and served as local postmaster. The postal job afforded him the opportunity to keep abreast of state and local news by perusing publications that came into his office. He also talked politics with prospective voters as they stopped by to pick up their mail. That Lincoln, an ardent Whig, could obtain the appointment as postmaster, a coveted political plum, at a time when Jacksonian Democrats dispensed all federal patronage attests to the strengths of his interpersonal skills and capacity to form useful friendships. Although he later observed in an autobiography written during his 1860 presidential campaign that the post was "too insignificant to make his politics an objection" (presumably to Democrative operatives), odds are strong that Lincoln obtained and retained appointment as postmaster through the intervention of someone he befriended in the opposite political party.[32]

In 1834, at the age of twenty-five, Lincoln won election to the Illinois House of Representatives. He quickly set out to master the details of legislation and policy. At the suggestion of his more established and socially connected colleague John Todd Stuart, whose cousin Mary he would eventually marry, Lincoln also began to study law. He was re-elected three times. Midway through his tenure, Lincoln's Whig colleagues selected him as their floor leader. As spokesman for the minority, he played a pivotal role in persuading both Whigs and Democrats to finance an intricate network of internal improvements and to relocate the state capital from Vandalia to Springfield, to which he had moved.

During his third year in office, Lincoln confronted slavery as a political issue for the first time. Angered over increasing abolitionist sentiment in the North and fearful that Nat Turner's slave rebellion in Virginia would be followed by others, southerners began pressing Northern state legislatures to pass resolutions sustaining slaveholders' rights to their "property." With Lincoln voting no, the Illinois House passed a resolution 77 to 6 condemning the spread of abolitionist societies, conceding the legality of slavery where it existed, and denying the federal government the right to abolish slavery in the District of Columbia. Together with a colleague, Dan Stone, Lincoln offered a separate resolution. As had the majority, Lincoln and Stone condemned abolitionist agitators and agreed that slavery was permissible in certain places under the Constitution. They saw fit, however, to put it on the record that they believed that slavery was "founded on injustice" and was "bad policy."[33] Diverging from the rest, they also declared that Congress had the right to abolish slavery in the District of Columbia. They expressed the hope that Congress would act in accordance with the majority of the city's residents in approaching the issue.

That Lincoln so early in his career felt the need to inform his constituents of his personal opinion, especially when it differed from theirs, says much about his character. Because of the heavy influx of southern-born settlers into Illinois, many if not most of its residents harbored little affection for abolitionists or for blacks. The legislature forbade free blacks from taking up residence in Illinois. The lopsided nature of the vote in favor of the initial resolution suggested that Lincoln took little political risk in breaking with his colleagues in that his vote had not been needed for the measure to pass. Still, that he felt the need to go on record with regard to what he thought of slavery and whether and where Congress might forbid it, is telling.

Shortly after he offered his resolution, in an address before the Young Men's Lyceum of Springfield, Lincoln cited "reverence for the laws" as the only antidote to mob rule, which, if left unchecked, he prophesied, would bring an end to the American experiment of self-government.[34] Speaking on the heels of the murder of an abolitionist editor and an outbreak of lynchings, Lincoln proclaimed the enforcement of laws essential to the survival of liberty. He made the case for extending its provisions to slaveholders and abolitionists alike. While Lincoln clothed his rhetoric in evenhandedness, his listeners were well aware that the recent acts of vigilante violence were directed against blacks and their white sympathizers, neither of which enjoyed much popular support. By extending the law's protection to those out of public favor, he argued, the majority could preserve the liberty of all as well as majority rule itself.

Having advanced in state politics as far as he thought it possible for a Whig in an overwhelmingly Democratic state, Lincoln set his sights on federal office. Attempting to maneuver his way into a "safe" congressional seat, he proposed that incumbents rotate after each term in Congress. Lincoln's turn to fill the seat came in 1846. Once elected, he threw himself into the central controversy of his tenure, the war with Mexico. Lincoln became one of its most ardent opponents. He went so far as to suggest that President James K. Polk had taken the country into war on the false pretext that the United States had been attacked on its own territory when, in fact, its troops had been ordered into Mexico. For the second time in his career, Lincoln had taken a position he knew to be unpopular among his constituents. His stand was, however, very much in accord with the national leadership of the Whig Party, which sought to capture the White House in 1848. Some have surmised that, knowing he would have to vacate his seat, Lincoln was angling for a federal appointment.[35] In opposing the war, Lincoln, however, was also voicing his opposition to the extension of slavery, one of the war's primary objectives. At the war's conclusion, Lincoln supported the ill-fated Wilmot Proviso, which would have banned slavery in territory acquired from Mexico.

His hopes for high political office dashed, Lincoln returned to Illinois and built a thriving law practice. Most presumed that his career in electoral politics had ended. Such might have been the case had Senator Stephen A. Douglas (a Democrat from Illinois) not introduced the Kansas-Nebraska bill, which would allow voters of newly organized territories to vote on whether to permit slavery within their borders. Douglas had introduced this bill to obtain support for his plan to build a transcontinental railroad along a northern route, beginning in Chicago. Southern Democrats were then backing an alternative route beginning in New Orleans. To Lincoln, the possible opening of new territory to slavery represented not just the perpetuation of a practice he considered morally wrong but a direct threat to the social mobility of whites. "Slave states are places for poor white people to remove from, not to remove to," Lincoln would say. "New free states are the places for poor people to go to and better their condition."[36]

The introduction of the Kansas-Nebraska bill propelled Lincoln back into politics. Back on the stump, he displayed a passion he had exhibited in prior years.[37] When the Supreme Court ruled in the Dred Scott case that owners of slaves were free to take their human property into areas where slavery had been banned, Lincoln joined the debate with renewed intensity. One authority on Lincoln's pre-presidential career maintains that, unlike in his previous runs for office, Lincoln's motives in challenging Douglas were rooted more in policy concerns than in furthering personal ambition.[38]

Lincoln was particularly troubled by the cynicism Douglas conveyed when he insisted that he "cared not" whether slavery (in a territory) be "voted up or down," just that the question be decided fairly. Douglas, Lincoln said, had "no very vivid impression that the Negro is a human; and consequently has no idea that there can be any moral question in legislating about him."[39] Much as Lincoln may have empathized with the slaves, his primary concern at this stage of his career was with preserving opportunities for the advancement of whites through economic competition. In the words of historian Richard Hofstadter, Lincoln was the "greatest dramatist" for such upward mobility.[40] "I happen, temporarily, to occupy the White House," Lincoln, as president, told the 166th Ohio Regimen. "I am living witness that one of your children may look to come here as my father's child has."[41]

Lincoln had been willing to tolerate slavery where it was, satisfied that the framers of the Constitution had restricted its practice to one area. He also believed that they, through their subsequent actions, had and set it on the road to extinction. All this changed when the Supreme Court breathed new life into what he had thought was a dying institution. When he campaigned for the United States Senate and, later, the presidency, Lincoln cast himself as the intellectual and ideological heir to the framers and presented his opponents as the true radicals who sought to take the nation down a path quite different from the one the framers had charted. Lincoln helped to forge a new electoral, and eventually a governing, coalition of disparate elements that shared his overall view. His coalition included former Free Soil Party members, Democrats opposed to extending slavery, northern Whigs, German and other immigrants, and nativists. Lincoln kept his coalition together by focusing on what united its members (opposition to the extension of slavery and the threat it posed to white liberties) and shied away from social issues that might divide them (immigration, temperance, and religion).

When several states opted to secede from the Union rather than accept the results of a free election, held in accordance with the Constitution, Lincoln chose "to accept war" rather than allow the Union to be destroyed.[42] Once engaged in the conflict, he used his powers as commander in chief to do what he insisted he could not do under the Constitution the during peacetime. Paradoxically, Lincoln acknowledged the enemy's claim that slaves were "property" so that he might confiscate such property, an action permissible under the Constitution during periods of war and insurrection. Through his powers as commander in chief, his issuance of the Emancipation Proclamation, as a war measure, and his support for a constitutional amendment forbidding slavery throughout the United States, Lincoln had achieved what he once believed impossible. He had brought an end to slavery in his country.

Just as he would not compromise over the extension of slavery before the war, Lincoln refused entreaties to shorten the conflict by rescinding his action. The restored Union he would bring into being would be one bereft of slavery. By the time the South sought terms similar to those he offered before the war began, Lincoln had broadened the war's objectives to include emancipation. With nearly 200,000 blacks fighting for the Union cause in what had become a war of attrition, Lincoln would not go back on his promise. He had as much of a practical reason for clinging to his position as he did a moral one.

Of the black soldiers and sailors, Lincoln inquired, "Why should they give their lives for us with full notice of our purpose to betray them? . . . If they stake their lives for us they must be prompted by the strongest motive . . . the promise of freedom. And the promise being made, must be kept."[43] Thus, late in his life, the man who, in his younger days, had yearned to make his fellow citizens know of his existence, proclaimed himself to have been an "instrument, under Providence, of the liberation of a race."[44] A convergence of circumstance and character had rendered this possible.

Theodore Roosevelt: The Umpire

Upon Theodore Roosevelt's death, the National Association for the Advancement of Colored People (NAACP) opined that even when he yielded to his worst impulses, Roosevelt believed that he had been in the right.[45] This character trait was sufficient, in the organization's opinion, to allow it to set aside, at least temporarily, its criticism of him for having strayed from his natural impulse in an important instance.[46] "That he [Roosevelt] was our friend," its publication, *The Crisis*, observed, "proves the justice of our cause, for Roosevelt never championed a cause which was not in essence right."[47] The NAACP knew its man. Franklin Delano Roosevelt said that the presidency was "pre-eminently a place for moral leadership,"[48] but no president better personified this aspect of the presidential role than had his fifth cousin Theodore.

The first President Roosevelt fought the hardest when he was convinced that he was doing more than just pursing a policy, but was upholding the right. ("Aggressive fighting for the right is the noblest sport the world affords.") Roosevelt's list of would-be and actual wrongdoers was long. It included "malefactors of great wealth" (greedy corporations), "the lunatic fringe" (leftists), "scavengers" of the nation's natural resources (lumbermen and polluters), and Columbian "blackmailers" (who refused to cede Roosevelt territory to construct the Panama Canal at the price he offered). In disputes between representatives of labor and capital, Roosevelt saw himself as representing a "third party," the general public.[49] He envisioned his role as head of the federal government as that of a disinterested umpire, mediating disputes between two organized minorities on behalf of an impacted but unorganized majority. Roosevelt's sense of what was right in both domestic and international affairs emanated less from a consistent set of principles than from his confidence in his ability to discern.

Theodore Roosevelt was born in New York City on the eve of the Civil War. His father's family had resided on Manhattan Island since 1644, when the Dutch still ruled New Amsterdam. (It was rechristened New York in 1667 by its new colonial rulers, the British.) Roosevelt's grandfather Cornelius Van Schaack Roosevelt, an importer of glass, a banker, and a land speculator, was among the city's early millionaires. The future president's father, Theodore Roosevelt Sr., devoted much of his life to charitable enterprises, political reform, and parenting. In his autobiography, President Roosevelt said that his father was the best man he ever knew. (FDR would later use this same appellation for his favorite presidential predecessor, Theodore Roosevelt.) He also set down a list of failings his father would not tolerate. Among them were selfishness, cruelty, idleness, cowardice, and untruthfulness.[50] Whatever Roosevelt's detractors would say about him, few, if any, would accuse him of displaying these failings. Another of his father's bêtes noires was hypocrisy. "What was wrong in a woman could not be right in a man," the Victorian elder told his progeny of two girls and two boys.[51] Had he substituted class for gender, he would have anticipated the later progressive impulses of his son perfectly. "A man who has never gone to school may steal from a freight car," President Roosevelt observed, "but if he has a university education, he may steal the whole railroad."[52]

As president, Theodore Roosevelt sought to instill his father's values in his fellow citizens. While he was prepared to use government to ameliorate social dislocations, hardships, and other by-products of unrestrained industrialism and laissez-faire capitalism, Roosevelt, unlike many of his fellow reformers, insisted that the best way to improve the human condition was through collective improvement of individuals. "Much can be done by wise legislation and by resolute enforcement of the law," he said in 1906. "But still more must be done by steady training of the individual citizen, in conscience and character," he added.[53] Roosevelt intended all of the social and economic policies he put in place as president to level the playing fields on which individuals, whatever their stations in life, competed. While he expanded the role that the federal government played in economic affairs, Roosevelt was not a redistributionist. As president, he did not establish any federal entitlements.

Once free to compete on equal footing (if sometimes as a result of government intervention), Roosevelt believed, Americans could and should make their way in the world by practicing the very rugged individualism whose excesses he had bemoaned. In this sense, he had more in common with the Gilded Age capitalists than he admitted. Like the industrial titans, Roosevelt believed that vigorous competition built moral character. However, Roosevelt also thought that the federal government should ensure fair competition by preventing anyone from "weighing-in with one foot already on the scale." He would prevent unfair competition primarily through his personal intervention, not by creating institutions designed to control or shape human behavior.

Referring to his office as a "bully pulpit," Roosevelt used it as a platform from which to preach values such as self-control and social responsibility.[54] His sermons consisted of more than the advocacy of policies he favored. Often, they were exhortations on the makings of good citizenship and upright character. Relying on the major media of his day—which consisted almost exclusively of mass-circulation daily newspapers and newsreels—Roosevelt used speeches, press releases, and articles that he either penned or ghosted. He also orchestrated staged events—such as the first White House conferences and the appointment of blue ribbon commissions—to dramatize issues he considered important in ways no president had before. Stories about Roosevelt's forceful personality and his six children—their antics and their exotic pets—made their way into the press as often as did the president's policy pronouncements. Of his capacity to attract and hold the limelight, Roosevelt's daughter Alice said that he "always wanted to be the corpse at every funeral, the bride at every wedding, and the baby at every christening."[55] Not even Roosevelt's most severe critic ever thought him dull.

Theodore Roosevelt was particularly proud of his father's lineage. Financially secure and far removed from earlier generations that had engaged in trade, Roosevelt and the sons of other prominent families saw themselves as society's "natural" (if not ideal) rulers. They were early champions of civil service reform. Who better than they (all men of breeding, means, character, and education) could best discern the nation's interests or advance them in a more "disinterested" fashion? Roosevelt and his elite colleagues did not trust this role to political appointees, whose principal loyalties were to party patrons. Nor were they willing to assign this role to nouveau riche "arrivistes," who might use it to further their own interests. Roosevelt and the sons of many other wealthy families sensed a special obligation to treat those they regarded as the lower orders fairly and in a spirit of justice. Practitioners of noblesse oblige, they believed they knew better what was best for wage earners than did workers, their proclaimed spokesmen, or their employers.

Roosevelt received his first taste of what he would regard as boss-ridden, corrupt politics when President Rutherford B. Hayes nominated Theodore Roosevelt Sr. to the post of customs collector for the Port of New York.

Through the appointment, Hayes intended to signal his support for civil service reform, a favored cause of the elder Roosevelt. U.S. Senator and New
York political boss Roscoe Conkling, who had little use for Hayes, civil service, or reformers, blocked the elder Roosevelt's confirmation in the Senate.
The prolonged controversy took its toll on Roosevelt Sr., who died a year
after its conclusion. The affair left the younger Roosevelt wary of party regulars. After he had entered politics, he took care not to alienate them beyond a
certain point. As a budding politico, Roosevelt aptly described the strengths
and failings of both clubhouse politicians and their reformist antagonists.
"The machine as such," he said, "had no ideals at all . . ." while the "ideals of
many of the silk-stocking reformers did not relate to the questions of real and
vital interest to our people."[56] If there was a breech to be filled, Roosevelt saw
himself as the person best able to fill it.

While Roosevelt developed his sense of duty and service from his father,
he acquired his flair for the dramatic from his mother, Martha ("Mittie")
Bulloch Roosevelt, a flamboyant socialite from antebellum Georgia. Out of
loyalty to her southern relatives, many of whom fought for the Confederacy,
she successfully dissuaded Roosevelt's father from joining the Union army.
(Like many men of means, the senior Roosevelt took advantage of the law
that allowed him to pay a substitute to fight in his stead.) Roosevelt's
biographers, as well as his two sisters, believed that he looked upon his
father's avoidance of military service with embarrassment. They and others
attributed the militarism Roosevelt displayed throughout his life to his long-
held desire to redeem the family honor.[57]

Roosevelt's father also taught him that he could, through hard work,
reshape much of his environment, if not his world. For the young Roosevelt,
the process began with his physique. Roosevelt started out in life a "sickly,
delicate boy" who suffered from severe asthma. Among his early memories
were recollections of his father sitting up with him on many nights, seeing him
through scary seizures.[58] One day, the senior Roosevelt announced that it was
time for his son to make his body.[59] Father and son installed a gymnasium in
their home. There, Roosevelt set his mind and body to the pursuits of what he
would later call the "strenuous life." As he became a steady practitioner of that

life, he experienced the power of physical exercise as an antidote to depression. "Black care," he observed, "rarely sits behind a rider whose pace is fast enough."[60] Commentators took to describing him as a "locomotive in trousers."

As he made his father's values his own and took to exhibiting his mother's vivaciousness, Roosevelt was slow to develop diplomatic skills. On a grand tour of Europe with his family, the ten-year-old Roosevelt—already a devotee of Abraham Lincoln, whose funeral cortege he had observed from his grandfather's window—encountered a son of Jefferson Davis, former president of the Confederacy. "Some sharp words" were exchanged, he recalled.[61] He did not have to record at whose instigation they began. A decade later, while discussing post-graduation plans with Harvard classmates, Roosevelt blurted out that he was "going to try to help the cause of better government in New York City." A peer who witnessed the conversation wondered whether Roosevelt was "the real thing, or only the bundle of eccentricities" that he appeared.[62] While he would learn to conceal some of his inner thoughts, Roosevelt never lost his boyish exuberance. "You must remember that the President is about six," British Ambassador Cecil Spring-Rice wrote home.[63]

As president, Roosevelt saw his role as steering the nation on a steady course between two volatile, self-interested factions. These were the "lunatic fringe" (on the left) and the "selfish rich" (on the right).[64] As he donned the cloak of the "trust buster," Roosevelt maintained that his only intention was to save the captains of industry from their own obstinacy.[65] "I wish that capitalists would see," he would say, "that what I am advocating . . . is really in the interest of property, for it will save it from the danger of revolution."[66] When he found the industry titans' myopia not only excessive but harmful to the public interest, Roosevelt intervened. He both broke and established precedent in 1902 when he settled a coal strike that threatened to become a national emergency. Roosevelt justified his intervention in what had been a private dispute between labor and capital by stating that he was obligated to act in the name of "a third party, the great public, that had vital interests and overshadowing rights in such a crisis."[67] Eight years earlier, Grover Cleveland had also intervened in a labor dispute, but in a vastly different manner. Cleveland had thrown the weight of the federal government behind management when he sent federal troops to confront workers striking against the Pullman Palace Car Company.

To persuade mine operators to participate in settlement talks, Roosevelt raised the prospect of using federal troops to operate the mines with J. P. Morgan, whose railroads ferried the coal to destinations across the country. The administration's principal concern, he declared, was the orderly distribution of coal to homes and businesses before winter cold set in. The settlement Roosevelt helped hammer out awarded the miners a 10 percent raise, reduced hours, and set precedent for presidential arbitration in future disputes. Roosevelt's successful intervention pleased the general public—and shielded his party from the wrath of coal customers. At the 1905 inaugural festivities that followed Roosevelt's triumphal re-election, he beamed with pride as miners unfurled a banner that proclaimed, "We honor the man who settled our strike."[68] Roosevelt's penchant for standing guard over the public interest was the animating force behind all of his economic policies that he dubbed the Square Deal. (These are detailed in chapter 5.)

Although a genuine aristocrat, belonging to a class that regarded the nation's governance as its birthright, Roosevelt came to embrace the Jeffersonian ideal of a natural aristocracy of virtue and talent, if not outright meritocracy. When he went to the Badlands to drown his grief after the simultaneous deaths of his first wife and his mother, Roosevelt learned that his personal fortune and his superior education counted for little in the Wild West—where one had to prove one's worth every day. Placed in charge of a military command during the Spanish-American War, Roosevelt, clad in a custom-made uniform from Brooks Brothers, forged an effective fighting force out of cowboys, ranchers, gunslingers, former bandits, New York socialites, immigrants, athletes, and more than a few Harvard men. As he worked to level all playing fields, Roosevelt's preeminent role remained that of steadfast referee, albeit of a most activist cast.

Gerald R. Ford: The Healer

"For myself and for our nation, I want to thank my predecessor for all he has done to heal our land," Jimmy Carter proclaimed at the outset of his inaugural address. He would later joke that it proved the most memorable line of his entire speech. In his tribute to Gerald R. Ford, however, Carter gave voice to feelings many Americans shared. Although he served as president for only 895 days, and was the first person to succeed to that office without ever being elected president or vice president, Ford left an indelible mark. He did it more through the quality of his character than through any policies he enacted. After more than a decade of "credibility gaps," "imperial presidencies," "Saturday night massacres," "enemies lists," and illegal cover-ups, the public was most content to have as its president a person devoid of pretext, who toasted his own English muffins, and who gave every appearance of, as one writer put it, being "a happy, normal man."[69] Not perhaps since Ike retired to Gettysburg had the American people seen one of themselves in the Oval Office.

Ford failed to have a significant effect on domestic policy primarily because of the contentious tenor of his times, the nature of the issues he confronted, and the disinclination of a heavily Democratic Congress to work with a Republican president. With Ford and Congress pulling in opposite directions on how to address inflation and the recession that spanned from November 1973 through March 1975, stalemate ensued. Yet of the sixty-six vetoes he handed down, Congress overrode Ford only twelve times.[70] Ford's efforts to hold the line on federal spending, which the October 25, 1975, *New York Daily News* headline "Ford to City: Drop Dead" captured, took a toll on his popularity. In the international arena, détente, the policy Nixon put into play in order to reduce tensions with the Soviet Union—never popular with the Republican right—continued on autopilot in the face of increased Soviet adventurism. Stymied at many turns, Ford focused primarily on the major challenge that awaited him, demonstrating that the American system of government worked. He met it through the high ethical standards he set for his administration, the high number of exceptionally capable individuals he appointed, and the strength of his character.

Gerald Ford, like fellow midwesterners Harry Truman and Dwight Eisenhower (whose portraits he displayed in the cabinet room), did not enter public life aspiring to be president. Elected to Congress at the age of thirty-five, Ford's highest aspiration had been to be Speaker of the House. That would entail repeatedly winning re-election in a relatively safe district and making his way up the legislative ladder with the help of colleagues. After Ford had served in the House for twenty-five years with his party acquiescing to what appeared to be permanent minority status, the highest position that Ford obtained was that of minority leader. He had already decided to retire from that post and from Congress when Nixon, already the subject of congressional and criminal investigations, selected Ford to succeed the disgraced Spiro T. Agnew. (Nixon's first vice president resigned on October 10, 1973, after pleading nolo contendere to charges of tax evasion and money laundering.)

This was not the first time that fate had smiled kindly on Jerry Ford. He was born in Omaha, Nebraska, in 1913 and was initially named after his bio-logical father, Leslie Lynch King, a wealthy wool merchant. During his infancy, the future president's parents divorced.[71] He and his mother then moved to Grand Rapids, Michigan, to live with his maternal grandparents. Not long afterward, his mother married a local paint salesman named Gerald R. Ford, who adopted his wife's son and gave him his name. (The Fords would go on to have three more sons.) Young Jerry proved a good athlete and an adequate student. He played center on his high school's football squad and was named to the all-city team. Ford took care to record that he made the National Honor Society and graduated in the top 5 percent of his high school class.[72] He was also an Eagle Scout. He made friends easily and was known for his pleasant disposition.

With the Great Depression taking its toll on the family business, Jerry took on odd jobs, mowing lawns and working concession stands at local parks. One of his jobs was flipping hamburgers at a restaurant across the street from his school. One day, while he was at work, a man appeared at the restaurant and abruptly identified himself to the seventeen-year-old as Leslie King, his biological father. King had heard about Jerry's athletic achievements and decided to seek him out and perhaps show him off to friends. Ford's estranged father explained that he and his wife had driven to Detroit to pick up a new Lincoln and decided to drive home through Grand Rapids. He handed the youth twenty-five dollars and invited him to spend the summer with him in Wyoming. Ford declined. A half century later, he wrote:

That night was one of the most difficult of my life. I don't recall the words
I used to tell my parents what had happened, but I do remember that the
conversation was a loving and consoling one. My stepfather loved me as
much as he did his own three sons. I knew how much he wanted to help
me and how lacking in financial resources he was. Nothing could erase the
image I gained of my real father that day: a carefree, well-to-do man who
really didn't give a damn about the hopes and dreams of his first-born son.
When I went to bed at night, I broke down and cried.[73]

There were limits to how far Ford would go to achieve his ambitions. To
have accepted King's invitation to Wyoming, in Ford's mind, would have
shown both disrespect and disloyalty to the man who had supported and
helped nurture him. He would not allow King to buy his affections. Nor
would he need to. Pooling their resources, Ford's football coach and a group
of University of Michigan alumni supplied him with a scholarship and found
him a job in Ann Arbor that helped him meet expenses. Ford continued playing football and was voted Michigan's most valuable player. Believing law a
more stable occupation than professional sports, he turned down contracts
with the Green Bay Packers and the Detroit Lions.

Figuring out how to pay law school tuition, however, proved a steep challenge, however, Ford accepted jobs as a boxing coach and an assistant football
coach at Yale University. He then applied to its law school. The admissions
committee, convinced he would not have sufficient time for his studies,
rejected him. Undeterred, Ford persuaded Yale officials to allow him to take a
few law classes on a trial basis. Eventually he gained admission and graduated
in the upper third of his class. While at Yale, Ford kept up on events in war-
torn Europe. Inspired by the reform-oriented campaign of presidential hopeful
Wendell Willkie, an internationalist, Ford abandoned his isolationist sentiments and joined Willkie's campaign as a volunteer. He was among the thousands of young people crammed into the convention galleries chanting, "We
Want Willkie." After his graduation in 1941, he practiced law briefly in Grand
Rapids with a Michigan classmate before enlisting in the Navy. Lieutenant
Ford became a war hero when, after surviving a tornado that swept through his
ship, he organized efforts that extinguished a fire in the ship's boiler room.

Unlike other war-heroes-turned-politicians, Ford neither boasted about his military record nor allowed his political operatives to publicize it.

Two years after his discharge, Ford, in what many deemed a politically suicidal move, challenged an entrenched incumbent Republican, Representative Bartel J. Jonckman, in a primary. Republican U.S. Senator Arthur Vandenberg—who supported the Marshall Plan and other policies Democratic President Harry Truman enacted to contain the spread of Soviet Communism—and who had been feuding with Jonckman—threw the weight of his formidable organization behind Ford. At thirty-five, Ford took his seat in the House. By his second term, Ford, again through the intervention of watchful and kindly elders, landed a coveted seat on the House Appropriations Committee. One biographer said that Ford approached both work and his colleagues with the earnestness of a Rotarian, "taking nothing for granted, claiming no greater knowledge than he actually possessed, and seeking the counsel of his elders."[74]

While in the House, Ford exhibited the rock-solid midwestern conservatism that characterized so much of his party at the time. He favored balanced federal budgets, a strong national defense, and civil rights. In 1963, a group of Young Turks led by Ford protégé, Illinois congressman Donald Rumsfeld, successfully managed Ford's campaign for chairman of the House Republican Conference, his party's third-highest leadership post. He toppled sixty-seven-year-old incumbent Charles Hoeven. Later that year, Lyndon Johnson named Ford to the Warren Commission. In 1965, in the aftermath of Johnson's landslide, in which the Republicans lost thirty-seven House seats, Ford's Young Turks again helped catapult him into a high party post. This time, Ford's target was incumbent minority leader Charlie Halleck. With the exception of civil rights legislation, Ford opposed most of Johnson's domestic initiatives. He criticized the manner in which Johnson prosecuted the war in Vietnam as well as what he called the president's "unhealthy passion for secrecy."[75] In response, LBJ leveled two insults at Ford that critics and satirists would repeat during his presidency: (1) that Ford had been playing football for too long without wearing a helmet and (2) that Ford could not walk and chew gum at the same time.

When he became president on August 9, 1974, Ford's fate was to extricate the nation from messes his two predecessors had left behind, both of which had badly divided the nation at home and undermined its effectiveness abroad: the war in Vietnam and the myriad of scandals that went by the name Watergate. Ford appeared to strike the right tone in the first words he uttered as president. "My fellow Americans, our long national nightmare is over," he said in an obvious reference to Watergate. Most of his fellow citizens thought that Ford had squandered his opportunity to heal the nation a month later, when Ford issued Nixon an unconditional pardon for any crimes he may have committed in his tenure as president. Gallup reported a drop in Ford's approval rating from 71 to 49 percent.[76] Editorials excoriated him. Without citing a scintilla of evidence, some charged that Ford had entered into a secret deal with Nixon prior to taking office. Waiving executive privilege, Ford testified in public before a House subcommittee to allay such suspicions. He maintained that the pardon was his only means of truly putting Watergate behind him and the rest of the nation.

In March 1975, Hanoi, in violation of the Paris Peace Accords Nixon had negotiated, launched a full-scale invasion of South Vietnam. Appearing before a joint session of Congress, Ford requested $1 billion in aid to South Vietnam. He was furious when Congress turned him down. Yet Ford, determined to be a constitutional president, yielded to constitutional and political realities. Rather than seek assistance through surreptitious means, he declared that, as far as the United States was concerned, the war was "finished."[77] However, Ford added one important exception: the fate of refugees, known as "boat people," whom few nations would accept. Ford ordered American naval vessels to pick up all that they could locate. When Congress rejected his request for funds to assist in their rescue, Ford turned up the heat. Through his personal intervention, 130,000 Vietnamese immigrants took their place within American society. "To do less would have added moral shame to humiliation."[78] That was not Jerry Ford's way. He would always regret that he had not been able to do more.

Ronald Reagan: The Lifeguard

When he was eleven years old, Ronald Reagan got his hands on one of his mother's favorite books, *That Printer of Udell's: A Story of the Midwest*, by

Howard Bell Wright. The inspirational novel told the story of how Dick Falkner, the impoverished son of an alcoholic father, became a figure of considerable influence in his community. After finding his way to the Disciples of Christ Church, Falkner advances a plan, which he proclaimed consistent with Christ's teachings, to redress poverty. Through his skills as a communicator, Falkner persuades the town to put his ideas into practice. The book ends with Falkner being elected to Congress, where he expected to be of "wider usefulness."[79]

"I want to be like that man," Ronald said to his mother after he shut the book. He also expressed a desire to join the Disciples of Christ, his mother's church, into which he was subsequently baptized. The parallels in the path Reagan's life would take and that of this fictional character are unmistakable: both displayed a deep commitment to a set of principles and used superior rhetorical skills they had developed to help secure their adoption. After he became president, more than a half century later, Reagan informed Wright's daughter-in-law that he had found a role model in Falkner and that he had tried to follow his example ever since.[80]

There were other similarities in the lives of the fictional Falkner and the real Reagan. Early in the novel, Falkner encounters the body of a homeless man lying in the snow. The same year that Reagan read Wright's book, he found his father lying in the snow, arms outstretched and smelling of alcohol. Embarrassed, he tried to ignore what he had seen, but ended up grabbing the older man by the overcoat, dragging him indoors, and putting him to bed.[81] Reagan had heard that his father had a "weakness" he could not control. This incident marked the first time he witnessed its effects.[82]

Reagan was born on February 6, 1911, in Tampico, Illinois, the second son of Nelle (Wilson) and Jack Reagan. Reagan derived his sense of self-discipline, sunny disposition, and flare for dramatics from his mother, a Protestant fundamentalist. He acquired his charm, skill at storytelling, sense of humor, interest in politics, and pride in all things Irish from his Catholic father. Before Ronald reached his teens, his family lived in six towns. The moves, necessitated by his father's shuffling from job to job, meant that Ronald and his brother, Neil, were always the new kids in school. One year they attended four different ones.[83] On a campaign visit to Monmouth, Illinois, in 1976, Reagan confided in an old acquaintance that the only time in his life when he had been truly terrified was when a bunch of the town's children chased him home from school.[84]

The constant moving during his childhood impeded Reagan from making permanent attachments to people. Countless people who observed him as an adult noticed that Reagan allowed himself to get close to very few people other than his wife Nancy, who recalled that he kept a part of himself concealed even from her. Reagan's Hollywood experiences may have reinforced this tendency. After he became president, aides would come and go without his appearing to pay much attention. In a sense, in Reagan's mind, his White House was not all that different from a movie set in which support staff and extras entered and exited from scene to scene and from picture to picture. Reagan confessed that he had learned as a child to compensate for the absence of close friends by developing his imagination: "As a kid I lived in a world of pretend."[85]

This imaginative capacity and the intense powers of concentration it helped him develop may account for Reagan's success as an actor. "He fit into any kind of role you put him in," recalled his high school drama instructor.[86] A one-time girlfriend commented that Reagan "had the inability to distinguish between fact and fantasy."[87] Making a similar point another way, Hollywood colleagues and White House aides would recall that the public Reagan was no different from the private one. Reagan's intense capacity to block out everything around him as he let his imagination be his guide served him particularly well during his days as a sports announcer, when he could describe entire plays to audiences with no facts at his command other than periodic updates and statistics he received from miles away by telegram. During breaks, he would regale friends with his impersonations of President Franklin D. Roosevelt delivering a "fireside chat."

In addition to his imagination, Reagan used reading, writing, and, eventually, plays and movies as forms of escape. His capacity to banish from his thoughts any trace of unpleasantness culminated at times in self-deception. He provided no better attestation to this than when, in his later years, he described his childhood as "sweet," "idyllic," and carefree—in the Tom Sawyer, Huckleberry Finn sense.[88] (By all accounts, it was nothing of the kind.) Reagan's capacity, as one adviser noted, to "blank things out" would adversely affect his presidency as members of his staff, bereft of a figure strong enough to compensate for Reagan's inattention to detail, would undertake missions without filling him in fully about the scope of their activities.[89]

Unlike his fellow Californian president, Richard Nixon, who started life in similar circumstances (though without the alcoholism at home), Reagan did not see himself as a victim. He regarded life's challenges as opportunities rather than crises and would allow nothing to dampen his overpowering optimism. "We make our life a struggle, when life should be a song," he wrote in a poem he composed as a high school student that appeared in his yearbook. Reagan believed that God had a plan for each individual and that God would put providers of assistance into people's paths as they were needed.[90] By the time he became president, he had come to believe that God also had a plan for the United States. He had long been approaching the idea that he was the Lord's assistant.

Reagan had, in a sense, played such a role earlier in life, when at age sixteen he became a lifeguard at Lowell Park, where the Rock River ran through Dixon, Illinois. After putting in ten-hour days, he would often return after hours to watch over, and sometimes rescue, swimmers who sneaked in for late-night dips, thinking they had not been detected. Reagan would carve a notch into a log every time he saved a life. By the time he gave up his post, he had carved 77 notches. Reagan derived satisfaction in imagining that the people he saved would continue along their life's journey to complete whatever task the Lord set for them. He came to like the attention he received as a lifeguard. "It was like a stage," Reagan later said, of his elevated lifeguard chair. "Everyone had to look up at me."[91]

Before he went into politics, Reagan had made his way in three industries that were coming into their own at the time he entered them: radio, motion pictures, and television. Each provided ample opportunities for him to develop his skills as persuader and performer. In the early 1930s, Reagan was a successful sports announcer and radio personality. His good looks, affable nature, and a call from a helpful friend landed him a Hollywood screen test. He made over fifty films, mostly in the range of B movies made to pair with expected blockbusters in double features. Always on time, always prepared, and always understanding of the team aspect of making movies, Reagan became a favorite among Hollywood executives. While he never acquired the fame or the standing of some of the leading matinee idols of the era, Reagan always had work.

Once it became steady and plentiful, he relocated his parents to southern California and became their principle source of support. From 1947 through 1952, and again from 1959 through 1960, Reagan served as president of the Screen Actors Guild. The position afforded him ample opportunities to hone his negotiating skills. It also first exposed him to the tactics, both surreptitious and confrontational, through which communist agents, loyal to Moscow, sought to infiltrate the movie industry. In the 1950s, with television still in its infancy, Reagan made the transition into that new and growing medium. As he hosted and occasionally performed on the program GE Theater, which aired on CBS immediately following the popular Ed Sullivan Show, Reagan became known to millions. Off the set, he doubled as a corporate spokesman, pitching General Electric products and delivering pep talks to its employees at plants across the country.

By the time he sought his first public office at the age of fifty-five, Reagan had developed a self-confidence unmatched by any other twentieth-century politician save for his first political hero, Franklin D. Roosevelt, whose campaign button Reagan had worn on his bathing suit as a lifeguard.[92] He would carry into the political arena traits that had become second nature to him as a lifeguard, sports announcer, actor, union president, and corporate spokesman: self-discipline, personal courage, an easygoing manner, a capacity for holding the attention of audiences, and deeply held beliefs.

To Reagan, public office was never an end in itself but an arena in which to attain goals he deemed important to his state and nation. Not surprisingly, he regarded elected positions he held as roles he would play for a limited time as he worked to enact his vision. He may have been only half joking when, asked what he would first attempt as California's governor, he said, "I don't know. I never played a governor." As president, he marveled at how anyone could succeed in that office who had not first been an actor. Once he had taken on a part, Reagan never stepped out of character. Aides would recall his never setting foot in the Oval Office, even on weekends, without his signature jacket and tie. He reserved jeans and informal attire for Camp David and his ranch in California.

Even while in excruciating pain, seriously wounded by a would-be assassin, Reagan the actor walked, shoulders back and suit jacket buttoned, into The George Washington University Emergency Medical Unit. Outside of public view, he collapsed. How Reagan comported himself under these circumstances, and his quip to the medical team that awaited him, "Tell me you are all Republicans," reassured a worried nation and attested to his personal courage. Few presidents gave voice to the feelings of a nation as well as Reagan did when he eulogized the crew that perished in the *Challenger* disaster or when he paid tribute to the "boys of Pointe du Hoc" on the fortieth anniversary of the D-day invasion. As he came to embody the central role in American political life, Ronald Reagan, once the "king of the Bs," showed himself superior to many of the leading men who preceded him. Most appropriately, his principal biographer, Lou Cannon, titled his study of Reagan's presidency *The Role of a Lifetime*.

Thomas Jefferson: The Philosopher

Historians have had much difficulty discerning what exactly made Thomas Jefferson tick. Jefferson would be pleased. A man of the Enlightenment, Jefferson would prefer that he be evaluated according to his ideas and actions rather than on his underlying personal motivations. Conscious of the role he played as a founder of what he termed a "rising nation," Jefferson carefully preserved his voluminous correspondence, in which he revealed for posterity his thoughts on suitable governmental structures, the results of his scientific inquiries, and even his taste in wines. Yet he destroyed letters to his wife, as well as any correspondence he might have had with his mother. That Jefferson, inscrutable though he often was, produced one of the few transformational presidencies in American history is reason enough to probe into the character of a man one biographer has appropriately called the "American Sphinx."[93]

Thomas Jefferson was born on April 13, 1743, on his family's plantation in what is now Albemarle County, Virginia. He was the oldest of eight children. His father, Peter, was a self-made, self-taught man of the frontier. A planter and surveyor with a love of adventure, the young Peter Jefferson augmented his holdings substantially when he married Jane Randolph, a member of one of Virginia's most prominent families. Peter died when Thomas was fourteen, leaving Jane, their children, and an estate that included sixty slaves behind. Long after Jefferson had come of age, he retained in his mind an idealized vision of his father, whom he idolized. (In his later years, Jefferson regaled his grandchildren with stories of Peter's heroic physical strength.[94]) It requires no stretch of the imagination to conclude that to Thomas Jefferson, his father was the prototype of the yeoman farmer in whose hands the freedoms gained in the American Revolution would be secure.

Jane Randolph appears to have exerted less of an influence on Thomas than had her husband—or at least less of a positive one. Their relationship appears to have been strained. He suffered a migraine headache immediately after she died 1776. Yet, in a letter to a kinsman in England, he relayed news of her passing as a mere matter of fact. Of his mother's family, Jefferson wrote in his autobiography, "They trace their pedigree far back in England and Scotland, to which let everyone ascribe the faith and merit he chooses."[95] For him to have attributed any importance to his mother's lineage would have been at odds with the image of himself as the quintessential American commoner, who believed in an aristocracy based on virtue and talent rather than on wealth and social standing. Such sentiments notwithstanding, Jefferson never shed the bearing of the Virginia aristocrat. Nor did he show any qualms about drawing upon his mother's powerful connections to advance his career and fortify the financial position of his family. He more than approved when his eldest daughter married a Randolph cousin.

At the age of sixteen, Jefferson received permission from his father's executors to enroll at the College of William and Mary. He became absorbed in the active social life of Williamsburg, then Virginia's capital. He learned to dance, to play the violin, and to hold his own in conversation. He also came under the influence of mathematics and natural philosophy professor William Small, the sole noncleric on the college's faculty. Under Small's tutelage, Jefferson read all the leading philosophers of the Scottish and French Enlightenments. He poured over the writings of John Locke, Francis Bacon, and Isaac Newton, and through Small, he also became an intimate of colonial governor Francis Fauquier and of George Wythe, one of Virginia's most learned lawyers.

In the company of such luminaries, Jefferson attended elaborate dinners where the conversation was as celebrated as the cuisine and entertainment, if not more so. Jefferson put the social skills he developed in such settings to good use later on as a diplomat and as a politician. He would also mentor younger men of promise, just as Small, Fauquier, and Wythe helped shepherd him. James Madison, James Monroe, Meriwether Lewis, and William Short were among Jefferson's numerous protégés and acolytes.

Jefferson completed two years of formal study. For the following five years—twice the amount of time aspiring lawyers of the era spent preparing for the bar—Jefferson, under the tutelage of Wythe, read widely in history, philosophy, and ethics. He also acquired a firm grounding in civil law, common law, and parliamentary procedures. After practicing law for two years, Jefferson won election to the House of Burgesses in 1769 and immersed himself in legislative committee work. He found that he had a knack for expressing himself clearly and concisely on paper.

Disliking the personal confrontations inherent in debate, Jefferson shied away from oratory. He would later write disparagingly of the capacity of fiery orators such as Patrick Henry to sway audiences (and juries) by appealing to emotion rather than to reason. Another reason Jefferson may have eschewed public speaking was that he possessed a weak voice. At the Continental Congress, Jefferson, in the words of John Adams, "though a silent member" was "prompt, frank, explicit and decisive" in committees and conversation.[96] Placed on the committee charged with drawing up a declaration of independence, Jefferson became its principal draftsman because of the "elegance of his pen," Adams remembered.[97] Back in Virginia, again applying skills Wythe had taught him, Jefferson drew up new sets of laws for what had become the state (or commonwealth) of Virginia. He would consider his authorship of the statute that disestablished Anglicanism as Virginia's official religion among his greatest achievements.

In 1779, Jefferson's fellow legislators elected him governor. His lack of executive and military experience impeded his effectiveness during wartime. Jefferson did little to fortify the state in advance of invading British forces. He also failed to use his skills as a writer to rally the public in the face of invasion. (His lack of activity in this regard suggests that he believed citizens would tend to their own defense.) When the legislature evacuated its temporary post in Charlottesville, Jefferson, his term having expired, failed to accompany them westward. Critics later accused him of vacating his post. In an uncharacteristic move, Jefferson later took to the floor of the legislature to clear his name.

Although he maintained that his primary interests were his farm and his books, Jefferson always kept one eye fixed on politics when he was at home. It appeared that every time he returned to his estate after relinquishing a public post, he instantly began plotting his next return. As a businessman, Jefferson proved less successful than his neighbor to the north, George Washington. Nor did he possess Washington's capacity for self-discipline or self-denial in his private affairs. Continually in debt, Jefferson continued to spend lavishly on food, wine, books, and works of art.

To allay his grief after his wife died in childbirth ten years into their marriage, Jefferson accepted Congress's call to succeed Benjamin Franklin as ambassador to France. He found the ways of the diplomat, which put a premium on indirectness rather than frankness, appealing. But when he became Washington's Secretary of State, Jefferson found for the first time that he could not avoid the kind of direct confrontations he so detested. Alexander Hamilton, as Washington's secretary of the treasury, would cross verbal and written swords with him on multiple occasions. Hamilton proved Jefferson's equal in intellect and as a writer and political organizer and Jefferson's superior as an orator and debater.

These two men found themselves on opposite sides of most questions of domestic and foreign policy. Behind the scenes, both rallied their respective partisans to defend their point of view and to cast aspersions on the character and ideas of the other. When Washington appeared to favor Hamilton's proposals for federal assumption of state debts, incurred during the Revolutionary War, a national bank, and a standing army, Jefferson increasingly, but not all that openly, tried to undermine the policies of the administration of which he was part. To counter the influence of the *Gazette of the United States*, a newspaper that served as Hamilton's leading propaganda organ, Jefferson founded a rival partisan journal, the *National Gazette*. To finance its operations, he put its editor, Philip Freneau, on the State Department's payroll, ostensibly as a translator. Jefferson also steered government printing business Freneau's way.

When Hamilton, whose own publication enjoyed similar government largesse, complained that Jefferson had used government funds to discredit Washington's administration, Jefferson denied the charge. He assured Washington, "in the presence of heaven," that he had played no role in Freneau's operation or that he, directly or indirectly, sought to influence what appeared in Freneau's publication.[98] Such news would have come as a surprise, not only to editor Freneau, but also to Representative James Madison, whom Jefferson beseeched on multiple occasions to "pick up" his pen and "cut [Hamilton] to pieces" on the pages of Freneau's publication.[99]

Anxious to preserve harmony within his administration, Washington wrote the two feuding cabinet officers and asked them to attempt to reconcile their differences. After declaring himself the injured party, Hamilton offered to heal whatever differences he could. Jefferson suggested, however, that he could not comply because Hamilton had undermined the people's liberty. Rather than defend his policy positions on their merits, Jefferson resorted to *ad hominem* attacks against his adversary. In a reference to Hamilton's lowly origins, Jefferson called his cabinet colleague "a man whose history, from the moment at which history can stoop to notice him, is a tissue of machinations against the liberty of the country which has not only received him and given him bread, but heaped its honors on his head."[100] Jefferson's outburst validates the views of one scholar who spoke of Jefferson's tendency to divide the world into "rogues" (those who opposed his point of view) and "honest men" (those who agreed with it).[101]

Perhaps in the heat of the moment, Jefferson had forgotten that Washington, who had risen above the station of his birth, might not be receptive to the tactics

Jefferson had used to undermine his rival. When it became apparent to him that Washington would side with Hamilton in most policy disputes, Jefferson began to describe the president as "a hollow hunk of his former greatness."[102] If Jefferson saw Hamilton as depraved, he found it politically useful to depict Washington as deceived.

Washington and Jefferson had a permanent falling out when Jefferson's privately expressed opinions of the president became public. Unhappy that Washington supported the Jay Treaty, which Jefferson believed compromised American interests to the British, Jefferson suggested in a letter to a friend that Washington was an "apostate" to the cause for which the American Revolution had been fought.[103] When his letter made its way into print, Jefferson panicked. Fearful of how Washington might retaliate, and unsure whether he would be able to work his way back into Washington's good graces, Jefferson turned to Madison for help. "Think for me on this occasion, and advise me what to do," Jefferson wrote.[104]

In contrast to Washington's council of war approach (in which officers debated options in the presence of all who would be affected by them), Jefferson preferred to make policy through "an intimate circle of friends" who shared his views.[105] To minimize the risk of personal confrontations (the kind in which he had engaged while in Washington's cabinet), and to spare himself the discomfort of having to choose among competing advice and advisers, Jefferson more often met with individual cabinet members separately than with his cabinet collectively assembled.

In his relations with Congress, Jefferson had his loyal lieutenants introduce legislation. He left it to these allies, often through the partisan press that he continued to fund, to answer his critics. This approach allowed him the luxury of maintaining the fiction that as president he was merely deferring to the wishes of Congress, which he insisted was the preeminent branch of government. With regard to real and perceived opposition, Jefferson used every means at his disposal to either win over doubters or render them ineffective. Those who he could not win over through the soundness of argument or the force of his personal charm, Jefferson would seek to circumvent, disarm, or remove from office in multiple ways (defeat at the polls, government reorganization, and impeachment).

During his last year in office, Jefferson, upon the recommendation of Secretary of State James Madison, imposed an embargo on all American trade with warring France and the United Kingdom. His purpose was to protect American shipping from seizure by either belligerent. His objective was to compel France and the United Kingdom, through means short of war, to respect the trading rights of neutral countries. In adopting the embargo, Jefferson discounted the warnings of Secretary of the Treasury Albert Gallatin that sanctions would not achieve their objective and would instead inflict greater harm on the U.S. economy than upon those of the warring powers.

Rather than abandon the policy when Gallatin's fears came to pass, Jefferson sought to enforce the embargo through increasingly draconian means. It would seem that his primary motivation was to bludgeon the public—in which he had invested high hopes—into submission. During Jefferson's final months in office, he reverted to a course he had taken as governor and as secretary of state when he had faced defeat and failure. He spent increased amounts of time at Monticello and all but ceased being president as he awaited the inauguration of Madison, his handpicked successor. While Jefferson did not resign his post, he might just as well have. "Never did a prisoner released from his chains feel such relief as I shall on shaking off the shackles of power," he said on leaving office.[106] This time he might actually have meant it.

Franklin Pierce: The Weakling

Few have seriously argued that Franklin Pierce was an effective president. But for the sectional strife that grew in intensity on his watch, he would receive even less attention from historians than he already does. Whatever actions Pierce took as chief executive resulted more from his unwillingness to offend those to whom he was beholden or had reason to fear than from deeply held convictions. Traditional accounts of Pierce's presidency discuss his excessive drinking and his concern for the fragile health of his wife, Jane Appleton Pierce. Her health deteriorated steadily after she and Franklin witnessed the

death of their sole surviving son in a train wreck shortly before his father's inauguration. Pierce's frustrations as president resulted from the same character
flaws that had helped render his domestic life a shambles even prior to their
child's death.

The fecklessness Pierce displayed in office contrasted sharply with the
intensity he exhibited when pursuing the multiple political offices he held,
including the presidency. Pierce attained his ultimate goal of becoming president as a result of a coalescing of personal attributes (a genial nature, good
looks, and unbridled ambition) and political circumstance (a stalemated
Democratic nominating convention, plus the party's need for a nominee who
could run equally well in both north and south).

The son of a Revolutionary War hero who was twice elected governor of
New Hampshire, Pierce was a graduate of Bowdoin College. There, his most
notable achievement was his befriending future novelist Nathaniel
Hawthorne, who would write Pierce's campaign biography. A few years later,
Pierce would wed the daughter of the college's president. Owing in part to his
father's popularity and connections, Pierce, at the age of twenty-four, was
elected chairman of the Hillsborough town meeting. A year later, he won election to the lower house of the state legislature. The next year, at twenty-six, he
became the youngest speaker in its history. At twenty-eight, Pierce was elected
to Congress.

Before too long, two obstacles arose that cast a cloud over what seemed to
be a promising political career: (1) Jane's aversion to politics and (2) Pierce's
fondness for alcohol.

Three years after taking his House seat, Pierce was named by the New
Hampshire state legislature to the United States Senate. This made him at
thirty-four the youngest member of that body. Bowing to pressure from Jane,
Pierce resigned in the fifth year of his six-year term and returned to New
Hampshire to practice law. It remains unclear to what extent Pierce's drunk-
driving accident (in which he ran over an elderly woman while driving a
horse-drawn carriage) contributed to this decision.

Again to please his wife, Pierce declined subsequent offers to return to the Senate
as well as an opportunity to serve as President James K. Polk's attorney general.

Pierce did, however, accept the chairmanship of the New Hampshire Democratic Party, a post that enabled him to keep his hand in the political thicket. One writer described Pierce in this period of his life as a man "at war with himself." He was simultaneously a politician craving to practice his calling and a devoted husband trying to honor a commitment he had made to his wife.[107] Alcohol may have been a means through which he tried to resolve this tension.

Aware that battlefield successes had propelled Washington, Jackson, and W. H. Harrison to the presidency, Pierce schemed to obtain a military commission and a command during the U.S.-Mexico War. He did not bother to inform Jane.[108] After being thrown from his horse on two successive days, Brigadier General Pierce won the respect of his men when he refused to be carried off the field in the midst of battle. Although he emerged from the war not quite the hero that generals Zachary Taylor and Winfield Scott had become, Pierce had added an important line to his résumé.

On the eve of the Democratic convention in 1852, Pierce engaged in a series of machinations—again behind his wife's back—that would lead to his nomination and subsequent election. When the convention deadlocked between three better-known contenders (Stephen A. Douglas, Lewis Cass, and James Buchanan), Pierce directed his surrogates to advance his name. Within his native region, Pierce remained popular because he supported the Wilmot Proviso, a Congressional provision that would have banned slavery from new territories acquired from Mexico. Though Pierce had supported the Compromise of 1850, which tipped the congressional balance toward the North by admitting California as a free state, Southerners appreciated Pierce's support for the accompanying Fugitive Slave Act, with its severe provisions. With Whigs badly divided over the slavery issue, Pierce won the general election in a landslide (capturing 254 electoral votes to Winfield Scott's 42).

Once in the White House, Pierce maintained the sectional compromise that had facilitated his nomination and election. He named to his cabinet three northerners, three southerners, and a representative from the border slave state of Kentucky. Secretary of War Jefferson Davis (who hailed from Mississippi) soon emerged as the strongman in an otherwise weak administration. Before long, Pierce was seen as playing the part of handmaiden to

Southerners angling to expand the reach of slavery. He tried, but failed, to help them further this objective by acquiring Cuba.

Pierce's vigorous enforcement of the Fugitive Slave Act led to increased abolitionist agitation in the North. This growing abolitionist activity, in turn, fanned southern militancy. Through the manner in which Pierce handled the case of Anthony Burns, a runaway slave who had taken up residence in Boston, Pierce displayed his political obtuseness. Burns's neighbors and prominent Massachusetts politicians had joined with abolitionists in protesting Burns's detention and anticipated forced return to the south. When his master offered to sell Burns his freedom, the local U.S. attorney, a Pierce appointee, refused, with Pierce's approval, to allow Burn's friends to complete the transaction. Pierce instructed his subordinates to "incur any expense" to execute the law to its fullest extent and sent federal troops to Boston to carry out his instructions.[109] Burns was marched to the docks to the sounds of rolling drums and past buildings bedecked with black bunting.

A more tempered response might have kept sectional passions in check. Pierce's action radicalized public opinion on both sides of the Mason-Dixon Line. "We went to bed one night old fashioned conservative, Compromise Union Whigs [and] waked up stark mad abolitionists," proclaimed textile baron Amos A. Lawrence.[110] Abolitionist William Lloyd Garrison publicly burned a copy of the Constitution. Southerners, rejoicing in this victory, began pressing for others.

Pierce stepped on another political land mine when he endorsed Stephen A. Douglas's Kansas-Nebraska bill, which repealed the ban on slavery Congress had, as part of the 1820 Missouri Compromise, placed in all territory north of the 36°30' north parallel, save for what became the state of Missouri. Five out of seven members of Pierce's cabinet opposed Douglas's bill. Davis and one other colleague favored it. Pierce asserted that the measure was consistent with the Jacksonian principle (of popular sovereignty) because it allowed the residents of future states, rather than Congress, to decide whether to permit slavery. Pierce's position diverged not only from those of most northern Democrats (who also considered themselves Jacksonians), but also from all of his presidential predecessors, including several, who had owned slaves.[111] Pierce threw the full weight of the presidency behind the measure, which he signed into law on May 30, 1854. His action triggered a rush of new settlers on opposite sides of the slavery issue into Kansas, culminating in a small civil war.

Why had Pierce acted as he had? He was both weak and duplicitous. Following a path of least resistance, Pierce found it easier to sacrifice the political legacies of his fellow northern Democrats than to offend southern ones who had helped put him in office. Rather than use the high standing he enjoyed among southern politicians to entice them to tone down their demands, Pierce allowed himself to become a tool of the firebrands. While it cannot be known whether another president facing similar circumstances might have been better able to calm tensions and dull sectional divisions, Pierce lacked the courage to try. In the absence of any conviction over which he was willing to take risks to advance, and unconcerned about the moral issues inherent in slavery, Pierce bent in the direction in which the wind was blowing the strongest. All the while, the United States drifted toward civil war.

James Buchanan: The Blockhead

James Buchanan served in more state and federal offices than any other president before or since. He served in the Pennsylvania state legislature, the U.S. House of Representatives (for ten years), the U.S. Senate (also for ten years), and as ambassador to Russia (under Jackson), secretary of state (under Polk), and ambassador to Great Britain (under Pierce). Despite all this experience, Buchanan achieved little of note in any of these offices. He was more or less a timeserver, carefully calculating his next move up the American equivalent of what Benjamin Disraeli called a "greasy pole." Although they appointed Buchanan to high posts out of political obligation, presidents did not rely on his counsel. Andrew Jackson thought Buchanan an "inept busybody."[112] James K. Polk, tired of Buchanan's meddling in the departments of other cabinet members, considered dropping him from his cabinet but decided instead to act as his own secretary of state.[113]

The only cause to which Buchanan appears to have been dedicated was his own advancement. Haughty by nature and embittered at having had to serve under men he considered his inferiors, Buchanan was determined to do things in his own way. During his lengthy climb to the presidency, he had grown cynical about the political process and the motives of other politicians. He betrayed a cavalier attitude toward ethics, both public and private, and seemed to believe that most everyone else did as well. Complacent and set in his ways, Buchanan was hardly the kind of president capable of thinking or acting anew at a time when the nation required such an ability in its president. He failed as president not because he was weak but because, as one biographer has noted, he pursued the wrong policies vigorously.[114] President Buchanan is best remembered for sitting on his hands as states began to secede from the union. He adopted this posture, however, only after he failed to obtain an objective he had first sought.

Buchanan exhibited a relentless drive at an early age. His father was an orphaned Irish immigrant and his mother an impoverished country girl. One of the presidents to be born in a log cabin, Buchanan put himself through Dickinson College and became a lawyer. He held a few minor political appointments before he won election to the state legislature at the age of twenty-three. Although he cited his fealty to the Federalist Party as the reason for his candidacy, Buchanan confided to his father that his main objective in seeking office was to attract better clients.[115] While he was not the only ambitious young man of modest background to court the daughter of an iron magnate in his area, those who knew Buchanan best insisted that what most attracted him to Ann Coleman was her father's money.[116]

Ann died mysteriously after breaking off their engagement. Four months later, Buchanan won a seat in Congress. "I saw that through a political following I could secure the friends I then needed," he recalled years later.[117] From the time he arrived in Washington, Buchanan began plotting to become president. He tried and failed three times to win the Democratic Party's nomination. He prevailed on his fourth attempt primarily because he was out of the country when the Kansas-Nebraska Act was being debated. Once nominated, Buchanan and his minions made certain that nothing derailed him on his path to the White House. After the election, investigators uncovered multiple frauds that had occurred during the recent election in several states that worked to the Democrats' favor. One clerk in Philadelphia admitted forging 2,700 naturalization forms so that recent immigrants could cast ballots.[118] A congressional investigation later revealed that government funds had made their way to the Know Nothing Party, which Democrats expected to siphon votes away from the new Republican Party in closely contested states. This would allow Buchanan to eke out a narrow win in those states and pick up their electoral votes. Buchanan was even reported to have personally selected which of the third party's newspapers would receive these funds.[119]

In selecting his cabinet, Buchanan put a greater premium on social compatibility than on regional or political diversity. Conspicuously absent was anyone known to be allied with Stephen A. Douglas, the man Buchanan had defeated for the 1856 Democratic presidential nomination. Buchanan let it be known during the transition that he had his own ideas as to how to handle the ongoing slavery dispute. His declared fealty to strict constructionist principles and professed respect for the separation of powers notwithstanding, Buchanan wrote to sitting justices of the Supreme Court, urging them to take the slavery debate out of "politics." By that, he meant denying Congress jurisdiction over whether to constrict the spread of slavery.[120] In his inauguration address, Buchanan took sides in a long-brewing dispute when he condemned antislavery agitators in Kansas but not their proslavery adversaries. Feigning disinterest in how the Supreme Court might come down on the slavery issue, Buchanan pledged to abide by whatever decision it reached. Some noted with suspicion that he had engaged in lengthy conversation with Chief Justice Roger Taney on the inaugural stand.[121]

Two days after Buchanan was inaugurated, the Supreme Court handed down the Dred Scott decision. In a vote of 7 to 2, it declared unconstitutional any federal legislation banning slavery from the territories on the grounds that it violated the rights of slaveholders to carry their property wherever they wished. Buchanan dropped the pretext of impartiality when he requested that Congress approve a constitution for the proposed new state of Kansas. Congressional approval of this measure would have admitted Kansas to the union as a slave state. Antislavery spokesmen argued that the referendum in which voters approved the constitution had been unfairly administered. They also maintained that the document provided no mechanism for slavery to be banished from Kansas, should this prove to be the majority's wish. Ignoring such protests, Buchanan fought for its approval. He played both nice and nasty with representatives and senators. His administration dangled patronage, government contracts, mail routs, shipyards, and cash before undecided—and, presumably, malleable—legislators. It also fired thousands of federal employees who had obtained their posts through the intervention of politicians who opposed the bill.[122] Douglas, having staked his reputation on the principle of popular sovereignty, balked at what he regarded as a boldfaced disregard of it.

The rift between the two men shattered the Democratic Party, which up to that point had been the only political party competitive in both the North and South. After the House refused to admit Kansas on Buchanan's terms, the president tried to convince Kansans to adopt the proslavery constitution in a specially called referendum in exchange for an additional land grant and immediate admission into the union.[123] Kansas voters spurned his offer. Buchanan attempted to oversee a fair referendum that would have revealed the true sentiments of the majority of the voters in the territory. As the battle wore on, Buchanan's true goal became clear. He sought rapid admission of an additional slave state as a means of restoring the political balance between slave and free states in the U.S. Senate. This, he reasoned, was the only way to avert secession.

As Kansans stood their ground and secessionists began preparing to leave the Union, Buchanan did nothing. He voiced his opposition to secession and opined that he considered it unconstitutional.[124] Yet this self-proclaimed strict constructionist—who had intervened in the internal operations of two other branches of government and attempted to bribe voters in a territorial election—claimed that he lacked the power to prevent it. Had he been willing to follow the example of Stephen A. Douglas's hero, Andrew Jackson, Buchanan would have secured for himself a higher place in history. ("Old Hickory," who also considered secession unconstitutional, had sent federal troops to South Carolina to compel compliance with federal laws. See chapter 4.) Instead, he left for his successor the worst situation that ever awaited an incoming president in all of American history.

Woodrow Wilson: The Prime Minister

"I cannot explain Woodrow Wilson to myself," Owen Wister reflected in 1930. The novelist continued:

If an obscure teacher of history, with no backing but his own gifts, becomes President of Princeton, and leaves behind him storm, schism, and fury; becomes Governor of New Jersey, and leaves behind him, storm, schism, and fury; goes to the White House and creates storm, schism, and fury; arrives in Paris the hope of the world, and leaves Paris amid storm, schism, fury, and disillusion, you will admit that he is a very extraordinary person."[125]

Wister did not have to add Wilson's controversial and unsuccessful effort to obtain Senate ratification of the Versailles Treaty, which he brought home from Paris, to make his point. Wister, though a partisan, loyal to the memory of his friend and Wilson critic, Theodore Roosevelt, voiced sentiments that many of Wilson's admirers shared. Actually, Wilson was not all that difficult to understand. Simply put, he insisted on having his way on all things he deemed important. When circumstances were favorable, he met with dazzling success. When they were not, he could not or would not adapt.

Wilson was born December 28, 1856, in Staunton, Virginia. During his infancy, Wilson's father, a prominent Presbyterian minister, moved the family to Augusta, Georgia. The shadow of the Civil War and Reconstruction hovered over Wilson's childhood. Wilson's first recollection was hearing a neighbor report that Lincoln had been elected president and that war would follow.[126] During the war that followed, Wilson's father's church functioned as a makeshift hospital for Confederate soldiers.

Religion played a central role in Wilson's upbringing. Wilson's mother was a daughter and sister to Presbyterian clerics in addition to being the wife of one. Her brother, an early hero and role model of Wilson's, became a center of controversy among southern Presbyterians when he publicly embraced Darwin's theory of evolution.[127] Wilson's entire family rallied to his uncle's defense. Like his fellow Presbyterians, Wilson believed that he was among the God's elect, "selected" to further the Lord's mission on earth. He expressed a "longing to do immortal work."[128] Observing him in prayer, one minister noted that Wilson "prayed like a man who knew God not only as . . . a doctrine in theology or an ideal in ethics, but as an experience in his own soul."[129] Of Wilson's demeanor at the Paris Peace Conference, John Maynard Keynes wrote that the president's thought process and temperament were more theological than intellectual.[130] This characteristic may account for the sense of certainty Wilson exuded while advancing political arguments.

As a child, Wilson listened intently to his father's sermons and closely watched the manner in which he led congregations in prayer. By the time he emerged as an orator in his own right, Wilson demonstrated a capacity to hold the attention of audiences. He won acclaim as one of the most eloquent and inspiring speakers of his age. One of his listeners found Wilson's diction "beautiful in its simplicity" and recalled that he spoke "clearly, distinctly, in a loud tone, and with perfect enunciation."[131] Wilson's father had taken care to push him in this direction. The elder Wilson had his son write down what they had discussed in conversation. He would then have him prepare several drafts until he was satisfied that the boy had expressed his ideas with precision. A stern disciplinarian, the minister would belittle his son in front of others as a means of enforcing his compliance to rules he had established.[132] Some have attributed Wilson's refusal to compromise with figures he could not dominate to an unconscious desire to stand up to his father.[133]

By the age of sixteen, Wilson was already an admirer of all things British, especially of nineteenth-century statesman and prime minister William Gladstone. He came to share his hero's advocacy of free trade and laissez-faire economics. The young Wilson carefully studied the speeches of Gladstone and other British politicians and historical figures, such as Edmund Burke. He committed long passages to memory. Sometimes he would retreat to the woods and recite them out loud. By the time he entered college, Wilson harbored dreams of his acting as prime minister, heading a party committed to noble purposes, and persuading his peers to enact his program through the force of his eloquence.

After a year at Davidson College, Wilson transferred to Princeton and, upon his graduation, enrolled at the University of Virginia's school of law. At every institution of learning he attended, Wilson made debating his primary extracurricular activity. At Princeton, he reorganized the debating society into a model parliament, in which parties competed for the approval of audiences through their capacity to persuade them of the rightness of their arguments. Envisioning himself as a future politician, he took, partially in jest, to signing calling cards as "Thomas Woodrow Wilson, Senator from Virginia." By the time he reached law school, he had dropped the "Thomas" in favor of the more alliterative name, by which he would become known to the world.

Finding public eloquence a nobler and more forthright form of persuasion than private negotiation, Wilson bemoaned what he saw as a decline in American oratory. In his senior thesis—and later in his doctoral dissertation that became the book *Congressional Government*—Wilson criticized Congress for dividing power among multiple committees and subcommittees. Finding the dispersal of power an inefficient and unaccountable means of conducting the public's business, Wilson advocated making the executive the preeminent branch within the American system of government. Wilson was fully aware, of course, that what made the British Parliament function was, not the persuasiveness of its orators before the House of Commons, but the centralization of power it awarded the majority party through the prime minister and the party discipline the ruling party imposed. As president, Wilson would attempt to make policy by extending the reach of his office to the majority party in Congress, thereby making the historical and constitutional separation of the executive and legislative branches permeable. When his party controlled Congress, the first six years of his eight-year presidency, Wilson pulled this off with considerable success.

After gaining admission to the bar, Wilson practiced law for a short time in Atlanta but soon shifted his ambitions toward academia. After taking his Ph.D. at Johns Hopkins in 1885, Wilson taught at Bryn Mawr, Wesleyan, and Princeton. His oratorical skills made him a popular lecturer on campus. Through his writings on historical subjects and issues of the day, Wilson won considerable note as a public commentator. In 1902, he became the first noncleric to serve as Princeton's president. "I feel like a new prime minister," he asserted at the outset of his tenure, and before long, he was all but functioning in such a role.[134] Prior to his ascension, Wilson demanded and received complete powers over faculty appointments and removals. He settled into a pattern of proposing ideas on short notice and ramming them through. With hardly a dissenting voice, Wilson organized the university into major departments, revised the curriculum, raised academic standards, built new facilities and dormitories, and, in what would be his most significant achievement, hired fifty young tutors ("preceptors," as Wilson called them) of outstanding promise. When a trustee questioned the location of a particular laboratory, Wilson replied that as long as he was Princeton's president he would "dictate the architectural policy of the university."[135]

Five years into the job, Wilson lost two major battles. While these back-to-back defeats would shorten his tenure at Princeton, they would also help propel him into other arenas in which to demonstrate his particular brand of leadership. In 1906, without notice or discussion, Wilson proposed abolishing upper-class eating clubs and replacing them with four-year resident colleges at which students of all four classes, together with some faculty, would reside and take their meals. Responding to alumni opposition, the trustees shelved Wilson's plan. In what would become a lifelong practice, Wilson broke relations with friends on the faculty who had opposed him.[136] In prime ministerial fashion, Wilson, having seen his plan repudiated, considered resigning. He would do precisely that after he suffered an even more humiliating defeat.

When the trustees voiced support for a plan to situate the university's graduate college on a site a dean recommended and for which the administrator obtained a donor, Wilson, favoring a different location, argued that what was at stake was not the site on which to erect buildings but the independence of the university. As would a prime minister who had dissolved parliament and called new elections, Wilson took his case to those he termed his "constituency" (alumni who chose the trustees). Disdainful of controversy, the initial donor withdrew his gift. When the dean produced an even larger pledge from a second donor and appeared to have retained the support of the trustees, Wilson capitulated.

At this juncture, New Jersey Democratic leaders sounded Wilson out about his availability to run for governor. His battles against privilege at Princeton had captured considerable headlines. Party bosses concluded that they could easily sell Wilson in the increasingly immigrant-dominated urban wards. Opinion leaders in New Jersey and elsewhere were already weighing Wilson's possibilities as a presidential contender. Before tendering him the gubernatorial nomination, party leaders demanded in writing Wilson's assurance that he would not, if elected, "set about fighting and breaking down the existing Democratic organization and replacing it with his own."[137] Having received it, they did not pay attention when, in his acceptance speech and in subsequent interviews, Wilson assured party reformers that he would enter office beholden to no one but the people. Running in 1910, a year in which Democrats fared well across the country, Wilson won handily, carrying with him an overwhelmingly Democratic lower house of the legislature, the Assembly. The New Jersey Senate, which was not up for election that year, remained Republican.

In his first order of business, Wilson stunned his initial backers when he made good on his pledge that, as governor, he would be unbossed. Rather than ask the legislature to appoint to the U.S. Senate the leader who had initially proposed him for governor and who fully expected Wilson to return the favor, Wilson threw his weight behind the man who had won a nonbinding primary. With direct primaries and direct election of U.S. Senators ranking high on progressives' agenda, Wilson's action endeared him to reformers across the country and propelled him to top-tier status as a presidential hopeful in the run-up to the 1912 Democratic National Convention.

During his first year as governor, Wilson steered to passage bills that established binding primaries, workers' compensation, and state regulation of utilities. He pressed through a corrupt practices act as well as measures permitting referendum, recall, and commission forms of government. Wilson easily had his way with the Democratic Assembly. During his first year as governor, the Republican Senate chose not to stand in his way. This changed during his second year, after the electorate put the Republicans in control of both legislature houses in 1911. New Jersey's "prime minister" appeared at a loss when faced with a new set of circumstances. He ceased appearing before Democratic caucuses, with the party now in the minority, and failed to develop a legislative strategy for working with the Republican majority. Spending increasing amounts of time away from the state, Wilson fell back on a veto strategy. One biographer found his behavior predictive of what lay ahead: "He had to hold the reigns to do the driving alone; it was the only kind of leadership he knew."[138]

In his first six years as president, Wilson reverted back to the leadership style that had served him so well in his early days as university president and governor. The beneficiary of a major split within the Republican Party, which resulted in his having two principal opponents (sitting president William Howard Taft and former president Theodore Roosevelt), Wilson was elected president in 1912 with 42 percent of the vote. (In the Electoral College, Wilson received 435 votes, Roosevelt 88, and Taft 8.) Democrats won comfortable majorities in both houses of Congress. In his inaugural address, in prime ministerial fashion, Wilson proclaimed that the electorate selected the Democratic Party its instrument to affect change. Claiming a mandate, the American "prime minister" set out to implement his program.

He became the first president since John Adams to address joint sessions of Congress in person. During his first year as president, Wilson appeared before Congress five times. As he had in New Jersey, Wilson also met with Democratic majority party caucuses. Drawing upon the increased attention, which newly elected presidents habitually received, Wilson used his popularity and prestige, often through the press, to entice legislators to approve his program. The fruits of his early and relentless labors included lower tariffs, implementation of a federal income tax on individuals, creation of the Federal Reserve System, enactment of the Clayton Antitrust Act, and establishment of the Federal Trade Commission. In his second year, Wilson pushed through Congress measures to restrict child labor, establish an eight-hour day for railroad workers, and create workers' compensation for federal employees. (These measures and their effects will be discussed further in chapter 5.)

In the international arena, where Wilson believed the president could act unilaterally, Wilson embarked on a confused attempt to advance the cause of democracy in Mexico. (On one occasion, he appeared to be supporting at least two different contenders for the Mexican presidency, during its civil war.) With the outbreak of war in Europe in 1914, Wilson attempted to steer a neutral course. Initially angered at Britain's naval blockade and seizures of American merchant ships, American public opinion turned when a German submarine attacked the British ocean liner *Lusitania*, killing 128 Americans. Resisting pressures to declare war on Germany, Wilson declared that there was such a thing as a nation being "too proud to fight."[139] Tensions eased when Germany, acceding to Wilson's ultimatum, temporarily suspended unrestricted submarine warfare.

With his backers proudly proclaiming that "he kept us out of war," Wilson won re-election by one of the narrowest margins in American history. (He received 49 percent of the popular vote to Charles Evans Hughes's 46 percent and prevailed in the Electoral College 277 to 254.) On the eve of his second inauguration, Wilson, in a speech to Congress, called for "peace without victory."[140] He cited imperialism, militarism, and balance-of-power politics, all of which he condemned as the causes of the war, and proposed that an international body be established to arbitrate future disputes.

Wilson saw his hopes of keeping the United States out of the war dashed when Germany resumed unrestricted submarine warfare and sank three American ships. In his speech to Congress on April 2, 1917, Wilson made the case for war. As he made the case for American intervention, Wilson spoke more of the need to uphold abstract principles than he did of upholding national interests. "The world must be made safe for democracy," Wilson declared as he promised a "war to end all wars" as a means of making that goal a reality. The United States, he said, "would fight for . . . the rights of those who submit to authority to have a voice in their own Governments, for the rights and liberties of small nations, and for the universal domination of right by such a concert of free peoples, as shall bring peace and safety to all nations, and make the world itself at last free."[141] In articulating these lofty objectives, Wilson spoke only for the United States. (The "concert of free peoples" phrase referred to the League of Nations concept he had advanced in January.) Within months over two million soldiers were headed to France.

Cognizant of the nation's wariness about what Jefferson had called "entangling alliances," Wilson resolved that the United States would fight not as one of the Allied Powers, but as an "Associate Power." His failure to make American participation in the war conditional on the Allies' acceptance of the war aims he would advance in his "Fourteen Points" proved a major mistake. The United States entered the war at a time when the Allied Powers were as close as they ever would come to losing the war. This was the time to have pressed France and the United Kingdom to commit themselves to the same goals as had the Americans. But Wilson demurred. In January 1918, again in a speech before Congress, as he officially presented the Fourteen Points, Wilson returned to an idea he had advanced on two previous occasions, a League of Nations to preserve the subsequent peace.

As one contemporary commentator saw it, Wilson's "associated" partners regarded his Fourteen Points not as "sincere tender," but as a "ruse of war designed to lure the German people to surrender and overthrow their government.[142] In October 1918, the German government informed Wilson of its willingness to seek an armistice based on the Fourteen Points. In granting the armistice and pressing the Allied powers to do the same, the American prime minister allowed Germany to believe that he had the power to commit not only the United States but also the Allies to the just peace he had promised. On this, he would fail to deliver.

Wilson sowed the seeds of the future catastrophe that would befall him when, on the eve of the 1918 elections, he denounced the Republican Party, which was showing signs of a resurgence. In a letter released October 25, Wilson explained that the Republican minority had "unquestionably been pro war," but "anti-administration." He urged voters to give him a "free hand" by electing a Democratic Congress. "The election of a Republican Congress," Wilson insisted, "would . . . be interpreted on the other side of the water as a repudiation" of his leadership.[143] As he had in New Jersey, Wilson made little effort to work with his political adversaries after they had attained control of the legislative branch. Wilson even raised the stakes when he announced that he would head the American delegation to the Paris Peace Conference and declined to name any active Republicans to it. If he was not consciously daring the Republican Senate to defeat the treaty he would bring home, Wilson was clearly betting that his personal popularity in Europe and at home would be sufficient to compel the Senate to ratify it.

Because the United States had not fought the war for territorial or other discernible interests, Wilson hoped to play the part of a disinterested arbiter at the peace conference. John Maynard Keynes, attached to the British delegation, found it odd that Wilson had arrived with no proposals of his own to press on his fellow delegates.[144] Perhaps the president believed that his oratorical skills would have the same effect on delegations assembled in Paris as they had on Democratic Congresses. Or he may have assumed, as one diplomat speculated, that he would be up against "counterparts of his own spirit."[145] This was hardly an apt characterization of the wily David Lloyd-George or the cynical Georges Clemenceau. Through his direct participation in the talks, Wilson put himself at a disadvantage. As he later admitted, he hastily agreed to provisions he had not thought through in response to pressures of the moment.

Once the deliberations were underway, Wilson's counterparts set about dismantling, qualifying, and redefining nearly all of his Fourteen Points. Whenever Wilson protested that his erstwhile allies were making a mockery of promises he had made to the peoples of the world, they conditioned their support for the one item they knew Wilson most wanted—the League of Nations—on his acquiescence to their compromises. According to David Lawrence, a former student of Wilson's who covered the conference as a journalist, Wilson went along with their demands because he believed that the League, acting as a "continuing peace conference," would undo mistakes he and others had made in fastening the treaty.[146]

During his two visits to Europe, Wilson never availed himself of several assets at his command. Europeans still depended heavily upon the United States to supply them with food. Their governments had borrowed heavily from the United States during the war and would borrow even more before the treaty took effect.[147] Wilson never used these economic advantages as bargaining leverage. Nor did he, as he would later attempt at home, seek to use his popularity with the people of Europe to persuade the representatives of other governments to follow his lead. Wilson let what Keynes called his "moral influence" dissipate, first by agreeing to ban the press from the proceedings and, ultimately, by not leaking his side of the story to the press as a means of applying the pressures of public opinion to his counterparts.[148] While the talks dragged on, American armies were still stationed in Europe.

Back in Washington, Wilson found the Senate unwilling to approve the treaty in the absence of written assurance that only Congress would continue to determine whether to deploy U.S. combat forces in battle. Wilson would not agree to such reservations. While he insisted that the treaty did not negate Congress' constitutional and legal right to declare war, Wilson stiffened his adversaries' resolve when he declared that the treaty imposed a "moral obligation" on its signatories to surrender some of their sovereignty. Wilson insisted that, were the Unites States to add reservations, he must extend to other nations the right to do the same. After Wilson's principal antagonist, Republican Senate Majority Leader and Foreign Relations Committee Chairman Henry Cabot Lodge, publicly disagreed, the British government voiced agreement with the senator's position. Still, Wilson would not budge.[149] Refusing to acknowledge, let alone bow to, political realities, Wilson, responding to Democratic entreaties that he compromise, blurted out, "Let Lodge compromise . . ."[150]

Repeating a scene he had played at Princeton, Wilson attempted to go over the head of the senators. He embarked on a national speaking tour to rally public opinion behind the treaty. His prediction that he would draw sizable and favorable crowds proved accurate. But with Lodge maintaining that he too supported the League, the public found it difficult to discern the precise difference between the two men's positions. With the war concluded, it was also ready to move on to other issues. The physical collapse Wilson suffered in the latter stages of the trip and the debilitating stroke that hit him after his return to Washington effectively removed him from the public debate over the treaty as the Senate began its deliberations.

From his sickbed, Wilson instructed his fellow Democrats to oppose the treaty whenever it came up to the Senate floor with the reservations attached. The Senate brought the treaty to a vote on three occasions. In November 1919, it voted down Wilson's original version in a straight party vote. When it considered the treaty with the Lodge reservations attached, a coalition of Democrats and "irreconcilables" (senators opposed to the treaty with or without reservations) defeated it. Cognizant that the public favored American participation in the League, Lodge brought the treaty, again with the reservations tacked on, to a final vote on March 19, 1920. With twenty-one Democrats disregarding Wilson's instructions and voting in its favor, the measure failed to carry by only seven votes.

For a time, Wilson fantasized that voters would regard the 1920 election as a referendum on the League and therefore provide the Democrats with a substantial victory. His hopes dissipated by the Harding landslide, Wilson looked to 1922 and 1924 for vindication. Over the years, numerous analysts have offered competing theories to explain why Wilson did not rise above his natural stubbornness in order to assure American entry into an institution he had strived so hard to create. Some maintain that Wilson's illness affected his reasoning powers.[151] Lodge was of the view that Wilson's personal hatred for him was so great that the president would oppose anything that had the Senator's ideas affixed to it.[152] This certainly squares with Lloyd-George's attribution of Wilson's failure to his "refusal to give up personal animosity.[153] Some speculated that Wilson's wife, acting as his gatekeeper, kept unpleasant news from him, thereby depriving him of important facts. Yer in her memoir, she recalled beseeching her husband to "accept the reservations and get this awful thing settled."[154] In his last public address, Wilson continued to predict his ultimate vindication. "I have seen fools resist Providence before," he said, "and I have seen their destruction, as will come upon these again—utter destruction and contempt. That we shall prevail is as sure as that God reigns."[155]

Richard Nixon: The Cynic

At the age of twelve, Richard Nixon declared to his mother his intention not only to become a lawyer but to become a certain kind of lawyer. "I will be an old-fashioned kind of lawyer," he told her, "a lawyer who cannot be bought."[156]

For weeks, Nixon had been listening to his parents discuss the unraveling Teapot Dome scandal, in which officials in the Warren G. Harding administration leased federal oil reserves to private interests in exchange for kickbacks. Lawyers featured prominently in the scandal. They had advised corrupt officials as to how they might swindle the public and defended the guilty before congressional investigators and juries.

The Teapot Dome scandal had particular resonance with the Nixon family. The Elk Hills oil reserve, one of three sites that Harding's secretary of the interior had, in exchange for personal gain, allowed private interests to exploit, was not far from where they lived. Even closer to home, oil had been discovered on a site in Santa Fe Springs, California—a site Nixon's father had once rejected in favor of another plot of land in Whittier, California, where he located the gas station and grocery store that secured the family's livelihood. For years, the elder Nixon ruminated over what might have been, thinking, perhaps, that fate had cheated him.

His son Richard also came to regard himself as a victim. He grew to resent those he considered less deserving, less hard working than himself, but who had risen to prominence and power through wealth, privilege, and connections—many of whom he would later clash with (Congressman Jerry Voorhis, State Department official Alger Hiss, Senate hopeful Helen Gahagan Douglas, John F. Kennedy, and much of the Washington press corps). When up against them, Nixon gave tirelessly of himself to defeat them. He described the source of his bitterness, and how he went about overcoming obstacles to attain what he felt was rightly his: "What starts the process, really are laughs and slights and snubs when you are a kid. . . . But if you are reasonably intelligent and if your anger is deep enough and strong enough, you learn that you can change . . . attitudes by excellence, personal gut performance, while those who have everything are sitting on their fat butts."[157] Attitudes he sought to change were those belonging to people with the capacity to reward him: the public. When this method failed, Nixon may well have regarded the excesses that eventually brought him down merely as attempts to even the score.

The story of Nixon's rise could have been lifted right out of a Horatio Alger novel as testimony to the American dream. Nixon all but made this very comparison in his speech accepting the Republican nomination in 1968.How the boy who pledged to become a principled, incorruptible lawyer became the man who was overheard on tape half a century later discussing the payment of "hush money" to criminals in his employ and the sale of ambassadorships should keep historians and psychologists busy for decades, if not centuries.

The story began in the grocery store, where young Richard was put to work to help out his family. His day started at 4:00 A.M., when he would head to nearby Los Angeles to pick up the produce. Relatives recalled that he departed especially early so friends wouldn't observe him performing such menial tasks. As a boy, Nixon was reserved, studious, sensitive, and musically inclined. He learned to read while quite young and was seen poring over newspapers while his peers stuck with picture books.[158] (It was from the pile of newspapers gathered around him that Nixon learned the full details of the Teapot Dome episode.[159]) He was also prone to daydreaming. Mostly, he dreamed of getting away—from the store, the gas station, and the farms and orange groves that surrounded them. He would recall lying awake at night listening to train whistles and dreaming of traveling to far off places.[160]

Nixon biographies habitually speak of the two personalities that lived side by side in the man who became President Nixon. There was his lighter side, which people attribute to the influence of his mild-mannered, well-educated, Quaker mother, Hannah Milhous Nixon. No one has ever taken issue with Nixon's depiction of her, in his remarks to the White House staff on his last day as president, as a "saint."[161] There was also Nixon's darker side, which many trace to his father, Frank, a grammar school dropout with a violent temper and an argumentative disposition. One Nixon associate wrote of conspiring with others on Nixon's staff, and even with Nixon, to prevent the dark side of his personality from taking over.[162]

In addition to hard work, financial worry and personal loss characterized much of Nixon's youth. Both an older and a younger brother of Nixon's succumbed to tuberculosis. (Hannah and Frank Nixon had five sons.) The costs of their medical care imposed a tremendous burden on his family. An outstanding student, Richard won a scholarship to Harvard but could not attend because his family could not afford his travel and living expenses. He enrolled instead at Whittier College, where again he compiled an outstanding academic record, proved a star debater, and won election as student government president on the promise that he would persuade the college administration to allow dancing on campus. It was at Whittier that Nixon had his first encounter with certain types of opponents. The Franklins, a fraternity-style organization comprised of sons of the town's wealthier families, dominated student life on campus. Nixon organized a rival organization of the self-identified have-nots.[163] Taking the name Orthogonians, the group elected Nixon its president during his freshman year. It functioned as his ready-made campaign organization during his subsequent successful runs for student government posts.

After graduating Whittier, Nixon won a scholarship to Duke Law School. Pouring all of his energies into his studies and part-time jobs he took to help meet expenses, Nixon acquired the nickname "Gloomy Gus." Nixon expressed pride in having acquired a reputation for developing an "iron butt," which he took as a tribute to his determination to succeed.[164] Unable to land a job at a Wall Street law firm after graduation, Nixon practiced law with two firms in Whittier. He worked briefly in Washington, D.C., with the Office of Price Administration after the outbreak of World War II, before joining the navy as a lieutenant.

Finding the prospect of retracing his earlier steps in Whittier unappealing, Nixon leaped at the chance when local businessmen asked him to run for Congress in 1946 against ten-year incumbent Jerry Voorhis. An ardent New Dealer, Voorhis appeared an anachronism in a district that had been trending Republican. Under the tutelage of California political consultant Murray Chotiner, Nixon ran what contemporary commentators would term a "negative campaign." He harped on Voorhis's acceptance of support from a political action committee known to have had communist affiliations. But in fact, the organization Nixon denounced carried a name that was similar to that of the group that had actually endorsed Voorhis. Democrats charged that Nixon had intentionally set out to deceive voters. Whatever pangs of guilt Nixon may have felt he assuaged with the knowledge that Voorhis was "a millionaire's son."[165] Having come from virtually nowhere, after winning the election Nixon had now both a job and a promising future.

While in the House of Representatives, Nixon participated in two events that shaped the rest of his political career. House leaders selected Nixon as one of a handful of junior members to partake in a fact-finding tour of war-torn Western Europe. He returned from that six-week sojourn (his first trip to Europe) an enthusiastic supporter of the Marshall Plan, which Congress was then considering. The experience awakened in him what became a lifelong fascination with international affairs. The extensive reading on foreign policy he commenced, the international contacts he made, the broadened outlook he developed, and the ongoing conversations he undertook with foreign policy experts all began with this trip. The experience clearly appealed to Nixon's "lighter side."

Nixon's second formative experience in the House and how he would remember it would bring his darker side to the surface. As chairman of a subcommittee of the House Un-American Activities Committee, Nixon, in the role of prosecutor, exposed the duplicity and perjury of former State Department official Alger Hiss, who had denied having been a communist and a Soviet spy.[166] Nixon emerged from the experience a hero to conservatives, convinced that the Soviets had infiltrated the American government. He also reaped the animus of liberals, who either believed Hiss innocent, resented being proved wrong, or believed that Nixon made it possible for Joseph R. McCarthy to destroy the reputations and careers of others on less sound evidence. Years later, Nixon expressed bitterness that someone like Hiss—the recipient of the finest possible education, a judicial clerkship with Oliver Wendell Holmes, and prestigious professional opportunities—would betray his country, and that so many members of the American intellectual elite had risen to his defense.[167]

Nixon's next brush against this set came when he opposed Hollywood starlet and friend of Eleanor and Franklin Roosevelt, Representative Helen Gahagan Douglas, in the 1950 campaign for U.S. Senator from California.[168] While each side rigorously attacked the other, Nixon received the bulk of criticism. While Nixon never actually called the liberal Douglas a "communist," his outburst that she was "pink right down to her underwear" appeared calculated to imply that she was. This campaign revealed, for the first time in public, how Nixon might react under stress.[169] He won by 680,947 votes.

Two years later, Republican leaders tapped Nixon to run for vice president on Dwight Eisenhower's ticket. After critics charged that Nixon had unethically tapped into a campaign fund that donors had set up to cover his political expenses, Nixon went on television, then in its infancy, to refute them. Assuming the pose of the hard-working, earnest Orthagonian, he gave a full accounting of everything he and his family owned, right down to his wife's "respectable Republican cloth coat." Along the way, he lambasted his wealthier Democratic opponents for taking advantage of tax loopholes and tax shelters, and for maintaining secret funds of their own.[170] While his effective performance saved his place on Ike's ticket, Nixon came away from the experience convinced that he had been the victim of a double standard liberals had devised to smear him. The episode may have reinforced doubts Eisenhower harbored about his running mate. Through a combination of circumstances—including a series of presidential illnesses, Eisenhower's disdain for partisan politics, and Nixon's growing interest in foreign policy—Nixon became one of the most active and well-known vice presidents up to that time.

His razor-thin loss to John F. Kennedy in the presidential race of 1960 marked a turning point in the ongoing struggle for dominance between Nixon's lighter and darker sides. Viewed from one perspective, some might find it remarkable not that Nixon lost that close contest but that he had come as close to winning it as he had, given the number of mistakes he made during the campaign, the anemic state of the economy, the perception that American prestige had declined abroad, and the unpopularity of Kennedy's Catholicism in certain parts of the country. (In many areas, Kennedy trailed the rest of the Democratic ticket.)

Nixon's errors included his agreeing to debate the lesser-known and highly charismatic Kennedy on television; his reluctance to make greater use of the still-popular incumbent, President Eisenhower; his ill-considered commitment to campaign in all fifty states (prompting a last-minute scramble to small, electorally poor states); his waffling over whether to intervene after civil rights leader Martin Luther King Jr. was arrested on trumped-up charges; and his slamming of his knee on a car door, which necessitated a hospital stay of several days. Most of these errors resulted from Nixon's insistence on running his own campaign and failing to delegate even minor decisions. When the ballots had been counted, Nixon lost the popular vote to Kennedy by less than 0.1 percent. Kennedy pulled ahead of Nixon by 118,000 votes. In the Electoral College, Kennedy received 303 votes to Nixon's 219, with fifteen going to Virginia Senator Harry Byrd. Although he had lost, his mistakes notwithstanding, Nixon had made a favorable impression on half of the electorate.

Putting his focus elsewhere, Nixon saw other factors as responsible for his defeat. Undoubtedly, he was correct in concluding that Kennedy, the son of one of the country's richest men, had outspent him considerably. (Kennedy once joked about his father being unwilling to pay for a landslide.[171]) During his eight years in the Senate and six years in the House, Kennedy had not established a reputation as a policy or political heavyweight. This did not stop some reporters from covering him as if he had. The press, smitten with his charm, failed to cover Kennedy's private, often reckless, personal indiscretions. Again, Nixon and many of his supporters also saw a double standard at work. Liberal intellectuals and commentators would denounce Nixon as a "red baiter," while failing to criticize Kennedy for refusing to state whether he approved of the Senate's censure of the liberals' bête noire, Senator McCarthy, for conduct unbefitting a senator.[172]

Above all, perhaps, were allegations that Kennedy allies in Cook County, Illinois, Texas, and elsewhere had committed multiple acts of fraud. Kennedy told of receiving a call from Chicago mayor Richard J. Daley in which he was assured that, "with a little bit of luck and the help of a few close friends," he would carry Illinois.[173] How Nixon must have seethed upon hearing that in salons from Harvard to Georgetown to Hollywood his detractors joked that if such had indeed been the case, it had been done for a good cause. Yet, presented with evidence of rampant electoral abuses, Nixon eschewed advice from party figures, including President Eisenhower, that he demand recounts and contest the results in disputed states.

Publicly, Nixon maintained that he ruled out these options because he did not want to "tear the country apart" by questioning the legitimacy of the new president at the height of the Cold War.[174] Confident that his supporters would stick with him, and believing that at forty-seven he would have another opportunity to run for president, Nixon—already known as Tricky Dick to his enemies—may not have wanted to add "sore loser" to the terms critics used to describe him. That he privately believed he had won the election is beyond dispute. "We won but they stole it from us," he announced to friends at a post-election holiday party.[175] Nixon came away from the experience determined never to be outspent or outgunned again. Having proved unable to withstand the combination of Joseph P. Kennedy's money and the electoral shenanigans of Dick Daley (in Illinois) and Lyndon Johnson (in Texas), Nixon would learn to beat them at their game when his chance came again.

Nixon's political career nearly derailed with his defeat for governor of California in 1962. At what he termed "his last press conference," he announced the day after he lost that the press would not "have Nixon to kick around anymore."[176] Yet, again through a combination of circumstances (including domestic unrest, an unpopular war, and a divided opposition) and his own hard work (especially his tireless campaigning for GOP candidates in 1966), Nixon was elected president in 1968. In a three-way contest that included incumbent Democratic vice president Hubert H. Humphrey and Alabama governor George C. Wallace, running as an independent, Nixon emerged the victor, carrying 43 percent of the vote, with Humphrey taking 42 percent and Wallace 13 percent. (In the Electoral College, Nixon received 301 votes to Humphrey's 191 and Wallace's 46.)

The first president in over a century to take office with his party in control of neither house of Congress, Nixon advanced a series of domestic initiatives that appeared calculated to disarm and divide the Democratic opposition. More interested in foreign than domestic affairs, Nixon delegated much of what he attempted domestically to subordinates. His instructions to John Ehrlichman, head of the Domestic Policy Council, was to do whatever he needed to when it came to environmental policy, just so long as it kept the president "out of trouble."[177] Leonard Garment, who handled cultural matters for Nixon, attributed the astronomical increases in arts funding that Nixon obtained to his desire to "soften his image" and to confound his detractors by catching them off guard—a favorite Nixon pastime.[178] While the extent to which Nixon actually believed in all he advanced in the domestic sphere may never be completely known, he left a legacy of government intrusion into the economy and spending increases unmatched by most of his Republican predecessors, and several of his Democratic ones.[179] Commentator Mark Shields proclaimed Nixon the nation's "last liberal president."[180] Few conservatives disagreed. (Nixon's domestic initiatives are discussed extensively in chapter 5.)

Initially, Nixon's stated intention to invest most of his efforts in foreign affairs appeared a good omen, given his experience in the area and with the nation bogged down in an unpopular war and with 530,000 of its soldiers in Vietnam. Nixon resolved that he would bring American participation in the war to an end through a three-pronged strategy. The first was the gradual withdrawal of American troops from Vietnam, replacing them with American-trained Vietnamese troops. (This came to be known as "Vietnamization.")

The second consisted of persuading North Vietnam's principal benefactors, the Soviet Union and the People's Republic of China, to press North Vietnam to make concessions at the negotiating table. Nixon sought to entice them to do this by granting each much of what it most wanted. He offered the Soviet Union concessions in strategic arms limitations talks, making parity their principal objective. Among the fruits of Nixon's *détente* policies were the Anti-Ballistic Missile Treaty and the Strategic Arms Limitations Treaty, both of which Nixon signed in 1972. Both would be eclipsed in subsequent years by Reagan's more aggressive, "we win, you lose" approach to the Soviet Union.

China received, in addition to the reversal of a decades-old American policy of maintaining that the Chinese Nationalist government, headquartered on Taiwan since 1949, was the legitimate government of all of China, promises of future trade as well as intelligence the United States had about the posting of Soviet troops along China's northern border. While Nixon stunned the world with his surprise announcement in 1971 that he would visit the People's Republic of China the following year, Nixon's shift in American policy was not as sudden as it appeared. One year prior to his election as president, Nixon made the case for ending China's "isolation" from the United States in an article in *Foreign Affairs,* titled "Asia After Vietnam."[181] Nixon carefully fudged the Taiwan issue, conceding that it was part of China, but committing the United States to the peaceful resolution of the island's political status.

During and after his presidency, Nixon maintained that, even in the absence of their perceived capacity to apply leverage to North Vietnam, he would have followed the approach he followed toward the U.S.S.R. and the P.R.C. because it was in the best interest of the United States. While Nixon's sustained outreach to the two rival communist powers did reduce world tensions, they did little to dissuade Hanoi from continuing its assault against South Vietnam. Both countries, each suspicious of the other, continued supplying North Vietnam with arms as they negotiated with Nixon and his administration. Nixon demonstrated his resolve to the North Vietnamese, the third aspect of his strategy, by escalating aerial bombings of major targets and mining harbors.

With the success of so many of Nixon's foreign policy objectives hinging on the outcome of secret back-and-forth negotiations with so many governments, both principals and go-betweens, Nixon grew increasingly concerned about possible leaks and the impact they might have on discussions. His efforts to keep them to a minimum set in motion forces that would eventually cut short his presidency.

Angered that the Pentagon Papers—documents detailing how his predecessors had, step by step, increased American military involvement in Vietnam—had made their way to the press, Nixon went to court to suppress their publication. After the Supreme Court allowed the *New York Times* and the *Washington Post* to print them, Nixon authorized a special White House unit (dubbed the "plumbers") to identify the sources of the leaks and prevent future ones. As they proceeded, Nixon and his retainers failed to distinguish between what was in the national interest and what was in the personal or political interest of a particular president.

In his first post-presidential televised interview, Nixon summarized the attitude that prevailed in his White House from the top down when he told David Frost that, "When the president does it, that means that it is not illegal." On the famous Watergate tapes, Nixon can be heard ruminating about using the power of his office to take reprisals against his political enemies.[182] The break-in that led to Nixon's participation in the cover-up that brought him down had been directed not against suspected national security risks but against the headquarters of the opposition's political operatives. Before long, the light and dark sides of Nixon's personality merged. While presidents as far back as Washington resisted sharing with Congress documents detailing transactions between presidents and their advisers, Nixon claimed executive privilege, not as much to protect policy discussions as to shield lawbreakers from prosecution. When the Supreme Court ordered Nixon to release the Watergate tapes, he yielded them. Days later, after the contents of the self-incriminating tapes were made public, he resigned.

Ironically, the most enduring reminders of Nixon's time in office remain all the reform-oriented measures, enacted in the aftermath of Watergate, that continue to hover over American politics. Terms such as "special prosecutors," "campaign finance legislation," "financial disclosures," "campaign contribution limits," "whistle-blower protections," and "offices of government ethics" all came into common usage and attained special significance in the wake of the president who, as a boy, vowed to become the kind of lawyer who could not be bought. "Always remember, others may hate you, but those who hate you don't win, unless you hate them, and then you destroy yourself," Nixon said to his White House staff on his last day as president.[183] This remains the best summation of his presidency and character.

3

VISION

$\mathscr{M}$ost who have run for president articulated a vision for the nation they hoped to lead. As political scientist Thomas C. Cronin aptly said, "You cannot be a successful president unless you can project a vision about the purpose of America."[1] While most great presidents came to office with a sense of vision, the American people have elected very few visionaries. The handful they did elect exhibited more than occasional pragmatism. While they clung to their ends, they were willing to compromise—over their means, and on issues they awarded a low priority.

In the Oval Office, vision has become manifest in five ways. Some presidents achieved major policy goals that ultimately proved beneficial to the nation after articulating a clear sense of what they intended to do during their campaigns (Jefferson, Lincoln, Wilson, and Reagan) or upon succeeding to office (T. Roosevelt and Truman). Others offered up a vision in response to issues that came to the fore after they had taken office (Kennedy in the case of civil rights and George W. Bush after the attacks of 9–11). Others (L. Johnson) showed extraordinary vision in some areas and virtually none in others. Several presidents, perceiving themselves primarily as managers (Van Buren, Cleveland, Taft, and G. H. W. Bush), responded to events as they unfolded (some with considerable skill). And a handful (Jackson, Polk, and A. Johnson) implemented visions that proved harmful to the long-term interests of the nation. The stories of their presidencies suggest that it is important for great presidents not only to have a sense of vision but to display the right vision, both for their times and for all times. (Once again, W. H. Harrison, J. A. Garfield, and G. W. Bush were not evaluated.)

Of the nation's forty-three presidents, four presidents demonstrated the clearest and most correct vision for their country, and most correct vision for the country in their times, as well as for ours.

FOUR PRESIDENTS RECEIVE A SCORE OF 5:

Abraham Lincoln

Ulysses S. Grant

Theodore Roosevelt

Ronald Reagan

EIGHT PRESIDENTS RECEIVE A SCORE OF 4:

George Washington

Thomas Jefferson

James Monroe

Zachary Taylor

Woodrow Wilson

Franklin D. Roosevelt

Harry S Truman

John F. Kennedy

TEN PRESIDENTS RECEIVE AN AVERAGE SCORE OF 3:

John Adams

John Quincy Adams

Benjamin Harrison

William McKinley

William H. Taft

Warren Harding

Calvin Coolidge

Dwight D. Eisenhower

Lyndon B. Johnson

Bill Clinton

ELEVEN PRESIDENTS RECEIVE A SCORE OF 2:

James Madison

Andrew Jackson

Martin Van Buren

James K. Polk

Rutherford B. Hayes

Chester A. Arthur

Grover Cleveland

Richard Nixon

Gerald Ford

Jimmy Carter

George H. W. Bush

SIX PRESIDENTS RECEIVE THE SCORE OF 1:

John Tyler

Millard Fillmore

Franklin Pierce

James Buchanan

Andrew Johnson

Herbert Hoover

This chapter offers glimpses of how five presidents acted on the vision set forth for their presidencies: Thomas Jefferson, Abraham Lincoln, Theodore Roosevelt, Lyndon B. Johnson, and Ronald Reagan.

Thomas Jefferson

After mounting a spirited campaign, Thomas Jefferson handily defeated incumbent president John Adams in the election of 1800. Prior to the passage of the Twelfth Amendment, however, the electors did not cast separate ballots for president and vice president. After Jefferson and his vice-presidential running mate, Aaron Burr, each received seventy-three votes in the Electoral College, the House of Representatives declared Jefferson the winner on the thirty-sixth ballot. In one of the great paradoxes in American history, this logjam in the House was broken only after Jefferson's most ardent political adversary, Alexander Hamilton, whom Jefferson regarded also as a personal enemy, beseeched colleagues in the lame-duck Federalist House help put Jefferson over the top.[2]

Jefferson's ascension to the presidency marked the first time in American history that power passed peacefully and by virtue of election from one political party to its opposition. With this thought in mind, Jefferson referred to his election as the "revolution of 1800." Some saw it as a counterrevolution in the sense that Jefferson had pledged to govern according to the principles of 1776, from which he had argued the Federalist Party had strayed. In his years in opposition, Jefferson identified a series of things he wanted the federal government to do, as well as things he wanted it to stop doing. All sides readied themselves for a profound change. The only question on most minds was how rapidly and how forcefully Jefferson would proceed.

Jefferson's vision for America was rooted in the Enlightenment. Like most of the other founders, Jefferson had been deeply influenced by the writings of John Locke; Charles-Louis de Secondat, Baron de La Brède et de Montesquieu; Adam Smith; David Hume; and other philosophers of the era. Unlike Washington, Adams, Madison, and the other founders, Jefferson was also heavily influenced by more radical ideas that Jean-Jacques Rousseau and other philosophers advanced at the tail end of the French Enlightenment. Jefferson took a somewhat different view of human nature, the role of government, and the virtues of popular democracy than did most of the other founders.

Jefferson did not quarrel with the gloomy assessment of human nature that Madison, Hamilton, and Jay posited in *The Federalist*, in support of the division of power among three distinct branches of government, with appropriate checks and balances placed on each. "It may be a reflection on human nature, that such devices should be necessary to control the abuses of government," Madison observed in Federalist Paper No. 51, "But what is government itself, but the greatest of all reflections on human nature? If men were angels, no government would be necessary. If angels were to govern men, neither external nor internal controls on government would be necessary."[3] Jefferson, however, did not believe that this needed to be a permanent condition. While Jefferson did not think that all men could become angels, he did believe that education, proper nurturing, and widespread dissemination of scientific knowledge *could* make them less base, acquisitive, and selfish.

With this as his guiding view, Jefferson placed greater faith in the ability of popular majorities to decide public questions correctly than did the other founders. He hoped that great questions of the day would be decided in an atmosphere in which the public had access to accurate and complete information. As this became more commonplace, Jefferson was more willing than some of his colleagues to modify existing rules and political institutions to facilitate social equality and reflect improvements in the human condition. His often-cited pronouncements that a "little rebellion" every now and then was a "good thing" and statutes and constitutions be allowed to expire with a generation should be viewed in this context. His belief in the gradual perfectability of humanity gave rise to the vision that guided his presidency.

The future that Jefferson envisioned was one in which communities of yeomen farmers lived harmoniously, free from the dictates of a distant federal government. According to Jefferson, government's proper role was to guarantee conditions that allowed such an agrarian society to flourish. As he described in the Declaration of Independence, government was an instrument established by the governed to secure the natural rights the people had been given by their Creator. To ensure that the federal government remained confined to this limited role, Jefferson argued that it be allowed to exercise only powers specifically granted it in the Constitution. With the national government restrained, Jefferson believed that participatory democracy would prevail at the local level. There, similarly situated citizens would enact wise policies by majority vote. Jefferson expected that such a society of equals would be motivated by communitarian values as well as by individual self-interest.

Jefferson did not want government to be run by a few rich and well-born men as had been the case in in colonial Virginia. He sought instead to make it easier for men from humble origins to participate in government. He intended most of what he achieved prior to becoming president (removing primogeniture and entailment from Virginia inheritance laws, disestablishing the Anglican Church in Virginia, establishing universal public education, banning religious tests for holding office, and reducing property requirements for suffrage) to advance this goal. Once such unnatural distinctions had been eradicated and men were free to compete and cooperate on equal footing, Jefferson believed that a "natural aristocracy" of rulers would emerge. Well-informed majorities among these free yeomen would elect highly educated, publicly spirited leaders. Jefferson felt that universal education would keep both leaders and those they led virtuous. "If a nation expects to be ignorant and free . . . it expects what never was and what never will be," he would say.[4] Jefferson cringed at the prospect of a charismatic leader, particularly a military hero, seizing power by flattering an uneducated mob. (He feared the ascendency of a man like Andrew Jackson for precisely this reason.)

While serving as ambassador to France, Jefferson had seen the squalor that had taken hold in European cities and observed how powerful interests, skillful in court politics, used their influence to produce policies that worked to their benefit. He had seen farmers migrate to cities and accept work in primitive factories for meager wages. (Jefferson thought that such practices created a sense of dependency among the workers that was inconsistent with free government.) He concluded that the liberties of the many were put in jeopardy whenever one class or faction took control of government and used its powers to enrich itself. As Washington's secretary of state, Jefferson became persuaded that Secretary of the Treasury Alexander Hamilton's plans for debt assumption and the Bank of the United States had been calculated to introduce into the New World practices he had come to detest in the Old. Jefferson formed the first organized opposition party in the new nation primarily to resist the Hamilton system.

While he regarded broad political participation as a safeguard of liberty and sought to extend it, Jefferson saw the abundance of arable land in the American west as a means through which his exalted yeomen farmers could retain their independence from commercial and manufacturing interests, concentrated in the east.[5] As president, he set out to make land available to more people by nearly doubling the size of the "empire of liberty." While president, he transferred more than four million acres a year into private hands.[6] Jefferson expected additional lands to come into his orbit in any of three ways: military conquest, diplomacy, and displacement of Native Americans. The continent's first occupants, he argued, would either adopt the practice of farming privately owned tracts or risk losing tribal lands to future white settlers.[7]

Jefferson might have thought that those "who tilled the soil were the chosen people of God," but he recognized that the most successful among them had their soil tilled by others. Slavery had made it possible for Jefferson to live the life of the mind and to participate in the public sphere. It would do the same for other whites of lower stations whom Jefferson intended to raise up. Jefferson acknowledged, nonetheless, that slavery was a violation of natural rights and condemned the injustice and violence on which it was based.[8] He grew, however, increasingly ambivalent about the institution as he acquired increased influence and political power. With Southern planters comprising the core of his political constituency, Jefferson chose not to disturb an institution peculiar to his region. As president, he helped expand it into others.

In the early days of the new republic, Jefferson worked to banish slavery from the Northwest Territory (which became the states of Illinois, Indiana, Michigan, and Ohio). As president, however, he allowed it into the Louisiana Territory, which he had acquired. As these new lands were settled, current and aspiring slaveholders would take with them a significant portion of the growing slave population. This might reduce the threat of slave insurrections. Somehow, in Jefferson's mind, an institution he proclaimed an "abominable crime" would become less lethal and odious if spread out across wider territory.[9] By the end of his life, he essentially threw up his hands in frustration over his inability to devise a solution to what he recognized as a festering problem. He condemned the Missouri Compromise of 1820, which allowed Congress to place limits on where slavery might be practiced, a repudiation of his "states rights" policies.

At the outset of his presidency, Jefferson signaled that he intended to govern as he had promised in his campaign. He released all prisoners who had been convicted under the Alien and Sedition Acts, which he had, while in the opposition, denounced. As he had promised, he reduced the federal debt, federal outlays, and federal taxes. During his first seven years as president, Jefferson presided over a booming economy. Surpluses ran on average $5.1 million (equal to 0.8 percent of estimated GDP). The national debt fell from $83.0 million at year-end 1800 to $65.2 million at year-end 1808. Jefferson slashed defense outlays, suspended all ship construction, and pared Adams's navy of thirteen frigates down to seven. Turning his attention away from the Atlantic and toward the Mississippi River, the principal trade artery to the port of New Orleans, Jefferson invested instead in gunboats. Historians attribute the nation's state of military unpreparedness on the eve of the War of 1812 to Jefferson's cutbacks on defense.

Jefferson's "empire of liberty" agenda received a boost from an unexpected source early in his term. Anxious to reduce the number of borders the United States shared with foreign governments, Jefferson contemplated seizing control of the Louisiana Territory from Spain, which maintained a weak military presence in North America. After learning that Spain had ceded Louisiana to France, Jefferson instructed emissaries to ascertain Napoleon's willingness to sell the port of New Orleans to the United States. In need of funds to finance renewed hostilities with the United Kingdom, and having abandoned his plans to re-establish a French presence in North America after he had failed to supress the Haitian revolution, Napoleon offered to sell the entire territory for $15 million. Jefferson accepted at once.

By his own admission, Jefferson's acquisition of territory through purchase violated one of his most sacred principles—and one on which he based his candidacy for president: limiting the power of the federal government. He had vociferously argued that the federal government could only exercise powers the Constitution expressly granted it. On the question of whether the federal government might acquire territory in the manner Jefferson proposed, the Constitution was silent. Jefferson's first impulse was to seek a constitutional amendment, authorizing territorial purchases. Fearful that Napoleon might withdraw his offer while Congress and state legislatures debated the soundness of both amendment and purchase, he abandoned this idea. In words that anticipated those Lincoln would use half a century later, Jefferson argued, "to lose our country by a scrupulous adherence to written laws, would be to lose the law itself."[10]

The purchase safely behind him, Jefferson commissioned the Lewis and Clark expedition to survey the newly acquired terrain. Reports of their exploration captured the public imagination and sparked not only interest in new settlements but dreams of a continental United States.

Having waged and won a battle in Congress against many of his fellow partisans to acquire Louisiana, Jefferson shied away from taking on other projects he favored but for which he could find no explicit authorization in the Constitution, such as a federal role in education and federal spending on internal improvements. Nor did he seek authorizing constitutional amendments. His "Jeffersonian" successors, citing the absence of such expressed authorizations, would veto such measures.

In the international area, Jefferson believed that governments, like individuals, should adhere to a common moral standard. Long opposed to paying tribute to secure the safety of American ships on the high seas, Jefferson, early in his term, refused the demand of the pasha of Tripoli for $250,000 in tribute and an additional $25,000 annually. When the pasha declared war, Jefferson sent a naval fleet to the Mediterranean to impose a boycott. After Barbary pirates seized an American ship and took its crew captive, U.S. forces bombarded Tripoli and set fire to the captured vessel. The pasha released the hostages, but not before Jefferson agreed to pay a ransom of $60,000 for each of the three hundred sailors. Thus, Jefferson wound up paying the pasha substantially more than the blackmailer initially demanded. In an attempt to save face, Jefferson tried to justify his decisions by issuing a lofty tribute to the spirit of republican government. Under a government "bottomed on the will of all," he said, "the life and liberty of every citizen become interesting to all."[11]

Surprisingly, Jefferson did not seize on the incident as an opportunity to increase defense expenditures. He suffered dire consequences as a result. In order to shield American merchant ships from hostile fire or capture during the Napoleonic wars, Jefferson persuaded Congress to enact an embargo, suspending all foreign trade with France and the United Kingdom. He took this action after a British navy ship, which had been denied permission to search an American merchant vessel for possible deserters from the British navy, fired upon the American ship. In response, Jefferson closed American ports to all British ships and issued a call for a 100,000-member militia.[12] At the suggestion of Secretary of State James Madison, Jefferson opted for the embargo as a means of pressuring the British and the French to respect the trading rights of the neutral United States. Both saw the measure as an alternative to war, which they believed the United States lacked the capacity to wage. Neither considered what course they might follow in the event these economic sanctions failed to achieve their purpose.

Nor had they weighed what impact the embargo might have on the American economy. In the fifteen months since it began, American international trade fell from $247 million (equal to 35.5 percent of estimated GDP) in 1807 to $111 million in 1809. Federal revenue fell from $16.4 million in 1807 to $7.7 million.[13] Estimated real GDP contracted by 5.8 percent during Jefferson's last year in office, and merchants commenced widespread smuggling. Lacking an alternative to his policy and unwilling to abandon it, Jefferson vigorously enforced the embargo with every the means at his disposal. As increasing numbers of his fellow citizens disregarded his edict, Jefferson grew resolute, even ruthless, in his actions.

He sent the army to police the frontiers and the navy to patrol harbors, in violation of his own admonition against using the military for policing purposes during peacetime. He authorized searches in the absence of warrants. He urged state attorneys general to initiate libel suits against editors who had criticized him and his policies. In a most creative betrayal of his strict constructionist principles, he advised friendly governors that First Amendment protections did not apply to the states.[14] In his last year in office, Jefferson had incarcerated more people for violating the embargo than Adams had for violating the Alien and Sedition Acts, which Jefferson had so heatedly denounced. Many of those he ordered arrested were prosecuted not for smuggling but, as had been so under Adams, for dissenting from official policy or criticizing the government. Worried that it might not be possible to execute all the guilty, Jefferson advised prosecutors to send "full statements of every man's case, that the most guilty may be marked as examples, and the less suffer long imprisonments, under reprieves from time to time."[15]

As the embargo crisis dragged on, Jefferson and Madison appeared befuddled that so many of their fellow citizens would so wantonly and openly defy the law and that they proved so unwilling to forego luxury goods to advance an important principle.[16] They failed to consider that, while wealthy planters such as themselves were foregoing imported china, fabrics, books, and wines, those they claimed to represent—sailors, stevedores, store clerks, merchants, artisans, and craftsmen—were losing their livelihoods. And what of all those yeomen farmers whose crops were rotting on American wharfs?

Having set out on a policy based on a principle, Jefferson found it difficult to either admit error or reverse course. Garry Wills aptly attributed Jefferson's stubbornness to his propensity to see universal principle and sacred duty in every political decision he made. "Whatever he was doing at the moment had a radiantly eternal rationale," Wills observed.[17] The embargo situation did not lend itself to the kind of mental somersault in which Jefferson engaged during the discussions about the Louisiana Purchase, when he resolved to sacrifice a lesser principle to advance a greater one. Seeing no way out, Jefferson counted the days that remained before he could turn his office over to his designated successor. Yet the "empire of liberty" he established over a continent remains.

Abraham Lincoln

From the time he entered public life until his death, Abraham Lincoln adhered to two basic principles: (1) respect for the rule of law and (2) opposition to slavery. "If slavery is not wrong, nothing is wrong. I cannot remember when I did not so think and feel," he remarked late in his presidency.[18] Much as he hated slavery as an institution, restricting its spread was as far as Lincoln thought he could go while remaining faithful to the Constitution.

Lincoln maintained that when Jefferson committed the United States to the principle that all men are created equal he intended those words to apply to all people. Seeking support for his own position in the actions of the founders, Lincoln noted that the Continental Congress had expressly forbidden the practice of slavery in the Northwest Territory in 1787. In his address at Cooper Union, delivered in February 1860, Lincoln went to great lengths to demonstrate that a majority of signers of the Constitution favored the gradual elimination of slavery. He thought that slavery was on a path toward extinction until Congress passed the Kansas-Nebraska Act, which opened up vast new unsettled territories to it, and the Supreme Court handed down the *Dred Scott* decision, which allowed it to spread into territory that had been declared free. These back-to-back changes in the existing political climate propelled Lincoln back into elective politics after a six-year hiatus. Having previously ruled out going on the offensive against slavery where it existed, he now found himself waging a defensive battle to prevent it from entering places where it had not previously been sanctioned. Lincoln made restricting the spread of slavery the central issue in his campaigns for senator and president. Two issues on which Lincoln refused to compromise during his presidency were the expansion of slavery and the preservation of the Union.

In his first inaugural address, Lincoln asserted that he had "no purpose directly, or indirectly, to interfere with the institution" (of slavery where it was already practiced). He added that he did not believe he had the "lawful right" to do so and added, perhaps disingenuously, that he had "no inclination" to do so.[19] He took a different view, however, when it came to accepting its extension into new territories. "We have just carried an election on the principles fairly stated to the people. Now we are told, in advance, the government shall be broken up, unless we surrender to those we have beaten," he wrote.[20] Here was a third principle on which he would not yield: majority rule.

Lincoln resolved that if civil war were to result, his adversaries would have to commence hostilities. As he told them in his first inaugural address, "In your hands, my dissatisfied fellow countrymen, and not in mine, is the momentous issue of civil war. . . . You have no oath registered in Heaven to destroy the government, while I have the most solemn one to preserve, protect, and defend it."[21] In his second inaugural address, four years later, he characterized them as those who would "make war rather than let the nation live."[22] In spite of his reassurances, which were genuine, Lincoln's Southern critics knew that his acting in conformity with his campaign promises encompassed the repeal of the Kansas-Nebraska Act and the reversal of the *Dred Scott* decision, whether through a change in the composition of the Supreme Court or by constitutional amendment. They feared, with some justification, that Lincoln's concept of "Union" would result in a permanent shift in the political balance of power in both Congress and the Electoral College in favor of free states. Over time, such a majority might disturb slavery where it existed.

Once engaged in the Civil War, Lincoln found his opportunity to uphold the rule of law and to destroy slavery simultaneously. With so much of the southern economy dependent upon slave labor, Lincoln justified the Emancipation Proclamation on grounds that the Constitution permitted him as commander in chief to reduce the enemy's capacity to wage war by confiscating enemy property—human and otherwise. Whether slaves were set free by advancing Union armies or whether they freed themselves by running toward Union lines or just running away, much of this "contraband" joined the Union's fighting forces. More than a decade after Lincoln's assassination, African American statesman Frederick Douglass commented on just how revolutionary this purportedly reluctant action on the part of the man who identified himself as a conservative actually was:

> Under his wise and beneficent rule we saw ourselves gradually lifted
> from the depths of slavery to the new heights of liberty and manhood. . . .
> We saw our brave sons and brothers laying off the rags of bondage and
> being clothed all over in the blue uniforms of the soldiers of the United
> States. . . . We saw two hundred thousand of our dark and dusky people

responding to the call of Abraham Lincoln, and with muskets on their shoulders, and eagles on their buttons, turning the high footsteps to liberty and union under the national flag. . . . We saw the Confederate States, based upon the idea that our race must be slaves, and slaves forever, battered to pieces and scattered to the four winds.[23]

With the war appearing at a standstill in the summer of 1864, and with casualties on both sides mounting, Lincoln felt public pressure to rescind his Emancipation Proclamation as a means of restoring the Union through negotiation. He refused. Having achieved what he had previously thought constitutionally impermissible during peace, Lincoln would not betray the African American soldiers and sailors who had swelled Union ranks on the basis of his promise. When he took that stand, Lincoln believed he would lose his bid for re-election. His political fortunes reversed when Atlanta fell to General Sherman, and General Sheridan took control of Virginia's breadbasket, the Shenandoah Valley. Lincoln's terms of peace were clear: unconditional surrender, a resumption of constitutional government, and acceptance of the Emancipation Proclamation. (He simultaneously sought passage of the Thirteenth Amendment, which forbade slavery in the United States.) In holding to these points, the once crafty and extraordinarily flexible politician had become an ideologue.

In addition to preserving the Union and employing his powers as commander in chief to issue the Emancipation Proclamation, as president Lincoln advanced an economic agenda to which he had adhered since his early days as a Whig state legislator. He pressed Congress to enact a series of laws designed to boost economic growth through increased investments in the nation's infrastructure and that would enable, through their own initiative, Americans of humble origins to rise. Lincoln signed laws that established a uniform national currency, allowed the federal government to charter national banks, increased tariffs, authorized homesteading on unoccupied federal lands, created a Department of Agriculture to distribute scientific information to farmers in order to improve productivity, provided land grants to establish and endow state colleges and universities, and authorized the building of a transcontinental railroad. To finance the Civil War,

Lincoln and a Republican Congress sold war bonds and, for the first time, had the federal government directly tax the incomes of its citizens.[24] Together, these measures (which will be discussed further in chapter 5) shaped the development of the U.S. economy for the rest of the nineteenth century and beyond.

Interestingly, none of the measures he signed excluded African Americans, other people of color, or members of minority groups from participating in them. Moreover, one of the last bills Lincoln signed established the Freedmen's Bureau to help former slaves to receive education and vocational training so that they might improve upon their condition and take full advantage of his other enacted initiatives. Lincoln pressed Congress to provide equal pay to those serving in the military, whatever their race, and equal benefits to their survivors, again regardless of race. He also rendered it possible for African Americans to testify as witnesses in federal courts. His signing legislation banning racial discrimination in Washington, D.C., street cars kept them integrated after Jim Crow policies extended their grasp to the city a half century later.[25]

In a speech he delivered and in a letter to a military governor shortly before his death, Lincoln gave some hint of how he hoped to approach the difficult question of Reconstruction and the extension of citizenship to the former slaves. Noting that 10 percent of Louisiana's 1860 voting population pledged allegiance to the Union, held elections, established public schools for the benefit of both blacks and whites, and empowered its legislature to grant franchise to blacks and approved the still-pending Thirteenth Amendment, Lincoln proclaimed it a possible template for the readmission of other seceded states to the Union. As he spoke, his future assassin, John Wilkes Booth, who had been among his listeners, vowed that would be the last speech Lincoln would ever give. It was.

Theodore Roosevelt

After he left office, Theodore Roosevelt admitted that when he assumed the presidency, he had no "deliberately planned and far reaching scheme of social betterment."[26] On most domestic issues, Roosevelt improvised as he went along. When it came to conservation and foreign policy, however, Roosevelt had indeed entered office with a strong sense of what he wanted to achieve.

Roosevelt came to conservation practically from birth. His father had helped found the Museum of Natural History in New York City. As a young child, Roosevelt began a collection of stuffed birds. By the time he left for college, his house had taken on the trappings of a miniature zoo. Later, he helped launch the Boone and Crockett Clubs to preserve wildlife from the ravages of hunters and industry. The time he spent in the Dakota Badlands, largely in solitude, enhanced his appreciation for nature's restorative powers. Had he never become president, Roosevelt's name would still be widely known because of his exploits as an explorer and his writings about natural history and wildlife. Roosevelt came to the presidency believing that government should play a role in conserving the nation's natural resources.

During his early years in office, Roosevelt established the nation's first federal bird preserve, off Pelican Island, Florida. Before long, it had become part of the Roosevelt-established National Wildlife Refuge System. Roosevelt set aside more than fifty such preserves, established Crater Lake National Park, protected the Grand Canyon, brought over 230,000,000 acres under federal control, and initiated federal irrigation and reclamation programs.

In taking these measures, Roosevelt donned the garb of the arbitrator, just as he had during the 1902 coal strike. Staking out what he considered middle ground between laissez-faire capitalists and conservationists, Roosevelt cast himself as the spokesman for future generations, which had a vested interest in preserving forests, wildlife, and open space. He repeatedly made the case that the preservation, use, and replenishment of natural resources was the best way to assure continued economic prosperity. Roosevelt maintained that since industry is properly concerned with maximizing immediate profits, the federal government needed to play an active role in regulating the use of resources under its jurisdiction. He believed that state governments were too beholden to local corporate interests to perform this function impartially.

Roosevelt entrusted many regulatory powers to his trusted adviser Gifford Pinchot, a fellow patrician who had studied at the French National Forestry

School. Pinchot was the prototype of the expert to whom progressives sought to delegate much public policy in the early twentieth century. In 1905, Roosevelt prodded Congress to establish a Division of Forestry within the Department of Agriculture. This brought under one roof all government entities responsible for forests. He then named Pinchot to head it. Over the next four years, Roosevelt steadily added to Pinchot's empire. Armed with the power to charge companies fees for cutting timber and grazing cattle on federal lands, Pinchot raised more funds through such assessments than Congress had appropriated. He used those monies to fund conservation initiatives Congress had not authorized. Not unexpectedly, Congress sought to rein in Roosevelt and his appointee. Hours before legislation took effect that brought the funds Pinchot raised to the treasury and barred government officials from bringing additional acreage under federal control without congressional approval, Roosevelt placed an additional forty thousand acres under Pinchot's protection.

Turning his attention to other areas, Roosevelt steered to passage the Newlands Reclamation Act of 1902, which allowed the government to collect fees in exchange for constructing dams on federal property and providing irrigation to arid lands.[27] He won approval of the American Antiquities Act of 1906. The measure granted the president the power to establish national monuments on his own authority. Roosevelt created eighteen such monuments before he left office in early 1909. Late in his tenure, he sought to extend his efforts beyond his presidency by drawing the nation's governors into conservation policies. "I did not usurp power," Roosevelt wrote in his autobiography, "but I did greatly broaden the use of executive power."

As President William McKinley's assistant secretary of the navy, Roosevelt aggressively pressed for war against Spain. Eager to test the strengths of American military power, Roosevelt and many others regarded the decaying Spanish empire as the perfect foil. Cuba's struggle for independence enjoyed considerable sympathy in the United States. With the great powers of his day engaged in a race for colonies, Roosevelt became an early and ardent imperialist. As president, he restructured the army and used its engineers to build infrastructure in the territories the United States acquired from Spain. Sensing American unease as a colonial power, and beset with insurrection in the

Philippines, Roosevelt, once president, lost his appetite for colonies. He retained, however, his vision of the United States playing a vigorous role on the world stage.

In his approach toward other nations, Roosevelt relied on the twin pillars of diplomatic engagement and military strength. "Speak softly and carry a big stick" became both his motto and guiding inspiration.[28] Roosevelt's concept of the stick entailed enhanced military preparedness. By fueling the nation's military might, Roosevelt sought to increase American influence in the world as well as to deter possible aggressors. In the course of his presidency, Roosevelt deployed troops to protect American interests abroad, enforce diplomatic agreements, and keep the peace. All his life, Roosevelt maintained an active interest in military preparedness and naval history and strategy.

When he was twenty-three, Roosevelt published *The Naval War of 1812: Or the History of the United States Navy during the Last War with Great Britain*. It remains a classic in military history. While serving on the Civil Service Commission during Benjamin Harrison's administration, Roosevelt lectured at the Naval War College. He aslo formed a mutual admiration society with its president, Alfred Thayer Mahan. At the time, Mahan was working on his book, *The Influence of Seapower upon History: 1660 to 1783*. Its overall thesis was that nations that dominated the seas and its commerce proved successful in war. Taking his cues from Mahan, Roosevelt greatly increased the size of the navy.

So that the United States could emerge as a Pacific power as well as an Atlantic one, Roosevelt worked to further American dominance of the Caribbean and establish an arc of influence in the area between the territories of Alaska and Hawaii. To implement that strategy, he set out to build what he would consider the crowning achievement of his presidency, the Panama Canal. Once in operation, the canal shortened by eight thousand miles the distance between the two American coasts by sea. When Columbia sought to extract a greater amount of funds than Roosevelt had agreed to pay for the site for the canal, Roosevelt instigated Panamanian secessionists to wage a war of independence against the Columbian government. With American troops stationed nearby, the war ended in hours, the United States recognized the new nation of Panama, and work began on the canal. Roosevelt's impetuousness in this instance, his use of gunboat diplomacy to help arbitrate disputes, and his assertion of an American right to maintain order throughout the Western Hemisphere—upon which he acted on multiple occasions—proved harmful over time to American standing in Latin America. Unlike his successors, however, Roosevelt never used the military to advance the interests of private corporations.

Toward the end of his tenure as president, Roosevelt sent the Great White Fleet of sixteen sparkling battleships around the world. "No single thing in the history of the new United States Navy has done as much to stimulate popular interest and belief in it as the world cruise," Roosevelt later wrote.[29] A British newspaper summarized Roosevelt's intentions accurately when it recorded, "Next time Mr. Roosevelt or his representatives appeal to the country for new battleships they will do so to people whose minds have been influenced."[30]

When it came to foreign affairs, even more so than in the domestic area, Roosevelt preferred to go it alone. Of his decision to launch the fleet on its journey, he reflected, "I determined to move without consulting the Cabinet, precisely as I took Panama without consulting the Cabinet. A council of war never fights, and in a crisis the duty of a leader is to lead and not take refuge behind the generally timid wisdom of a multitude of councilors."[31] Roosevelt's practice was to make his case to Congress after first building sufficient public support for what he sought to achieve. When legislators balked at the cost of sending the navy around the world, Roosevelt suggested that he had enough funds to send the fleet halfway and would leave it to Congress to explain why it would not finance the ships' return.

With the "big stick" he had built firmly in his grasp, Roosevelt reverted to the role he played so skillfully in the domestic one, that of arbiter. He received the Nobel Peace Prize for his successful brokering of an end to the Russo-Japanese war in 1905. A year later, he resolved a dispute between France and Germany over Morocco. His display of naval strength in the Caribbean enticed Germany and Britain to settle debt claims against Venezuela, while his dispatch of troops to Alaska prompted Britain to resolve its dispute with the United States over Alaska's boundary with Canada. After he left office, Roosevelt expressed great satisfaction in the fact that while he served as president, the United States remained at peace. "There was no nation in the world with whom a war cloud threatened, no nation in the world whom we had wronged, or from whom we had anything to fear," he recalled.[32] He attributed the emergence of what he called "the peace of righteousness" to his preventative policies.

Lyndon B. Johnson

Few presidents aspired to do more in office than did Lyndon Johnson. A man of gargantuan appetites and ambitions, Johnson wanted nothing less than to break the record of his hero, Franklin Delano Roosevelt. who had greatly expanded the role of the federal government in American life. Johnson wanted to pick up where FDR had left off. If Roosevelt provided old-age pensions through the Social Security Act, Johnson bestowed the elderly with medical insurance through Medicare. If FDR envisioned protecting Americans against "certain hazards and vicissitudes of life," LBJ attempted to eradicate poverty altogether. If Roosevelt won re-election by the widest margin in American history in 1936, LBJ exceeded Roosevelt's showing in 1964.

Johnson's fixation with quantification often led him to equate the number, size, and costs of programs with success. On the flyleaf to his memoirs, he itemized one thousand bills along with dates on which he signed them into law. His silence in the book as to which ones actually achieved their stated goals says volumes about Johnson. In a misbegotten attempt to convince Americans that his Vietnam policies were working, Johnson's Pentagon regularly released body counts of the fallen, as if victory consisted primarily of U.S. troops inflicting higher casualties on the Vietcong than vice versa.

Johnson's greatest and most lasting legacy resulted from procedural changes he made that were less costly than either the Great Society or the Vietnam War, but did more to spur economic development in the southern states and elsewhere than had all programs he and his predecessors initiated with the intent of achieving precisely that. This Johnson did after venturing into controversies that the "sainted" Roosevelt had carefully avoided. Lyndon Johnson made the extension of civil and voting rights to all Americans a major priority of his administration.

While Senate majority leader, Johnson's record on civil rights and much else hardly qualified him as a "profile in courage" in the sense that his predecessor had used the term in a best-selling book.[33] Although Johnson could rightly boast that he had steered to passage the first civil rights bill in over eighty years, his liberal critics, including baseball great Jackie Robinson and several northern Senators, were quick to point out that Johnson attained this feat by rendering the measure toothless.[34] Some went as far as to request that President Eisenhower veto it. After he became president, however, Johnson did not hold back on civil rights. He asserted that he wanted to be "president of *all* the people." "I wanted power," he told one biographer, "to give things to people—all sorts of things to all sorts of people, especially the poor and the blacks."[35] This was not Johnson telling one of his tall tales. The briefest look at his actions as president suggests that he meant what he said. While historians will long debate the efficacy of many of Johnson's Great Society social programs, none will question that the civil and voting rights measures that he passed forever changed the character of his native region and of his country and for the better.[36]

Lyndon Johnson was born August 27, 1908, in Stonewall, Texas, and grew up in Johnson City, fifty miles west of Austin. While his family occasionally experienced hard times due to fluctuations in prices of corn and real estate, in which his father was heavily invested, Johnson's origins were not as humble as he pretended. Relatives of both sides of his family, including his father, served in the state legislature. Both of his parents had been to college and had taught school. Both had been smitten with the economic populism that spread through the region while they were growing up. (They spent their first date listening to William Jennings Bryan address the Texas legislature.) While serving in the legislature, Johnson's father took positions that anticipated those that his son would espouse in Congress and as president. The elder Johnson favored higher state funding of rural schools, regulation of railroads, relief for farmers, women's suffrage, and protecting the civil liberties of German Americans during World War I. He broke with populists such as Bryan in his opposition to prohibition and to the Ku Klux Klan.

Between his junior and senior years at Southwest Texas Teacher's College, Lyndon took a job as principal and teacher at Welhausen School in Cotulla,

Texas, near the Mexican border. His predominantly Mexican American students were among the poorest in the state. Johnson, whom many of his college classmates found "full of himself" and "difficult to take," took a personal interest in his young charges.[37] More interested in politics than in education, Johnson landed a job as chief of staff to a newly elected Texas congressman through family connections. To Johnson's dismay, his boss proved anything but an enthusiast of FDR's New Deal. At the intersession of a more liberal member of the Texas delegation, FDR named Johnson, then twenty-six, to head the National Youth Administration in Texas. Johnson raised a few hackles when he, unlike other administrators of New Deal programs in the south, steered funds to African Americans.

Running for the House of Representatives in a special election to fill a vacancy in 1937, LBJ ingratiated himself to FDR through his outspoken support for Roosevelt's unpopular proposal to pack the Supreme Court. Roosevelt assured Johnson a long career in Washington when he persuaded the Rural Electrification Administration to bend its rules to build a hydroelectric project to bring cheap electricity to farm cooperatives in Johnson's district. Two years later, again with FDR's help, Johnson procured a naval air station for Corpus Christi. Careful to cultivate and never antagonize his state's power structure, LBJ steered contracts to the politically influential engineering firm of Brown and Root. He became a leading spokesman for Texas ranching and oil interests. Johnson would serve twenty years in Congress, however, before he voted for a civil rights bill. He called Harry Truman's civil rights program "a farce and a sham." In a burst of sophistry rare even among segregationist demagogues, Johnson said that he opposed the measure's antilynching provision on grounds that it brought only one form of murder under federal jurisdiction.[38]

Elected to the Senate in 1948, Johnson became minority leader in 1953 and majority leader in 1955. Under the tutelage of Senator Richard B. Russell of Georgia, Johnson embarked on a strategy to position himself as more moderate on civil rights than his fellow southern senators. Russell, a diehard opponent of integration, had seen his hopes for his party's presidential nomination blocked by northern liberals. To spare his protégé from suffering a similar fate, Russell advised Johnson to distance himself from the segregationist bloc. Declaring himself no friend of integration, Johnson, with Russell's backing, maintained that it would be inappropriate for him as Democratic leader to sign the Southern Manifesto. (Drafted by self-proclaimed constitutional expert Sam Ervin, who would later head the Senate Watergate investigation, the Southern Manifesto pledged southern Democrats to oppose the implementation of the *Brown v. Board of Education* decision.)

Adopting the stance of the honest broker, Johnson guided to passage the Civil Rights Act of 1957, a priority of President Eisenhower. In exchange for agreements with southern Democrats not to filibuster the bill, Johnson inserted language that provided for jury trials for people accused of violating the law's provisions.[39] This, many claimed, is what rendered the statute meaningless. Johnson's success in steering it to passage, however, persuaded him and many others that a presidential nomination might not be beyond the realm of his possibilities. Furthering that objective had been his principal objective as he made the numerous machinations that produced the 1957 civil rights bill.

After failing to obtain the 1960 presidential nomination through an insider strategy, which entailed having Senate colleagues who felt beholden to Johnson swing their states' delegations his way, Johnson joined John F. Kennedy's ticket and was elected vice president. Unhappy and bored in the nation's second-highest office, Johnson privately voiced disappointment that Kennedy failed to consult with him on policy and legislation.[40] After some hesitation, Kennedy in 1963 sent what would become the Civil Rights Act of 1964 to Congress. Kennedy did invite the vice president to sit in on meetings he convened with legislators who opposed the bill. In conversations with former Senate colleagues, Johnson complained in the most graphic of terms about the indignities his college-educated African American cook endured every time she drove his official car back to Texas from Washington.[41]

Five days after Kennedy's assassination, Johnson urged a joint session of Congress to pass the civil rights bill as a memorial to his slain predecessor. Veteran observers of Johnson's actions in 1957 expected him to weaken the legislation in order to pass it, just as he had the earlier bill.[42] Yet Johnson, who had built a career and a reputation on brokering such compromises, surprised them. When the measure stalled in the Senate, he let it be known that he was prepared to see all other business put on hold until after the measure had passed. He threw himself into the debate, working the phones, dangling patronage, and issuing threats. He reached out to Republican minority leader Everett Dirksen, who delivered the votes of all but a tiny handful of his thirty-six-member caucus for cloture and for final passage. Republican votes proved indispensable for surmounting southern Democratic opposition. After Johnson signed the bill into law, he remarked to an aide that he had delivered the South to the Republicans well into the future.[43]

Less than a year later, in response to violent attacks by state and local law enforcement officers on peaceful marchers in Selma, Alabama, Lyndon Johnson proposed the Voting Rights Act of 1965. Mindful of the attention politicians paid to voter sentiment, Johnson concluded that, once African Americans obtained and exercised the vote, they would use it to attain other rights and favorable policies. "They can get the rest themselves if they get this—and they can get it on their own terms, not as a gift from the white man," he said.[44] Adopting the civil rights anthem as his own clarion call, Johnson declared before Congress that, "We *shall* overcome." He related his experience as a young man trying to uplift his impoverished students in Cotulla. "It never occurred to me in my fondest dreams that I might have the chance to help the sons and daughters of those students and to help people like them all over the country," he said. "But now I do have that chance," he continued, "and I will let you in on a secret. I mean to use it."[45] It was his finest moment as president.

Ronald Reagan

"There are no easy answers," Ronald Reagan liked to say, "but there are simple ones."[46] Of all who served as president of the United States, none came to office with a more clearly articulated vision of where he wanted to take the nation than Reagan. Like Jefferson and Jackson, Reagan came to office universally known as a spokesman for a significant political movement. If his two nineteenth-century predecessors promulgated their ideas through partisan newspapers and personal letters, Reagan's preferred medium was speeches. As Gerald Ford remarked, Reagan's "public speeches revealed more [about Reagan] than [did] his private conversations."[47] In the course of a political career that spanned several decades, Reagan delivered, in various forms, essentially the same speech. He began formulating its strong free-market, anti-communist, and anti–Soviet expansion message during his days as a corporate spokesman for General Electric. He delivered it for the first time to a television audience on October 27, 1964, in an eleventh-hour campaign appeal on behalf of Barry Goldwater. From that moment until he departed the public stage, Reagan's supporters would refer to all he had said simply as "the speech."

In multiple versions of that speech, Reagan would proclaim that God had a divine plan for the United States and had imposed on its citizens a special obligation to preserve and extend freedom. Reagan offered nothing less than a complete reversal in the direction in which the nation had been headed prior to his inauguration a president. On the domestic front, he sought major reductions in marginal tax rates and fewer regulations on the economy. He argued that such measures would unleash the creative entrepreneurial impulses of the American people.

Internationally, Reagan sought nothing less than having the United States prevail in the Cold War. This he sought to do by increasing U.S. military strength while challenging the Soviet Union economically, politically, and in the "war of ideas." Through such an approach, sustained over time, Reagan was convinced that the Soviet Union could be relegated to the "ash heap" of history. Reagan regarded Marxism as contradictory to human nature because it held out the prospect of perfecting human beings through various forms of social engineering and oppression. Reagan also viewed the détente policies of his three predecessors as tantamount to appeasement because of the Soviet Union's propensity to cheat on arms limitation agreements. Reagan regarded the choice before the West not as one between war and peace but between confrontation and capitulation. He argued that the decisions the United States made, as it entered the final decades of the twentieth century, would determine whether it would preserve what Abraham Lincoln had termed "the last best hope" on earth, or set it on a course that would lead to "a thousand years of darkness."[48] Reagan made keeping Lincoln's dream alive the primary mission of his presidency.

As president, Reagan saw himself rescuing not one person at a time—as he once had as lifeguard—but standing guard over, if not saving, an entire civilization. As a child, he assimilated his mother's belief that "God had a special plan" for every person.[49] Reagan's daughter Maureen recalled that his mother had a way of making people feel they had within them the power to change the world.[50] Reagan came to believe that about himself. Reagan's childhood pastor Ben Cleaver, an early mentor, taught him that the Disciples of Christ Church believed that the United States had a mission to save the world from autocrats.[51] Donn Moonmaw, the pastor at Bel Air Presbyterian Church, where Reagan worshipped while in California, said that Reagan derived his faith more from what he regarded as his personal relationship with God than from his reading of scripture.[52]

Similarly, Reagan came to his policy positions from personal experience. After leaving the White House, Reagan took issue with critics' claims that he had cut income tax rates upon the recommendation of supply-side economists. Instead, he attributed his beliefs about taxation to what he had personally experienced at earlier stages of his career. He explained that when he reached the peak of his earning capacity as an actor and found himself in the 94 percent tax bracket, he decided it was no longer profitable for him to accept additional work when he knew that he could only keep six cents out of every dollar he made after a certain point.[53] He concluded that each time he or someone else in his bracket declined work for this reason their refusals resulted in others, who earned substantially less, also going without work. Reagan recalled that one movie scene, in which only he and a horse appeared on camera, required a support staff of seventy to make.[54]

Through this anecdote, Reagan had intuitively summarized the concept of the "excess burden of taxation" known to economists. (This concept, also know as the "deadweight loss from taxation," holds that the total cost of any tax includes not only the revenue the government collects but also the value of output lost through the reduction or rearrangement of productive activities in response to the tax.[55]) If, as president, Reagan could reduce marginal income tax rates to a reasonable level, this excess burden, he reasoned, would shrink. This, he expected, would create many new, better-paying jobs as businesses invested in new, high-risk industries, while middle-and lower-income households retained more of what they earned. In his memoirs, Reagan confessed to another motivation for tax reductions: reducing the size of the federal government. Richard Neustadt, a shrewd observer of many presidencies, attributed what Arthur M. Schlesinger Jr. termed Reagan's "tolerance of higher deficits" to his desire to curb appetites for increased federal spending.[56]

It took Reagan a long time to embrace the principles of reduced taxes and limited government for which he became so well known. From his youth well into his acting career, Reagan remained a committed New Dealer. He characterized the politics he had practiced during his early years in Hollywood as that of a "near hopeless hemophilic liberal."[57] He had idolized Franklin Roosevelt for the decisiveness with which he responded to the Great Depression, the optimism he projected to a despondent nation, and the skills he brought to bear as a communicator. Reagan also felt personally indebted to FDR for establishing programs that made it possible for Reagan's father to obtain work. (The elder Reagan served as head of the Works Progress Administration in Dixon, Illinois.)

From what his father told him, Reagan concluded that professional bureaucrats had transformed a program Roosevelt had intended to provide people with emergency, one-time, stopgap assistance into a permanent way of life. All his life Reagan remained true to what he considered the founding spirit behind Roosevelt's New Deal—the maintenance of safety nets for the truly needy. As president, Reagan did not seek to unearth FDR's entitlement legacies, including old-age pensions, disability pensions, unemployment compensation, and survivors' benefits provided under the Social Security Act. Instead, Reagan set his sights on curbing the growth of entitlement programs that came into being as part of Lyndon Johnson's Great Society and that expanded under Richard Nixon.[58]

Reagan's drift into the ranks of militant anti-communists began in the late 1940s, about the same time that he was beginning to sour on the tax code. While president of the Screen Actors Guild, Reagan became acquainted with tactics that organized minorities used to force their will on the majority. He observed how communist infiltrators would pack meetings, shout down speakers, seize control of the floor. He had seen them attempt to intimidate figures of influence, often by retaining thugs to beat them up. One day, Reagan received an anonymous telephone call while on the set. "There's a group being called to deal with you. They're going to fix you so you'll never act again," the caller said.[59] The studio supplied him with a pistol.

"I discovered it firsthand," Reagan later said, "the cynicism, the brutality, the complete lack of morality in their positions, and the cold-bloodedness of their attempt, at any cost, to gain control of that industry."[60] Politically, Reagan threw his support behind President Truman's containment policies abroad. In Hollywood, he worked to prevent communist-infiltrated unions from becoming the preeminent bargaining agent between actors and studios.[61] He began reading about communist theory and practice. By the time he became president, Reagan knew all the arguments communists made to advance their case. He had also become alert to the inherent weaknesses in their ideology, especially the premise that humans could forever be made to behave in ways at odds with their sense of self-interest.

Through his sharp intuition and active imagination, Reagan could envision what most defense and policy experts could not: a world bereft of the Soviet Union and the omnipresent threat of nuclear war. With the exception of Reagan, nearly everyone across the political spectrum, ranging from strident anti-communist hawks to peace activists, assumed that the Soviet Union was a permanent fixture in the world. Analysts on the right and the left took it as a given that Soviets could expand their military capability indefinitely. Policy debates centered on how the United States should respond. Should it, together with its NATO allies, seek to match its adversary's military strength, weapon by weapon? Or should they seek to contain the Soviets through détente and the capping of weapons production?

During the 1960s and 1970s, Reagan gradually came to the conclusion that the Soviet Union had a much smaller economy than Sovietologists both inside and outside the CIA claimed. Doubting experts' estimates of Soviet GDP, Reagan took to telling jokes that had as their theme Soviet citizens' complaints about poor living standards. One concerned a man who went to the transportation department to order an automobile. The man fills out the forms, has them processed through various agencies, and finally goes to the last office to make his payment. The Soviet official says, "Come back in ten years and get your car." He asks, "Morning or afternoon?" The man in the agency says, "We're talking about ten years from now. What difference does it make?" He replies, "The plumber is coming in the morning."[62]

Behind these jokes were flashes of insight. If, as Reagan intuited, the Soviet economy was considerably smaller than published estimates suggested, the U.S.S.R. would have great difficulty maintaining its current armed forces, let alone increasing them and developing new technologically advanced weapons systems. Concluding that the Soviet economy could not sustain a military buildup, Reagan decided to exploit this weakness. If he could goad the Soviet Union into an arms race, the additional defense outlays it would have to make would cause its creaking economy to collapse. This would either cause the communist empire to implode or force the Kremlin to sue for peace.

Reagan's intuition proved correct. After the Soviet Union dissolved, CIA analysts reviewing economic data not previously available concluded that they had for decades significantly overestimated the size of the Soviet economy. They had grossly underestimated Soviet defense outlays as a percent of its GDP. CIA analysts boosted their estimates of Soviet defense outlays during the 1980s from a range of 9 to 11 percent of GDP to a range of 15 to 17 percent of GDP. Other post–Cold War estimates put Soviet military outlays as high as 27 percent of GDP during the 1980s. Initiating a major military buildup, Reagan boosted U.S. defense outlays to a peak of $273.4 billion (6.2 percent of GDP) in fiscal year 1986 before allowing it to settle at $303.6 billion (5.62 percent of GDP) in fiscal year 1989. With its much larger and now surging economy on which to draw, the United States easily afforded Reagan's increase in defense outlays. The Soviet Union could not.

Confident that his insight about Soviet economic weakness was correct, Reagan stood by his strong defense initiatives, even in the face of intense public opposition both in Western Europe and within the United States. Reagan was aghast at the thought of nuclear war and thought it immoral that his predecessors had agreed to a deterrence strategy based on mutually assured destruction. Unlike arms control experts of the era, Reagan did not think that negotiating new treaties with the Soviet Union to limit the number of nuclear warheads or their delivery systems was an effective means of reducing the likelihood of war. Instead, Reagan supported increasing the size and scope of U.S. nuclear power so that the United States could apply increased leverage once the Soviet Union conceded the weakness of its economy and inability to sustain an arms race. Reagan surprised critics who urged a freeze on nuclear weapons when he proposed eliminating intermediate-range missiles in Europe and embraced the goal of abolishing nuclear weapons altogether.

Reagan became increasingly captivated by the possibility of land-, sea-, and space-based defensive systems that could intercept incoming missiles. Most scholars now cite Reagan's insistence on developing the Strategic Defense Initiative (SDI) as the reason General Secretary Mikhail Gorbachev agreed to reduce hostilities. The Soviet Union simply could not afford to develop new technologies to counter or compete with SDI. Reagan and Gorbachev signed the Intermediate Nuclear Forces Treaty on December 7, 1987, eliminating all intermediate-range nuclear missiles in Europe as Reagan had proposed. By 1991, 2,692 such weapons had been destroyed, 846 by the U.S. and 1,846 by the Soviet Union.

Through the power of his vision, Reagan, like Washington, Jefferson, and Lincoln before him, made possible what many if not most of his contemporaries thought inconceivable. Just as the country's founders in their youths could not have imagined swearing allegiance to any sovereign other than the British monarch, and Lincoln, well into middle age, could not see a way to abolish slavery under the Constitution, few in Reagan's generation, including his recent predecessors, had visualized a world without the Soviet Union looming large. Through his resolve, Reagan actualized his vision in a manner set forth by one of his favorite founders. "We have it in our power to begin the world over again," Thomas Paine had written. Reagan made this quotation part of his speech accepting the Republican presidential nomination in 1980. It became a guiding spirit of his presidency. "We have every right to dream heroic dreams," Reagan proclaimed in his first inaugural address. He never stopped.

Reagan also had the ability to see new dangers that lay beyond the horizon. At one juncture during his first of four meetings with Gorbachev, after noting that both of their countries had been born in revolution, Reagan suggested that the two leaders "keep an eye on another revolution," then heating up just as the Cold War was winding down. He warned his counterpart about "a fundamentalist Islamic revolution . . . which teaches that the way to heaven is to kill a non-believer." Reagan noted that he, a professed Christian, and Gorbachev, a committed atheist, were equally at risk.[63]

4

COMPETENCE

*C*ompetence is the ability of a president to achieve his policy objectives and to respond effectively to unforeseen events. To succeed in office, a president must communicate his ideas to other political actors and to the public, and persuade both to follow his lead. He must be able to navigate through, and sometimes bridge, the institutional barriers inherent in the American political system. A president's success can be seen in the influence he commands at *both* ends of Pennsylvania Avenue and elsewhere (foreign capitals, state and local governments, the media, the judicial system, the private sector, pressure groups, his political base, etc.). "Influence" is the ability of a president to persuade would-be allies and adversaries to take his preferences into account as a means of advancing their own. While a president certainly must be competent in order to do this, and therefore succeed, the mere possession and demonstration of competence is by no means a sign of greatness. Some presidents were quite successful in advancing policies that proved detrimental to the national interest.

Participants in surveys of presidential greatness have not always been mindful of this. Some have been too preoccupied with the institutional history of the office and how the presidency emerged as the dominant branch within the American government to notice. This has been particularly evident in how they have rated Andrew Jackson, who consistently places among the near great presidents. That Jackson possessed extraordinary political skills, a forceful personality, courage, determination, organizational ability, and even charisma—all of which he used to get his way—is beyond question.

Presidential scholars rightly regard Jackson's particular use of the veto (negating bills because he *disagreed* with them rather than primarily because he doubted their constitutionality) as a significant step in making the president an ongoing and important part of the legislative process. They correctly see Jackson's characterization of himself as the voice of the people, using his popularity as political capital to curb the power of special interests, as foreshadowing Theodore Roosevelt's portrayal of himself as a steward of the people, who used the bully pulpit of his office in similar ways. They hail Jackson for unifying the executive branch by making all appointees answerable to him and keeping the nascent bureaucracy responsive to him as the people's representative, through his deft use of his patronage powers (the spoils system). They make note of how Jackson used his leadership of the political party he helped create to break down institutional barriers inherent in the separation of powers.

As they praise Jackson for exerting such a strong influence on events, not many of his evaluators, in marking their ballots in surveys, considered whether the policies that Jackson rammed through were the right ones for the United States. A close inspection of some of them invites the conclusion that the nation might have been better served by a president who had a different agenda than Jackson's, or, barring that, proved less competent than Jackson. Through his effective use of the veto, for instance, Jackson achieved his stated goal of destroying the Second Bank of the United States. His success came at a tremendous cost, however, precipitating the Panic of 1837, the second worst depression in American history. Jackson's blatant disregard of judicial decisions resulted in one of the gravest violations of human rights the U.S. government ever committed, the forced relocation of the Cherokee from the southeastern United States on the Trail of Tears, to what is present-day Oklahoma. With his forces in control of Congress, Jackson rammed his measure through and justified it by citing majority support for his action. This in his mind was sufficient to warrant setting aside treaties and opinions of the Supreme Court. Many who laud Jacksonian democracy for its "populist" and majoritarian aspects ignore the mob-rule passions it sometimes ignited and underplay the political corruption and election fraud that often accompanied it.[1]

Those who tend to equate competence with greatness sometimes attribute presidential failures to the absence of competence. Yet they do not always apply this criterion consistently. Harry S Truman, another of the near greats, is seldom faulted for his failure to enact most of his legislative agenda. Instead, scholars credit him with having pressed for civil rights, national health care, and a greater federal role in housing—none of which passed while he was president. Curiously, they give short shrift to Ulysses S. Grant and Benjamin Harrison for their failed efforts to safeguard the rights of African Americans. Unlike Truman, neither is habitually hailed as being ahead of his time. Grant is repeatedly marked down for allegedly overlooking corruption among those he appointed and for trying to protect those accused of misdeeds. Yet Truman skates by unscathed in spite of the scandals that engulfed several of his cronies.

These contradictions reveal yet another flaw inherent in most presidential surveys: their inability to allow evaluators to acknowledge that a president can be extraordinarily competent in some aspects of their job and extraordinarily incompetent in others. Not all of Truman's programs proved as transformative as the Marshall Plan, nor did all his appointees have the character and vision of George Marshall and Dean Acheson. Likewise, Grant's administration was more than the sum of petty scandals, which have attracted the most attention from scholars. If ability to select able advisers is indeed a fair measure of presidential competence, Grant's appointment of Hamilton Fish as secretary of state, Benjamin Bristow as secretary of the treasury, and Amos T. Akerman as attorney general were as inspired as Truman's selection of George Marshall, Dean Acheson, or any other of the "wise men" whose services he retained.[2] That Truman also named to high posts people as wanting in aptitude and ethics as those presidents too readily dismissed as failures (Grant and Harding), James David Barber made clear in his book *The Presidential Character: Predicting Performance in the White House*: "His personal physician played the commodities market, then lied about it to Congress; his Appointments Secretary went to jail for fixing a tax case; one of his secretaries accepted the gift of not one, but seven deep freezers. It was a ragtag crew, a buzzing clot of 'five-percenters' and 'influence peddlers,' flitting around Washington making arrangements for a price."[3] Barber failed to note that as a senator Truman tried to block the appointment of a prosecutor who showed interest in going after Truman's political benefactor, Kansas City political boss Jim Pendergast, and that as president he fired the U.S. attorney who had succeeded in sending the corrupt politician to jail. While many Truman biographers fail to make note of such actions on his part, most of Grant's have fixated on his willingness to stand by an assistant accused of wrongdoing.

Presidential scholars will long wrestle with the paradox of Ronald Reagan being more attuned to the economic disintegration of the Soviet Union than were multiple intelligence professionals and simultaneously appearing oblivious to what aides in close proximity to him were doing, purportedly to advance his agenda. They will likewise marvel at the meticulous care with which John F. Kennedy and Bill Clinton crafted their foreign and domestic initiatives and the recklessness with which they conducted their private affairs, which in Kennedy's case might have threatened his continuance in office and, in Clinton's, actually did.

This chapter considers five presidents who used their carefully acquired competence to achieve what they regarded *and what history has subsequently confirmed* to have been in the nation's best interests: Thomas Jefferson, Abraham Lincoln, Franklin Delano Roosevelt, Dwight D. Eisenhower, and Ronald Reagan. (Others, including Theodore Roosevelt, Calvin Coolidge, Harry S Truman, and John F. Kennedy, are examined in subsequent chapters.) Each of these five, under immediate consideration, projected an extraordinary self-confidence that they, in turn, used to inspire the public, associates, and their fellow actors on the political stage to follow their lead. In some instances, their belief in their capacity to persuade was high enough to cause them to display the kind of hubris that led them astray. So certain were Jefferson and FDR of their capacity to rally public opinion behind them that they forged ahead with ill-considered policies in the face of political realities that preordained failure. Jefferson wound up stymied when he attempted to enforce his embargo; FDR suffered a similar fate when he tried to pack the Supreme Court.

Whatever the pressures of their moment, each of these five—most of the time—kept their focus on the policy objectives that they most wished to achieve.

They proved extraordinarily flexible, however, about the means through which they sought to attain them. On occasion, each found it necessary to stand up to important elements within their respective political bases in order to achieve objectives that they deemed essential to the nation's well-being. Most made masterful use of the technology of their day to communicate their message to the American people. Jefferson and Lincoln, both extraordinarily talented writers, made use of special messages, correspondence, and intentional leaks to get their points across. Even before he became president, Lincoln sent carefully worded speeches and public letters across the country by telegraph to waiting newspaper editors. When radio was a new medium, both Ronald Reagan and Franklin Delano Roosevelt learned to use it to their advantage. Reagan subsequently made the transition to television. Comfortable in front of a camera, he complemented his highly honed oratorical skills (which he shared with Kennedy) with powerful visual backdrops.

Operating under the assumption that people are policy, all five selected able advisers who entered their administrations with a record of significant achievements behind them, which they compiled independently of the president who appointed them. Yet none became beholden to any single adviser. All remained focused on their ultimate policy objectives. All set a general tone for their administration. None let excessive attention to detail draw them away from their overall goals or confuse their priorities. All delegated widely, but only up to a point. Each of the five, while well known to millions, allowed few to penetrate through the armor they had carefully constructed around themselves. All had taken office aware that their ability to succeed depended, in part, upon the image of themselves they had cultivated in the minds of citizens and significant political actors. Like George Washington, none stepped out of character.

The focus of this chapter will shift then to four presidents whose failings can be directly attributed to their lack of competence: James Madison, Herbert Hoover, Lyndon B. Johnson, and Jimmy Carter. To the extent that they shared common flaws, all acted in accordance with how they believed things *should* or *might* work rather than in response to the realities of situations in which they found themselves. Whatever their pre-presidential reputations (Madison was widely respected as the "Father of the Constitution" and Hoover as the "Great

Engineer" and humanitarian), as president, none was able to command sustained public support. Johnson held it for a time, when, after the assassination of Kennedy, he turned a national tragedy into an opportunity to pass Kennedy's program. He saw it atrophy when he and the nation paid a steep price for the way he increased American participation in the conflict in Vietnam. Having come to power on a wave of public dissatisfaction with scandals and policy failures that had come to characterize politics as it was practiced in Washington, D.C., Carter let detail consume him. He also had difficulty setting priorities and establishing in the public mind a fixed idea of what he sought to achieve and how. Of this group, only Madison won re-election—and that was before the consequences of his ill-fated war had become manifest.

SEVEN PRESIDENTS RECEIVE A SCORE OF 5 FOR COMPETENCE:

George Washington

Andrew Jackson

James K. Polk

Abraham Lincoln

Theodore Roosevelt

Franklin D. Roosevelt

Dwight D. Eisenhower

SEVEN PRESIDENTS RECEIVE A SCORE OF 4:

Thomas Jefferson

James Monroe

Zachary Taylor

William McKinley

Calvin Coolidge

Harry S Truman

John F. Kennedy

TWELVE RECEIVE A SCORE OF 3:

John Adams

John Quincy Adams

Martin Van Buren

Ulysses S. Grant

Chester A. Arthur

Grover Cleveland

Benjamin Harrison

Woodrow Wilson

Gerald Ford

Ronald Reagan

George H. W. Bush

Bill Clinton

EIGHT PRESIDENTS RECEIVE A SCORE OF 2:

John Tyler

Millard Fillmore

Rutherford B. Hayes

William H. Taft

Warren G. Harding

Lyndon B. Johnson

Richard Nixon

Jimmy Carter

**FIVE PRESIDENTS RECEIVE A
SCORE OF 1:**

James Madison

Franklin Pierce

James Buchanan

Andrew Johnson

Herbert Hoover

(W. H. Harrison, J. A. Garfield, and G. W. Bush were not evaluated.)

Thomas Jefferson

As president, Thomas Jefferson proved successful in persuading others to follow his lead. Before the public, he continually drew upon his superior talents to make his case through the dominant political medium of his day, the printed word. In more private settings, he won over doubters through personal charm. Those Jefferson could not bring into his orbit he learned to circumvent through tactics he developed in his years as a legislator, lawyer, diplomat, cabinet secretary, vice president, and opposition leader. When these proved ineffective, Jefferson sought to remove the most recalcitrant from their posts or curb their influence through whatever legal means he found available. When working with Congress and members of his administration, Jefferson relied more on informal influence than on the formal exercise of power. He created within his coterie of advisers a sense of camaraderie and a unity of purpose. To them and among his many followers, Jefferson imparted a sense of ownership of the policies he advanced.

With his authorship of the pamphlet *A Summary View of the Rights of British America*, written and widely circulated in 1774, Jefferson—then a member of the House of Burgesses—became a widely known and much-respected figure in legal and political circles across the eastern seaboard. In this pamphlet, Jefferson made many of the arguments he would repeat two years later in the Declaration of Independence. He argued that, because the colonies had been settled by individuals acting voluntarily, and had not been conquered by an invading army, their inhabitants were entitled, under English common law, to the same rights as all British subjects. Foremost among them, Jefferson wrote, was the right to be taxed only by legislatures of their own choosing. He ended with an appeal to the king to spurn the advice of parliament and grant the colonists their full rights as English citizens.

Two years later, with the Continental Congress poised to declare the colonies independent of British rule, Jefferson's colleagues turned to him to set their reasons to paper. John Adams attributed Jefferson's selection as drafter of the Declaration to the "eloquence" of the Virginian's pen.[4] By the time he became president, Jefferson had perfected the practice of—as contemporary political consultants might put it—getting his message out. After his return home, Jefferson revised Virginia's laws, stripping them of the vestiges of British practices that were inconsistent with the freedom and equality of opportunity that Jefferson wished to encourage. Other states were quick to follow Jefferson's lead in reforming their penal codes, disestablishing official churches, providing for public schools, restructuring inheritance practices, and expanding the franchise. Through his voluminous correspondence to opinion leaders, Jefferson made known his views on major issues of his day, fully expecting that what he said would reach wider audiences. He relied on this technique for the rest of his life.

Upon his election as president, Jefferson took care to convey to allies and adversaries alike that he remained cognizant of the circumstances that surrounded his election. Having easily defeated incumbent Federalist president John Adams in the popular vote, Jefferson, through a yet to be amended flaw in the original Constitution, received an equal number of votes in the Electoral College as had his running mate, Aaron Burr. This tie meant that the outgoing Federalist House of Representatives would select the next president. (This was discussed in greater detail in the previous chapter.) When wavering Federalist representatives sought reassurance from Jefferson that he would retain the national bank that Hamilton had put into place, and that he would not remove all remaining Federalists from their government posts all at once, Jefferson at first vowed that he would not go in with hands tied. His emissaries, however, signaled on Jefferson's behalf, and supposedly at his instruction, that he would go slow, presumably on both matters. Jefferson used his inaugural address, which he knew would be the focus of much attention, as an opportunity to repeat this promise and set forth the course he intended his administration to follow.

In crafting his message, Jefferson took care to address simultaneously two distinct publics: celebratory Democratic-Republicans, eager for power and patronage, and jittery Federalists. "Every difference of opinion," he said "is not a difference on principle. We have called by different names brethren of the same principle. We are all republicans, we are all federalists." While the "rightful" will of the majority would prevail, Jefferson insisted, power would be exercised in "reasonable" fashion. (All knew that Jefferson would determine what was reasonable.) He also acknowledged that the minority possessed equal rights with the majority and pledged that, as president, he would protect those rights. To do otherwise, he said, would constitute oppression. At the very least, Jefferson had reassured the Federalists, who had eased his path to the presidency, that he was not the Jacobin that many presumed him to be. Having delivered that reassurance, Jefferson began to put his stamp on his administration.

Mindful that his opponents had presented him as an enemy of religion, Jefferson sought to reassure clerics that they and their congregations had nothing to fear from his ascendancy in a letter intended for wide distribution. In opting to send it to the Baptist Association of Danbury, Connecticut, Jefferson was conveying a second message as well. Victims of religious persecution, whether at the hand of the recently disestablished Anglican Church or other dominant religious orders, Baptists looked kindly on Jefferson's election, primarily because of his known advocacy of religious freedom. In his communication, Jefferson wrote that he envisioned not the destruction of organized religion but a "wall of separation" between church and state. One of his biographers found it no coincidence that on the same day that Jefferson mailed the letter, he received an attention-getting 1,235-pound cheese from a Baptist congregation in Massachusetts. (The public was invited to taste what became the most famous cheese in American history. Jefferson made sure that samples of it were sent to key supporters of his throughout the country.) In a public demonstration of his support for religion, Jefferson attended a Baptist service in the House of Representatives with the preacher who had presented him with the cheese.[5]

As president, Jefferson did away with a practice Washington and Adams followed when he declined to deliver his annual message to Congress in person. (He disliked the pomp and circumstance of such formalities and was never a gifted orator.) At the same time, he found other ways to communicate his goals to Congress and to disseminate them to the public. He invested considerable time preparing his messages, which he knew would be widely read. He began the process by asking each cabinet officer to provide him with suggestions. He then wrote a draft and circulated it to them, eliciting further advice. Aware of the powers of symbolism, Jefferson, through nonverbal and nonwritten means, found ways to present himself as president, as the embodiment of republican ideals. Eschewing carriages, parades, and other trappings associated with British coronations, Jefferson walked from his boarding house to the Capitol to take the oath of office. Casting himself in the role of his country's "first citizen," Jefferson opted not to receive the British ambassador in formal attire, as was the custom. Instead, Jefferson wore a simple coat and slippers, cut at the heels. Picking up on the president's intentions, the ambassador described Jefferson's comportment as "a state of negligence actually studied."[6]

With the cooperation of the partisan press, Jefferson acquired a reputation for accessibility. Believing him approachable, ordinary people wrote him about their problems, to convey their views, or to seek his help. Jefferson answered a good many of them personally. During his first year in office, he received 1,881 letters and wrote 677.[7] Before long, lithographers and engravers began turning out prints of the president's image for a public eager to purchase them.[8] He granted, on occasion, audiences to uninvited and unexpected visitors.

Although Jefferson had professed that Congress (and especially the popularly elected House of Representatives) was the preeminent branch of the government, he found multiple, and sometimes surreptitious, ways to assert himself in the legislative process. Jefferson would have his supporters on Capitol Hill introduce legislation, sometimes drafted at the executive mansion. He would then carefully monitor the progress of bills he favored. Often, he would meet in private with key legislators, individually or in groups. To forge personal ties with senators and representatives, Jefferson hosted small dinner parties three times a week. On different nights, Federalist and

Democratic-Republican lawmakers would attend, often accompanied by their spouses. In addition, Jefferson invited diplomats, members of his administration, and personal friends. Presiding over a round table, Jefferson regaled his guests with stories about people whom he had known (such as Washington and Franklin) and great events in which he had participated.

John Adams captured the essence of Jefferson's charm when he remarked that one "can never be an hour in this man's company without something of the marvelous."[9] One scholar noted that Jefferson's dinners not only afforded him opportunities to forge new alliances but also represented the few times when Washington, D.C., society could actually see the president.[10] Invitations to Jefferson's table became highly coveted status symbols. After his guests had departed, Jefferson carefully recorded who had attended, where they sat, and, sometimes, what they discussed.

In working with his five cabinet officers, Jefferson routinely routed incoming mail to the affected department heads. He required that they then furnish him with drafts of their intended responses. This approach kept him informed about what was transpiring within his administration. If he disagreed with a subordinate's action or policy, Jefferson would resolve the matter in private. He preferred such one-on-one conversations to full cabinet meetings, which more readily lent themselves to personal confrontations, which Jefferson found quite distasteful. As would become Franklin Delano Roosevelt's custom nearly a century and a half later, Jefferson assigned similar tasks to different individuals. He also worked through both official and nonofficial channels to achieve his aims.

In the diplomatic endeavors to purchase the Louisiana Territory, Jefferson operated through at least three emissaries. He made his opening move through Robert R. Livingston, the U.S. ambassador to France. He then sent Virginia governor James Monroe, a former ambassador to France, as his personal representative to assist in the talks. At the same time, Jefferson kept his friend Samuel du Pont de Nemours apprised of his intentions, confident in that the businessman would relay whatever information Jefferson wanted him to at Napoleon's court. The one time in Jefferson's presidency when his political skills—and his powers of persuasion, public and private—failed him was during the embargo crisis (covered in the previous two chapters). It was also among the few occasions when he allowed his political philosophy to override his best instincts.

Abraham Lincoln

Throughout the Civil War, which dominated his presidency, Lincoln, assisted by only two aides, maintained a very active correspondence, drafted innumerable speeches, and received a steady stream of visitors. Probably one of the least isolated presidents, Lincoln was always soaking up information and disseminating ideas. To this day, many continue to draw inspiration from his letters and speeches. In its brevity, the address that Lincoln delivered at Gettysburg better captured the essence of the American creed than has any pronouncement made since. Through the simple phrase "new birth of freedom," Lincoln told the world that Union soldiers, both fallen and surviving, had given new meaning to the principles on which the United States was founded and that the Union for which they fought would emerge from the war an even freer place than had been the one for which they had taken up arms. Lincoln may have varied his choice of words to suit different venues, but he kept his basic message clear and consistent.

As a communicator, Lincoln readily availed himself of the latest technological advances. He spent countless hours at the telegraph office, keeping abreast of news from the front and sending orders to generals. He made ample use of rails and barges to move armies, supplies, and even himself to the scene of battle. He understood that his personal presence underscored the sincerity of his commitment to the task before him and for which he had asked so many others to sacrifice. He found that his personal presence was an effective way to maintain morale among those in whose name he governed and those who served under his command. Lincoln made it his practice to review every regiment that passed through Washington, regardless of the amount of time it took or the state of the weather. He reviewed troops, often with his hands extended as he made his way through the line, stopping along the way. He visited the wounded. He called upon his generals in the field and spent time with the troops. Word of Lincoln's resolve, sense of purpose, and concern for their welfare got around.

Lincoln sought out information from many sources, displaying great curiosity about most things. He kept abreast of the press and his mail. He referred to the time he spent hearing out people from all walks of life who called upon him as his "public opinion baths." He probed eyewitnesses to battles for their impressions, in the same fashion as he kept up with political developments in the home states of visiting acquaintances and total strangers. He sought to acquaint himself with military strategy through books he checked out of the Library of Congress. He took an interest in the engineering methods that determined the shape of military fortifications. He made personal visits to subordinates, counterparts, and colleagues, be they generals or cabinet members, senators or congressmen, often at their homes. He sent emissaries to places he could not go himself, such as Charleston in the weeks preceding his decision to resupply Fort Sumter, and to foreign capitals. Having obtained the presidential nomination over better-known aspirants, Lincoln subsequently named his three major rivals to his cabinet. Confident in his ability to check their ambitions, if he could not earn all of their loyalties, Lincoln reasoned that he could draw on the talents and contacts of each as he set in motion a strategy to win the war. He concluded that the hopes any had of replacing him as the party's standard bearer rested on their succeeding in tasks he had delegated to them. Keeping his cabinet unified, and controlling rivalries, tested Lincoln's strength as a manager.

Lincoln spent considerable time mediating disputes between Secretary of State William Seward and Secretary of the Treasury Salmon P. Chase. Although once considered more ardent in his opposition to slavery than Lincoln, Seward came to advocate a go-slow approach to emancipation. Lincoln put up with Chase's sometimes open scheming against him because of the skill the treasury secretary displayed in obtaining adequate funding for the war. Alerted by senators that talk of dissention within Lincoln's cabinet was making its way around Washington, Lincoln convened a meeting of his cabinet and invited key senators to attend. One by one, he asked the cabinet secretaries whether rumors of discord within the cabinet were true. All replied in the negative. Afterward, Lincoln requested the resignations of the feuding Seward and Chase. He then declined to accept them. The appearance of harmony was thus preserved for several critical months.

Persuaded that Chase could no longer camouflage his political ambitions as the 1864 election neared, Lincoln replaced him. His renomination assured, Lincoln appointed Chase chief justice of the United States that same year. In doing so, Lincoln reiterated the rationale he had used to justify his retention of Chase in his cabinet. For Chase to advance his ambitions, Lincoln argued, he would first have to acquit himself ably as chief justice.[11] At that particular moment, Lincoln needed a chief justice who would not, as had the deceased Chief Justice Roger Taney (once Jackson's attorney general), try to thwart emergency measures Lincoln had undertaken in the face of mounting insurrection (such as his temporary suspension of *habeas corpus*).

Lincoln's ability to forego past slights, not hold grudges, and appoint people based on what he believed to be their ability to achieve his goals were much in evidence throughout his presidency. In selecting his second secretary of war, Lincoln turned to Edwin Stanton, who had held the same post under James Buchanan. Years earlier, Stanton had both shunned and publicly ridiculed Lincoln when the two had worked together on a legal case.[12] Lincoln, aware of this, named Stanton to the post just the same. Lincoln subsequently found a way to back up Stanton, whom he considered a loyal subordinate, while countervailing him at the same time. Early in the war, Ohio Congressman Thomas Corwin, accompanied by Cincinnati businessman Simon Wolf, requested that Lincoln pardon the soldier son of a constituent. The young soldier had left his post without permission in order to visit the bedside of his dying mother. He was subsequently found guilty of desertion and sentenced to be executed. Lincoln explained that Stanton, alarmed at the high number of pardons Lincoln had issued for such infractions, threatened to resign if he continued his practice. Instead, he telegraphed the soldier's commanding officer that the soldier was not to be shot until he had received subsequent instructions from the president. Lincoln then assured his worried visitors that he had no intention of issuing future orders. Three years later, upon learning that the soldier had been killed in the Battle of Cold Harbor, Lincoln expressed pride that he had done the right thing.[13]

In 1863, after receiving a similar visit by a woman so emotionally distraught that she failed to supply him with the name of her husband, also accused of desertion, wrote General Meade, "If there is a man by the name of King under sentence to be shot, please suspend execution till further order and send record."[14]

When it came to implementing his objectives, Lincoln showed himself the master of his administration and, until he found a commander to whom he could impart his trust, the major strategist of the war. While he would seek advice from his cabinet and from others before he took action, Lincoln neither put things to a vote among subordinates nor sought consensus. When he issued the Emancipation Proclamation, he convened a cabinet meeting, informed the attendees of his decision, and declared that he did not wish their "advice about the main matter," which, he said, he had already "determined for himself."[15] He then sought their input on style, the manner of implementation, and legal issues. A most productive discussion followed.

Shortly after becoming president, Lincoln had to decide how he would handle the immediate crisis at Fort Sumter, the last remaining federal enclave in what sought to become the Confederate States of America. He decided to resupply the installation, thereby leaving it to the enemy to decide whether to let the supplies through or commence hostilities. When it chose the latter course, Lincoln acted decisively. With Congress not in session, evoking his authority as commander in chief, he called up 75,000 members of the militia, suspended habeas corpus, called up 45,000 troops, authorized the purchase of munitions, and ordered a blockade of Southern ports. Upon his request, Congress, upon its return months later, ratified his actions retroactively.

In his slow but steady march toward issuing the Emancipation Proclamation, Lincoln followed public opinion as much as he led it. Knowing where he wanted to come out, Lincoln, in his public pronouncements on the slavery question, put forth option after option until emancipation remained the only one that carried with it the furthering of the Union's cause. Lincoln began his administration promising not to disturb slavery where it existed. Later on, he tried to persuade slaveholders to accept compensated emancipation. Consistent with his often-stated view that the Constitution permitted Congress to ban slavery in territory it controlled, Lincoln signed legislation that outlawed slavery in the District of Columbia. He also abolished the slave trade and meted out stiff penalties to violators. In August 1862, in a meeting with black leaders, Lincoln urged that all blacks emigrate, on the grounds that their presence in the country was the cause of the war. A discouraged Frederick Douglass pronounced Lincoln's comment equivalent to blaming a horse for its own theft.[16]

Lincoln did not inform his visitors that he had already decided a month prior to their meeting with him to issue a preliminary Emancipation Proclamation. He wanted to hold off his announcement until after the Union forces had won a significant military battle. He felt that if European powers that had abolished slavery throughout their empires believed that the North would prevail, they would be less likely to extend diplomatic recognition to the Confederacy. With British manufacturing dependent on raw materials from the Southern states, Queen Victoria's government harbored fewer reservations about presuming to take sides in a dispute that centered around the legal right to secession. The Emancipation Proclamation transformed the Northern cause into a war to end slavery as well as to preserve the Union. Absent a military victory that might affect British expectations, Lincoln had resisted Chase's demands for emancipation earlier in the war and reversed the emancipation decrees two of his generals had issued in territory that had fallen under their control after the battle of Antietam.

The preliminary Emancipation Proclamation Lincoln issued on September 28, 1862, gave slaveholders in seceded states an ultimatum to free their slaves within one hundred days. It contained provisions for compensation, providing they pledged allegiance to the Union. As he had done in the case of Fort Sumter, Lincoln left the decision in the enemy's hands. He had also showed those in the North who remained opposed to abolition that he had attempted more moderate measures, which slaveholders had rejected. By the time he issued his decree, public opinion had either caught up with him or had outpaced him. The Emancipation Proclamation took effect on January 1, 1863. As critics and cynics have noted ever since, it took effect only in territories that were still in rebellion, and therefore outside of Union control. In that literal and technical sense, the document freed no one. Yet, as the war dragged on, more and more Confederate territory did fall into Union hands. As word spread that Lincoln had issued his decree, slaves in territories beyond Union reach took matters into their own hands. Lincoln's expectation

that by confiscating enemy "property" he would weaken the enemy's capacity to wage war began to be realized. By that time, he had already turned his
attention to efforts to ratify the Thirteenth Amendment to the Constitution,
which banned slavery everywhere in the United States.

Looking back on Lincoln's actions with the benefit of hindsight and in full
possession of the facts, Frederick Douglass summarized Lincoln's position
and actions perfectly: "Had he put the abolition of slavery before the salvation
of the Union, he would have inevitably driven from him a powerful class of the
American people and rendered resistance to rebellion impossible. Viewed
from the genuine abolition ground, Mr. Lincoln seemed tardy, cold, dull, and
indifferent; but measuring him by the sentiment of his country, a sentiment he
was bound as a statesman to consult, he was swift, zealous, radical, and determined."[17] By the time Douglass uttered these words, Lincoln, who as a young
man yearned to "make any human being remember that he had lived," had, as
Stanton pronounced, become part of the "ages."[18]

Franklin D. Roosevelt

Unlike Thomas Jefferson, Andrew Jackson, or Ronald Reagan, Franklin
Delano Roosevelt did not enter the presidency identified as a spokesman
for a particular ideology or political movement. "I am a Christian and a
Democrat, that's all," Roosevelt told a reporter who inquired about his
philosophy. In the words of historian Richard Hofstadter, "at the heart of
his New Deal was not a philosophy, but a temperament."[19] Former
Supreme Court justice Oliver Wendell Holmes tapped into that sentiment
when he declared Roosevelt the possessor of a "second-class intellect, but
a first-class temperament."[20] Sharing this view, Winston Churchill declared
that meeting Roosevelt was like opening a bottle of sparkling champagne.
Unlike Washington, Jefferson, Madison, Jackson, Grant, Wilson, Eisenhower, or even Hoover, his forlorn predecessor, Roosevelt did not enter
office with a record of substantial accomplishments behind him. Weeks
before his election as president, columnist Walter Lippmann proclaimed

Roosevelt "an amiable man . . . who, without any important qualification for the office, would very much like to be president."[21]

Yet, even without a well-defined philosophy of government, FDR, through his penchant for action, genial disposition, and widespread application of that well-known temperament, did more than had any president before him to transform the presidency into the dominant branch of the federal government, and to increase the role the federal government played in American life. Roosevelt did not view challenges through the lens of ideology. Nor did he approach them primarily through the perspective of personal experience. Roosevelt was primarily an experimenter. "It is common sense to take a method and try it," he explained. "If it fails, admit it frankly and try another. But above all, try something."[22] Through this approach, Roosevelt guided the nation through two of the most severe crises in its history, the Great Depression and World War II.

Of course, there was more to FDR than either Lippmann's characterization of him or his own presentation of himself as a Christian, a Democrat, and an experimenter betrayed. Like his fifth cousin and role model, Theodore Roosevelt, FDR grew up with a strong sense of noblesse oblige. The son of an older father—who had a grown son by a previous marriage—and the only child of a doting and overprotective mother, Roosevelt was the principal focus, not only of his parents' attentions, but also of scores of servants, governesses, and tutors, while he was growing up. He had it drilled into him as a child and as a young man that the privileges that were his came with obligations. Roosevelt's sense of duty came into clearer focus when, as a student at Groton School, he came under the influence of its headmaster, Endicott Peabody.

An elite preparatory school patterned on the English model, Groton took as its mission the inculcation of "manly Christian character" in boys deemed destined to lead their nation.[23] Theodore Roosevelt was Peabody's *beau ideal* of the kind of leader Groton would train. Theodore was a soldier, athlete, explorer, devotee of books, and amateur historian, as well as a patriot and a believer in God. As preparation for their special calling, students at Groton adhered to a heavily regimented schedule of chapel attendance, athletics (primarily football), and courses in a classical curriculum. If Franklin Roosevelt, by background and bearing, felt an obligation to those less fortunate than himself, his battle against the polio he contracted in his late thirties instilled in him a sense of empathy.[24] Both at school and early in his political career, Roosevelt's companions and colleagues found him arrogant and haughty. Behind his back, some suggested that Roosevelt's first two initials stood for "Feather Duster."[25] While he would never lose his habit of tossing back his head and peering through his pince-nez before delivering a line he knew would go over well with audiences, the Roosevelt who re-entered the political arena in 1924, when he delivered the nominating speech for Alfred E. Smith at the Democratic National Convention, was noticeably different from the one who had departed public life years earlier to seek a cure for his illness.

Roosevelt's struggle to conquer his disease, whether in physical therapy, personal reflection, or in the company of fellow patients in Warm Springs, Georgia, marked the first time that FDR set out to achieve something important entirely on his own. Other than their affliction, his neighbors at Warm Springs had little in common. They came from many backgrounds, from all walks of life, and from all parts of the country. Roosevelt made himself the leader of his new community He purchased the facility and threw himself completely into its operations. It was there that he demonstrated qualities he would later exhibit as president. As he tried to create a positive atmosphere, especially for children, and saw how others had come to depend on him, Roosevelt's own disposition improved.

After he became president, Roosevelt projected to the world the same contagious optimism that those children of Warm Springs had come to recognize.[26] Behind the mask of gaiety and nonchalance, which Roosevelt projected to the world, was an intense ambition. So that he might keep his hopes for higher office alive, Roosevelt worked to conceal the extent of his paralysis from the public. To create the illusion that he could walk, Roosevelt would shift his body weight from a cane he held in his right hand to the arm of a companion whose elbow he grasped with his left hand while dragging one leg forward. He would then repeat the process with the other leg.

Destined to preside over a nation in which, he said, one third of which was "ill-housed, ill-clad, and ill-nourished," Roosevelt raised the nation's spirits through the promise he made to take bold action and the sympathy he voiced for those who suffered the worst effects of the economic turndown. Even prior to his election as president, Roosevelt found ways to dramatize to the country that his presidency would represent a significant departure from the past. Breaking with tradition, Roosevelt flew to the 1932 Democratic National Convention to deliver his acceptance speech in person. He intended this action as a means of conveying his sense of urgency. Once president, he issued reassurance to the public ("The only thing we have to fear is fear itself") and a warning to Congress (that if it did not respond to his call for emergency action, he might proceed on his own). He made his administration's mission the revitalization of the nation's financial system and economy and the protection of society's most vulnerable from what he called the "vicissitudes of life."[27] (How well he succeeded in all of this will be examined in the next chapter.)

Roosevelt's successes as president would have been inconceivable without the extraordinary self-confidence that he felt and projected. As Hofstadter observed, whatever the nature of the problem before him, Roosevelt remained confident that "he could do no wrong."[28] He committed his greatest political mistake as president when, in the aftermath of his record-breaking 1936 re-election landslide, without preparing the country he embarked on his ill-conceived and ill-fated scheme to pack the Supreme Court. He recovered from that defeat in time to render his greatest services to his country, his masterful nudging of the United States away from its post–World War I isolationism and his extraordinary performance as commander in chief during World War II.

Many Roosevelt biographers have noted that Roosevelt's conception of the presidency was that of himself in the job. He delighted in the gamesmanship of politics. No stickler for organization charts or bureaucratic niceties, Roosevelt tasked several aides with similar assignments. This served a dual purpose: assuring that he received more than one perspective on an issue and that he had at his command more information than anyone else. Roosevelt compensated for whatever toll this practice took on the morale of his staff through his playful manner and the cheerful atmosphere he maintained around him. There were the daily cocktail hours, for example, at which the president demonstrated his skills at mixing martinis and invitees observed the president's rule that they not discuss business. (Exchanges of gossip and jokes were encouraged, if not required.) As would George W. Bush two generations later, Roosevelt assigned nicknames to members of his inner circle. Key White House aide Harry Hopkins was "Harry the Hop"; Secretary of the Treasury Henry Morgenthau Jr. became "Harry the Morgue."

The ambiance he established about him and his appreciation for bureaucratic snafus were in evidence in a memo Roosevelt wrote to his budget director:

I agree with the Secretary of the Interior. Please have it carried out . . . that fur-bearing animals remain in the Department of the Interior.

You might find out if any Alaska bears are still supervised by a) War Department b) Department of Agriculture c) Department of Commerce. They have all had jurisdiction over Alaska bears in the past and many embarrassing situations have been created by the mating of a bear belonging to one department with a bear belonging to another Department.

s/FDR

P.S. I don't think the Navy is involved but it may be. Check the Coast Guard. You never can tell![29]

Roosevelt invented new ways to communicate with the American people—and keep the pressure on Congress. He held press conferences twice a week. In a break from past practice, reporters no longer had to submit written questions in advance. Roosevelt used his exchanges with scores of reporters, gathered around his desk, as occasions to launch trial balloons, make announcements, and keep himself informed. While previous presidents had used radio to their advantage, Roosevelt, rather than merely deliver formal addresses through this medium, introduced what he called "fireside chats." Prepared in a conversational tone and delivered in a folksy manner, the broadcasts were Roosevelt's way of bonding himself to his listeners. Walking the streets of an American city on a hot summer night, passersby could hear Roosevelt's voice booming out of the multiple windows opened above.

Whether in fireside chats, speeches, or press conferences, Roosevelt presented dangers the nation faced and his proposals to resist them in terms that the average person could understand and through his use of powerful metaphors. He likened Italy's decision to join in a war against France to the sticking of a pointed dagger into the back of a neighbor. Retaining the neighbor theme, Roosevelt likened his making American destroyers available to the British to lending a garden hose to a neighbor to put out a fire. (His use of "fire" as a metaphor for war that would spread unless tended to early was lost on no one.) According to Roosevelt, the United States would become an "arsenal of democracy" through the arms buildup he recommended.[30]

Elected and re-elected in the expectation that his principal focus would be on domestic concerns, Roosevelt gradually shifted his concerns to international affairs after the Japanese invaded China in 1937. Having suggested that the nations of the world "quarantine the aggressor," Roosevelt voiced disappointment when his advice went unheeded. "It's a terrible thing to look over your shoulder when you are trying to lead and find no one there," he told an aide.[31] Although White House mail and rudimentary opinion polls recorded that the public was somewhat supportive of Roosevelt's stance, Congress was not. Roosevelt found himself summoning his energies as much to thwart congressional attempts to pass a constitutional amendment forbidding the nation from going to war in the absence of a national referendum as he did to enact new defense initiatives.

Unlike domestic affairs in which he was willing to find his way through experimentation, Roosevelt came to office with a clear idea of what was in the best interests of the United States in international affairs. Having served as assistant secretary of the navy during the entire Wilson administration, Roosevelt continued to monitor world events long after the war had ended. With a rudimentary understanding of German, Roosevelt, as he listened to Adolf Hitler's speeches over the radio, picked up upon the fürher's ability to manipulate listener sentiment and mobilize audiences. Earlier than most other American and European policymakers, FDR discerned that not everything Hitler said was intended only for domestic consumption. He fully expected the Nazi dictator to carry out the aggressive threats he was making and that he would not be placated by appeasement. For a time, however, FDR kept his conclusions to himself, fearful that voicing them might jeopardize his chances of remaining president. He pressed to do all he could short of war to enable the United Kingdom, then under steady bombardment, to remain free of Nazi subjugation. He declared this strategy the key to keeping the United States out of the war.

With world tensions rising, Hitler, in rapid sequence, annexed Austria, unleashed *Kristallnacht* (officially sanctioned violence against Jews), marched into the Sudetenland, conquered what remained of Czechoslovakia, occupied Norway and Denmark, invaded Poland, brought France to its knees, and bombarded Britain. In 1939, Roosevelt persuaded Congress to amend the Neutrality Act so that Britain could purchase arms and munitions for cash and be allowed to transport them across the Atlantic on its own ships. (He pressed the bounds of the law when he ordered military convoys to escort the foreign vessels home.) A year later, Roosevelt pushed for and obtained, by the narrowest possible vote, congressional approval for a peacetime draft. He dramatically increased defense expenditures. When Britain could no longer afford to purchase munitions, Roosevelt locked arms with Wendell Willkie, his Republican opponent in the 1940 election, and made the case for lending them.

After the Japanese attack on Pearl Harbor, Roosevelt lost no time shifting his priorities. "Dr. New Deal," he told a trusted aide, had been replaced by "Dr. Win the War."[32] The implication was clear that he would bring to the effort the same energy and resolve he had to the battle against the Great Depression. The can-do spirit with which Roosevelt mobilized the full industrial might of the United States in the war effort galvanized millions into action and left a lasting impression in many minds. One who took particular inspiration from Roosevelt's capacity to set, meet, and even exceed goals was thirty-year-old Ronald Reagan. Four decades later, Reagan, as president, recalled to historian David McCullough Roosevelt's ability to motivate:

He gave confidence to the people. He never lost faith in this country for one minute. I remember him when he . . . said that he was going to ask for 50,000 planes a year, and I remember when the American press tore him to ribbons for that. . . . They said that . . . this was impossible. It couldn't happen. But when you look at what this country did starting from the low point of Pearl Harbor in 44 months—something like 350,000 planes and hundreds of thousands of tanks and trucks and every kind of weapon, we truly were the arsenal of democracy.[33]

As he briefed the nation in a fireside chat about the D-day invasion, then underway, Roosevelt led the nation in prayer. On another occasion, he instructed his radio audience, "get out your maps," so that they might follow his account of the world's situation. (In advance of his talk, newspapers obligingly printed maps of the world.) On visits to veterans' hospitals, Roosevelt established instant camaraderie with the wounded. Sometimes he would even show them his disabled legs. Relying on his instincts, his experience in World War I as Wilson's assistant secretary of the Navy, and his ability to read people, Roosevelt assembled an able crew of generals and backed them to the fullest. In assessing his own performance as president, Roosevelt likened himself to a quarterback of a football team. "I know what the next play is going to be, but cannot say what the play after that will be until the next play is run off," he said.[34] In his inimitable way, Roosevelt scored more touchdowns than most presidents.

Dwight D. Eisenhower

"Organization cannot make a genius out of an incompetent," Dwight D. Eisenhower observed. "On the other hand," he added, "disorganization . . . can lead to disaster."[35] When Eisenhower was elected president in 1952, no one doubted that the man who had assembled and planned Operation Overlord (involving the largest armada in history)—otherwise known as the "D-day" invasion—knew how to organize. As president, Eisenhower introduced to the presidency organizational elements that have become permanent fixtures. They include the positions of chief of staff, national security adviser, congressional liaison, and science adviser, as well as multiple committees, councils, and agencies scattered across the government.

By the time Eisenhower left office, admirers claimed that he had the government functioning as efficiently as a Swiss watch. Humorist Harry Goldin opined that Eisenhower's major contribution was that he proved that the nation could get along *without* a president. Tapping into this vein, stand-up comics joked about the "Eisenhower doll." You wound it up, they explained, and it stood for eight years. Assessments historians made after Ike left office were not all that different. They changed their minds in recent decades after they examined his opened presidential papers, which showed him to be a more hands-on president and more astute political operative than many had thought at the time he was in office. His reputation also received a boost as historians appraised the performance of his immediate successors.

Even the briefest perusal of his biography reveals that Eisenhower, in contrast to the three men who followed him in office, had not aspired to be president from an early age. Upon the conclusion of World War II, both parties sought to persuade Eisenhower to run for president. He expressed no interest. During the run-up to the 1952 election, Eisenhower changed his mind after he concluded that only his presence at the head of the Republican ticket would advance two objectives he considered crucial to the nation's short- and long-term interests: the election of a Republican president and bipartisan acceptance of containment policies toward the Soviet Union. Because the Republicans had lost the last five presidential elections, many questioned whether the two-party system would survive at the national level. Denied any responsibility for the nation's governance, save for the two years the Republicans controlled Congress (from 1947 to 1949), Republican leaders, in Eisenhower's view, had taken to making increasingly irresponsible statements as a means of appealing for votes. Two of these spokesmen that he particularly came to dislike were senators Joseph R. McCarthy and Walter Jenner.

The disinclination of Senate Republican leader Robert A. Taft, the presumed frontrunner for the GOP nomination, to endorse the containment policies that guided American Cold War strategy during the Truman administration factored heavily into Eisenhower's decision to run in 1952. (These are discussed in greater detail in chapter 6.) As chief of staff to the army from 1945 to 1948, Eisenhower had helped devise and implement many of the policies Taft opposed. He had also been called back into military service as the first commander of the North Atlantic Treaty Organization (NATO), the centerpiece of the United States' defense posture. Taft had voted against it. Aware of his popular appeal, Eisenhower sensed that he could defeat Taft for the party's presidential nomination and go on to win the general election. No other Republican could make such a claim. Thus, Eisenhower became one of the few presidents since Washington who could accept the presidency almost entirely on his own terms. He won with 55 percent of the vote. Four states of the former Confederacy—Texas, Virginia, Tennessee, and Florida, all still part of the "solid" (Democratic) south—contributed to his Electoral College land-slide (442 to 89). Although he proclaimed his victory a "mandate for change," Eisenhower's actions as president suggest he considered it more a mandate for continuity with a bit of fine-tuning.

Eisenhower organized his presidency around one central vision: how to wage the Cold War effectively. His strategy rested on the twin pillars of deter-ring Soviet aggression and maintaining a strong economy. Regarding both as indispensable to national security, Eisenhower weighed all policy options against their capacity to advance one or both of these objectives. He immedi-ately ruled out the possibility of committing American troops every place the Soviets or their surrogates probed for Western weaknesses. Such an approach, he reasoned, would necessitate the establishment of a garrison state. And the costs of maintaining such an enterprise would inflict irreparable harm upon the American economy through high taxes, high interest rates, or inflation. Eisenhower considered the exceptionally high quality of life the American people enjoyed in comparison with their counterparts in the com-munist world a powerful weapon in strengthening Western resolve during the Cold War. He was determined to maintain it.

In a reversal of Truman's defense posture, Eisenhower cut back on conven-tional forces. Through what became known as the "doctrine of massive retalia-tion," he invested instead in the cheaper option of nuclear superiority. Its underlying assumption was that would-be aggressors, once they understood that attacking the U.S. or its allies would assure their own physical destruction, would be deterred. With the Soviets in possession of nuclear capability, but still without the capacity to develop the necessary intercontinental missiles to launch a surprise nuclear attack, Eisenhower's strategy appeared to be both a safe bet and a chance for the West, after years of depression and war, to obtain some breathing room. As he cut back on conventional forces by one-third, Eisenhower increased spending on aircraft, missiles, and nuclear weapons. Although Congress occasionally criticized Ike for spending too little on defense, it never raised the ceilings he set in his budgetary recommendations.

Impressed that the Marshall Plan had established a favorable view of the United States in Europe, Eisenhower devoted increased attention to public diplomacy. He consistently backed multiple vehicles through which the United States could compete in the war of ideas with the Soviet Union. He was an early advocate of the Voice of America and, as president, broadened the number of countries that participated in the Fulbright Exchange Program. He was also a booster of Radio Free Europe, a creation of the National Committee for a Free Europe that John Foster Dulles helped organize, before he became Eisenhower's secretary of state. While still the army's highest official, Eisenhower had spoken out in favor of revising school curricula to include greater discussion of world affairs. As president, he established the United States Information Agency, within the State Department, to foster cultural exchange and enhance global understanding of the American way of life. Eisenhower became an advocate for the "sister cities" concept, which grew out of a White House conference he sponsored in 1956.

Eisenhower's and Dulles's penchant for placing all countries, in their minds and in their allocation of foreign aid, into one of two camps—one allied with the United States and one in the Soviet orbit—proved a less effective means of building support for the United States in other parts of the world. Sometimes it proved self-defeating as the Soviet Union threw its muscle behind indigenous nationalistic movements in newly independent nations that had once been colonies of European powers.[36] It may also have stalled by a half century the establishment of closer economic and political ties between the world's two largest democracies, the United States and India. In the name of anticommunism, the Eisenhower-Dulles approach led the United States to disregard human rights abuses committed by dictators who sided with the United States against the Soviet Union. As a consequence, much of the public in those countries began to hold the United States responsible for shoring up repressive regimes in their countries. Marxist revolutionaries took to exploiting those grievances.

The United States would reap a bitter harvest in parts of Asia, Africa, and Latin America for allowing the CIA to initiate covert actions to overthrow freely elected governments in the 1950s that American policymakers deemed too left-leaning. On Eisenhower's watch and at his direction, the CIA orchestrated coups against governments headed by Mohammed Mossedeq in Iran (replacing him with the shah), Jacobo Arbenz Guzman in Guatemala (replacing him with a military junta), and Joseph Lumumba in Congo (participating in his subsequent assassination). Its botched attempt to topple Sukarno's government in Indonesia helped to create a significant leftist, anti-American insurgency movement that had not previously existed.

In handling the Soviet Union, Eisenhower proved a master in achieving his overall objective of maintaining peace through superior strength, even if his administration seemed at times inconsistent and contradictory. While Eisenhower discoursed about "atoms for peace," peaceful "coexistence," "wars of ideas," cultural exchanges, and "goodwill missions," Dulles spoke of "rollbacks," "agonizing reappraisals," "brinkmanship," and the "liberation of captive peoples." Dulles's rhetoric, broadcast over Eisenhower-initiated media, sometimes created the impression that the United States would physically come to the aid of Eastern Europeans who sought to throw off their Soviet oppressors. Yet in 1956, when Hungarian rebels, perhaps inspired by American propaganda broadcasts, took to the streets against their communist masters, the United States stood idly by. As a matter of public policy, the decision not to risk a nuclear war with the Soviet Union in the heart of Europe was prudent. Yet the perception that the United States had raised expectations among so-called captive peoples that it would not help them fulfill, in the short-run at least, produced a tightening of the Soviet Union's grip over the people of Eastern Europe.

In a manner reminiscent of his hero and role model, George Washington, Ike brought to his presidential advisory system practices he had used during war counsels. By allowing stakeholders to participate fully in policy deliberations, Eisenhower increased the likelihood that he would hear all points of view and that all participants, satisfied that they had had their say, would help implement whatever was decided. This approach served Eisenhower well as he contemplated how to respond to France's request for military assistance in 1954. Ho Chi Minh's nationalistic forces had just defeated colonial troops in the town of Dien Bien Phu in the northern part of Vietnam. Dulles and Vice President Richard Nixon favored sending American forces to assist the French. Eisenhower wanted to know first whether the congressional leadership and American allies would support such an action. Their reluctance to express immediate support ranked high among the reasons why he rejected the idea. Because Ike treated Congress as a full partner in foreign as well as domestic policy and took its leaders into his confidence, he avoided the mutual mistrust and suspicion that came to characterize relations between the branches during the administrations of most of his successors. Drawing upon his own military experience, Eisenhower concluded that such a war in Southeast Asia "would absorb our troops by the divisions."[37]

Upon entering the White House, Eisenhower voiced dissatisfaction with the quality of the intelligence he received form the CIA about Soviet military capabilities and intentions. In 1955, he secretly directed the CIA to develop a high-altitude reconnaissance aircraft, the U-2, to provide surveillance of the U.S.S.R. He simultaneously directed the Air Force to research and develop reconnaissance satellites. Once the U-2 became operational in 1957, Eisenhower depended on the intelligence provided by aerial surveillance to satisfy himself that no missile gap between American and Soviet weapons capabilities was developing, as administration critics charged.

Having built up the nation's nuclear stockpile to the point at which he believed it had achieved superiority, Eisenhower hoped he might be able to attain some kind of rapprochement with his communist adversaries. His hopes that he could achieve this vanished on May 1, 1960, when the Soviet military unexpectedly downed the last U-2 Eisenhower had authorized to be sent over Soviet territory. The Soviets withdrew the invitation they had issued for Eisenhower to visit the U.S.S.R., and its leader, Nikita Khrushchev, used the incident as a pretext for cutting short a summit meeting with Eisenhower, British prime minister Harold MacMillan, and French president Charles DeGaulle. The relaxation of tensions that Eisenhower hoped to produce would be delayed for a decade.

Eisenhower applied the savings from cuts in defense spending to balancing the budget. He also expanded the reach of entitlement programs his predecessors began, bringing an additional 10.5 million Americans into the Social Security program. In making domestic policy, Eisenhower assembled a bipartisan consensus that was not dissimilar from the one he had put together in support of his defense initiatives. At his request, Congress established the Department of Health, Education, and Welfare to oversee the New Deal legacies he inherited and expanded. Fearful that budget deficits would produce inflation, Eisenhower did not propose significant cuts in income tax rates as a means of spurring economic growth. During his eight years in office, high marginal rates kept the growth rate artificially low, averaging 2.5 percent, and the economy suffered three recessions. The first ran from July 1953 through May 1954, the second from August 1957 through April 1958, and the third from April 1960 to February 1961.

Eisenhower's most significant domestic achievement, which he justified in terms of national security, was the Federal Highway Act of 1956. This legislation, exclusively an Eisenhower idea, appropriated $25 billion to construct more than forty thousand miles of limited access Interstate highways over the next decade. The federal government put up 90 percent of the funds, raised through a federal gas tax, with participating states providing the remaining 10 percent. The idea of an integrated network of federal highways had been germinating in Eisenhower's mind since 1919, when a military convoy he participated in took two weeks to cross the country. In proposing what became the interstate highway system, Eisenhower declared that, in the event of an attack or invasion, the nation would need to vacate cities rapidly and move soldiers rapidly about.

After the Soviet Union launched *Sputnik* in the fall of 1957, Eisenhower sought to reassure the public that it had no reason to fear for its security. His reassurances emanated not from complacency but from sound intelligence he had been obtaining from U-2 reconnaissance flights. Moreover, Eisenhower did not protest *Sputnik*'s flight over the United States because he wanted to establish the legal precedent that unmanned satellites, unlike airplanes, could fly over the airspace of all nations. Having established this precedent, the United States launched its first spy satellite, *Corona*, in 1959. One year later, this program was providing valuable intelligence about the Soviet Union. In response to growing fears, if not panic, about supposed Soviet superiority, Eisenhower, in close cooperation with the Democratic Congress, backed three measures that significantly strengthened the defense capability, intellectual wherewithal, and economic prosperity of the United States: the National Education Defense Act of 1958, which provided for expanded science education and foreign language instruction and allocated millions of dollars in loans to college students; the National Aeronautics and Space Act, which established NASA; and the Defense Reorganization Act of 1958, which established the Advanced Research Projects Agency (ARPA). (ARPA developed ARPANET, which became the Internet.)[38]

Another form of hysteria that President Eisenhower quieted down was McCarthyism. With the election of a Republican president, many expected Republican senator Joseph R. McCarthy of Wisconsin to cut back his probe of security risks within the executive branch and defer to the Justice Department. When McCarthy kept up his attacks, Eisenhower worked behind the scenes to discredit him.

When McCarthy demanded that Marxist-oriented writings be removed from United States Intelligence libraries around the world, Eisenhower, in a commencement speech at Dartmouth College, admonished his listeners not to "join the book burners." "Do not think you are going to conceal thoughts by concealing evidence that they ever existed," he said.[39] When McCarthy requested personnel records of thousands of government employees, Eisenhower forbade government agencies from surrendering them, claiming executive privilege. After McCarthy crossed a line in Eisenhower's view—when he questioned the patriotism of army personnel who had denied special privileges to McCarthy's former staffers—Eisenhower worked through Vice President Nixon and other intermediaries to line up conservative support for the Senate's censure of the Wisconsin senator. After the vote, McCarthy issued an apology to the American people for having supported Eisenhower's election.

Eisenhower's limitations as a public speaker and his "hidden hand" management style impeded him from making as strong a contemporaneous defense of his policies as he might have. Had he done more to trumpet his achievements, Eisenhower might have given historians of previous eras more to work with than popular perceptions, in advance of the release of his papers. But Eisenhower preferred to entrust his place in history to the American people. They responded in kind. Of all who have served as president since Truman, Eisenhower is the only one never to see his public approval rating fall below 50 percent. After he left the presidency, Eisenhower took stock of how well he had done his duty. "The United States never lost a soldier or a foot of ground in my administration. We kept the peace. People asked how it happened—by God, it didn't just happen. I'll tell you that."[40]

He considered keeping public morale in the United States high during some of the most challenging and dangerous periods of the Cold War an important part of his legacy. "Optimism and pessimism are infectious," he observed, "and they spread more rapidly from the head downward."[41] Campaigning, speechmaking, and the demands of politics were not chores he relished. Nor did these tasks come easily to him. Yet, as president, they were among the duties he was required to perform. And Dwight D. Eisenhower was never one to shirk duty. In the third person, he described what an ordeal campaigning was and how he prepared for such an undertaking:

Armed with a card on which he or an assistant has written three or four words to remind him of the particular subjects he must mention, and the local candidates for whom he wants to express support at this stop, he awaits cessation of the crowd's clamor—which he fervently prays will consume at least two minutes of his allotted seven. Then he launches into a talk that he is convinced, by his battered memory, must certainly fail because it has been delivered over and over again, never-ending and tiresome. But he quickly feels within him a transformation. Although as he came out to the platform, he was bored, resentful, or even sorry for himself, invariably he is anxious to make his planned points. . . . He seems to feel that he owes it to these people to expose them to his beliefs, his convictions, his hopes, and his aspirations for our country.[42]

All in all, he pulled off this and so much else rather well.

Ronald Reagan

"I wasn't a great communicator," Ronald Reagan insisted in his farewell address to the nation, "but I communicated great things."[43] He had it half right. *What* he said and how he said it mattered at a time when the nation—after a series of failed presidencies and years of high inflation, high unemployment, and repeated setbacks in the international arena—was ready to embark on a different course. That Reagan was able to persuade his fellow citizens to follow the one he proposed was no small achievement. In making his case, Reagan displayed several gifts that he had spent the better part of a lifetime perfecting.

One was a reassuring, melodious voice, which, in the words of one biographer, was "tinged with a hopeful cadence."[44] Reagan's mother had taught him how to lower his voice, speaking barely above a whisper, in order to hold the attention of and establish intimacy with his audience, and then how to raise it in order to project the sincerity of his passion. As a boy and as a young adult, Reagan listened carefully to sermons and radio broadcasts, paying special attention to his then role model, Franklin Delano Roosevelt. When Reagan beseeched his party in 1976 to present its case in bold colors rather than pale pastels, he was speaking primarily about policy. But he was also expressing his own disappointment at having seen his party's fortunes suffer after nominating lackluster candidates. One journalist later observed that if Reagan's voice was a gift, his delivery, "which sounds so natural, is the result of hard work and careful preparation."[45]

Along with that melodious voice, Reagan possessed and conveyed a certain presence. As early as high school, Reagan had a way of "sauntering across the stage" and drawing all eyes to him, "even when he was not speaking."[46] Through his body language, Reagan exuded a sense of command. After he became president, his staff went to great lengths to make maximum use of this attribute. Among the most enduring images of his time in office were of Reagan walking through the American cemetery at Normandy; reviewing caskets of fallen U.S. soldiers, victims of terrorist attacks in Lebanon; and his singling out for praise, during his State of the Union addresses, ordinary Americans who had performed heroic actions. Reagan projected strength, confidence, and reassurance even in situations for which he could not have prepared. When a moderator attempted to turn off Reagan's microphone in the midst of a skirmish over the procedure for a candidates' debate, the Californian, recalling a line from a 1947 movie, blurted out to the audience's delight, "I paid for this microphone . . . !"[47] And having suffered a near fatal injury during an assassination attempt, Reagan insisted on walking into the hospital emergency room, unaided and with his jacket buttoned.

In dealing with his peers and especially with his adversaries—be they the Democratic speaker of the House Tip O'Neill or Soviet leader Mikhail Gorbachev—Reagan's practice was not to begin negotiations by seeking an early consensus or offering to split differences. He would take a firm stand early on and wait for his opposition to make concessions. Anxious for a deal, his negotiating partners would often leap at his first or second offer. House Speaker Tip O'Neill considered Reagan a master at knowing how to extract 60 percent from his opposite and return at a later time for the rest.[48] Reagan would remind fellow Republicans and conservatives that someone who agreed with them 80 percent of the time was hardly their adversary, let alone their enemy.

When congressional Democrats, who held a majority in the House, resisted Reagan's tax cuts—his highest domestic priority during his first year—Reagan made an appeal for public support in a nationally televised address. Representatives later complained of their telephones being tied up for hours with constituent calls and being inundated with mail. Reagan worked the phones as well. He met with wavering members of Congress—both in formal White House settings and over drinks and burgers at Camp David—and turned up the heat. In the end, Reagan pulled sixty-three House Democrats his way. (Many represented districts he had carried in the 1980 election.) One Democratic leader wrote afterward that he was not sure he had ever seen Reagan's equal.[49]

Although Reagan came to his political views more by experience and instinct than from what he read, Reagan did read widely on subjects that interested him and that he deemed important. One aide recalled watching Reagan "dive into the details of the federal revenue code," putting his mastery of memorization to good use in his negotiations with representatives and senators.[50] The president, who had difficulty identifying the faces of some people he had named to cabinet positions, went to great lengths sounding out experts of all persuasions to advise him on nuclear weaponry, Soviet strategy, and Russian history. "He only had five or six ideas," Margaret Thatcher said of Reagan, "but all of them were big and all of them were good."[51]

In areas where Reagan was less well informed, or invested little time, his propensity to delegate to subordinates whose abilities and judgments he was unlikely to second guess got the best of him. Reagan's secretary of state George Shultz noted that the president accepted "uncritically" and "wishfully" advice that was sometimes "amateurish and even irresponsible."[52] (Examples of such recommendations are provided in chapter 7.) Aware of her excessively optimistic husband's tendency to take people at face value and expect the best of them, Nancy Reagan "did the worrying" for both halves of the first couple.[53] As the occasion warranted, she helped bring into his orbit people who would watch out for his interests and move out those she suspected were either disloyal or interested in moving agendas of their own.

After Reagan refused to acknowledge that he had in fact sanctioned the trading of arms for hostages, triggering the Iran-Contra scandal, Nancy's sense of danger and the president's strengths of character together salvaged his presidency. After the scandal had come to light, Reagan made a series of well-received staff changes and reorganizations. More importantly, Reagan, unlike his immediate predecessors and successors, declined to assert executive privilege, a constitutionally protected means of withholding from

Congress and investigators details of communications he had had with key advisers. This—along with his reputation for honesty; his willingness to suffer embarrassment should those materials be made public; and the highly persuasive speech he delivered to the nation, in which he conceded having made errors, even if he could not recall them—enabled Reagan not only to survive the scandal but to end his presidency on the highest possible note by negotiating the beginning of the end of the Cold War.

James Madison

By any standard, James Madison was among the most brilliant men ever to serve as president. He was also one of the least competent. Were it not for the role he played in crafting and securing ratification of the Constitution and the Bill of Rights, Madison would place even lower than he does in surveys assessing presidential greatness. As president, he exhibited two flaws that proved fatal to his administration: he proved too much of an ideologue, and he viewed challenges more through the eyes of the legislator he had been than through those of the executive he had become. The defining event of Madison's presidency, the War of 1812, need not have been fought. By the time he waged it, Madison, through a series of mistakes he had made earlier in his presidency, had rendered victory almost impossible.

Before he became Jefferson's secretary of state, Madison had spent his entire career in legislative bodies. He served in the Virginia House of Delegates, the Continental Congress, and the U.S. House of Representatives. He had also been a delegate to the Virginia convention in 1776, the Annapolis convention of 1786, and the Constitutional convention in 1787. In all of these assemblies, Madison became a master at legislative compromise and at assembling coalitions. His peers recalled that Madison always came across "as the best informed man on any point in debate."[54]

From the moment he and Jefferson began what historian Adrienne Koch termed the "great collaboration," Madison provided the form and much of the substance to the set of ideas that became known as "Jeffersonian democracy."[55]

With Jefferson the more skillful politician and the better political organizer, it fell to Madison to fashion Jefferson's philosophical musings into a coherent philosophy. As opposition leader and as president, Jefferson looked to Madison to iron out wrinkles and smooth over inconsistencies in his statements, letters, and pamphlets.

In voicing their opposition to Hamilton's economic policies, which presupposed a strong central government, Jefferson and Madison argued for strong state governments, a weak central government, a strict interpretation of the Constitution, and legislative supremacy over the executive and judicial branches of government. Within Congress, they assigned a leading role to the House of Representatives, which at the time was the only arm of the federal government directly elected by the people. Jefferson and Madison argued that the Bank of the United States was unconstitutional because the power to charter banks was not among the functions the Constitution authorized Congress to do.

When he purchased the Louisiana Territory, Jefferson demonstrated that as president he was willing to yield a philosophical point in order to advance what he believed to be a greater objective: the empire of liberty. Interestingly, with Madison serving as secretary of state when the purchase was negotiated, Jefferson limited his more ideological colleague's role to reassuring strict constructionists that the president had not abandoned them when he committed what was at least an extra-constitutional, if not unconstitutional, act. When his subordinate found this task particularly onerous, Jefferson advised Madison that the "less said" about the matter "the better."[56]

Paradoxically, the one time Jefferson followed Madison's advice on international affairs, he brought upon himself and the country what was probably the greatest catastrophe the United States suffered in the three decades since it won its independence. Unable to win a war against one or two European superpowers, and unwilling to endure the continued disruption of its trade with one or both of the warring powers, Jefferson and Madison settled on an embargo as a halfway measure. By denying France and the United Kingdom access to American goods, they hoped to entice both foreign governments to respect American rights on the high seas. Neither man had anticipated how long the embargo would need to stay in place in order to be effective. Nor did they have in mind, when they imposed it, a fallback position in the event that their policy failed to achieve its objectives. (The embargo was discussed in further detail in chapters 2 and 3.)

That Madison could recommend such a course to his superior underscores the truth in Fisher Ames's observation that Madison was prone to "too much theory and wants that discretion that men of business commonly have."[57] Showing signs that he recognized his policy to be a mistake, but not knowing how to change course without enduring a loss of face, Jefferson all but threw up his hands in despair. With Congress poised to repeal the measure on the eve of his inauguration, President-elect Madison, a colleague observed, was "inclined to hug the embargo, and die in its embrace."[58]

Madison's provincialism, in contrast to Jefferson's worldliness, together with his limited practical experience, led him to develop a worldview that bore little relationship to how individuals and nations responded under certain circumstances. Madison was the first secretary of state not to have been abroad prior to his appointment. As both a cabinet officer and as president, Madison had little feel for how other nations regarded the United States and few, if any, foreign contacts.

As president, Madison proved Washington's and Jefferson's inferior in filling major posts. Whereas Washington sought out the most able men, and Jefferson selected men of standing who had earned his trust in prior associations with him, Madison made his picks with an eye toward pleasing sectional, factional, and even familial blocs within his governing coalition. When Senator Samuel Smith of Pennsylvania objected to Madison's designating Jefferson's secretary of the treasury Albert Gallatin as his secretary of state, Madison named Smith's brother, Robert, a known incompetent, to the most important post in the cabinet and left Gallatin at the Treasury. Aware of Robert Smith's deficiencies, but also mindful of the influence of his powerful brother, Jefferson had appointed Robert to the less important job of secretary of the navy. To head the War Department, Madison turned to William Eustis, whose sole qualifications were his New England residence and his service as a hospital surgeon during the Revolutionary War. To replace Smith at the Navy Department, Madison appointed Paul Hamilton, an ineffective former governor of South Carolina and a known alcoholic.[59] These early decisions impeded Madison's effectiveness as commander in chief when he found himself directing the very shooting war Jefferson had averted.

With the charter of the Bank of the United States scheduled to expire in March 1811, at the end of Madison's second year in office, Gallatin began to press for its renewal. Aware of Madison's prior opposition to the Bank, Gallatin persuaded the president that it was necessary for maintaining financial stability and promoting economic growth. With assurance from Madison that the president accepted the Bank's legitimacy, on the grounds that its constitutionality had not been challenged during its almost two-decade existence, Gallatin turned his attentions to Capitol Hill.[60] Madison failed, however, to use his influence with Congress when the Bank's charter came up for renewal. His nearly religious belief in legislative supremacy all but ruled out his engaging in private lobbying or acting through surrogates in the manner of the more flexible Jefferson. Moreover, Madison proved reluctant to appear to be going back on statements he had made decades earlier in opposition to the bank, which its opponents were certain to cite. When the bill to renew the Bank's charter tied in the Senate, Madison's vice president George Clinton, a Republican of the old school and no friend of Madison's, cast the deciding vote against it. As a result, Madison was left with insufficient means to raise funds to finance a war he could and should have avoided. (For more on Madison's approach to the economy and international affairs, see chapters 6 and 7.)

With the British impressing American soldiers, impeding neutral powers from trading with France, and instigating Native American attacks against American settlers in the Great Lakes region, Madison issued a series of increasingly threatening protests. When these failed to produce results, "war hawks" in Congress, led by newly elected Speaker Henry Clay and Representative John C. Calhoun, buoyed by public opinion primarily in the south, pressed for war. Clay was particularly anxious to annex the British colony of Canada. On June 1, 1812, Madison asked for a declaration of war against the United Kingdom. The resolution passed the House by a wide margin. With New Englanders staunchly opposed, it cleared the Senate by a margin of only six votes.

Given the lack of American preparation and the country's anemic military posture, this was hardly the optimal time for the new nation to engage in a war of choice. Perhaps Madison reasoned that the British government, already engaged in conflict with Napoleonic France, was not in the position to mount a strong defense of Canada. Jefferson advised Madison that Canada would easily fall to the Americans—an assertion unsupported by reliable intelligence. Upper Canada (modern Ontario) had become home to thousands of loyalists who had fled the United States after the American Revolution. In Lower Canada (modern Quebec), francophones feared that the predominantly protestant and secularist United States would disestablish the Roman Catholic Church as the official church of one or more new states. Neither group wanted its region to join the United States, and both fought valiantly against invading American forces. Moreover, with the British parliament voting to cease impressing American sailors the day before Congress declared war, Madison could easily have claimed victory before the war had begun.

The land war went badly from the beginning. True to a promise he made as a candidate for president, Jefferson had left as his legacy a standing army of limited size. This meant that state militias would carry out most of the fighting. Many of these proved reluctant to engage in combat outside their respective states and unwilling to serve under commanders not from their states. Congress, aware of these problems, increased the size of the standing army from twelve thousand to thirty-five thousand at the outset of the war. Nevertheless, the unclear command structure of the army and continued political interference in its operations hampered its effectiveness. After a series of setbacks on land, the United States fared better in its naval operations. In a major turning point that may have assured continued American independence, Commodore Oliver Perry seized control of Lake Erie, denying the British control of the Mississippi River.

Like the embargo that preceded it, the war remained unpopular in New England and elsewhere, where disrupted shipping caused financial ruin. Apt at exploiting internal American divisions, the British exempted New England from its blockade of U.S. ports. Smuggling continued unabated. Several northern states convened at Hartford to consider their options. Some threatened secession. With Napoleon's defeat in April 1814, the British government was able to turn its full attention to North America. Having dismissed Eustis as secretary of war, Madison also sacked Eustis's replacement, John Armstrong Jr., after British troops made their way to Washington, D.C., and burned the White House and the Capitol in August 1814. Frustrated, Madison sent a delegation abroad to negotiate an end to hostilities. Although the Treaty of Ghent did not resolve any issues cited in the war declaration, Madison opted to accept a stalemate. Unaware that the war had ended, British troops mounted a major assault against New Orleans two weeks after the treaty was signed. In fending them off, General Andrew Jackson's forces produced an impressive and decisive victory, which dampened whatever hopes the British might have had of resuming hostilities.

In spite of his multiple failures as leader of an ill-considered war, Madison redeemed part of his reputation through the stoicism he exhibited during the ordeal and for the respect he showed for civil liberties during the conflict. If his rigid adherence to constitutional principles rendered Madison ineffective early in his tenure, it also decreed that he stand steadfast behind the Bill of Rights during the darkest days of the war. In stark contrast to the jailing of administration critics under the Alien and Sedition Acts (under Adams) and during the embargo (under Jefferson), not a single person was charged with treason or libel at any time during Madison's presidency.[61] Picking up on this aspect of Madison's leadership, John Adams opined that "notwithstanding a thousand faults and blunders," Madison's administration helped "establish more Union" than had his three predecessors put together.[62]

Herbert Hoover

"That man has offered me unsolicited advice for six years, all of it bad," President Calvin Coolidge said of the man who would succeed him.[63] Coolidge did not like Herbert Hoover, but he respected his abilities. When the lower Mississippi River overflowed its banks during the great flood of 1927, Coolidge sent Hoover, then commerce secretary, to direct the relief efforts. Hoover commandeered railroads and commercial barges to rescue the homeless and ferry supplies at no cost. He helped the Red Cross raise an unprecedented $8 million. Press accounts of Hoover's successes reminded the American public of the legendary efforts he made during World War I to fend off starvation in war-torn Europe.[64]

Hoover's multiple successes notwithstanding, there was something about the "Great Engineer" that Coolidge, the sullen and self-effacing Yankee, could not abide. Beyond earshot, Coolidge referred to the much-admired Hoover as "Wonder Boy."[65] Coolidge, having spent nearly all of his adult life in elected office, had kept his ear close to the ground. Valuing practical experience, diligence, and common sense more than anything else in colleagues and subordinates, Coolidge had little patience for self-proclaimed or media-crowned experts. To him—and to many others—Hoover, who had not run for office before being elected president at the age of 54, appeared the quintessential expert. A year into the Great Depression, one journalist recalled the sense of anticipation that had accompanied Hoover's inauguration. "We summoned a great engineer to solve our problems for us; now we sat back comfortably and confidently to watch the problems being solved," she remembered.[66] Andrew Mellon—who served as secretary of the treasury under Harding, Coolidge, and Hoover—having expected less of Hoover, was also less disappointed. He considered Hoover "too inclined to have his own solution of problems, frequently unsound."[67]

While Theodore Roosevelt and Woodrow Wilson had paid lip service to the idea that politics could be removed from governing and that government could be reduced to a science, Hoover made the proper functioning of government machinery along scientific principles a goal unto itself.[68] Hoover failed as president not because he sat idly by and waited for market forces to right the economy, as many believed—mistakenly, at the time—but because he aggressively pursued policies that ran in a direction counter to what the nation and its economy most needed. In setting his course, Hoover, sometimes consciously, disregarded advice from people even more expert than he on the causes of the Great Depression and how they might be addressed. As his first presidential benefactor, Woodrow Wilson, anticipated, "I have the feeling that [Hoover] would rather see a good cause fail than succeed if he were not the head of it."[69]

Unlike Jackson, Lincoln, Truman, and several other presidents, Hoover had never experienced failure before he became president. Born in West Branch, Iowa, in 1874 and orphaned by the time he was nine, Hoover went to live with a wealthy uncle in Willamette, Oregon. He gained admission to the newly opened Stanford University on the strength of superior mathematical skills. Foreshadowing his future difficulties as a communicator, Hoover's evuators found his verbal skills poorly developed.[70] One associate, years later, compared listening to Hoover speak to bathing in a tub of ink.[71] In public and in private, Hoover was all graphs, statistics, and charts. When he ran for president, his handlers attempted to "humanize" him by releasing to the press photographs of the candidate playing with his dog.[72]

After his graduation from Stanford in 1895 with a degree in engineering, Hoover's work as a mining engineer took him to several continents.[73] A millionaire by the time he was forty, Hoover turned his complete attention to public service. When war broke out in Europe in 1914, he supervised the evacuation of 120,000 stranded Americans. His subsequent efforts on behalf of dislocated and starving Belgians earned him the title, the "Great Humanitarian." After the United States entered the war, President Wilson designated Hoover as the nation's food administrator and granted him the authority to set prices and production goals for farmers, hire packers, cut deals with exporters, and enlist freight companies. According to one account: "As the United States became early in 1918 the only available source of supply for the feeding of millions of men and animals . . . the President, acting through Mr. Hoover, became a dictator of world affairs unprecedented in history."[74]

Placing a premium on voluntarism and individual sacrifice, Hoover encouraged the public, through posters and advertisements, to observe meatless Mondays and wheatless Wednesdays and to plant victory gardens. In so doing, Hoover managed to meet his goals without having to resort to compulsory rationing. After the war, Hoover distributed food, clothing, and supplies across war-ravaged Europe. His work led him to the Paris Peace Conference. In *Economic Consequences of the Peace*, John Maynard Keynes dubbed Hoover "the only man who emerged" from the war and its after-math "with an enhanced reputation."[75]

Both parties tried to recruit Hoover as their presidential candidate in 1920. Hoover agreed to serve as secretary of commerce under Warren G. Harding after requesting and obtaining the responsibility of overseeing federal agencies in other departments that regulated business. Insiders took to referring to Hoover as "secretary of commerce and undersecretary of everything else." In his multiple roles, he practiced a form of management he termed "associationalism."[76] Often described as "corporatism" when practiced in other countries, "associationalism" connoted government partnering with business and labor to promote industrial and social harmony. Using the principles of scientific management, and explicitly rejecting the laissez faire approach, Hoover tried to eliminate what he regarded as wasteful competition. While he preferred to minimize explicit regulations, he encouraged price fixing and division of markets among competing firms in the same industry. Replicating the extension services of the Department of Agriculture, Hoover sought to make the Department of Commerce into a source of information and technological advice for nonagricultural businesses.

As the Republican presidential nominee in 1928, Hoover easily defeated Democrat Alfred E. Smith, winning 58 percent of the vote. (In the Electoral College, the margin was 444 to 87.) In addition to his personal popularity and public satisfaction with the prosperity of the Coolidge years (see chapter 5), Hoover benefited from Smith's Catholicism and from the Democrat's opposition to Prohibition. In 1929, six months into his presidency, the stock market crashed. From a high of 381.17 on September 3, the Dow Jones Industrial Average plunged to 298.17 on October 24, or Black Thursday. It fell to 230.17 on October 29, or Black Tuesday. Hoover declared the "fundamental business of the country, that is the production and distribution of commodities," to be sound.[77] With only 3 percent of the public owning shares of stock, few saw any reason to take issue with his assessment. Stock market crashes had occurred before and would again, without igniting depressions. Hoover, however, committed a series of blunders that turned what might have been a normal recession into the Great Depression.

After first misdiagnosing its causes, Hoover implemented policies that not only failed to improve the situation but actually made it worse. Hoover and Mellon attributed the crash to stock speculators bidding up share prices to irrational heights. To soften the adverse effects of the crash on the broader economy, Mellon pushed the twelve Federal Reserve banks to cut their discount rates by 1 percentage point. At Mellon's urging, Hoover prodded Congress to enact a one-year, 1-percentage point, across-the-board reduction in individual and corporate income tax rates for 1929.[78] Once these two actions had been taken, Mellon advised allowing the market to bottom out so that stocks would again reflect their true worth.

At this point, Hoover reverted back to associationalism. Because he believed that high wages were the cause rather than the result of American prosperity, he pressed corporate executives not to reduce the number of their employees or to cut wages. While business leaders attempted to comply with Hoover's requests for a time, slack in demand eventually forced them to reduce output, resulting in their laying off workers and slashing wages. Hoover responded with a series of public works programs intended to put Americans back to work. His public works program drove federal spending up from $3.320 billion (equal to 3.4 percent of GDP) in fiscal year 1930 to $4.598 billion (equal to 8.0 percent of GDP) in fiscal year 1933. Reviewing Hoover's initiatives, FDR's economic adviser Rexford Tugwell observed that "the New Deal owed much to what he [Hoover] had begun."[79] None of this spending, however, turned the economic tide.

Most historians today accept economist and Nobel laureate Milton Friedman's conclusion that misguided monetary policies the Federal Reserve persued caused the unprecedented economic contraction that occurred between August 1929 and March 1933. Friedman's much heralded analysis of these policy failures has caused intellectuals of all ideological persuasions to reassess previously held views about what policymakers in the 1930s did that produced this result. Most believe that the Federal Reserve should have expanded the money supply instead of contracting it, as the Fed did. Less widely known, perhaps, is that leading economists in Hoover's time, with whom he enjoyed professional relationships—Yale University's Irving

Fisher being the most famous—warned Hoover to change course and begin reinflating the money supply.[80] Had he chosen to follow this advice, Hoover could easily have persuaded the Federal Reserve to go along. (Prior to 1935, two of the seven members of the Federal Reserve Board served at the pleasure of the president, while the remaining five were presidential appointees serving staggered ten-year terms.)

Hoover's inattention to these economists' warnings proved calamitous. Rather than act as Fisher suggested, Hoover demonized Wall Street, sermonizing about greed, avarice, and the short selling of shares.[81] He urged the Senate to establish what today is known as the "Pecora Commission," to identify financial wrongdoing. Part of the Great Engineer's blindness to what was transpiring around him stemmed from his failure to appreciate what Fisher and others were telling him and, perhaps, to his having absorbed the suspicion and distrust he heard his neighbors voice about banks, bankers, and paper money while he was growing up in the west. Hoover better understood the physical processes involved in the production of goods and the application of natural resources, such as the precious metals he had mined in the early stages of his career, than he did finance.

Without a push from the president the Federal Reserve was not poised to reverse its policy. In the 1920s and beyond, most bankers and many economists adhered to the antiquated real bills doctrine. This held that central banks should lend to commercial banks based on their "real bills," a nineteenth-century term for high-quality short-term loans to businesses that were to be repaid through the production of goods and services. Under this theory central banks would restrict credit during downturns and expand it during boom times. All along, there had been dissenters from what had become the prevailing orthodoxy. Nearly a half-century before the Great Depression, British economist Walter Bagehot proposed the loosening rather than tightening of credit during economic downturns.[82] Ironically, Federal Reserve Bank of New York Governor George Harrison had been pushing his colleagues to adopt precisely this approach. Had Hoover voiced support for this view, Harrison might well have prevailed. Having made up his mind in the absence of real evidence that speculation had caused both the stock market crash and the subsequent economic downturn, the man Coolidge termed Wonder Boy was more interested in punishing perceived perpetrators than he was in seeking a way out of the financial distress that plagued him and the nation.

The collapse of U.S. investment abroad caused a large inflow of gold to the country in 1930 and well into 1931. Under normal conditions, these gold inflows should have increased reserves and caused commercial banks to increase the money supply by making new loans to businesses and consumers. The Federal Reserve, however, counteracted, with apparent presidential acquiescence, what would have been a monetary expansion by selling government bonds and reducing its loans to commercial banks. The Federal Reserve also failed to perform its principal function as lender of last resort to commercial banks. Instead of extending loans to troubled commercial banks to avoid runs and prevent widespread failures, the Federal Reserve largely closed its discount window. Through three rounds of bank failures in October 1930, March 1931, and March 1933, the Federal Reserve's loans to commercial banks actually fell from $1.29 billion in 1928 to $0.12 billion in 1933.[83] Economist Richard Timberlake found that in the years during which Hoover was president, "the commercial banking system would have had $1.05 billion more in reserve assets for its own production of loans and deposits if the Federal Reserve had not existed."[84]

In October 1931, Hoover organized the National Credit Corporation as a voluntary cooperative through which commercial banks could extend loans to other banks facing runs. After a few loans had been made, Hoover observed, "Its members and the business world threw up their hands and asked for government action."[85] On January 22, 1932, Hoover signed legislation establishing the Reconstruction Finance Corporation (RFC), which was capitalized with $500 million from general revenues and authorized to issue another $1.5 billion in debt. Hoover instructed the RFC to lend to commercial banks as well as to nonfinancial corporations and state and local governments. Essentially, he had established a new entity to perform the lender of last resort role that the Federal Reserve had abandoned. The RFC did not begin to function at full capacity until well into Franklin Delano Roosevelt's administration, which may be one reason Hoover receives so little credit for one of his few constructive undertakings as president.

Ironically, at the time he acted, Hoover's embrace of the RFC contributed to his rising unpopularity. He had shown himself willing to provide money to banks, businesses, and state and local governments at the same time that he opposed providing public relief to individuals on the grounds that such a policy would stifle individual initiative. He opted instead to provide such relief, but to conceal the federal government's role so as not to increase demand. Much of it flowed in the form of aid to state and local governments, which passed it on. With Hoover intent on hiding what he was doing, increased numbers of homeless Americans christened the groupings of makeshift shelters in which they hovered "Hoovervilles." As the Great Depression wore on, Hoover's once legendary public relations skills failed him. The president allowed himself to be photographed feeding his dog White House table scraps practically within sight of breadlines in the nation's capital. A neon sign at a Democratic rally best captured the public mood: "Herbert Hoover: He Fed Europe and Starved America."[86]

Hoover made one of his worst blunders when he signed the Smoot-Hawley Tariff Act into law on June 17, 1930. Although other sectors of the U.S. economy had prospered during the 1920s, farm income had been declining since 1920. This decline was due in large part to the additional acreage Hoover had brought into production as food administrator during World War I. In 1928, Hoover pledged to help farmers by increasing tariffs on agricultural imports. Weeks before he signed Smoot-Hawley, 1,028 economists, including Fisher, signed an open letter to the *New York Times*, urging Hoover to veto the bill.[87] Rather than heed their warnings, Hoover entered into intricate negotiations with legislators to establish rates, industry by industry. Hoover's signing the bill into law precipitated a decline in world trade flows on an epic scale. U.S. imports declined from $7.034 billion in 1929 to just $2.402 billion in 1933, while U.S. exports fell from $5.886 billion in 1929 to a mere $2.044 million in 1932.

Together, collapsing tax revenues and Hoover's spending initiatives produced mounting budget deficits. Harboring a businessman's conventional aversion to deficits, Hoover then pushed through the largest tax increase in U.S. history up to that time. In 1932, individual income tax rates jumped from a range of 1.125 to 25 percent to a range of 4 percent on taxable incomes over $4,000 ($50,425 in 2000 dollars) to 63 percent on taxable income over $1,000,000 ($12,606,149 in 2000 dollars); corporate tax rates rose from 12 to 15 percent; estate taxes jumped from a range of 1 to 20 percent to a range of 1 to 40 percent on taxable estates above $10,000,000 ($126,061,493 in 2000 dollars). The gift tax was reinstated, and bank depositors began paying a two-cent tax on each check they drafted. Again, had Hoover sought advice, he would have found that no school of economic thought advocated increasing taxes during a depression. John Maynard Keynes, with whom Hoover was well acquainted personally, had already warned that budget deficits should be allowed to expand during economic downturns.[88]

Anyone who harbored illusions that Hoover could be re-elected in 1932 was disabused of them when newsreels showed the U.S. Army being turned on by veterans who had traveled to Washington, D.C., to demand early payment of promised bonuses. By some accounts, Army Chief of Staff Douglas MacArthur exceeded Hoover's orders in precipitating this action. Unbeknownst to the press and to most of the marchers, Hoover and his wife had secretly supplied the protesters with food and blankets days before MacArthur took action.[89] In his last, and perhaps most fatal, act of misjudgment, Hoover the expert celebrated when the Democratic National Convention settled on Franklin Delano Roosevelt as its presidential nominee. Having remembered Roosevelt from the latter's days as assistant secretary of navy in the Wilson administration, Hoover concluded that FDR would be the easiest of all the available Democrats to defeat.[90] His prediction anticipated by four decades a similar assessment the next engineer to serve as president (Jimmy Carter) made about a former actor who had closely followed Roosevelt's career.

Lyndon B. Johnson

A master legislator by instinct, experience, and temperament, Lyndon Johnson, in the opening months of his presidency, succeeded in persuading his former congressional colleagues to pass not only the historic Civil Rights Act of 1964 but also to enact three other measures of his slain predecessor's legislative agenda: tax cuts, federal aid to education, and a war on poverty. With the size of the Democrats' legislative majorities substantially increased by Johnson's landslide re-election in 1964, Johnson enacted even more precedent-shattering measures during the historic 89th Congress.

Biographers, former aides, and contemporaneous commentators all noted the meticulous attention Johnson paid to Congress. He was constantly working the phones, seeking out opinions, counting votes, and checking up on a bill's progress, as he put it, "from cradle to grave."[91] "Merely placing a program before Congress is not enough," Johnson would say. "Without constant attention from the administration, most legislation moves through the congressional process with the speed of a glacier."[92] Enacting legislation was how Johnson primarily conceived of his job as president. He was less inclined to intervene in bureaucratic turf battles, check up on how well a law that he signed was being implemented, or inquire as to whether all the funds he spent on domestic programs were achieving the intent of the legislation he helped enact.

Speedy passage of bills was Johnson's primary concern. As soon as one measure had passed, Johnson would move on to the next. In that sense, Johnson never made the transition from Senate majority leader to president of the United States. Once, Johnson voiced surprise that passage of one of his favorite bills, the antipoverty program, put at loggerheads two groups he regarded as part of his governing coalition: urban political machines and advocates for the poor. He had intended, through the bill, to recreate FDR's National Youth Administration and Civilian Conservation Corps. Instead, in the area of job training, for instance, he wound up subsidizing nongovernment organizations, which competed with city governments for federal funding. Nor had he anticipated that the Legal Services Program, which provided the poor with legal advice in civil cases, would become a vehicle though which community action groups took state and local governments to court.[93]

Some of Johnson's frustrations resulted simply from the manner in which he crafted bills. Rather than establish pilot programs that could be replicated if found successful, Johnson and Sargent Shriver, his principal poverty adviser, opted for mammoth programs, spanning multiple cabinet departments. By taking this approach, Johnson assured that disagreements would occur over what legislation intended and that inefficiencies would result in its implementation. His aims, also, were nothing less than grandiose. Under the rubric of the Great Society would fall bills to create two new cabinet departments (Housing and Urban Development and Transportation), Medicare and Medicaid, and measures to protect the environment, increase aid to education, outlaw discrimination in housing, end restrictive immigration practices, support the arts, create a public broadcasting system, and protect consumers.

For a man intent on transforming so many aspects of American civilization, Johnson showed a surprising lack of curiosity about the workings of public policy. By his own admission, he read whatever proved immediately useful. He used statistics, findings, and recommendations in government reports, to disarm critics—only to forget them once legislative opposition subsided. He also seemed not to understand how people on opposite sides of important policy debates, often within his own administration, could quote some of his statements in support of their position.

One case in point was the speech Johnson delivered at Howard University after passage of the Voting Rights Act, in which he appeared to advocate equality of results rather than equality of opportunity: "You do not take a person who, for years, has been hobbled by chains and liberate him, bring him to the starting gate and say, 'You are free to compete with the others,' and still justly believe that you have been completely fair. . . . We see . . . not just equality as a right and a theory, but equality a fact and equality as a result."[94]

Generally regarded as the beginning of affirmative action, Johnson's words appeared to contradict assurances he had made, while making the case for other legislation, that the federal government would not award special consideration to persons based on race. By the end of Johnson's tenure in office, many who identified themselves as liberals openly argued over whether goals and timetables constituted hiring quotas and whether either was permissible under the antidiscrimination legislation Johnson had signed.

It is unclear how well Johnson understood that, because of pressures that had come to the surface during his presidency, the New Deal coalition (of union households, immigrants and their children, African Americans, southern whites, big city machines, Catholics, and Jews), which had made the Democratic Party the dominant force in American politics for a generation, and the bipartisan coalition through which he operated were beginning to crumble. He did comprehend that, as a result of his civil rights policies, southern whites were beginning to fall away from his base, and that urban unrest had produced a backlash against further civil rights initiatives among certain northern voters. The irony was not lost on him that college students, who had benefited from his efforts to broaden educational opportunities, seemed to oppose him the most.

Yet Johnson appeared at a loss in how to respond to the many challenges that confronted him. The "ways of the fixer" he had so perfected over the years and had served him well in the Senate did him little good in the White House once the twin foreign and domestic catastrophes known as the "war in Vietnam" were in full bloom. "I knew from the start," he told one writer, "that . . . if I left the woman I really loved—the Great Society—for that bitch of a war on the other side of the world, then I would lose everything at home.[95] His assessment was much on the mark.

Mindful of the pollitical damage the Republican Right inflicted upon Democrats a generation earlier—when it blamed the Truman administration for failing to prevent Mao Zedong's forces from winning the Chinese civil war and for pursuing a "no-win" strategy in the Korean conflict—Johnson resolved that he would not give such would-be opponents the opening they needed. ("I will not be the first president to lose a war," he insisted.) He concluded that the best way for the Democrats to retain power—so that he could continue to advance his domestic agenda—was to keep the Right at bay. It was almost as if he regarded his gradualist escalation of the war as the price he was willing to pay the hawks so that he could continue to build the Great Society undisturbed.

During the election of 1964, Johnson's Republican opponent, Senator Barry Goldwater, promised a more aggressive defense of the independence of South Vietnam than the one Johnson was waging. He advocated bombing cities in North Vietnam, mining its harbors, and permitting the use of tactical nuclear weapons, at the discretion of commanders on the ground. Johnson, presenting himself as a peace candidate, adopted the pose of a less trigger-happy and a more responsible leader, who could be trusted to resist communist aggression through more moderate means.

In response to what Johnson proclaimed was an unprovoked attack by North Vietnam on American naval ships in international waters on August 4, 1964, Johnson asked Congress to pass a resolution authorizing him to take "all necessary action" to protect American military personnel in the area. Three days later, Congress passed the Gulf of Tonkin Resolution, a measure Johnson would repeatedly cite as authorization for the war he ultimately waged against North Vietnam. Declassified years later, intelligence after action reports indicated that no such attack of the kind Johnson described had taken place and that earlier intelligence findings and testimony by Secretary of Defense Robert McNamara to the contrary had been at best incomplete.[96] Johnson never requested that Congress declare war against North Vietnam. That, together with his failure to share with congressional leaders the war's true costs and his repeated dares to Congress to cut off funding for the war if it disapproved of his policies, soured relations between Johnson and the Congress he needed to enact legislation he favored.

Months after he won the 1964 election, in response to an attack on an American base at Pleiku, which killed 6 and wounded 116, Johnson retaliated with an air strike against North Vietnam and followed up with additional bombings. In July 1965, after several days of high-level talks, Johnson acceded to General William Westmoreland's request that 125,000 additional troops be sent to defend American installations in South Vietnam. He matter-of-factly informed the nation of his decision at a midday news conference.[97] Johnson's attempt to underplay, if not conceal, a major change in American policy gave rise to what would be called the "credibility gap." When Johnson succeeded to the presidency on November 22, 1963, 16,000 American troops were in South Vietnam. A month before Johnson announced this major escalation, the number stood at 60,000. Three years later, approximately 550,000 American troops were in South Vietnam.

Johnson's failure to prepare either the Congress or the country for the sacrifices that lay ahead or the reasons that justified them may have stemmed from his failure to have developed in his own mind a set of goals he hoped to pursue and a sense of what American interests he hoped to advance by escalating American participation in the conflict. According to most accounts, he made his strategy as he went along, responding to changed situations on the ground. A respected columnist of the era had it right when he observed, "The laws of politics do not allow even the mightiest nation to win a victory it cannot define."[98]

In his 1966 "guns and butter" State of the Union Address, Johnson said that the nation was strong enough and economically secure enough to pursue its objectives in South Vietnam and to continue building the Great Society at home.[99] Yet he had already hidden from Congress and the public the true costs of the war. He delayed asking for a tax increase in order to forestall congressional debates over priorities. "Those damn conservatives . . . are going to use the war as a way of opposing my Great Society," he told a group of advisers months earlier.[100] As inflation made both the war and the domestic programs he had earlier enacted more costly, Johnson instructed departments and agencies to trim their budget requests. (Late in his term, he succeeded in obtaining a 10 percent surtax from Congress to finance some of the costs of the war.)

As a commander in chief, Lyndon Johnson violated a principle that had been among his hallmarks when it came to enacting legislation. "Don't assume anything," he had said; "make sure every weapon is brought to bear . . . keep everybody involved . . . don't let them slacken."[101] As the situation in Vietnam worsened and casualties mounted, Johnson made no effort to draw upon the advice of people with greater expertise, whose experience exceeded his own. Instead, he relied on the complacent if not smug group he inherited from Kennedy. (By 1967, many of them had come to harbor doubts of their own about policies they had recommended.) When freshman Democratic Senator George McGovern presumed to raise with Johnson the history of the region into which the president had poured an excess of a half-million soldiers, the president exploded. "Goddamn it, George, you and Fulbright and all you history teachers. I haven't got time to fuck around with history. I've got boys on the line out there. I can't be worried about history when there are boys out there who might die before morning."[102]

Fearful that, by hitting the wrong target, American bombing might bring either the Soviet Union or China into the war—both of whom had been supplying North Vietnam with arms—Johnson personally selected bombing sites from the White House. Unable to comprehend the motivations of his principal adversary, Johnson at one point declared his intention to request $1 billion from Congress to fund a rural electrification project along the Mekong River valley.[103] "What does Ho [Chi Minh] want?" Johnson blurted out at aides. He never got it into his head that the communist leader, who had driven the French out of Indochina, would rather have South Vietnam than either the New Deal or the Great Society. Nor had the master legislator come to appreciate the distaste his fellow citizens had for prolonged, inconclusive wars. Because he had defined his strategy and tactics better than Johnson had, Ho could afford to wait as the levers of American democracy—a free and uncensored press, the capacity of Congress to hold hearings and conduct investigations, and the right of the people to petition their government—forced a change in American policies and presidents.

Jimmy Carter

Jimmy Carter seemed too good to be true. The former one-term governor of Georgia began his campaign for the presidency by promising never to lie to the American people. He promised a government "as honest and truthful and fair and idealistic and compassionate and filled with love as are the American people."[104] Only in the aftermath of the back-to-back traumas of Vietnam and Watergate could a man who talked like that ever be elected president. Carter, columnists Rowland Evans and Robert Novak observed, "was allergic to all efforts at eloquence."[105] His inability to inspire in the manner of Franklin Delano Roosevelt or John F. Kennedy furthered the impression that he was genuine. To symbolize that he would comport himself differently as president than had his more imperious predecessors, candidate Carter had himself photographed carrying his own luggage. After being sworn in as the nation's thirty-ninth president, Carter, his wife

Roslyn, and their nine-year-old daughter, Amy, exited their limousine and walked back to the White House, waving to the crowds.

In addition to restoring trust in government, Carter promised to reduce wasteful spending, revise the tax code—which he termed a "national disgrace"—and introduce zero-based budgeting. (This concept required departments and agencies to justify their entire budgets, as opposed to only their requested increases.) Carter's failure to articulate a grand vision for the country coincided perfectly with the public's lack of desire for one. During his journey to the White House, Carter displayed many of the idiosyncrasies that would characterize his presidency: a meticulous attention to detail, extraordinary self-discipline, an understanding of the powers of symbolism, and a tendency toward self-righteousness. The first three characteristics proved insufficient to persuade others to follow his lead, and the fourth actively impeded their cooperation.

Born on October 1, 1924, in Plains, Georgia, Carter was the eldest son of James Earl Carter, a prosperous peanut farmer, and Lillian Gordy Carter, a registered nurse. Relatives on both sides of the family had participated in Georgia politics for generations. A conservative Democrat, Carter's father opposed FDR's agricultural policies that paid farmers to slaughter hogs and withdraw acres from cotton production in order to increase commodity prices.[106] Discipline in the Carter household was strict; Carter recalled receiving several whippings from his father between the ages of four and fifteen. One came after young Jimmy had taken a penny from a church collection plate. Carter's mother, known to all as "Miss Lillian," was more of a free spirit and more of a social liberal—especially with regard to race—than her husband. Late in life, she became a Peace Corps volunteer in India.

All through school, Carter was able to read beyond his grade level. After taking additional math courses at Georgia Institute of Technology, he won admission to the U.S. Naval Academy in Annapolis, Maryland, and graduated 59th in a class of 820. Carter studied nuclear physics at Union College before working on the program to launch the first atomic submarine, the U.S.S. *Nautilus*, under Admiral Hyman Rickover. Known for exacting standards, Rickover exerted a powerful influence over Carter. He took the title of his first book, *Why Not the Best?*, from a question Rickover put to him about his grades at Annapolis.[107] Carter served in the Navy from 1946 to 1953. Upon his father's death, Carter returned to Plains to operate the family business. Applying modern techniques, Carter turned what had been a profitable small business into a thriving commercial enterprise. He became active in his community, serving on the local board of education and participating in regional planning and development councils. In 1962, Carter declared his candidacy for the state senate.

In the face of evidence that his narrow loss in the Democratic primary resulted from electoral fraud, Carter challenged the results. With the local press not showing much interest, Carter persuaded the *Atlanta Constitution* and other large-circulation newspapers to pay attention to his case. Readers who had long ago left Georgia contacted Carter to inform him that they had been recorded as having voted in the primary election. Also having voted, it appeared, were many of the deceased. After a judge invalidated the results of one precinct, Carter was designated the Democratic nominee. Republican opposition in the then one party state was minimal. After clearing two additional roadblocks, including a write-in challenge, he won election to the Georgia State Senate.

Carter came away from the experience suspicious of political organizations, clubhouse politicians, and political horse-trading. Aware that he might not have prevailed in his court challenge had he lacked financial means, access to excellent legal counsel, and family and other connections in the media, Carter made government reform and the integrity of the election process one of his signature issues. He would always stand guard against legislative apportionments that discriminated against populous areas, partisan gerrymandering that reduced the number of truly competitive seats, and election fraud. Regarding himself as a citizen (or even an amateur) politician, Carter would argue his causes on their merits and ways that suggested that he thought that those who opposed them were either personally dishonest or tools of special interests.

In his four years as state senator, Carter read each of the hundreds of bills that came up to the floor. By his own account, he became "an expert on many unimportant subjects."[108] After losing a closely contested Democratic primary for governor in 1966, Carter suffered a spiritual crisis. After numerous discussions and lengthy prayer sessions with his sister Ruth Carter Stapleton, an evangelist, Carter declared that he had been "born again." Four years later, during the Democratic primary campaign for governor, Carter, a moderate on racial issues, positioned himself to the right of another moderate, former Governor Carl Sanders. Posing as a populist, Carter derided his dapper opponent as "Cufflinks Carl." Carter's operatives in rural Georgia circulated photographs of Sanders, partial owner of the Atlanta Hawks, being doused with champagne by African American basketball players in a locker room victory celebration.[109]

As governor, Carter came to epitomize a new breed of elected officials in the "new South." As a group, they were well educated, fiscally conservative, and more supportive of integration and civil rights than their predecessors. On national policy, they were said to be more hawkish on defense than their liberal Democratic counterparts in the northern and midwestern states. *Time*, signaling that it considered Carter representative of this group, put him on its May 31, 1971, cover. In his governing style, Carter proved a master of symbolism. Making good on a campaign promise, he invited George Wallace, the one-time segregationist, to address the Georgia legislature. He balanced this gesture by hanging a portrait of Rev. Martin Luther King Jr., a Georgian, in the state capitol. Carter named a record number of African Americans to state positions.

After hosting several contenders for the 1972 Democratic presidential nomination in the governor's mansion, Carter concluded that he would make as good a president as any of his better-known guests. He turned his penchant for detail to mastering the recently adopted Democratic Party rules that significantly changed the way delegates would be selected. In 1976, more states would choose delegates through primaries and caucuses than ever before, and more delegates would be awarded on a proportional basis. One could win the nomination by placing first in a number of carefully selected states and picking up delegates in states in which one placed second or worse. All but gone were the days of boss-picked delegations and winner-takes-all primaries. To get a jump on his rivals and attract free media attention, Carter chose to compete in the Iowa caucuses, elevating their significance.

In early-deciding states, Carter built strong organizations. His campaign augmented local ground forces with hundreds of Georgia volunteers, known as the "Peanut Brigade," who stayed with local families or bunked in church basements. Campaigning as a moderate (or even as a conservative) against a field of better-known liberals in some places and (sometimes as a moderate or even as a liberal) against better-known moderates and conservatives elsewhere, Carter piled up delegates. At the time he accepted the Democratic presidential nomination, Carter was running thirty points ahead of the incumbent, President Gerald Ford, in the polls. On Election Day, Carter pulled ahead of Ford by 2 percentage points in the popular vote. His winning margin in the Electoral College was the narrowest since 1916 (297 to 240).

Carter's eventual difficulties with a heavily Democratic Congress sprang as much from his personality and cultural divides within the Democratic Party, as from ideological differences between Carter and his fellow partisans. Proud that he had won the presidency without having had to court party power brokers or representatives of special interests, Carter took office believing he owed nothing to the political establishment that he had defeated on the way to the nomination. As he looked toward Capitol Hill, and especially the House of Representatives, Carter saw similarities between leaders there and the very favor-trading, patronage-seeking clubhouse politicians who had tried to steal a state senate seat from him in Georgia. Democratic lawmakers who had run well ahead of Carter sensed as little obligation to the new president as he did to them. (He was the first Democrat to win without carrying a majority of Catholics, southern whites, and union households.) Carter's insistence on "holding the line on spending" opened deep fissures within his party, culminating with Senator Edward M. Kennedy's challenging Carter's re-nomination. As he had in Georgia, Carter presented himself as an advocate of "what was right" and those in Congress who opposed him as "captives" of special interests.[110]

The new speaker of the House proved to be as different a Democrat from Carter as it was possible to be. Thomas P. "Tip" O'Neill, a cigar-chomping, poker-playing, alcohol-drinking, patronage-dispensing Irish Catholic from Massachusetts. O'Neill, who was steeped in the traditions of the New Deal, never knew what to make of the teetotaling, born-again Southern Baptist from Georgia, who talked about balanced budgets, government reorganization, and reform. A mistake Carter's inaugural team made in assigning O'Neill's guests seats in the last row of the balcony at a Kennedy Center gala became a metaphor reporters used to characterize Carter's relationship with Congress. O'Neill took to referring to Carter's chief of staff Hamilton Jordan as "Hannibal Jerkin." Congressional complaints about unreturned telephone calls and the failure to receive advance notice about administration appointments and programs continued throughout Carter's tenure.

Carter did little to familiarize himself with congressional folkways or operating methods. He showed little appreciation for members' concerns or for their leaders' need to assert congressional prerogatives. Nor did he make much of an effort to forge personal friendships with many representatives or senators. Time spent with Carter, they discovered, was all business. Carter's manner of persuasion was to beseech his visitors to do the right thing. If he had invested the same amount of time in mastering how Congress functioned as he did in trivial matters, such as the scheduling of White House tennis courts, Carter might have been better able to advance more of his agenda. Frequently, he demanded more of Congress than its committees could handle at any one time. Toward the end of one session, O'Neill suggested to Vice President Walter F. Mondale that the administration pare down the twenty outstanding items it sought to enact to four or five priorities. As he reviewed Mondale's recommendations, Carter added eleven more items to the list. Carter noted afterward that he found it impossible to defer anything he felt needed to be done.[111]

In attempting to build a base of support that he might use as leverage in his negotiations with Congress, Carter, never a particularly persuasive speaker, continued to rely on symbolism. To underscore his commitment to economize and his lack of pretense, Carter cut back on White House limousines and other perks, lowered thermostats, banned the playing of "Hail to the Chief," sold the presidential yacht, enrolled his daughter in a Washington, D.C., public school, and walked her to class on her first day. For a time, he continued to hold town meetings. Once, he fielded calls from citizens over the radio. Clad in a cardigan sweater, suggesting his commitment to energy conservation, Carter delivered what the media termed a "televised fireside chat" on energy policy. Over time, the dichotomy between Carter's character and intelligence and his failure to deliver on his promises hurt his public standing.

In his second year in office, while his domestic program languished in Congress, Carter scored two major achievements in international affairs. He secured Senate approval of treaties transferring control of the Panama Canal to Panama and brokered the Camp David Accords, through which Israel returned the Sinai Peninsula, captured during the Six Day War in 1967, to Egypt in exchange for Egypt's recognition of the State of Israel. Carter was successful in both instances primarily because the complexities inherent in both issues required the very attention to detail and intense powers of concentration he possessed.[112] Carter also paid a price for concentrating on these matters almost to the exclusion of all others. While Carter was pouring over the details of every senator's perspective on the Panama Canal Treaty, the Senate picked away at his energy proposals. To produce the Camp David breakthrough, he secluded himself with his guests for thirteen days, studying maps, shuttling to and from cabins, and praying.

While Carter's energy and economic policies were inconsistent and often self-defeating (as will be demonstrated in the following chapter), his management style underscored perceptions that he was not quite up to the job of president. With inflation rising and gasoline costly and scarce in 1979, Carter canceled his vacation, returned to Washington, and announced plans to deliver what would have been his fifth speech on energy concerns. He retreated to Camp David, where for eight days he held an unbroken chain of meetings to elicit advice from business leaders, academics, clergy, and members of Congress. Upon the conclusion of this domestic "summit," Carter spoke on television about a "crisis of confidence" that struck to the very "heart and soul" of the national will.[113] (The media termed it the "malaise speech.") Initially, public reaction to what Carter had said was favorable. Days later, however, Carter undercut his own support when he announced that he was replacing half his cabinet. Rather than build public confidence in his leadership, Carter, through his announcement, created the impression that he was indecisive and that the nation was rudderless with him at the helm.

Having denounced the realpolitik approach to the Soviet Union his two immediate predecessors had taken, Carter sought to reorder American priorities in the Cold War. In a speech at Notre Dame University, Carter announced that the United States had broken free of its "inordinate fear of communism." He appeared to be making policy on the assumption that the Soviets had abandoned their aspirations to nuclear superiority and world dominance. He initiated negotiations to lock in strategic "parity" in nuclear weapons, postpone new weapons procurement, and eliminate nuclear weapons on the Korean peninsula. Carter also reassessed American practices of overlooking—or at not criticizing in public—human rights violations its purported anticommunist allies had committed. (His efforts are summarized in chapter 6.) When the Soviet Union responded to Carter's policies with renewed adventurism, which included the launching of proxy wars (especially in Africa) and the invasion of Afghanistan in December 1979, Carter reversed course. He cancelled American participation in the 1980 Summer Olympics in Moscow, started assisting anti-Soviet insurgents, and began an arms build-up that would accelerate under his successor.

Carter's presidency is most remembered for the thirteen-month stalemate that began when purported "students" tied to the revolutionary Islamic government in Iran stormed the American embassy in Tehran and held fifty-three American diplomatic personnel hostage. In what appeared to be at odds with his declared human rights policies, Carter had expressed solidarity with the shah of Iran shortly after taking office. After the shah was deposed, Carter allowed him to enter the United States to receive medical treatment. In response to this action, violent anti-American protests erupted throughout Iran. Although Carter worked ceaselessly to arrange the hostages' release, none of his efforts succeeded. Frustrated, he sought to free the hostages through military means. This rescue mission also failed. The sight of two American helicopters burning in the Iranian desert after colliding during a sandstorm, killing eight military service personnel, came to symbolize the paralysis of U.S. power during Carter's presidency and the haplessness of its president.

5

ECONOMIC POLICY

*H*ow should the economic policies of presidents be judged? The easiest way would be to rank their economic performance according to aggregate statistics such as the average growth of real GDP during their administration.[1] This approach, however, would tell only part of the story. Some presidents confronted economic crises during their time in office, while others were fated to govern under more favorable circumstances. While in the White House, some presidents confronted problems such as inflation, financial panics, recessions, and depressions. Others established or reformed institutions, laws, and regulations that influenced the workings of the American economy well beyond their tenure. Evaluating presidents solely by taking stock of how rapidly the economy expanded during their terms would ignore such long-term consequences of presidential actions.

A better way would be to assess what the economic conditions were during presidential administrations and how, based on the state of economic knowledge available at the time, presidents reacted to those conditions and to challenges that arose during their administrations. In this chapter, presidents are investigated with the following three questions in mind:

1. Did this president improve the performance of the U.S. economy during his time in office? Successful presidents employed the macroeconomic tools of fiscal, monetary, and tax policies to ameliorate crises, foster real

GDP growth, and maintain price stability. Unsuccessful presidents triggered recessions and caused sustained inflation or deflation.

2. Did this president improve the economic infrastructure of the country? Successful presidents employed good economic policies that solved social problems at a reasonable cost, increased productivity, strengthened the international competitiveness of American industries, and accelerated long-term growth of real GDP. Unsuccessful presidents adopted economic policies that failed to solve social problems while imposing excessive costs, reduced productivity, weakened international competitiveness, and decelerated long-term growth of real GDP.

3. Did this president sustain the social contract and expand the economic opportunities available to all Americans? In 1942, economist Joseph Schumpeter described a market economy as an ongoing process of "creative destruction" in which entrepreneurs are continually recombining labor and capital in innovative ways to produce new, superior, or cheaper goods and services.[2] Although creative destruction generates higher real income for all Americans over time, some businesses and individuals inevitably suffer short-term economic hardships as new firms and industries displace old ones. Conflicts arise between the market's need for freedom and the public's demand for fairness. Successful presidents balanced freedom and fairness, marshaled empathy, inspired confidence, provided transitional assistance to the displaced, and reformed the economic infrastructure to reduce such frictions, while preserving America's free market economy. Successful presidents enabled ordinary Americans, particularly those who may have suffered from past discrimination, to participate fully and freely in the economy, rising as far as their talents allowed, and enjoying the fruits of their labor. Unsuccessful presidents ignored conflicts or made unwise decisions that diminished public support for America's free market economy and consequently retarded long-term GDP growth.

With regard to economic policy, four presidents compiled excellent records.

FOUR PRESIDENTS EARNED A SCORE OF 5:

George Washington

Abraham Lincoln

Theodore Roosevelt

Ronald Reagan

SEVEN PRESIDENTS DID QUITE WELL, EARNING A SCORE OF 4:

James K. Polk

William McKinley

Woodrow Wilson

Calvin Coolidge

Dwight D. Eisenhower

John F. Kennedy

Bill Clinton

FIFTEEN PRESIDENTS COMPILED EITHER MIXED (JEFFERSON AND FDR) OR AVERAGE RECORDS, EARNING A SCORE OF 3:

John Adams

Thomas Jefferson

John Quincy Adams

Zachary Taylor

Millard Fillmore

Franklin Pierce

Ulysses S. Grant

Warren G. Harding

Rutherford B. Hayes

Chester A. Arthur

Benjamin Harrison

William Howard Taft

Franklin Delano Roosevelt

Gerald Ford

George H. W. Bush

SIX PRESIDENTS FARED POORLY, EARNING A SCORE OF 2:

John Tyler

James Buchanan

Andrew Johnson

Grover Cleveland

Harry S Truman

Lyndon B. Johnson

SEVEN PRESIDENTS FAILED, RECEIVING A SCORE OF 1:

James Madison

James Monroe

Andrew Jackson

Herbert Hoover

Richard Nixon

Martin Van Buren

Jimmy Carter

(W. H. Harrison, J. A. Garfield, and G. W. Bush were not evaluated.)

This chapter discusses the four excellent presidents as well as four extraordinarily competent ones—Wilson, Coolidge, Kennedy, and Clinton—in some detail. Their stories reveal some common approaches. Most economically successful presidents were genuinely interested in business and economics. They availed themselves of multiple sources of information both inside and outside their administrations and selected good advisers and competent department heads. Although willing to listen and learn from their advisers, and tolerant of divergent opinions, successful presidents did not become mired in indecision or vacillation. Nor did they resort to short-term gimmicks. Through the decisiveness they brought to bear, they instilled confidence in the public, reassured markets, and won approval for their programs in Congress. While often reacting to short-term challenges, these presidents developed coherent policies designed to boost long-term economic performance. As a result, their policies produced affirmative answers to the three questions posed above, pertaining to macroeconomic performance, economic infrastructure, and opportunity.

This chapter also looks at the failed presidents (other than Hoover, whose economic failings were discussed in chapter 4). None of these presidents, save for Carter and Hoover, showed much interest in business or economics. All of them chose poor advisers and incompetent department heads. Some were know-it-alls who would not listen to sound advice. Others were too ideologically rigid to adapt to changed circumstances. Still others were micromanagers who got lost in the details. Short-term political considerations rather than sound economics frequently drove their policies. While some of these failed presidents persuaded Congress to enact at least some of their economic programs, little of what they achieved passed muster when viewed through the lens of the three questions posed above.

This chapter also looks at two other presidents, Warren G. Harding and Franklin Delano Roosevelt, whose economic policies are rated average. Harding is discussed in conjunction with Coolidge because the latter continued his predecessor's economic policies. Coolidge's superior administrative skills, however, enabled him to achieve even greater success than Harding. Roosevelt's economic record combines brilliant successes and dismal failures. While FDR receives an average score, nothing about him or what he attempted to do was mediocre. For these reasons, his economic record will be examined in detail.

George Washington

Colonial America had a quasifeudal agricultural economy rigged to benefit wealthy planters. Without a bank, a circulating currency, or an adequate supply of gold and silver coins, most transactions involved barter or private bills of exchange. Colonial assemblies fixed interest rates, regulated prices, and proscribed arbitrage, futures, and speculation as "offenses against public trade."[3] They also had a tendency to proclaim debt holidays whenever crops were bad or prices were low. These were intended to protect landowners from impatient creditors in London. Compliant judges also used the just price doctrine to invalidate contracts after the fact when market prices proved unfavorable to local elites.[4]

Economic woes after the Revolutionary War compounded these colonial legacies. The Continental Congress defaulted on its war debt of $51 million, and the states encountered great difficulties in servicing their war debts of $23 million.[5] The market value of these debt securities fell by as much as 80 percent below their face value. Although the new United States desperately needed European equity investments and loans to finance its development, Europeans felt that investing or lending in this new nation was too risky. Under the Articles of Confederation, states imposed tariffs on interstate and international trade. The resulting collapse of trade and investment caused a deep recession and widespread unrest. Shays's Rebellion (1786–1787) sparked the convening of the Constitutional Convention on May 25, 1787, and ratification of the Constitution by the necessary minimum number of states on September 21, 1788.[6]

When George Washington became president on April 30, 1789, it fell to him to create an economic infrastructure that would spark recovery and sustain support for the new federal government. To help him do this, Washington selected as his secretary of the treasury Alexander Hamilton—who had the vision, knowledge, and determination to revive the listless U.S. economy. Hamilton had a unique perspective among the nation's founders. Born out of wedlock and into poverty on St. Croix Island, Hamilton learned international trade and finance as a young clerk in a counting house.[7] He concluded that an agricultural economy would eventually evolve into a stagnant, highly stratified society with a few wealthy, landowning haves and many have-nots without any opportunity. Hamilton wanted to transform the United States from a collection of quasifeudal fiefdoms dominated by wealthy planters into a national meritocracy in which individuals, whatever the circumstances of their birth, could rise as far as their ambition and talents could take them. He sought to create conditions conducive to this by restoring confidence in the credit of the United States, establishing a sound currency, and promoting industrialization.

Although a slaveholding planter who enjoyed a more privileged lifestyle than many if not most of his contemporaries, Washington was sympathetic to the establishment of financial institutions Hamilton proposed. Having risen to wealth and prominence as much by his wits as by chance after the circumstances of his birth denied him a commission in the British army, Washington was predisposed toward practices that provided incentives and rewarded risk taking. While commander in chief of the Continental army he had also seen how weak financial structures had threatened the young nation's security, even its survival as a free and independent nation.

With Hamilton providing most of the intellectual fervor and administrative capabilities to breathe life into the institutions he proposed, and with Washington lending his prestige to secure their establishment, the two set out to build America's economic structure from scratch. Choosing Great Britain as his model, Hamilton applied the Whig financial innovations of a funded government debt, a national bank, and a circulating currency of bank notes to help establish the United States as a creditworthy borrower.[8] He was convinced this financial system would increase the market value of war debt securities, reduce interest rates, encourage Europeans to invest and lend in the United States, and make the U.S. dollar as good as gold. Hamilton anticipated that a national bank could use Treasury debt securities as reserve assets (instead of scarce gold or silver) and as collateral for making loans to entrepreneurs.

Opposition to this system soon arose. Thomas Jefferson, then serving as Washington's secretary of state, echoed the complaints that Henry St. John, the first Viscount Bolingbroke, had voiced against the very system Hamilton wanted to import from England. These Whig practices, Bolingbroke argued, had made British society turbulent and venial. Bank of England notes had replaced true money (i.e., gold and silver), thereby encouraging industrialization and speculation in stocks rather than honest labor in agriculture. The Bank of England, Bolingbroke believed, promoted corruption by helping British ministers buy support in Parliament by arranging loans to wavering members on favorable terms.[9]

On January 9, 1790, Hamilton presented his *First Report on the Public Credit* to the House of Representatives. He proposed that the federal government assume full responsibility for the war debts of *both* the Continental Congress and the states, and that the federal government repay the full face value of all bonds regardless of their current market value or ownership (i.e., nondiscrimination). To create confidence in the federal government's ability to service these debts, Hamilton proposed a sinking fund that would use tariff revenues to pay interest.[10] Jefferson and his followers opposed nondiscrimination because many Revolutionary War veterans, having fallen on hard times, sold their IOUs at hefty discounts to speculators.

In his report *Operations of the Act Laying Duties on Imports*, issued the following April, Hamilton spelled out the nature of those tariffs. Although he realized that high tariff rates on certain imports could insulate infant American industries from international competition, Hamilton's primary objective was to maximize government receipts. He proposed moderate tariff rates averaging less than 10 percent on a broad base of imports. Higher rates, Hamilton asserted, would stifle legal imports, encourage smuggling, and reduce federal revenue.[11] To pass his debt assumption, sinking fund, and tariff proposals, Hamilton brokered a deal with Jefferson and his principal adviser, Representative James Madison, through which southern lawmakers gave these proposals their support in exchange for northern votes for the Residency Act. This measure moved the U.S. capital from New York City to Philadelphia in 1790 for ten years while a new federal city was built along the Potomac River. Though highly controversial, the nondiscrimination provision in the Assumption Act tripled the market value of financial assets held by the American public. As Hamilton had anticipated, this sparked a vigorous recovery.

In the *Second Report on Public Credit*, issued several months later, Hamilton proposed that Congress charter the Bank of the United States for twenty years. Patterned after the Bank of England, the Bank of the United States would be a private corporation, but the federal government would own 20 percent of its shares and supervise its operations. The Bank would make loans to the U.S. government, private businesses, and individuals; hold government deposits; issue a uniform national currency of Bank of the

United States notes; and regulate the money supply through its interactions with state-chartered banks. The Bank's initial capitalization would be $10 million payable over several years, of which $2.5 million would be in gold or silver, and the remainder in Treasury securities. This bond requirement would create an active and deep market for Treasury debt securities and would assure the Bank of substantial and secure profits.[12]

On February 8, 1791, the House of Representatives and the Senate passed a bank bill and sent it to President Washington. As was his custom, Washington circulated it to his cabinet for comment. Jefferson and Attorney General Edmund Randolph argued that the bill was unconstitutional because the Constitution made no provision for Congress to charter a bank.[13] Hamilton maintained that the federal government, as a sovereign power, had the authority to employ whatever means necessary to exercise its explicit powers, provided such means were not expressly prohibited, immoral, or contrary to other constitutional principles. Given that the Constitution granted Congress the power to levy taxes, borrow money, coin money and fix its value, and regulate interstate and international trade, he argued that establishing a bank was a logical way to exercise these powers.[14] Washington, persuaded by Hamilton's arguments, signed the bill into law on February 24, 1791.[15]

Finally, Hamilton's *Report on Manufactures*, issued in December of 1791, outlined his vision for an industrial America. Relying on arguments Adam Smith advanced in *The Wealth of Nations*, Hamilton refuted Jefferson's contention that agriculture was the only source of wealth. Hamilton endorsed free trade as the ideal the United States should pursue once it became a major economic power. However, he observed that free trade was impractical for a small developing economy such as the United States so long as large developed economies such as France and Great Britain pursued mercantilism.[16] He affirmed that all businesses except weapon manufacturers should be privately owned and managed. Nevertheless, he advocated a specific but limited role for the federal government in promoting industrialization. Hamilton wanted the federal government to disburse cash awards to spur innovation and scientific research; inspect manufactured goods to insure they met minimum quality standards; enact patent laws to encourage invention; and fund canals, harbors, and roads to expedite transportation.[17] While Congress laid these proposals on the table, Hamilton's ideological heirs, Henry Clay, Abraham Lincoln, and Theodore Roosevelt, subsequently moved them forward. Congress enacted them over the next two centuries.[18] None of this might have occurred if Washington had not appointed Hamilton and backed him to the hilt.

As he did on so much else, Calvin Coolidge had it right when he wrote, "Washington and Hamilton increased the success and greatness of each other."[19] They launched the first economic boom in U.S. history. Estimated real GDP grew about 7 percent a year from 1790 to 1796. Their highly successful partnership created the economic infrastructure that transformed the United States from a quasifeudal confederation of former colonies into a free market powerhouse.

James Madison and James Monroe

Through a combination of managerial incompetence and rigid adherence to ideology, President James Madison compounded the poor economic situation that he inherited from Thomas Jefferson. Madison's actions produced first inflation, then deflation, a speculative land bubble, and a protectionist trade policy. In a large way, Madison's decisions triggered the Panic of 1819, the first presidentially induced depression in U.S. history, which took hold during the administration of his successor, James Monroe. Because Madison, through his ineptness, allowed the Bank of the United States to go out of business when its charter expired in March 1811, he encountered great difficulty financing the War of 1812. With the British blockade of American ports reducing customs receipts by more than half, Congress passed a capitation tax of $3 million a year and excise taxes on alcohol and sugar to make up for lost revenues.[20] Although Congress authorized the borrowing of $61 million, Secretary of the Treasury Albert Gallatin could only raise $38 million.[21] Federal debt increased from a trough of $45.2 million (equal to 5.6 percent of estimated GDP) at year-end 1811 to $127.2

million (equal to 11.1 percent of estimated GDP) at year-end 1815. Finally, the Madison administration resorted to issuing $15 million in circulating Treasury notes.[22]

Inflation skyrocketed. From 1811 to 1816, the number of unregulated state-chartered commercial banks grew from 88 to 246,[23] increasing the circulation of state bank notes from $28 million to $68 million and ultimately driving prices 34 percent higher from 1811 to 1814.[24] Gallatin saw this inflation as "the natural consequence of the dissolution of the Bank['s] salutary regulating power."[25] After the War of 1812, Speaker Henry Clay proposed a Second Bank of the United States. Once an ardent Jeffersonian, Clay had opposed the First Bank of the United States. He changed his mind when he formulated his plan for "a functioning American System" of a national bank, protective tariffs, and federal funding for "internal improvements."[26]

Clay garnered political support for his plan from a coalition of entrepreneurs, manufacturers in New England and the Middle Atlantic states that favored protectionism, Louisiana sugar planters similarly worried about competition from imports, and farmers in the Midwest who wanted a federal transportation infrastructure to reduce the time and expense of moving their crops to market. Yielding to Clay's powerful coalition, Madison abandoned his hands-off approach and asked Congress to charter a Second Bank of the United States. On April 10, 1816, he signed the bill that Secretary of the Treasury Alexander Dallas and Clay produced.[27] In a repeat performance of how he had ineptly filled his cabinet at the outset of his administration (again, see chapter 4), Madison proceeded to name five partisan Republicans with little banking experience as the Bank's presidential directors and forced the Bank's board to select his second secretary of the navy, William Jones, as its first president.[28] Jones proved incompetent in his new role.

The Tariff Act of 1816, which Madison also signed, nearly doubled the average tariff rate on dutiable imports to 20 percent. The act departed from Hamilton's policy of modest tariff rates to maximize federal receipts and from Jefferson's advocacy of tariff reductions as a means of holding down prices and keeping American agriculture competitive. In effect, Madison established protectionism as the cornerstone of U.S. trade policy for more than a century. The only plausible explanation for Madison's ideologically inconsistent decision was a reversion to his previous habit of deferring to Congress.

Dallas and his successor at the Treasury, William H. Crawford, then used postwar budget surpluses to retire all of the circulating Treasury notes by 1817.[29] This monetary contraction caused prices to fall almost as dramatically as they had risen. They dropped by 27 percent from 1814 to 1817. Despite Madison's protective tariffs, many industries that sprung up during the embargo and the war were unable to compete with the lower costs and superior technologies of their European rivals once trans-Atlantic trade resumed. U.S. manufacturers suffered large losses that persisted until 1823.

Jones's tenure as president of the Second Bank was a comedy of errors. He appointed incompetent and corrupt branch managers. The Bank augmented rather than restrained the reckless lending by state banks that was fueling widespread speculation on western lands.[30] Consequently, Jones drained the Bank of its gold and silver reserves. Under pressure from Crawford, the Bank began to redeem state bank notes in gold and silver in August 1818.[31] Discovered to have been speculating in Bank stock, Jones resigned in January 1819.[32] A former speaker of the House, Langdon Cheves, became the Bank's second president, and he implemented Monroe's policy of monetary contraction.[33] The circulation of bank notes fell from $68 million in 1816 to $45 million in 1820, and prices declined another 27 percent before bottoming out in 1824.

Monroe's policy precipitated the long-in-the-making Panic of 1819, which burst the land speculation bubble. During this panic, many state-chartered banks failed, businesses closed, wages fell, and the unemployment rate escalated. Many Americans, especially Andrew Jackson, blamed the Second Bank for the Panic of 1819 and the subsequent depression. It was, however, Madison's failure to renew the charter of the First Bank as well as his appointment of the incompetent Jones as president of the Second Bank that allowed the reckless lending by state banks that inflated an unsustainable land speculation bubble.

Andrew Jackson and Martin Van Buren

Andrew Jackson carried into office with him a host of prejudices and resentments he had nurtured over a lifetime. It was the nation's misfortune that, as president, he acted on so many of them. "I have an opinion of my own on all subjects," Jackson said, "and when that opinion is formed I pursue it publicly, regardless of who goes with me."[34] As historian Richard Hofstadter noted, "Historians have never been certain how much his policies were motivated by public considerations and how much by private animosities."[35] The totality of Jackson's inconsistent and often irrational policies—often the products of personal pique—saddled his designated successor, Martin Van Buren, with the Panic of 1837 and a subsequent depression.

Born on the border between North Carolina and South Carolina in 1767, as a youth Jackson joined the Continental Army. At the age of fourteen, he was captured. When he refused to polish a British officer's boots, the officer struck him with his sword. Jackson emerged from the experience with permanent scars (both physical and emotional), a scrappy disposition, and an abiding hatred of all things British.[36] The only member of his family to survive the Revolutionary War, he apprenticed with a saddler, taught school, read law, and gained admission to the North Carolina bar. Jackson subsequently served as district attorney for the frontier community that became Nashville, Tennessee. When not dueling or gambling on horse races or cock fights, he collected debts for merchants and engaged in politics.

Prone to rage and violence, Jackson took on all he believed had besmirched the character of his wife, Rachel. (Unbeknownst to the Jacksons, they had wed before Rachel's divorce from her first husband had become final. Legally, this made her both an adulteress and a bigamist.) Jackson attributed the fatal heart attack Rachel suffered prior to his inauguration to smears his political opponents, especially Henry Clay, had spread about her during the campaign.

The slanders his wife endured rendered Jackson sympathetic to others close to him who had been accused of private indiscretions. His efforts on behalf of one such person triggered the "Petticoat Affair," which consumed a major portion of his first term as president. In 1829, the wives of Vice

President John C. Calhoun and several cabinet members shunned Margaret "Peggy" Eaton, the new wife of Secretary of War John Eaton. (Peggy's first husband, John Timberlake, committed suicide allegedly because Peggy was having an affair with Eaton; Peggy married Eaton shortly after Timberlake's suicide.) Jackson put the nation's business virtually on hold for two years while he relentlessly pressed Washington society to receive Mrs. Eaton. The stalemate ended only after Jackson removed the husbands of the offending hostesses from his cabinet and resolved to change his vice president during the next election.

Because of the financial losses he suffered as a young man, Jackson grew to abhor debt, land speculators, banks, and paper currency.[37] In 1795, he had received $20,000 in promissory notes from Philadelphia merchant David Allison for the sale of fifty thousand acres. Jackson used the notes to open a general merchandise store. When Allison defaulted on the notes two years later, Jackson lost his store, three thousand acres, and a number of slaves. In an 1833 letter to his protégé James K. Polk, Jackson confessed, "Everyone that knows me does know that I have always opposed the United States Bank, nay all banks."[38] He made an almost identical comment to Nicholas Biddle, the president of the Second Bank of the United States, with whom he was soon to cross swords: "I do not dislike your bank any more than all banks."[39]

The animus that Jackson came to display toward Biddle's bank was also rooted in politics. In 1824, Jackson won 43.2 percent of the popular vote but failed to win a majority in the Electoral College. Under the Constitution, the House of Representatives had to select a president from among the top three contenders in the Electoral College. Jackson believed that Speaker Henry Clay, whose fourth-place finish eliminated him from the balloting, used his influence in the House to elect John Quincy Adams. Jackson regarded Adams's subsequent appointment of Clay as Secretary of State as evidence of a "corrupt bargain." Jackson immediately launched his second presidential campaign, voicing his opposition to practically everything that Clay supported: a national bank, high tariffs, and the "American plan."

By 1828, every state except Delaware and South Carolina had decided to choose its presidential electors by popular vote.[40] Because most states had lowered their property requirements for voting—or abolished them alto-gether—the total vote rose from 356,038 in 1824 to 1,155,350 in 1828. Jackson cast himself as the champion of these newly enfranchised poor whites who had been "cheated" out of the presidency by eastern elites. He vowed to use the powers of the presidency to protect the masses from the rich and powerful few. Jackson's national persona as a "tribune of the people" contrasted sharply with his image in Tennessee, where he was re-garded as a spokesman for wealthy planters.[41] Due to his skillful use of the marketing tools of the era to mobilize newly enfranchised voters, Jackson won the popular vote by a resounding 59.5 percent and prevailed in the Electoral College 178 to Adams's 83.[42]

In his first annual message in December 1829, Jackson hinted at his opposition to federal funding of internal improvements. His key political adviser, Secretary of State Martin Van Buren, called Jackson's attention to a bill sponsored by Representative Richard M. Johnson that would have the federal government purchase stock in a corporation set up to construct a road in Kentucky from Maysville to Lexington. Seeking to reduce federal spending and debts, Jackson informed allies that he opposed federal financ-ing of such projects. In his veto message, he not only proclaimed the bill unconstitutional because the Constitution had not granted Congress the power to invest in such enterprises but also suggested that, even if the bill were constitutional, the bill bestowed a special privilege on some Americans that would not be available to all. This was the first time that a president cited philosophical objections as his reason for exercising the veto. The realization that Henry Clay, a resident of Lexington, Kentucky, might benefit from the road hardened Jackson's opposition.

Jackson, however, reserved his greatest wrath for another part of Clay's American System, the Second Bank of the United States.[43] Jackson heard rumors that the Bank's president, Nicholas Biddle, had secretly financed Adams's campaign. Biddle exuded the very aristocratic haughtiness and air of refinement that Jackson so despised. Biddle was the son of a promi-nent family, the recipient of a classical education, and the protégé of James Monroe.

In his annual message of December 1829, Jackson stated that "a large proportion" of the population questioned the constitutionality of the law that established the Second Bank of the United States.[44] To Jackson, the Bank was a large and powerful private institution, exercising governmental functions but unaccountable to the public or its duly elected government. The Bank's capital of $35 million was twice the size of all federal expenditures. Moreover, Jackson alleged that the Bank had failed to maintain a sound national currency. This allegation was unfounded. Although the Bank had a rocky start under its first president, William Jones, it had become under Biddle "the balance wheel of [the] banking system" that "regulated the money supply [and] restrained the expansion of bank credit."[45]

A year later, Jackson proposed making the Bank a subsidiary of the Treasury. By the fall of 1831, Jackson and Biddle appeared close to a compromise in which Jackson agreed to reauthorize the Bank's charter before it expired in 1836, in exchange for Biddle agreeing not to seek renewal of the Bank's charter prior to the 1832 presidential election and promising to make certain modifications in its operations.[46] At Senator Henry Clay's behest, however, Biddle, on January 6, 1832, requested that Congress renew the Bank's charter. Sensing that he had been double-crossed, and at the instigation of the man who had blocked his advance to the presidency in 1824 and who he believed hastened the death of his wife, Jackson, in the words of historian Robert Remini, "slammed into the Bank with the fury he normally reserved for Indians, British invaders, and cantankerous politicians."[47] When Congress renewed the Bank's charter, Jackson vetoed it. After rehashing conventional Jeffersonian arguments against the Bank's constitutionality, Jackson denounced the Bank as a special privilege that the government bestowed on a few, who use it for personal gain. Since the rest of the society did not share fully and equally in the Bank's profits, the Bank, according to Jackson, created artificial distinctions within society. Jackson maintained that the federal government, like nature, should "shower its favors alike on the high and the low."[48] Attesting to Jackson's skills as a party leader, Bank supporters in Congress failed to summon the two-thirds majority necessary to override his veto.[49]

As the 1832 presidential campaign unfolded, both Jackson and Clay, his principal opponent, took their respective cases to the people. A pro-Jackson newspaper proclaimed that Jackson's cause was of "democracy and the people against a corrupt and abandoned aristocracy."[50] Senator Daniel Webster, a leading advocate for the Bank, proclaimed Jackson guilty of encouraging class warfare, setting the poor against the rich primarily to settle political scores.[51] Returned to office with 56.5 percent of the popular vote and a 216-to-49 majority in the Electoral College, Jackson interpreted his re-election as a mandate to destroy the Bank. He would, however, continue to face pro-Bank majorities in both the House and in the Senate.[52] This set the stage for Jackson's second battle with the Bank's supporters.

In January 1833, Jackson ordered the withdrawal of Treasury deposits from the Bank. Jackson dismissed two successive secretaries of the Treasury after they refused to act on his instructions, citing their statutory responsibilities over Treasury deposits.[53] On October 1, 1833, Acting Secretary of the Treasury Roger B. Taney (the Senate blocked his confirmation) removed $10 million from the Bank and redeposited the funds into ninety state-chartered banks, whose directors were politically friendly to the administration. Jackson later rewarded the pliant Taney with an appointment as chief justice of the United States.

With Taney's action having depleted the Bank of its gold and silver reserves, Biddle demanded immediate repayment in gold or silver of many of the Bank's outstanding loans, triggering a recession in 1834.[54] Lacking any understanding of how banks operated, Jackson interpreted this retrenchment solely through the lens of politics. When a delegation of businessmen facing financial ruin called upon the president, Jackson revealed that the primary motivation for his war against the Bank had been to settle a political grudge match. After instructing his visitors to take their case to Biddle, Jackson proclaimed, "I tell you, gentlemen, it's all politics."[55] Unable to muster the votes necessary to reverse Jackson's actions or to override a likely veto, the Senate, for the only time in its history, passed a resolution censuring a president.

Meanwhile, South Carolina launched a war of its own against the federal government Jackson headed. Angered by the "tariff of abominations" enacted during John Quincy Adams's administration, its legislature sanctioned a "Nullification Convention," which declared the Tariff Acts of 1828 and 1832 unenforceable within the state's borders after February 1, 1833. State officials further threatened that South Carolina would secede from the union if the federal government sought by force to compel its residents to pay these tariffs. On December 10, 1832, Jackson declared the nullification doctrine contrary to the spirit and letter of the Constitution. On January 16, 1833, he submitted a bill to Congress authorizing him to use the military to enforce federal customs laws. To avert violence and dissuade other states from standing with South Carolina, Senator Henry Clay and Vice President–Elect Martin Van Buren devised an accompanying compromise measure that would gradually reduce all tariff rates in excess of 20 percent to a flat 20 percent by 1842. Congress enacted both Jackson's force bill and Clay's compromise tariff bill as a package. South Carolina subsequently repealed its nullification ordinance.

In response to the recession he ignited when he removed Treasury deposits from the Bank, Jackson pressed Congress to enact the Gold Coin Act of 1834, which devalued the dollar by 6 percent against gold, but not silver.[56] Over the next two years, gold inflows and Treasury deposits enabled the Jackson-favored state banks to expand their outstanding loans and circulating bank notes. Federal revenues from land sales soared from $4.9 million in 1834 to $24.9 million in 1836.[57] Economic growth picked up, but so did inflation.

In June 1836, Jackson signed the bill, which allocated $28 million of the federal surplus to the states. This short-term measure significantly aided Van Buren's campaign to succeed Jackson as president. Some states demanded payment in gold or silver; others requested that the Treasury place their shares in state-chartered banks. The withdrawal of $28 million and the conversion of approximately $5 million into gold and silver forced deposit-losing banks to reduce their outstanding loans and circulating bank notes immediately. Although the states eventually deposited most of this gold and silver in other state-chartered banks, it took time for deposit-receiving banks to make loans and issue bank notes. Consequently, Jackson's surplus distribution caused a severe monetary contraction of 33.6 percent that lasted well into 1837.[58] Jackson inflicted further economic havoc when, on July 11, 1836, he issued the Species Circular, which required payment in gold or silver for all purchases of federal lands. His goal was to phase out paper currency and thereby harm land speculators.[59] Both Jackson's surplus distribution and his Species Circular increased public demand for gold and silver coins. Deflation replaced inflation, the land speculation bubble burst, and federal receipts from land sales plummeted.

The culmination of Jackson's economic policies, rooted in political retribution, left the economy on the edge of crisis as Van Buren assumed office. An extraordinarily skillful political tactician, as evidenced by his acquired title, the "Little Magician," Van Buren lacked the stature, the will, and the clout that were necessary to modify Jackson's economic policies. One result of his inaction was the Panic of 1837. On March 22, 1837, less than three weeks after Van Buren took office, news reached New Orleans that the price of cotton in London had dropped by 17 percent.[60] Banks in the south and west suspended the convertibility of their notes into gold and silver, and the financial crisis spread. On May 10, all banks in New York City suspended convertibility.[61] Of the 729 state-chartered banks prior to the panic, 194 closed permanently.[62] The crisis seemed to ease in 1838 when former Secretary of the Treasury Albert Gallatin, now president of the National Bank of New York, organized the remaining banks in New York City to resume convertibility without assistance from the Van Buren administration.[63] Congress also repealed the unpopular Species Circular on May 31, 1838.[64]

These actions failed to alleviate the severe economic downturn. British investors, major purchasers of state bonds during the 1830s, turned away when the Morris Canal and Banking Co. defaulted on its obligations in August of 1839.[65] Banks outside of New York City and New England again suspended convertibility, and the now state-chartered Bank of the United States failed. Without federal assistance, states had incurred massive debts to build canals, harbors, and roads.[66] Jackson's policy had merely shifted government debt from a federal government that had ample revenues available to states that did not. Between January 1841 and February 1843, eight states and one territory defaulted on their obligations.[67] In Illinois, Abraham Lincoln, who led the Whigs in the legislature, feared for his political life as the state teetered toward defaulting on bonds he had persuaded colleagues of both parties to float in order to fund major public works projects. Creditors settled for fifteen cents on the dollar.[68]

Historians rightly see Jackson's presidency as an important milestone in strengthening the institutional powers of the chief executive. His unprecedented use of the veto resulted in future Congresses having to take presidential preferences into account when crafting legislation. His dismissal of cabinet officers who defied him centralized control of the executive branch in the president.[69] By taking his case to the people and claiming to govern in the name of the majority, Jackson pioneered techniques through which future presidents would draw upon their popularity to appeal to the public over the heads of Congress to advance their agendas.

Yet, by proclaiming Jackson a near-great president, primarily because of the lasting effects he had as president, historians have left their readers with the impression that the economic policies Jackson invested so much of his energy into were in the best interest of the United States. His victory over Biddle came at great cost to the young nation. Along with his subsequent actions, it helped cause the second worst depression in U.S. history. Among those who suffered the most were farmers, small business owners, artisans, and urban workers—the very elements in society that Jackson had vowed to protect. Jackson's policies injected unnecessary volatility into the nation's financial system. They paved the way for the panics and recessions that erupted frequently in the decades that followed the Bank's demise.

Few who write about him bother to ask whether Jackson might have achieved the legitimate objective of making the Bank more accountable to an elective government in ways that proved less damaging. As he demonstrated through his victory, Jackson had the political skills necessary to bring about other outcomes. He could have forced changes in the Bank's operations. He might, over time, have been able to force Biddle's removal and replace him with an official more to his liking. Instead, he chose to destroy his enemies, whatever the costs. The nation paid a tremendous price as a result.

Abraham Lincoln

Most accounts of Abraham Lincoln's presidency rightly devote most attention to his extraordinary skills as a politician and as commander in chief. Had Lincoln been less adept in his handling of the economy than he was in running the government and overseeing military strategy, the Union might well have lost the Civil War. Under Lincoln's skillful leadership, the 37th Congress enacted more economically significant legislation than had any of its predecessors. In terms of its lasting influence, that Congress rivaled those of the 63rd, which enacted Woodrow Wilson's New Freedom; the 73rd, which approved Franklin Delano Roosevelt's New Deal; and the 89th, which passed many of Lyndon Johnson's Great Society programs.

Lincoln demonstrated his economic prowess in how he chose to finance the war. In a special session that he convened on July 4, 1861, Congress authorized the Secretary of the Treasury to sell $250 million in Treasury notes at 7 percent interest, increased tariffs, and enacted the nation's first income tax. These were the first of many steps his administration took to fund a war that Lincoln knew would be costly. Between fiscal years 1862 and 1865, tariffs were the federal government's largest source of revenue. Before leaving office, President Buchanan had signed the Morrill Tariff Act of 1861, which increased the average tariff rate on dutiable imports from 21 to 38 percent. At Lincoln's prodding, Congress increased average tariff rates on dutiable imports to 48 percent.

Lincoln also relied on income and excise tax receipts to pay the costs of the war. The Revenue Act of 1861 imposed an income tax of 3 percent on individuals with incomes of $800 ($16,130 in 2000 dollars). The Revenue Act of 1862 required employers—for the first time—to withhold taxes from their employees' pay, and increased the tax rate on income above $10,000 ($176,600 in 2000 dollars) to 5 percent. Finally, the Revenue Act of 1864 imposed rates from 5 percent beginning at $600 to 10 percent on more than $10,000. Between fiscal years 1862 and 1865, income taxes raised $136 million. New excise taxes on manufactured goods generated another $126 million.

Despite these new taxes, mounting outlays in 1861 depleted the Treasury's gold. By year-end, contractors and soldiers were going unpaid. Federal spending had totaled $67 million in the fiscal year that ended on June 30, 1861. Outlays grew by a whopping 613 percent to $475 million in fiscal year 1862 and would continue to escalate to $1.3 billion in fiscal year 1865 (equal to 14.1 percent of estimated GDP). Late in 1861, Secretary of the Treasury

Salmon P. Chase suspended the free convertibility of the U.S. dollar into gold and silver at fixed prices. Forced to innovate, Congress passed the Legal Tender Act on February 25, 1862, which authorized the Treasury to issue $150 million in U.S. notes and required Americans to accept these notes—known as "greenbacks" because of the color of their ink—to satisfy their claims. Unlike previous currencies, U.S. notes were a fiat currency, backed only by the promise of the federal government rather than payable in gold or silver on demand. By the end of the war, Congress had authorized a total of $450 million in greenbacks. While issuing currency was a common means of financing wars in the nineteenth century, this practice produced significant inflation. From 1860 to 1865, prices rose by an estimated 96 percent.

Issuing currency, however, satisfied only a fraction of the federal government's borrowing needs. Having decided to sell bonds to the public, the Lincoln administration embarked on a sales campaign worthy of a presidential election. Lincoln turned to financier Jay Cooke to manage what became the model for bond drives in future wars. The administration posted placards, bought advertisements in newspapers, and recruited opinion leaders and celebrities to sell bonds. Cooke retained a sales force of twenty-five hundred, consisting of small town bankers, insurance salesmen, and real estate brokers. He used the telegraph to contact his subordinates and to confirm purchases. To encourage the broadest possible public participation, bonds were issued in small denominations, and sales offices stayed open late. Lincoln understood that in addition to raising money, bond sales would promote patriotism and maintain morale on the home front. As historian Philip Shaw Paludan noted, every purchase of a twenty-year bond connoted the buyer's faith that the U.S. government would be around to pay its debts when they came due.[70]

In addition to these short-term and sorely needed initiatives to finance the war, Lincoln also lobbied Congress to enact a series of laws that fundamentally reshaped America's economic infrastructure and expanded opportunities for ordinary Americans. Legislation to grant federal charters to commercial banks and to provide for a uniform national currency proved the most difficult of these measures to pass. (State banks lobbied strenuously against such features.) To persuade Congress to pass this legislation, Lincoln, Cooke, and their

associates and congressional supporters again mounted a spirited public relations campaign. Ads were placed in newspapers, and speakers were sent on
the road to overcome remaining Jacksonian resistance to a national banking
system. Lincoln personally lobbied recalcitrant northern Democrats and a
good many of his fellow Republicans to vote for the bill.

The National Bank Act of 1863 (with significant amendments passed in
1864 and 1865) established the Office of Comptroller of the Currency to
charter and regulate national banks. National banks were authorized to issue
up to $300 million in national bank notes secured by Treasury bonds. This
collateral requirement expanded the market for U.S. Treasuries, and simultaneously protected the public from losses on national bank notes in case of a
bank failure. At the same time, a 10 percent tax on state bank notes essentially
taxed them out of existence. Unlike the prewar period, when state bank notes
often traded with each other at significantly less than face value (because notes
issued by state banks often became worthless after a bank failure), all U.S.
notes and national bank notes were accepted at face value nationwide. By significantly reducing the cost and uncertainty of doing business across state
lines, the National Bank Act contributed to the emergence of large corporations operating nationwide during the remainder of the century.

Lincoln and Congress enacted a series of other measures that hastened the
emergence of a national identity throughout the United States. The Agriculture Act created the U.S. Department of Agriculture to provide extension services to farmers so that they could use scientific knowledge to improve their
productivity. The Homestead Act granted title to 160 acres of western land to
anyone who agreed to settle on it and farm it for five years. This law helped
thousands of Americans who had started out in life at the bottom rung of the
social ladder, as had Lincoln, to become self-supporting, independent citizens. Its passage sped up settlement in the Great Plains.

The Pacific Railway Act, another measure in which Lincoln had taken an
ardent interest, authorized subsidies and land grants to the Union Pacific and
Central Pacific companies. This sped up construction of the transcontinental
railroad. By one estimate, the companies received $500 million in grants as
well as control over huge sections of the West.[71] Finally, the Morrill Land

Grant College Act, which Lincoln also signed, awarded each state thirty thousand acres in or near its borders for each senator and representative it had been allotted in 1860. Proceeds from these land sales would be used to establish an "agricultural and mechanical" college. Most of the sixty-nine colleges that benefited from Morrill grants grew into the great state universities, now much admired around the world for the quality of their research and for the outstanding education and professional training they make available to millions. Thus, the Morrill Act laid the foundation for the broad access to higher education in the United States that fueled its emergence as a leader in scientific discovery and technological innovation that continue to this very day.

Lincoln biographers usually award all of the domestic measures enacted in 1862 little more than a sentence or a paragraph before returning their attention to Lincoln's other deeds. Historian Leonard P. Curry was right to have termed the avalanche of legislation Lincoln helped pioneer a "blueprint for modern America."[72] In the absence of the banking, higher education, and transportation systems it helped spawn, the United States might never have emerged as a world power.

Theodore Roosevelt

As he readily admitted, Theodore Roosevelt's approach to the economy was more eclectic than systematic. As related in chapter 2, he conceived of his role as president as that of the neutral umpire, mediating feuds among private parties on behalf of a larger group that had a stake in the ultimate outcome, the public. A well-informed, wily politician, confident in his own judgment, skillful in attracting support, and blessed with considerable people skills, Roosevelt knew when to confront problems head-on, when to work around them, and when to back off. His most predictable trait was his unpredictability. He used it to keep both allies and adversaries off-balance.

On January 21, 1895, the U.S. Supreme Court issued a decision in *United States v. E. C. Knight Co.* that severely limited the reach of the Sherman Antitrust Act, which Congress had passed five years earlier at the prodding of President

Benjamin Harrison. The Court held that manufacturing was a local activity and thus Congress could not regulate it under the interstate commerce clause of the Constitution.[73] Consequently, the second Cleveland administration and the McKinley administration brought antitrust actions under the Sherman Antitrust Act only against labor unions. This changed under Theodore Roosevelt. In 1902, the Justice Department, with the president's full knowledge and support, brought an antitrust suit against the Northern Securities Company, a conglomeration of three parallel northwestern railroads J. P. Morgan had assembled.[74] Although the Supreme Court did not expressly overturn the *Knight* decision, the Court ordered the dissolution of this conglomeration and expanded the scope of antitrust law to include virtually all business activities.[75]

When Morgan asked Roosevelt, in the midst of the Northern Securities case, whether he intended to attack the tycoon's other interests, the president replied that he would not, so long as Morgan and his associates did nothing wrong.[76] He might just as well have added the words, "in my opinion," after the word "wrong." Roosevelt did not initiate legal actions against corporations solely to punish lawbreakers. He intended that the very possibility of suits would encourage corporations to behave in a manner consistent with his idea of the common good. "Wrong" in Roosevelt's eyes was not simply and strictly the violation of laws. It constituted acting contrary to the public interest. Applying this yardstick, Roosevelt sometimes opted not to prosecute a corporation that he suspected of violating the law.

During the Panic of 1907, for example, he did not challenge U.S. Steel's acquisition of Tennessee Coal and Iron because he feared that such a prosecution might cause the demise of the investment firm Moore and Schley, which had pledged its Tennessee Coal and Iron shares as collateral for bank loans. Moore and Schley's going under, he sensed, would undermine his efforts to maintain public confidence as he tried to stabilize financial markets. Thus, Roosevelt proved more flexible in his approach to antitrust considerations than did his successor, William Howard Taft. Taking a more legalistic approach, Taft's administration initiated ninety such suits as opposed to Roosevelt's forty-four. Yet history remembers Roosevelt as the trust-buster. It also records that he enjoyed better relations with the nation's business community than did Taft.

When it came to the rights of organized labor and consumers, Roosevelt took a similar and equally pragmatic stance. He intervened in the coal strike of 1902 (discussed in chapter 2), not as an advocate for one side, but as a mediator. While his government was warring with Morgan over Northern Securities in court, Roosevelt enlisted Morgan's aid in extracting concessions from the coal magnates, whose product Morgan's railroads transported and used for fuel. Because the settlement granted workers a 10 percent pay increase and reduced hours, but did not recognize the union as the workers' bargaining agent throughout the industry, Roosevelt was able to claim that the settlement he had brokered did not harm the long-run interests of business.[77]

When convinced that legislation provided a sounder means of solving problems than either direct presidential intervention or litigation, Roosevelt sought it. On June 29, 1906, he signed the Hepburn Act, which empowered the Interstate Commerce Commission to set the maximum rates that railroads could charge customers.[78] Having noticed that soldiers under his command during the Spanish-American War had shunned canned foods, Roosevelt grew suspicious of the meatpacking industry. When Upton Sinclair's novel *The Jungle* focused the public's attention on unsanitary and unsavory procedures in food processing, Roosevelt pressed for passage of what became the Pure Food and Drug Act and the Meat Inspection Act.[79] In addition to enhancing public health and safety, these measures made American agricultural commodities and processed foods more attractive to foreign consumers and thus increased U.S. agricultural exports, important economic opportunities hardly lost on Roosevelt.

Roosevelt remained attuned to fluctuations in the economy. At a time when businesses and urban households were increasingly conducting major transactions by check, farmers still relied primarily on cash. Every fall, currency drained from banks as food processors paid farmers in cash. Every winter, currency would flood back into banks as farmers paid their debts in cash. National banks, however, were not always able to meet this autumnal peak in demand for currency because recurring federal budget surpluses reduced the available supply of Treasury debt securities needed as collateral for issuing national bank notes. Each year, economic growth increased the peak seasonal demand. Simultaneously the shrinking supply of collateral made it increasingly difficult for national banks to issue enough national bank notes to meet it. During this seasonal drain, short-term interest rates often exceeded 100 percent. Additional stresses during these periods of tight credit could be enough to trigger a recession.[80]

In 1903, Roosevelt began working with Senator Nelson Aldrich to relieve what had become known as the "form-seasonal elasticity problem." House Speaker Joseph Cannon, however, blocked their initiatives. In the absence of legislation, Roosevelt resorted to ad hoc measures. Among other things, his second secretary of the treasury, Leslie Shaw, accepted state and local debt securities instead of Treasuries as collateral for Treasury deposits. This freed up Treasuries for use as collateral for issuing additional national bank notes. Shaw also moved Treasury deposits into banks to offset seasonal fluctuations in other deposits.[81] While not sanctioned by law, these measures helped the United States avoid panics during Roosevelt's first six autumns in office.

They proved insufficient, however, to forestall a major economic crisis in 1907. On October 22, a fall in copper prices sparked a run on the Knicker-bocker Trust Company, rumored to have links with the copper industry. The run spread to other New York banks, and the Panic of 1907 ensued. Roosevelt and his one-time nemesis J. P. Morgan worked together to save the nation's financial system from collapse.[82] Morgan secured emergency lines of credit from foreign banks and organized key bankers to lend millions of dollars to other besieged banks around the country. In a dramatic gesture intended to instill public confidence, Morgan personally walked onto the floor of the New York Stock Exchange to buy large blocks of stock. Roosevelt, in an equally bold move, instructed his third secretary of the treasury, George Cortelyou, to deposit $68 million of Treasury funds in New York banks and to issue $50 million in Panama bonds and $100 million in Treasuries in order to provide additional collateral for issuing national bank notes. To demonstrate Roosevelt's personal involvement, Cortelyou set up command not far from Morgan's bank in New York to ride out the crisis. The panic subsided by December.

As a means of preventing further such crises, on January 7, 1908, Aldrich introduced a bill to allow the secretary of the treasury to issue additional currency during emergencies and to establish a National Monetary Commission to study the banking system and recommend additional legislation. Roosevelt mustered all his political skills to overcome the efforts southern Democrats and midwestern Republicans, both blocs equally suspicious of eastern banks, to block the bill. When fierce opposition stalled the measure in the House Banking Committee, Roosevelt met with Speaker Cannon to enlist his aid in getting the feuding factions to resolve their differences. Because of Roosevelt's personal and relentless intervention—which included his overseeing conference committee negotiations—Congress passed the Aldrich-Vreeland Act on May 30, 1908. When he left office the following March, Roosevelt was aware that his efforts had at best produced but a makeshift measure. He hoped that his successor, working with the National Monetary Commission, would be able to devise "some permanent plan."[83] While success eluded him in this last instance, Roosevelt demonstrated how a president determined to act and eager to find and follow the right approach can sustain and enhance the economic health of the nation.

Woodrow Wilson

Had Woodrow Wilson's presidency ended in 1917 rather than in 1921, he would primarily and justifiably be remembered as a domestic reformer and innovator who put the U.S. economy on sound financial footing. In 1912, Wilson was elected with a solidly Democratic Congress (51-to-44 in the Senate and 291-to-127 in the House). Seeing his role primarily as that of party leader in the mode of a British prime minister (see chapter 2), Wilson called Congress into special session to enact his progressive agenda soon after his inauguration. "No one can mistake the purpose for which the Nation now seeks to use the Democratic Party," he remarked in his inaugural address. "It seeks to use it to interpret a change in its own plans and point of view."[84] His vision of what that entailed included a number of economic reforms.

As president, Wilson made tariff reduction his first priority. To promote a sense of urgency and to keep public attention focused on Congress, Wilson reverted to a practice not used by presidents since John Adams. He presented his program in person before a joint session of Congress. Wilson made the case that lower tariffs would reduce consumer prices, and entice U.S. industries to invest in new facilities and equipment and upgrade products in order to remain competitive on the international market. Striking a Jacksonian pose, Wilson argued that lower tariffs reduced the special privileges that highly protected industries had enjoyed. Lower tariffs, he said, were inherently more democratic because they expanded consumer choice.

Continuing a practice he had pioneered in New Jersey, Wilson met with Democratic members of the committees that considered his proposals and addressed Democratic caucuses. To keep public attention on his recommendations, he complained to the press about industry lobbyists "swarming" around Congress.[85] Lower tariffs had been part of Democratic Party gospel since the Jeffersonian era. With progressives in both parties and all regions voting with their southern Democratic colleagues, Congress quickly passed the Revenue Act of 1913 (also known as the Underwood-Simmons Tariff Act).[86] The statute slashed the average tariff rate on dutiable imports from 41 percent to 27 percent and substantially increased the number of duty-free items. More significantly, it re-established a federal individual income tax to replace revenues lost from tariff reductions.

On June 23, 1913, while his tariff measure was making its way through Congress, Wilson returned to Congress to propose what would become the landmark domestic achievement of his presidency, the Federal Reserve. In 1911, the Aldrich-inspired National Monetary Commission had recommended that Congress establish a single privately owned central bank, the National Reserve Association (NRA). This new entity would hold the reserves of every commercial bank, issue a new currency (NRA notes), and lend to commercial banks.[87] Although bankers and business leaders generally liked the proposal, many Democrats opposed it, seeing it as an attempt to re-create the kind of national bank that Jackson had destroyed eighty years earlier. After studying the issue, Wilson decided to support the Commission's plan, with modifications that increased federal oversight of the NRA.

Immediately, key powers within Wilson's party mounted fierce opposition to his proposal. In the year before Wilson took office, a Democrat-led House banking subcommittee held public hearings that had cast commercial bankers in a very poor light. Witnesses had alleged that a "money trust" of prominent New York bankers had used their positions to dominate major industries through interlocking directorates.[88] William Jennings Bryan, who had been the Democratic presidential nominee in 1896, 1900, and 1908, and continued to act as spokesman for the party's agrarian and populist wings, appeared poised to lead the opposition to Wilson's initiative.[89] Wilson had appointed Bryan secretary of state in recognition of Bryan's standing and as a reward for his having eased Wilson's path to the 1912 Democratic presidential nomination. Fearful that the alleged money trust could exploit the proposed NRA to further consolidate industries, Bryan demanded that the federal government own and control any central bank it created. He implied that, should Wilson not agree to these terms, opposition in Congress might prove sufficient not only to block its passage, but to jeopardize Wilson's pending tariff bill. Bryan was clearly threatening the president.[90]

Wilson could not ignore such opposition. Nor could he yield to Bryan's demands without forfeiting the support of the business community, which controlled some of the votes the administration needed in order to enact banking reform, as well as other proposals. To bridge this political divide, Wilson worked together with House Banking Committee Chairman Carter Glass and Glass's Senate counterpart, Robert Owen, to reshape the National Reserve Association into what became the Federal Reserve System. Instead of one privately owned central bank, Wilson proposed between eight and twelve regional Reserve Banks.

The national banks in each region plus the state banks that chose to join the system would own all of the shares in the regional Reserve Bank and appoint six of its nine directors. However, a Federal Reserve Board in Washington, D.C., composed of the secretary of the treasury, the comptroller of the currency, and initially four other presidential appointees would supervise all of the Reserve Banks. Federal Reserve notes, which would replace U.S. notes and national bank notes, would be U.S. government obligations. Any profits generated by the Federal Reserve System above a fixed dividend to its member banks would accrue to the Treasury. Wilson's presidency might have ended on a happier note had he demonstrated in his handling of the Versailles Treaty the same creativity, dexterity, flexibility, and willingness to compromise that he showed in the drafting of this bill.

The Federal Reserve Act, which Wilson signed on December 23, 1913, contained many contradictory provisions. Some had been deliberately inserted so that competing factions could claim the resulting product as their own. As the head of a party that had voiced skepticism about central banks for decades, Wilson had achieved a victory that his two immediate Republican predecessors had been denied. He succeeded in establishing a federal institution to regulate the money supply, in part because the act contained a sufficient number of Jacksonian-sounding provisions and had left open the question of where power ultimately resided in the system. Future presidents would reap the bitter consequences of this lack of clarity.

Wilson demonstrated a similar legislative genius in the approach he took in seeking to overcome Jacksonian opposition to federal funding for internal improvements. The Federal Aid Road Act of 1916 authorized, for the first time since the Civil War, the disbursement of federal funds to the states for building roads. The allocation of these funds to the states was based on population, land area, and existing road mileage. To receive federal funds, states were required to match each federal dollar with a dollar raised by state taxes and to establish a state highway department that met the approval of the Federal Office of Public Roads in the Department of Agriculture. Subject to federal inspections, state highway departments retained full responsibility for road planning, construction, and maintenance.

Wilson pressed Congress to pass other progressive measures. The Clayton Antitrust Act of 1914 outlawed business practices such as discriminatory pricing and tie-ins. It banned interlocking directorates among banks, railroads, and large corporations; empowered affected individuals and firms to sue alleged violators of antitrust law for damages; limited the application of antitrust laws to labor unions; and set guidelines governing a company's acquisition of the stock of its competitors.[91] Enacted a few weeks earlier, the Federal Trade Commission Act established the Federal Trade Commission as an independent regulatory agency to enforce federal antitrust and consumer protection legislation.[92] Two years later, the Adamson Act mandated an eight-hour day and overtime for railway workers. Wilson hoped this would avert a nationwide rail strike and prompt other industries to follow suit.[93] Finally, the Keating-Owen Act forbade the sale of any goods assembled by children in interstate commerce.[94]

When war broke out in Europe in the summer of 1914, many Americans feared that Europeans would spark a stock market crash by shedding their $6 billion in American investments and repatriating their funds in gold. On July 31, the New York Stock Exchange suspended trading for four months. The next week, a gold outflow from the Bank of England ignited fears of another panic. Adroitly using the Aldrich-Vreeland Act, Wilson's secretary of the treasury, William McAdoo, issued $68 million in emergency currency, rising to $363 million, to prevent a panic. Fears that the European war would push the United States into recession also proved unfounded. Allied demand for American agricultural products and manufactured goods sparked a boom starting in December 1914 and lasting through August 1918. France and the United Kingdom were indeed liquidating many of their U.S. investments, but only to use the cash to buy supplies from American firms. Consequently, the United States, which had been a net debtor of $2.2 billion (equal to 6.4 percent of GDP) in 1914, became a net creditor of $6.4 billion (equal to 8.4 percent of GDP) in 1919.

American entry into what history would subsequently know as World War I in 1917 proved costly. Federal outlays rose from $713 million (equal to 1.7 percent of estimated GDP) in fiscal year 1916 to $18.5 billion (equal to 25.3 percent of estimated GDP) in fiscal year 1919. To fund the war effort, Wilson pressed Congress to pass the Revenue Acts of 1916, 1917, and 1918, which collectively increased the top individual income tax rate from 7 percent on income above $500,000 ($8,839,836 in 2000 dollars) to 73 percent on income over $1,000,000 ($11,434,263 in 2000 dollars). These acts also hiked the corporate income tax rate from 1 percent to 12 percent, levied an excess profit tax with rates from 20 percent to 60 percent (on profits that exceeded an amount determined by the rate of return on capital during a base period) in addition to corporate income taxes, and increased various excise taxes. Under Wilson, federal debt increased from $1.118 billion (equal to 3.3 percent of estimated GDP) on June 30, 1914, to $24.485 billion (equàl to 34.9 percent of estimated GDP) on June 30, 1919. To finance this debt, Wilson sold war bonds by employing many of the same marketing techniques that Lincoln had pioneered decades earlier. However, McAdoo decided that the Treasury, rather than private firms, would manage bond drives.

Instead of maintaining price stability by allowing interest rates to rise, the Federal Reserve helped the Treasury finance the war by keeping interest rates low through a doubling of the money supply.[95] This policy caused prices to increase by 109 percent from 1913 to 1919, inflicting punishing inflation on consumers. Wilson's Federal Reserve tightened monetary policy to curb postwar inflation. This stringency plunged the U.S. economy into a severe recession in January 1920 that lasted until July 1921. This contraction was brief but quite severe. Industrial output dropped by 23 percent, while the unemployment rate rose to 12 percent before recovering in 1922.

When Wilson inserted free trade into his Fourteen Points, he hoped that the League of Nations would both promote it and foster economic interdependence among trading partners to help sustain peace. But Wilson did not press the Allies to reduce trade barriers at the Paris Peace Conference. As he became increasingly preoccupied with peace negotiations and the congressional battle over ratification of the Versailles Treaty, Wilson all but ignored the mounting economic problems at home and abroad. The Army was rapidly discharging millions of veterans without any transitional assistance. In order to avert starvation in war-torn Europe, Food Administrator Herbert Hoover had encouraged American farmers to maximize crop production—yet neither he nor Wilson had prepared for what would happen once the war ended and European farmers resumed full-scale production. Without a plan to retire the marginal acreage that Hoover brought into production during the war, the agricultural economy remained depressed for a generation.

World War I had turned the global economy upside down. Between 1815 and 1914, U.S. presidents had been able to make economic policy decisions based solely on domestic considerations because the United Kingdom had maintained the international economic system. Now, the United States had displaced the United Kingdom as the world's economic superpower; the Federal Reserve had inherited the Bank of England's role as the guardian of the gold standard; and New York had displaced London as the center of international finance. Presidents now needed to incorporate international considerations into their economic policy decision making. Wilson, his many domestic achievements notwithstanding, did not fully understand the international responsibilities that had fallen on the United States, nor did he exercise the leadership that was needed to promote sustainable growth in the global economy. Perhaps he expected his much-heralded League to take on this leadership role. If this was so, his failure to obtain American entry into it brought consequences even more calamitous than those he had feared.

Warren G. Harding and Calvin Coolidge

President Warren G. Harding and his successor, Calvin Coolidge, compiled mixed records on economic policy. Like Wilson, both were successful on the domestic front but failed to exercise the leadership that was necessary to put the global economy on a path toward sustained growth and mutual cooperation among nations. On April 11, 1921, before a joint session of the 67th Congress meeting in special session, Harding laid out the domestic economic agenda for his administration. Its major components were higher tariffs, income tax reductions, reform of budgetary procedures to control federal expenditures, and the establishment of regulatory frameworks for the nascent radio and aviation industries.

Prior to Harding, there was no such thing as a federal budget. Departments individually petitioned Congress for their annual appropriations. The lack of a review process for these requests severely limited the president's ability to control and prioritize spending. Congress, in turn, lacked the power to audit departments to determine how they actually spent their appropriated funds. Harding signed the Budget and Accounting Act of 1921, which required the president to submit a unified budget to Congress before the beginning of each fiscal year. The act established a Bureau of the Budget in the Treasury Department (which later became the Office of Management and Budget in the Executive Office of the President) to review appropriations requests from each department and compile the budget. The act also created the General Accounting Office (subsequently renamed the Government Accountability Office) to audit and evaluate the effectiveness of expenditures on behalf of Congress. Harding appointed Chicago banker Charles Dawes to be the first budget director and fully supported his drive to reduce governmental waste. Together they reduced federal outlays by more than a billion dollars a year.

The deep recession that had begun in January 1920 finally reached its trough in July 1921. Secretary of the Treasury Andrew Mellon pressed Congress to lower the high income tax rates that had been enacted during World War I. Congress passed and Harding signed the Revenue Act of 1921 in November. This act lowered the top individual income tax to 56 percent on income over $200,000 ($1,924,022 in 2000 dollars), increased personal exemptions, introduced a preferential rate of 12.5 percent on capital gains, and abolished the excess profits tax, but increased the corporate income tax rate to 12.5 percent.

Plans to regulate and promote the emerging aviation and radio industries, high on Harding's priorities, proceeded at a slow pace. Aviation needed basic safety standards and a coherent network of airports. The explosive growth in the number of radio stations threatened to drown their signals in a sea of static. Harding directed Secretary of Commerce Hoover to develop regulatory bills for Congress. Coolidge signed both measures into law in 1927. Under the Air Commerce Act, the Aeronautics Branch of the Commerce Department began to make aviation safety rules, certify aircraft and pilots, and build a national system of lighted airways and radio beacons to aid in-flight navigation. The Radio Act established the Federal Radio Commission—subsequently renamed the Federal Communications Commission—to issue broadcast licenses and assign frequencies to reduce interference.

Having succeeded to the presidency upon Harding's death in 1923, Coolidge threw his weight behind Mellon's efforts to persuade Congress to continue lowering income tax rates. Together, the Revenue Acts of 1924 and

1926 lowered individual federal income tax rates to a range of 1.125 percent on income over $4,000 ($38,900 in 2000 dollars) to 25 percent on income over $100,000 ($973,000 in 2000 dollars). The 1926 act also abolished the gift tax and slashed the maximum estate tax rate in half to 20 percent. In 1928, the corporate income tax rate was reduced to 12 percent. Because of the Harding-Coolidge tax cuts, all sectors of the U.S. economy save for agriculture experienced a vigorous recovery throughout the 1920s. Real median income for urban households increased. The number of motor vehicles registered rose from 9.3 million in 1921 to 26.7 million in 1929. High school education became nearly universal. By the time Coolidge left office, 98 percent of all Americans paid no federal income tax.

Coolidge's deft handling of the Teapot Dome and other scandals involving actions of corrupt Harding appointees bolstered investor confidence. Shortly after Harding's unexpected death on August 3, 1923, the long-simmering Teapot Dome scandal broke into the open. A Republican member of Congress termed it "the most stupendous piece of thievery known to our annals or, perhaps to those of any other country."[96] It entailed the leasing of government oil reserves in Wyoming and California to private interests in exchange for bribes, gifts, and favors (See Chapter 2). As Coolidge entered the presidency, three separate congressional investigations into malfeasances that occurred under his predecessor were under way. Concerned that the independence of the executive be preserved, Coolidge took charge of the inquiry. He named two special prosecutors, one a Republican and one a Democrat, to ferret out corruption throughout the government. "Every law will be enforced and every right of the people and the Government will be protected," he declared.[97] As a result of their investigation, Harding's interior secretary, Albert Fall, went to prison. While his appointees gathered their facts, Coolidge removed Harry Daugherty, Harding's attorney general and head of the notorious "Ohio gang," from office and replaced him with Harlan Fiske Stone, whom he subsequently named to the Supreme Court. By the time Coolidge sought re-election—less than a year after he took office—the "Harding scandals" had faded from memory.

One sector of the economy that did not share in the "Coolidge prosperity" was agriculture. Increased use of motorized tractors allowed farmers to sell grain that had formerly been used to feed draft animals, and the resumption of peacetime agricultural production in Europe slashed foreign demand for American grain. As a result, grain prices fell dramatically, and farm income with it. A number of measures were considered to stimulate the agricultural sector. Voluntary reductions in acreage under production and higher tariffs on agricultural imports were among them. Secretary of Commerce Hoover proposed the establishment of farmers' cooperatives to improve marketing efforts. Senator Charles McNary of Oregon and Representative Gilbert Haugen of Iowa proposed that the federal government maintain a parity between grain prices and other prices based on their relationship between 1909 and 1914—an unusually prosperous time for American farmers. To maintain parity, the federal government would employ a variable tariff on agricultural imports and buy up surplus domestic products, exporting them at a loss. Because of farmers' objections, the McNary-Haugen plan did not concurrently impose caps on output. Coolidge realized this would only aggravate the fundamental overproduction problem because guaranteed high prices would simply encourage farmers to produce even more crops on marginal acreage. Twice Coolidge vetoed McNary-Haugen bills Congress had passed. (The McNary-Haugen approach inspired the European Union's Common Agricultural Policy, which produced "mountains of unsold butter and lakes of unsold wine" during the 1980s, much as Coolidge had foreseen.)

When it came to disentangling the complex, convoluted, and heavily entangled problems of war debts and reparations, neither Harding nor Coolidge demonstrated leadership, forethought, or vision. The United States had lent a total of $10.4 billion to the Allies—including $4.8 billion to the United Kingdom and $3.4 billion to France. Neither president was willing to forgive these loans. (In 1922, the World War Foreign Debt Commission negotiated repayment plans with fifteen countries that would retire $11.5 billion in debts over sixty-two years.)

France and the United Kingdom had expected to use German reparations, which ran to the tune of $16 billion, to help repay their U.S. loans. Germany's ability to pay these reparations was contingent, however, on its ability to increase its exports dramatically. That, in turn, rested on the willingness of the

United States and the Allies to lower their tariffs and to allow a surge of German exports that could displace some domestic manufacturing jobs in import-competing industries. Harding and Coolidge, as well as the electoral and congressional coalitions they led, remained protectionists. On May 21, 1921, Harding signed the Emergency Tariff Act, which raised tariffs considerably. Wilson had vetoed an identical bill on his last full day in office. On September 21, 1922, Harding signed the Fordney-McCumber Tariff Act, which increased the average tariff rate on dutiable imports from 27 percent to 38.5 percent.

In January 1923, Belgium and France occupied the Ruhr valley after Germany could not make a scheduled payment. German workers launched a general strike in retaliation, and the resulting loss in tax revenues led to hyperinflation. An impasse occurred: France would not reduce the amount of reparations it expected, and U.S. banks would not extend new loans to Germany until France did. In 1924, Coolidge convened an international conference that negotiated the Dawes Plan, under which German payments were reduced to $250 million a year and then scheduled to increase to $625 million a year over five years, while U.S. banks resumed making loans to Germany.

Neither Harding nor Coolidge understood that high U.S. tariffs and Allied repayment of U.S. loans were mutually exclusive goals. International trade expert Frank Taussig warned Harding that the Fordney-McCumber tariffs would make it hard for the Allies to make payments and at the same time might spark retaliation against U.S. exports. Indeed, thirty-three countries increased their tariffs on U.S. exports to those countries between 1925 and 1929. When the League of Nations organized a conference to negotiate tariff reductions in 1927, Coolidge's delegates—incredibly—demanded that Europe reduce its tariffs but refused to entertain discussion of any U.S reductions. Not surprisingly, the conference failed.

Franklin D. Roosevelt

When it comes to economic performance, Franklin D. Roosevelt is the most difficult president to evaluate. Roosevelt remained popular with a majority of the public throughout his presidency. Many admired him for his bold response to the most severe economic crisis in American history and avowed concern for society's underdogs. At the same time, an intense minority resented Roosevelt's more than occasional resort to "class warfare." A *New Yorker* cartoon captured this alternative view of Roosevelt in its depiction of one child in a wealthy neighborhood tattling on another for writing a bad word on the pavement. The word was "Roosevelt."

FDR forever redefined the relationship between the federal government and its citizens. He established the first federal entitlement programs, which he financed through payroll taxes. He expanded the reach of federal income tax to most households and extended federal regulations to every sector of the economy. His admirers contend that his policies pulled the United States out of the worst economic downturn in American history and transformed the nation's economic infrastructure. Even some of his critics credit him with saving capitalism and democracy at a time when many Americans believed that freedom's days were numbered and that dictatorship, whether under communist or fascist auspices, was the "wave of the future" (as Anne Morrow Lindbergh predicted in a best-selling book by this title).[98]

However, with the passage of time, a fuller and more objective picture of FDR's successes and failures in economic policy has emerged. Most economists and historians now agree that Roosevelt's war-related defense outlays, coupled with the Federal Reserve's expansion of the money supply to fund federal deficits, pulled the United States out of the Great Depression in 1942.[99] Much of their research demonstrated, however, that many of FDR's policies actually *prolonged* the nation's economic hardships during the 1930s. Roosevelt may have also felt this way. In *No Ordinary Time*, Doris Kearns Goodwin suggests, with ample evidence, that when Roosevelt pondered seeking a third term in 1940, the New Deal was waning and the economy was not showing signs of recovering any time soon. He reasoned that, with ill winds blowing on the international horizon, he might secure his place in history by applying his administrative skills and foreign policy experience in that arena.[100]

Like Hoover, Roosevelt did not understand the monetary causes of the deflation and resulting economic contraction that ensued between August

1929 and March 1933. While he took office determined to do something and, unlike Hoover, to be perceived as doing something, Roosevelt was uncertain as to what to do. Behind the ebullient optimism that Roosevelt projected lay a fundamentally pessimistic view of the economy. FDR believed that excessive competition in a free market economy inevitably led to overproduction and widespread unemployment and that, in the absence of government intervention, stagnation rather than growth would be the natural state of affairs.[101] While often linked to Theodore Roosevelt and Wilson, whose reformist impulses he shared, FDR diverged from his progressive forebears considerably in both his approach to the economy and his policies.

Theodore Roosevelt and Woodrow Wilson sought to enhance competition through their antitrust and regulatory policies. They regarded competition as a beneficial force that expanded economic output and employment, improved business productivity, and lowered consumer prices. In other words, they believed that competition in a free market economy increased the real income of most households over time. Consequently, neither sought to redistribute wealth or income through government intervention. Nor did they believe that the federal government should play any role in the economy other than that of a disinterested arbiter among various special interests on behalf of the public as a whole.

In contrast, FDR feared that competition was a destructive force, and his policies generally restricted it. Because he did not share his predecessors' view that a competitive market economy would create jobs and ultimately increase real household income, at least after the Great Depression had begun, FDR pressed for entitlement programs and for progressive taxes on corporations and wealthy individuals as a means of reducing income disparities. Instead of functioning as a neutral umpire among competing interests, the second President Roosevelt put the federal government on the side of groups such as organized labor that he believed had been consistently dealt a bad hand. These are the people to whom he promised a New Deal.

While the Great Depression was a worldwide phenomenon, the United States was among the last countries to recover from its ravages. Democratically elected governments in other market-oriented countries pursued policies different from

Roosevelt's and experienced recoveries well in advance of the United States.[102] Rather than study their successes and apply economic remedies that had worked elsewhere, Roosevelt and his advisers, to the extent that they looked abroad at all, remained fixated on corporatism, which Benito Mussolini introduced into Italy. In this, the New Dealers were not alone. Media magnate Henry Luce, publisher of *Time*, *Life*, and *Fortune* magazines, heavily publicized the Italian dictator's apparent progress. FDR's flirtation with Mussolini's corporatism proved but one of his many passing policy fancies. Rather than stay on any particular course, Roosevelt followed paths of economic experimentation and constant change.

While FDR's professed practice of trying something, admitting when it failed, and trying something else was certainly preferable to sticking with ineffective policies, Roosevelt's bob-and-weave methods injected unnecessary uncertainty into already rattled markets. He would simultaneously apply contradictory approaches and shift from one inconsistent policy to another, often on short notice. When Columbia University professor and economic adviser Raymond Moley presented the president with drafts of two different speeches, each supportive of an approach that was diametrically opposed to that of the other, Roosevelt instructed him to "weave the two together."[103] He either would not or could not decide on a certain course and stick with it. In the course of his presidency, Roosevelt would first follow, then "weaver together," and then ignore advice from five different camps of advisors battling for his ear.

- The *reflationists* advocated abandoning the gold standard and expanding the money supply until prices rose to their predepression level. This group included professor-turned-adviser George Warren and his colleagues outside the administration, Irving Fisher and John R. Commons. While Roosevelt proved sympathetic to their ideas at first, their influence with him waned after 1933.
- The *corporatists* included Secretary of Agriculture (and future Vice President) Henry A. Wallace, Columbia University professor Rexford Tugwell, and his Columbia colleague, Moley. This group was responsible for early New Deal legislation, which took its inspiration from

Italian-styled corporatism, such as the National Industrial Recovery Act and the Agricultural Adjustment Act.

- Budget Director Lewis Douglas in 1933, and Secretary of the Treasury Henry Morganthau Jr. thereafter, spoke for the *conservatives* with the support of financier Bernard Baruch and Senate Appropriations Committee Chairman Carter Glass, who had served with Roosevelt in the Wilson administration. This group favored a return to the gold standard and a reduction in federal budget deficits—an enduring Roosevelt objective—through spending cuts if possible, and higher taxes if not.

- The *Keynesians* included Secretary of the Interior Harold Ickes, Federal Reserve Chairman Marriner Eccles, and Roosevelt's "jack of all trades," Harry Hopkins. They favored running large budget deficits to provide relief to the needy as well as large-scale public works projects. Like the British economist from whom they took their name, this group discounted the effectiveness of monetary policy in raising the price level.

- *Structuralists* such as FDR aides Thomas Corcoran and Benjamin Cohen, both influenced by Supreme Court justices Louis Brandeis and Felix Frankfurter, argued that corporations had exploited the power they exercised in the marketplace to raise prices and depress wages. They advocated breaking up powerful corporations as a means of lowering prices, raising wages, and promoting growth. The influence of this group became ascendant in 1938.

If Roosevelt's advisers can be placed into warring camps, his meandering battle against the Depression can be divided into several phases. During the historic first hundred days of his presidency, FDR sought to cartelize the entire U.S. economy in order to decrease excessive production, increase consumer prices, guarantee business profits, and put the unemployed back to work through collective action. This meant, initially, ending destabilizing bank runs. Upon taking office, Roosevelt adopted as his own an idea that Hoover's secretary of the treasury Ogden Mills had proposed, a national bank holiday. Exercising powers granted to him under the Emergency Banking Act passed on March 6, 1933, Roosevelt ordered the nation's 17,308 banks to close their doors. Of these, 11,878 were found to be sound and were licensed to reopen a week later.[104] As Congress turned to long-term reform of the financial sector, Senator Carter Glass persuaded Roosevelt that commercial banks that had engaged in underwriting stocks, bonds, and insurance had caused the Great Depression by recklessly financing speculation. Glass pressed for legislation to separate commercial and investment banking, and to curb "ruinous competition" among financial services firms through financial product segmentation, cartelization, and price controls.[105]

Glass attributed the excessive number of bank runs and failures between 1929 and 1933 to geographical restrictions on branching that prevented small, undercapitalized rural banks with undiversified loan portfolios from merging with larger, well-capitalized urban banks with diverse—and therefore less risky—loan portfolios. In contrast, House Banking Committee Chairman Henry Steagall opposed the geographic deregulation that Glass favored because it would lead to a small number of banks operating nationwide. He saw Glass's bill, however, as an opportunity to advance a proposal of his own: mandated federal deposit insurance, which he thought would help avert future bank runs. While he did not share Glass's interest in separating commercial and investment banking, Steagall made federal deposit insurance his price for agreeing to Glass's proposal. Although Glass and Roosevelt had previously opposed federal deposit insurance, they acceded to Steagall's demand. Thus, one of FDR's most significant contributions to the future health of the banking system resulted not from presidential initiative but through Congressional logrolling, and even political blackmail.[106]

The Banking Act of 1933, often but incorrectly referred to as the "Glass-Steagall Act," mandated the separation of commercial and investment banking, authorized the Federal Reserve to regulate deposit interest rates, and established federal insurance for bank deposits. The Securities Act of 1933 required the issuers of new debt or equity securities to disclose all relevant financial information to potential investors. The Securities Exchange Act of 1934 regulated the secondary trading of securities through exchanges and broker-dealers, required the quarterly disclosure of financial information by publicly traded corporations, and established the Securities and Exchange

Commission. Congress passed other laws to regulate credit unions, savings banks, and saving and loan associations and to establish federal insurance for their deposits. While financial disclosure and antifraud provisions in these laws proved beneficial through time, these laws also contained many anticompetitive provisions that segmented financial services into separate industries, severely limited competition between and within them, regulated interest rates on deposits, fixed brokerage fees, and allowed states to regulate insurance premiums and loan interest rates. These anticompetitive provisions proved unnecessary and created structural rigidities that contributed to frequent recessions and other economic problems after World War II. Congress has repealed many of these provisions in recent years.

Under the influence of the reflationists, Roosevelt sought to reverse the general price decline during 1933 by devaluating the dollar. On April 5, he required private citizens to sell their gold to the Federal Reserve at the price of $20.67 per ounce. Twelve days later, he forbade gold exports. On June 5, he secured congressional approval to abrogate gold clauses in all contracts, requiring payments be made in U.S. currency. On June 12, an international conference convened in London to discuss currency stabilization. Representing the U.S. government, Harvard professor Oliver Sprague, believing he was speaking for his government, pressed for a return to the gold standard after a 20 percent devaluation of the U.S. dollar. Then Roosevelt sent Moley to London with new instructions: to negotiate an agreement with France and the United Kingdom to return to the gold standard without specifying exchange rates. On July 3, Roosevelt sent a message in which he completely reversed his position. His statement that he now opposed a return to the gold standard caused the conference to collapse.[107]

On December 28, FDR ordered the Federal Reserve to exchange of all of its gold with the Treasury for gold certificates at the price of $20.67 per ounce. Under provisions of the Gold Reserve Act (January 31, 1934), Roosevelt devalued the U.S. dollar by 59 percent by increasing the gold price to $35 per ounce.[108] As a result, domestic prices began increasing. This reflation was necessary to recover from the Depression. Roosevelt assured, however, that this policy would not stay in force when he appointed Marriner Eccles, an opponent of devaluation and reflation, to be Federal Reserve Chairman in November 1934. Eccles attributed the Depression to overinvestment by business, maldistribution of wealth, and under-consumption by poor households—not monetary contraction. Like Keynes, Eccles believed that monetary policy was largely ineffective. Under Eccles's leadership, the Federal Reserve did not expand the money supply significantly for the remainder of Roosevelt's first term. Thus, the recovery of price level sputtered.[109]

In addition to financial services reform, jobs and relief for the unemployed proved a second cornerstone of the first New Deal. On March 31, 1933, Roosevelt signed the Emergency Conservation Work Act, which established the Civilian Conservation Corps (CCC). Under its auspices, the government hired thousands of unemployed youths to restore the nation's forests and work on irrigation projects.[110] On May 22, FDR signed the Federal Emergency Relief Act, creating the Federal Emergency Relief Administration. Headed by Harry Hopkins, and prior to its abolition late in 1935, FERA provided $3.1 billion to states and local governments to hire unemployed workers to build small-scale public facilities. FDR then created the Works Progress Administration (WPA), the successor to FERA, by executive order on May 6, 1935. Congress funded the WPA generously each year, and, not surprisingly, signs of its undertakings were evident in every Congressional district.[111]

The WPA hired the unemployed directly. Its preference for maximizing the number of people employed, even if projects it undertook could have been completed with far fewer workers and at less cost, led its critics to deride the program as make-work and a boondoggle. Until its abolition in 1943, the WPA remained the largest and most visible of the New Deal agencies. The WPA also established the Federal Writers Project, the Historical Records Survey, and multiple arts projects. During their peak year of 1935, the WPA and the CCC employed 2.7 million and 459,000, respectively. While these measures provided jobs and hope to millions and useful work to the nation, they did not make much of a dent in the overall unemployment rate. In 1935, it stood at 20.3 percent.[112]

What the president liked most about the CCC and WPA was their capacity to rescue those they employed from the "threat of enforced idleness" that he believed would prove harmful to their "spiritual and moral stability."[113]

Roosevelt was proud of the high number of people he moved from relief rolls to federal payrolls, believing that work restored their sense of pride in themselves. (In attempting to lift people out of poverty through transfer payments and other methods, Lyndon Johnson rejected FDR's policy of requiring work for benefits. In the decades that followed, conservatives and moderates, including Daniel Patrick Moynihan, Richard Nixon, Ronald Reagan, Newt Gingrich, and Bill Clinton, worked to build work incentives and requirements into government assistance programs.)

Roosevelt embarked on other recovery efforts that took the form of newly established governmental agencies and planning entities. On May 18, 1933, Roosevelt signed legislation establishing the Tennessee Valley Authority to provide cheap electricity, flood control, navigation, and economic development to a badly depressed area spanning seven states. (Congress later rejected his request to create similar agencies in other major river valleys.) He pressed Congress to pass the National Industrial Recovery Act. Signed into law on June 16, 1933, Title I created the National Recovery Administration (NRA), and Title II established the Public Works Administration (PWA) within the Department of the Interior.

The NRA attempted to apply the apparent success of Mussolini's corporatism to the United States, while the PWA, a reflection of Keynes's "pump priming," had the government finance large-scale public works projects, funded by budget deficits.[114] Under the direction of General Hugh Johnson, the NRA created labor and management committees that negotiated 557 industrial codes determining minimum wages, maximum hours, child labor restrictions, and occupational health and safety rules. The NRA's thousands of rules and multiple codes, however, became especially onerous to small businesses. The PWA undertook approximately 34,000 construction projects, including airports, hydroelectric dams, highways, and the electrification of the Pennsylvania Railroad between New York and Washington, D.C. Unlike the WPA, the PWA had private construction firms enter a competitive bidding process and sought to get the best value for taxpayer dollars.

On May 27, 1935, in the case of *A.L.A. Schechter Poultry Corp. et al. v. United States*, the Supreme Court unanimously overturned Title I and the

NRA. It declared provisions authorizing the agency to infringe upon state authority an unreasonable stretching of the commerce clause and the delegation of legislative powers it awarded the executive branch a violation of the nondelegation doctrine.[115] By the time the court reached its decision, the NRA had become unpopular with both business and labor. While Roosevelt railed against the court for striking down such programs and would soon seek to pack it with justices more favorable to this kind of federal intervention, he never tried to revive Title I. Seeing no intrusion into the rights of the states or the private sector, the court allowed Title II to stand.[116]

To relieve what had been a decade-long depression in the agricultural sector, Roosevelt tried to increase commodity prices and farm income by requiring farmers to reduce their acreage under production and their output. On May 12, 1933, FDR signed the Agricultural Adjustment Act, under which the Agricultural Adjustment Administration (AAA) imposed taxes on food processors and paid subsidies to farmers who agreed to shrink output by plowing under their crops and slaughtering their livestock and poultry. During its three years in operation, the AAA increased farm income by 50 percent from its depressed level in 1932. Almost all of this increase, however, resulted from subsidy payments. Commodity prices barely budged. In *United States v. Butler*, the Supreme Court declared in a 6-to-3 vote that the AAA was invalid and unduly coercive.[117] In response, Congress passed the Soil Conservation and Domestic Allotment Act (signed on April 27, 1935), which authorized farm subsidies out of general funds to reduce acreage under production for soil conservation purposes. At FDR's request, Congress passed a second Agricultural Adjustment Act (signed on February 16, 1938), which enshrined an entitlement program of farm subsidies and production controls, most of whose benefits would eventually flow to the well-off and to large-scale agribusinesses.[118]

One of the few progrowth measures that Congress enacted during Roosevelt's first term was the Reciprocal Trade Agreements Act of 1934. Secretary of State Cordell Hull, a free trade advocate, convinced the president that foreign markets were crucial to American prosperity and that the United States should reduce its high tariffs. Roosevelt sought and received authorization from Congress to negotiate bilateral trade agreements and lower tariff rates by up to 50 percent in exchange for similar reductions for U.S. exports. From June 12, 1934, when it was signed into law, until it was replaced by other legislation during the Kennedy administration, more than sixty tariff reduction agreements were negotiated under this act.

No discussion of the first New Deal would be complete without making mention of FDR's so-called soak-the-rich policy, which was embedded in the Revenue Act of 1935. Signed on August 30, the act increased the top individual income tax rate to an unprecedented 79 percent on incomes above $5,000,000 ($93,181,818 in 2000 dollars). Roosevelt considered it immoral for millionaires, during hard times, to avail themselves of legal tax deductions and exclusions to avoid their full tax obligations. Eager to make an example of those he believed the worst offenders, Roosevelt abused the powers of his office when he ordered government agents to prosecute certain wealthy individuals against whom he harbored personal or political grudges. He also tried to shame people into compliance by making their names public.

Perhaps the most celebrated example of how Roosevelt acted in this regard was the manner in which his administration pursued former Secretary of the Treasury Andrew W. Mellon. In 1934, Morgenthau ordered the Internal Revenue Service (IRS) to investigate Mellon for tax evasion. (An IRS unit had already conducted an investigation and uncovered no wrongdoing on Mellon's part.) A recent Mellon biographer discovered a note in FDR's handwriting suggesting that if the president did not personally read Mellon's 1930 tax return, he certainly discussed it with aides. "Why not have [Attorney General] Cummings read [the tax return and] make it public?" he presumably wrote on a note attached to a memo.[119] In March 1934, Cummings did more than that. He issued a press release accusing Mellon and six others of tax evasion. This prosecution failed. Later, in 1937, Roosevelt demanded to see the returns of wealthy taxpayers and leaked their names and details about their returns to friendly reporters. A little more than a month later, IRS Commissioner Guy Helvering fingered a number of wealthy individuals that he claimed had avoided paying their fair share of taxes, even though he admitted that the deductions they took were "perfectly legal."[120]

Toward the middle of his first term, Roosevelt and Congress shifted their attention from relief and recovery to reforming American economic infrastructure.

This constituted the second New Deal. During his term as governor, New York became the first state to enact an unemployment insurance program. After his inauguration, Roosevelt had begun looking for an opportunity to create a federal system of social welfare benefits. In 1935, he decided to press for a federal entitlement program after he detected growing public support for more radical ideas being advanced by politicians and activists to his left. In 1933, Dr. Francis Townsend—who advocated a $200-per-month pension for all Americans of sixty years of age or older, financed by a national sales tax—acted as spokesman for an organization boasting five million. Senator Huey Long of Louisiana, his eye cast on the presidency, attracted considerable headlines with his "share the wealth" redistributionist rhetoric.

As a means of stealing their thunder and reducing poverty, especially among the elderly, Roosevelt pressed Congress to enact a federal system of old-age and disability pensions, unemployment insurance, and welfare benefits for poor families with children. He advocated financing these benefits through a joint employer-employee payroll tax, rather than through a sales tax or higher income taxes, as others proposed. Roosevelt reasoned that once workers paid their share of the payroll tax, they would feel a stake in the program's survival, as well as a right to benefits when they retired. Once this happened, Roosevelt predicted, "no damned politician" would ever seek to terminate the program.[121]

The original Social Security Act that Roosevelt signed into law authorized several programs, including the benefits listed above and grants to states for various health and welfare programs. An amendment enacted in 1939 added survivors' pensions for spouses and minor children of covered workers. Upon signing the act, Roosevelt articulated his vision not only for the program but for much of the New Deal: "We can never insure one hundred percent of the population against one hundred percent of the hazards and vicissitudes of life, but we have tried to frame a law which will give some measure of protection to the average citizen and to his family against the loss of a job and against poverty-ridden old age."[122]

Believing that workers stood at a great disadvantage when negotiating wages, benefits, and working conditions with their employers, Roosevelt tried to balance the scales by strengthening the union movement. He threw the weight of the federal government behind efforts to increase union membership, require employers to bargain in good faith with unions, and protect unions from unfair labor practices and violence. Under Roosevelt's leadership, Congress passed two major labor laws. The first was the National Industrial Labor Relations Act (NLRA; also known as the Wagner-Connery Act). In part a response to the Supreme Court's overturning Section 7(a) of the NIRA, which had established the right of private sector employees to engage in collective bargaining, this act again guaranteed the right to organize unions and established the National Labor Relations Board to investigate charges of unfair labor practices by employers. The second major labor law was the Fair Labor Standards Act, signed four years later in June of 1939. This act established a federal minimum wage, guaranteed time-and-a-half pay for overtime, and prohibited the employment of minors in "oppressive child labor."

As a result of Roosevelt's efforts, union membership increased from 11 percent of the workforce in 1933 to 27 percent of the workforce by 1941. Union-organized strikes and plant occupations won significant wage increases for their members, and the average hourly wage of production workers in manufacturing during that same time rose from $0.44 per hour in 1933 to $0.73 per hour in 1941, a real increase of 61 percent. However, some of the gains for employed unionized workers came at the expense of the unemployed. Manufacturing productivity rose by only 29 percent during the same period. Thus, the unit cost of labor increased significantly, slowing the decrease in the unemployment rate that would have otherwise occurred.

In 1936, economic recovery appeared to be underway. By the year's end, unemployment declined to 15.3 percent, and industrial production was 5.9 percent higher than it had been in 1929. Then Roosevelt made three major mistakes that pushed a weak but recovering economy into a recession that lasted from May 1937 to June 1938. During this recession, industrial production declined by 31.9 percent, and the unemployment rate soared from 11 percent in July 1937 to a high of 20 percent the following June. His first error was to press Congress for a new tax on retained earnings (the portion of after-tax profits that corporations do not pay out as dividends to their shareholders) ranging from 12 percent to 27 percent in addition to corporate income taxes. Rexford Tugwell persuaded Roosevelt that corporations would make better decisions if they had to finance their investments in new facilities and equipment from bank loans or newly issued stocks and bonds rather than from retained earnings. Having recently seen many indebted firms fail, the executives of surviving corporations were hesitant to take on new debt or issue new securities. Consequently, business investment, which had begun to increase in 1936, plummeted in 1937.

Roosevelt next attempted an ill-conceived monetary experiment. The commercial banks that had survived bank runs and Roosevelt's own bank holiday were, understandably, cautious. They wanted to hold large reserves at the Federal Reserve in excess of the regulatory required minimums. Secretary of the Treasury Morgenthau and Federal Reserve Chairman Eccles thought these excess reserves might trigger inflation (even though prices were still 19 percent below their level in 1929). To preempt inflation, the Federal Reserve doubled its reserve requirements between August 1936 and May 1937, and in response, commercial banks contracted their deposits and loans to build new excess reserves. The resulting credit contraction forced businesses to curb production and lay off workers.[123]

Roosevelt's third error was trying to balance the federal budget prematurely. To the extent that he subscribed to any economic philosophy at all, Roosevelt remained a deficit hawk all his political life. When he ran for president in 1932, he attacked Herbert Hoover for running up large deficits. In 1944, Roosevelt talked to advisers about paying off the entire federal debt after World War II. Upon the slightest signs of recovery, early in 1937, Roosevelt moved aggressively to balance the budget. Federal outlays fell from $8.42 billion (equal to 10.5 percent of estimated GDP) in fiscal year 1936 to $6.77 billion (equal to 7.7 percent of estimated GDP) in fiscal year 1938. As a result, the federal budget deficit fell from $4.30 billion (equal to 5.5 percent of estimated GDP) to $89 million (equal to 0.1 percent of estimated GDP).

When FDR saw the effects on the unemployment rate, he shifted policy directions once again. On the advice of Hopkins and Eccles, he abandoned spending restraint. In June 1938, Congress appropriated, at his behest, an additional $3.75

billion for relief and public works. He also veered away from his earlier support for corporatism and toward an activist antitrust policy. Roosevelt's attorney general Robert Jackson, whom Roosevelt appointed to the Supreme Court, was of the view that FDR "knew that there were evils in the suppression of competition and that there were evils in competition itself." Where the greater evil lay, Jackson wrote, Roosevelt "never fully decided."

War-related deficit spending and an accommodative monetary policy began to lift the United States out of the Great Depression, beginning in 1942. Defense spending increased federal outlays enormously from $6.8 billion (equal to 7.7 percent of estimated GDP) in fiscal year 1938 to $92.7 billion (equal to 41.9 percent of estimated GDP) in fiscal year 1945. The Federal Reserve belatedly began to increase the money supply in 1938. Prices finally exceeded their 1929 level in 1943. As the military draft absorbed workers, the unemployment rate—which still averaged 9.9 percent as late as 1941—finally fell to 4.7 percent in 1942.

To finance the war, Roosevelt pressed Congress to expand the scope of the individual income tax to include middle-income households and to raise rates to confiscatory levels. By 1945, individual income rates ranged from 23 percent on incomes above $2,000 ($19,133 in 2000 dollars) to 94 percent on incomes above $200,000 ($1,913,333 in 2000 dollars). Moreover, FDR persuaded Congress to institute the withholding of wages and salaries. Congress increased the top corporate income tax rate to 53 percent and imposed an excess profits tax, in addition to corporate income taxes, that eventually rose to 95 percent. Despite these tremendous tax increases, federal budget deficits rose to $47.6 billion (equal to 21.5 percent of estimated GDP) in fiscal year 1945, and the federal debt increased to $235.2 billion (equal to 106.2 percent of estimated GDP) on June 30, 1945.

During the war, the Federal Reserve's monetary policy was to keep nominal long-term interest rates low to help the Treasury service the growing debt. Because of the Federal Reserve's aggressive purchases of Treasuries, the money supply ballooned and inflationary pressures mounted. To disguise this inflation until the end of the war, Roosevelt instituted comprehensive wage and price controls. While prices doubled during the Civil War and World War

I, visible prices increased by only 18 percent from December 1941 to August 1945. These controls, however, deferred price and wage increases only until just after the war; prices rose by 31 percent between August 1945 and June 1950 instead of falling as they had after previous wars.

Before the war's end, Roosevelt added one more significant piece of legislation to America's economic infrastructure, the Servicemen's Readjustment Act of 1944, commonly referred to as the "GI Bill." It provided returning veterans with grants to pay for college or vocational training, one year's unemployment benefits, and loans to purchase a home or start a business. By 1951, 8 million veterans had received education benefits under the program, including the 2.3 million who attended colleges and universities. As a result of Roosevelt's vision and concern for those who had sacrificed to preserve the nation's freedom, the United States had at its disposal a highly educated workforce as it entered an increasingly competitive postwar economy.

John F. Kennedy

John F. Kennedy was one of the few presidents whose father had been an extraordinarily successful and entirely self-made businessman. "My father always told me that all businessmen were sons of bitches," Kennedy once quipped.[124] Whatever thoughts about his peers Joseph P. Kennedy might have shared with his children notwithstanding, his son John, as president, showed a genuine appreciation for entrepreneurship and a clear understanding of how tax and regulatory policies influence the economic health of the nation.[125] During his fourteen years in Congress, Kennedy had been a fiscal conservative. While he voted the standard Democratic line in favor of increasing the federal minimum wage and Social Security benefits, and against the Taft-Hartley Act, which labor leaders regarded as hostile to unions, Kennedy was not a proponent of the redistributionist policies of either FDR's New Deal or Truman's Fair Deal. As president, Kennedy continued Eisenhower's tight-fisted approach toward spending.[126] Indeed, Kennedy became so concerned over the number of groundskeepers at the White House that he called in his own gardener to review landscaping costs.

Kennedy approached economics with the mien of an earnest undergraduate, eager to raise the C he received in the subject at Harvard.[127] He relied on Chairman of the Council of Economic Advisers Walter Heller, who represented a new generation of Keynesian economists, and Secretary of the Treasury C. Douglas Dillon, a Republican with years of Wall Street experience who had served in the Eisenhower administration, to advise him. In his abbreviated presidency, Kennedy compiled the most pro-business record of any Democratic president since Grover Cleveland.

Throughout the eight-year Eisenhower administration, real GDP growth had averaged an anemic 2.6 percent per year. One month into Kennedy's term, the recession that candidate Kennedy had pledged to reverse, lifted. However, the new president worried that if real GDP growth did not accelerate, the U.S. economy would not create enough jobs fast enough to absorb the baby-boom generation as it entered the workforce. Consequently, the unemployment rate would rise, and the standard of living, already strained by the high individual and corporate income tax rates left over from World War II and the Korean War, would fall. Kennedy set as his objective 5 percent growth in real GDP per year. To achieve it, he agreed to a proposal Heller made that entailed reductions in individual and corporate income tax rates and a willingness to live with higher budget deficits for a time. Heller contended that the additional tax revenues the anticipated economic growth generated would eventually bring the budget back into balance.[128]

In choosing this course, Kennedy rejected conflicting advice from more orthodox Keynesians. Harvard Professor John Kenneth Galbraith, who had decried the emergence of "private affluence and public squalor" in his book *The Affluent Society*, urged Kennedy to stimulate the economy by spending considerably more on public works and unemployment assistance. If Heller's plan worked, Galbraith feared, Democrats would have a difficult time persuading the public to support continued and increasing government spending on social and other programs. "Once we start encouraging the economy with tax cuts," he warned, "it would sooner or later become an uncontrollable popular measure with conservatives. And tax cuts would be urged as a way of getting public expenditures down."[129] By opting for

Heller's plan over Galbraith's, Kennedy demonstrated a decisiveness that Franklin Delano Roosevelt had lacked. Instead of directing his subordinates to weave together contradictory recommendations, Kennedy made what he considered the best possible choice and pursued it vigorously.

The president unveiled his tax reduction plan in two stages. In 1962, Kennedy proposed a 7 percent investment tax credit (ITC) to increase the after-tax return from business investment in new equipment. Congress approved it in October.[130] After this victory, Kennedy proposed an across-the-board reduction in individual and corporate income tax rates in a speech before the Economic Club of New York on December 14, 1962. To offset some of the projected short-term losses in tax receipts, Kennedy also proposed to tighten tax deductions. Kennedy's announcement marked the first time that a president had recommended a significant tax cut while the federal budget was running deficits. Kennedy asserted that his intention was to make the economic pie bigger. Liberals and conservatives of the era understood that Kennedy's plan represented a major shift away from the then prevailing thinking, which placed a premium on using government to redistribute income rather than to promote growth through tax cuts.

Kennedy argued that the ITC, along with his proposal for a lower corporate income tax rate, would encourage businesses to purchase and install state-of-the-art facilities and equipment. This, he said, would increase business productivity and profits. Lower individual income tax rates, Kennedy maintained, would increase the incentives for individuals to work while simultaneously boosting business output. Higher levels of both consumption and investment, he continued, would bolster the demand for labor, creating more jobs and increasing real after-tax wages.[131] Galbraith, half jokingly, proclaimed Kennedy's remarks "the most Republican speech since McKinley."[132]

Passing a major tax reduction proved more difficult than Kennedy expected. Proclaiming Kennedy's tax cut an act of "fiscal recklessness," Eisenhower urged spending cuts to bring the federal budget into balance.[133] Other Republican leaders took issue with Kennedy's claim that tax rate cuts would not reduce the unemployment rate.[134] Traditional liberals bemoaned Kennedy's reluctance to spend more on public works. To win congressional support for across-the-board tax rate reductions among deficit hawk southern Democrats and their Republican allies, Dillon persuaded Kennedy to pare down spending increases on domestic programs. To secure support from liberal Democrats, Kennedy advisers assured labor leaders that lower income households would receive a disproportionate share of the tax cuts. After Kennedy agreed to drop the revenue-raising provisions, his proposal cleared the House on September 25, 1963. Lyndon Johnson obtained Senate approval for it the following January. The Kennedy-inspired Revenue Act of 1964 reduced marginal income tax rates for people in all brackets. The top rate fell from 91 percent to 70 percent in 1965, while the bottom rate dropped from 20 percent to 14 percent. The top individual rate applied to incomes over $200,000 ($1,091,255 in 2000 dollars). The act also reduced the top corporate tax rate from 52 percent in 1963 to 48 percent in 1965.

The Kennedy tax cuts produced the economic boom of the 1960s. Real GDP growth jumped from 2.5 percent in 1960 to 6.4 percent in 1965. The unemployment rate fell from 6.6 percent in January 1961 to 4.0 percent in December 1965. The combination of accelerating economic growth with the federal spending restraint that Dillon and congressional Republicans demanded slashed the budget deficit from $7.1 billion (equal to 1.3 percent of GDP) in the fiscal year 1962 to $1.4 billion (equal to 0.2 percent of GDP) in fiscal year 1965.

Kennedy's attempts to control inflation produced a showdown between his administration and the steel industry. His minions had persuaded the United Steelworkers Union to accept a 2.5 percent wage increase with the expectation that steel manufacturers would hold price increases to a similar level. On April 10, 1962, U.S. Steel President Roger Blough, whose company accounted for a quarter of all domestic steel production, informed Kennedy that it was raising its prices by 3.5 percent. One day later, Bethlehem Steel and Republic Steel followed suit.[135] At a press conference, Kennedy denounced these price increases as unjustifiable and contrary to the public interest. In private, he sanctioned the use of all the powers of his office to force the steel manufacturers to recant. His administration launched an antitrust investigation and threatened to haul steel executives before a federal grand jury.[136] Attorney General Robert Kennedy admitted that he ordered FBI agents to march into the offices of steel executives to probe their expense accounts. While Republicans complained about what they termed "Gestapo-like" tactics, Bethlehem Steel rescinded its price increase on April 11, 1962. U.S. Steel followed suit the next day.[137]

These highly publicized criticisms of steel executives caused business confidence in Kennedy to plummet. By June 26, 1962, the Dow Jones Industrial Average (DJIA) had fallen by 27 percent to 535.76. Backpedaling, Kennedy began courting business executives, going so far as to press regulatory agencies to pull back from plans to issue new regulations. As his proposed tax rate cuts began moving through Congress, equity markets responded. By November 1, 1963, the DJIA had risen to 753.73. After the tax cut bill won approval two years later, the DJIA peaked at 995.15 on February 9, 1966.

Kennedy concluded that the Reciprocal Trade Act that had governed U.S. trade negotiations since 1934 had become obsolete. He sought to replace it with new legislation authorizing the president to negotiate multilateral agreements to reduce tariffs across the board by 50 percent and to eliminate tariffs altogether on certain goods. Kennedy also proposed adjustment assistance to industries, firms, and workers adversely affected by trade liberalization. In September 1962 both houses of Congress enacted a bill containing all of Kennedy's major recommendations. Using its authority, he then proposed convening the sixth round of multilateral negotiations under the General Agreement on Tariffs and Trade (GATT). A GATT ministerial meeting with representatives of fifty countries convened in Geneva on May 16, 1963, to launch the "Kennedy Round" in recognition of the president's efforts on behalf of trade liberalization. During the Kennedy Round, tariffs were reduced on 70 percent of the dutiable goods in the United States and other developed countries.[138] Almost all of the reductions were on industrial goods; little progress was made on agricultural products.

To many Americans, nothing symbolized the spirit of Kennedy's "New Frontier" more than the space program. After the Soviet launch of *Sputnik* in 1957, the United States and the U.S.S.R. raced to see which would successfully launch the first person into space. On the heels of the successful flights of first Russian Yuri Gagarin and then American Alan Shepard only weeks apart in 1961, Kennedy upped the ante. Before a joint session of Congress on May 25, 1961, Kennedy set a goal "to land a man on the moon and return himself safely to earth" before the decade was out.[139] The projected cost of achieving this was between $30 billion and $40 billion. Given Kennedy's concerns about government spending, he went down this path with some trepidation. With Eisenhower and some scientists questioning whether a manned lunar landing program would generate sufficient additional knowledge to justify the extra costs, Kennedy pressed ahead. He regarded space as another arena of the Cold War where the West would have to compete with the Soviet Union.[140] Many had interpreted the Soviet launch of *Sputnik* and Gagarin's first flight as a loss of American prestige. On the heels of the Bay of Pigs fiasco, these factors weighed heavily on Kennedy's mind.

In the end, Kennedy saw a manned flight to the moon as a means of rekindling the kind of national unity and shared sense of purpose among the American people that he had experienced during World War II. Endeavoring to capture the imagination of the public, he likened the moon project to the Lewis and Clark expedition, George Mallory's climb of Mount Everest, and Charles Lindbergh's solo flight to Paris. "But, why, some say, the moon?" Kennedy said at Rice University. "Why does Rice play Texas? We choose to go to the moon, in this decade and do the other things," he said, "not because they are easy, but because they are hard, because that goal will serve to organize and measure the best of our energies and skills, because that challenge is one that we are willing to accept, one we are unwilling to postpone, and one which we intend to win, and the others, too."[141]

Kennedy considered the commitment he made to do this among "the most important decisions" of his presidency.[142] He forged ahead despite the opposition of much of the Republican leadership (who thought the moon program too costly), liberal Democrats (who clamored to divert space funds into social programs), and according to a Gallup poll taken during the month that Kennedy announced his plan, 58 percent of the public.[143] The euphoria that surrounded the landing of *Apollo 11* on the moon in 1969, and the nostalgia that still surrounds it, have obscured the relentless efforts

Kennedy made to sell his program to Congress and to the public. The moon program boosted real nondefense outlays for research and development by 242 percent, from 0.4 percent of GDP in fiscal year 1961 to 1.0 percent of GDP in fiscal year 1965. Because of space-related research and development, entirely new technologies emerged that accelerated America's economic development and enhanced its competitiveness well into the twenty-first century.

As some students of his presidency repeatedly point out, Kennedy did not achieve all of his legislative agenda during his short time in office. Lyndon Johnson won final approval for not only Kennedy's tax cuts but also the late president's proposals to increase aid to education, prohibit racial discrimination in public accommodations, combat poverty, and establish Medicare. They often fail to note, however, that many of these were on their way to passage the day Kennedy departed on his fateful trip to Dallas. With regard to his economic policies, Kennedy, through his vision, competence, and actions, demonstrated the truth of an old adage he liked to quote. During his time in office, a "rising tide" did indeed lift all boats.

Richard Nixon

Economic policy bored Richard Nixon. According to Herbert Stein, his chairman of the Council of Economic Advisers, Nixon grew impatient with the "dull, pedestrian and painful" choices inherent in economics and "yearned for the long bomb."[144] As president, Nixon threw many long bombs, many of which proved harmful to the U.S. economy. During his 1968 campaign, Nixon had opposed many of Johnson's Great Society programs and promised to clean up the "welfare mess" and to check swelling inflation.[145] Yet, as president, however, Nixon spent more on social programs than had any of his predecessors. To aid his re-election campaign, he pressed the Federal Reserve for an overly easy monetary policy. Its compliance ushered in the Great Inflation of the 1970s. Nixon also imposed waves of new regulations that impeded economic growth for a decade.

In January 1969, the month Nixon took office, the unemployment rate stood at 3.4 percent, and the inflation rate was 4.2 percent. Annualized real GDP growth, which was running at 6.5 percent during first quarter of 1969, slowed to 1.1 percent in the second. Alarmed at the rising inflation rate—which Nixon denounced as "the most disguised and least just of all the taxes that can be imposed"—Nixon sought to control it through the Keynesian tools of higher taxes and restrained spending rather than through a tighter monetary policy. On April 12, 1969, he proposed that Congress extend Johnson's 10 percent income surtax and place federal excise taxes on motor vehicles and telephones. Tinkering with his proposals, Congress created the alternative minimum tax and repealed the 7 percent ITC in order to increase taxes on businesses and wealthy households. It also increased the personal exemption and standard deduction in order to remove poorer households from the income tax roll. On December 30, Nixon signed the Tax Reform Act of 1969.

Higher interest rates and repealing the ITC significantly reduced the after-tax return on new business investments, and the resulting decline in business investment caused a recession from December 1969 to November 1970. Real GDP growth slowed to just 0.2 percent in 1970. Fearful that a recession might hurt his re-election, Nixon told advisers that his administration could handle inflation if necessary, but not unemployment. Nixon believed that the recession that had run from April 1960 to February 1961 contributed to his narrow loss of the 1960 presidential election. Consequently, Nixon pressed the newly appointed Federal Reserve chairman, Arthur Burns, to increase the money supply and lower interest rates. "You see to it—no recession," Nixon ordered him.[146]

Burns warned Nixon that excessive U.S. monetary growth since 1966 and booming economies elsewhere had caused the U.S. dollar to become overvalued relative to the French franc, German mark, and Japanese yen. At the same time, the Bretton Woods system of fixed exchange rates was effectively exporting U.S. inflation to other countries. Burns urged that the U.S. devalue the dollar by increasing the official gold price above $35 per ounce. Writing in *Newsweek* and operating behind the scenes, future Nobel Laureate Milton

Friedman urged Nixon instead to allow the dollar to float freely against other currencies. Preoccupied with Vietnam, Nixon declared that he did not "want to be bothered with international monetary matters."[147]

Although foreign policy remained Nixon's primary concern during his presidency, he understood that his administration needed to address some of the domestic concerns he had raised during his 1968 campaign if he was to be elected again in 1972. Shortly after taking office, Nixon announced his proposal to reform welfare. The number of Americans receiving cash payments from the Aid to Dependent Children (ADC) program had more than doubled from 3 million in 1960 to 8.4 million in 1970. Program rules favoring single-parent households were discouraging marriages and encouraging out-of-wedlock births among recipients. Daniel Patrick Moynihan, a Democrat who had advised both Kennedy and Johnson, recommended replacing the ADC program with a negative income tax, which guaranteed a minimum income to all households. Aware of Nixon's interest in pursuing Democratic constituencies, Moynihan argued that the program furnished the president with an opportunity to take on the veneer of a conservative reformer in the mode of nineteenth-century British prime minister Benjamin Disraeli, who had attracted support from recently enfranchised British workers. Moynihan suggested that Nixon might do the same among America's working poor.

Nixon threw his weight behind Moynihan's Family Assistance Plan. The program would have set a minimum income of $1,600 for a family of four plus a food stamp allowance. It also provided for job training and child care. Simultaneously, Nixon proposed increasing welfare payments to the aged, blind, and disabled.[148] Conservative Republicans opposed Nixon's plan because it federalized welfare, contained no work requirements, and increased federal outlays at least during the short term. Liberal Democrats, on the other hand, argued that the guaranteed minimum income that Nixon recommended was too low. The Democratically controlled House of Representatives enacted Nixon's recommendations by a vote of 243 to 155 on April 16, 1970. A coalition of Republicans and liberal Democrats on the Senate Finance Committee killed it later that year. Congress eventually passed a limited guaranteed income program, known as Supplemental Security Income, for the aged, blind, and disabled in 1972.

Nixon won congressional approval for his proposals to expand eligibility for food stamps and free school lunches. He also signed legislation increasing old age, survivor, and disability insurance benefits under Social Security by a combined 69 percent (34 percent after adjusting for inflation) and then locked in these real increases by indexing benefits for inflation beginning in 1975.[149] To pay for these additional benefits in subsequent years, Congress significantly increased the wage base and rate of the payroll tax in 1977 and again in 1983.

In his 1971 State of the Union Address, Nixon declared a war on cancer. At the behest of long-time donor and early mentor Elmer Bobst, chairman of Warner-Lambert (pharmaceutical) Company, and philanthropist Mary Lasker, Nixon won congressional approval for significant additional funds for cancer research. In his 1974 State of the Union Address, picking up where Truman left off, Nixon proposed a National Health Insurance Partnership that would have mandated universal coverage, provided federal subsidies to the self-employed and small businesses seeking to buy private health insurance, and awarded government health insurance to low-income persons not eligible for Medicaid. In his public comments, Nixon reflected on the financial hardships his family endured when tuberculosis struck two of his brothers. He well understood how a catastrophic illness could wipe out a family's savings and jeopardize plans for children's higher education and retirement. Vigorous opposition from the American Medical Association, which was fearful of "socialized medicine," and labor leaders who hoped for an even more generous plan after the 1974 elections doomed Nixon's proposals for universal health insurance coverage.[150]

Nixon had a federal budget surplus of $3.2 billion (equal to 0.3 percent of GDP) for fiscal year 1969. However, real outlays on entitlements rose by an average of 14.7 percent per year from fiscal year 1969 to fiscal year 1975, the fastest growth rate among all post–World War II presidents. Real domestic discretionary outlays also grew by an average of 6.3 percent a year during the same period. This constituted the second fastest growth rate under any administration since World War II. Despite an average decrease of 5.6 percent a year in real defense outlays, Nixon's uncontrolled spending ballooned federal outlays from $183.7 billion (equal to 19.4 percent of GDP) in fiscal year 1969 to $332.3 billion (equal to 21.3 percent of GDP) in fiscal year 1975, creating a budget deficit of $53.2 billion (equal to 3.4 percent of GDP).

While Nixon was gearing up his re-election campaign, annualized real GDP growth was a sluggish 2.3 percent in the second quarter of 1971. By July 1971, the inflation rate edged up to 4.6 percent, and the unemployment rate remained stalled at 6 percent. At the official price of $35, foreign governments held $7 for every $1 of gold in Fort Knox. A crisis began on August 9, 1971, when the British government demanded gold in exchange for $3 billion.[151] Nixon turned to his new Secretary of the Treasury, John Connally—the former Democratic governor of Texas and erstwhile protégé of Lyndon Johnson. More grounded in bravado than in either business or economics and aware of Nixon's penchant for long bombs, Connally suggested the New Economic Program (NEP), replete with numerous gimmicks calculated to attract attention.[152] Mesmerized by Connally's charisma and salesmanship, Nixon announced the NEP on August 15, 1971.

It included (1) a ninety-day wage and price freeze; (2) removal of the federal excise tax on motor vehicles and reinstitution of the 7 percent ITC; (3) closure of the "gold window," effectively ending the gold exchange standard; and (4) a 10 percent surcharge on all imports.[153] Conservatives derided his package both for its substance and its name, which was practically identical to the one Lenin assigned the draconian economic proposals he imposed after the Bolshevik revolution. From a domestic political perspective, the NEP boosted Nixon's approval ratings. Nixon's decision to follow Connally's advice made him the first president to impose wage and price controls during peacetime. His declaration, in defense of his action, that "we are all Keynesians now" astonished both conservatives and liberals. Fixated on his re-election, Nixon had not thought through what would happen once the ninety-day freeze expired.[154] With the deadline of December 13 fast approaching, Council of Economic Advisers Chairman Stein cobbled together Phase II of the plan, a complex system of wage and price controls that allowed the Federal Reserve to run an overly easy monetary policy designed to make the economy look good during the 1972 campaign, delaying the inevitable inflation until after the election.[155]

U.S. allies and trading partners, however, found the "Nixon shock" or "long bomb" profoundly disturbing. The NEP violated numerous international agreements, and undermined the stability of the Bretton Woods system of fixed exchange rates and the progressive liberalization of international trade that had supported global economic growth for two decades. On December 18, Connally pressed finance ministers from Europe and Japan to agree to an 8 percent devaluation of the U.S. dollar by raising the official gold price to $38.[156] Within two years, the system of fixed exchange rates gave way to floating exchange rates.

In Stein's assessment, Nixon's administration also imposed more new regulations on the economy than had any other since FDR's.[157] He signed into law the Occupational Safety and Health Act in 1970, creating the Occupational Safety and Health Administration to regulate safety at workplaces. Two years later, he signed the Consumer Product Safety Act, creating the Consumer Product Safety Commission to develop and enforce safety standards for more than fifteen thousand products not already regulated by other federal agencies.

While he was not by temperament an environmentalist, Nixon understood the salience of environmentalism as a political issue. Making the environment the theme of his 1970 State of the Union Address, he proclaimed that "clean air, clean water, open spaces—these should once again be the birthright of every American."[158] Strategically, Nixon placed himself between what congressional Democrats and environmental groups demanded and what business would accept.[159] Sometimes Nixon appeared to be in a race with Congress to prove which branch of government was more committed to the environment. Nixon won the first round when he established, by executive order, the Environmental Protection Agency (EPA) on December 2, 1970. The two officials he named to head it—William Ruckelshaus and his successor, Russell Train—proved two of the toughest regulators in American history. Both rigorously enforced a series of environmental laws that Congress enacted with Nixon's support, the best known being the Endangered Species Act (which protected the habitat of endangered species from development), the National Environment Policy Act (which required environmental impact statements on all projects involving federal funds), and the Clean Air Amendments Act of 1970 (which mandated a 90 percent reduction of the carbon monoxide from automobiles over five years and authorized the EPA to regulate stationary air pollution sources).[160] While Nixon did attempt to redress serious environmental degradations through these laws, many of the new regulations were hastily designed. Their drafters had not always weighed costs against benefits. Some environmental regulations, for example, mandated specific engineering solutions regardless of their cost or effectiveness in reducing pollution.

The strained relationship that characterized Nixon's relations with Congress toward the end of his administration began when Nixon vetoed the Clean Water Act of 1972. The president had proposed spending $6 billion in grants to state and local governments to upgrade sewage treatment facilities; Congress authorized $24 billion. After Congress overrode Nixon's veto by a vote of 247-to-23 in the House and 52-to-12 in the Senate, the president impounded most funds appropriated in excess of the $6 billion he favored.[161] Thus commenced a prolonged battle between the executive and legislative branches over spending priorities and constitutional prerogatives. In his blatant assertion of budgetary powers no previous president had claimed, Nixon appeared to be triggering a constitutional crisis. Prior presidents had declined, on occasion and with tacit support from key congressional leaders, to spend all appropriated funds on some programs. Nixon, however, upped the ante when he impounded between 17 and 20 percent of all domestic discretionary appropriations between 1969 and 1972.

With Nixon politically weakened by the Watergate scandal, Congress—by a vote of 401 to 6 in the House and 75 to 0 in the Senate—enacted the Budget and Impoundment Control Act of 1974, which, among other things, prevented future presidents from impounding funds without expressed approval from Congress. The act also established the Congressional Budget Office as a counterweight to the Office of Management and Budget.[162] Having begun a battle without the necessary votes to win it, Nixon did more than merely set himself up for failure; he inadvertently reduced the capacity of future presidents to control spending. He was neither the first nor the last president to weaken his office through clumsy and ill-considered attempts to strengthen it.

On January 11, 1973, Nixon introduced Phase III of the NEP. Under Phase III, price controls remained on food, health care, and construction, but other sectors were effectively lifted. Not surprisingly, the artificially suppressed inflation began to skyrocket. On July 13, Nixon announced another thirty-day price freeze, known as Phase IV. After August 12, all prices except food were gradually decontrolled.[163] To relieve high domestic food prices, Nixon embargoed delivery of 50 percent of international grain purchases contracted before June 27, 1973. Although the embargo was lifted in September, it damaged the reputation among international customers of American farmers as dependable suppliers and reduced U.S. agricultural exports for more than a decade.[164] The inflation rate rose to 8.7 percent in 1973, and annualized real GDP growth slowed dramatically from 10.8 percent in the first quarter of the year to a negative 2.1 percent in the third quarter.

In October 1973, when Arab governments embargoed oil exports to the United States because of its support for Israel during the Yom Kippur War, Nixon took a number of actions to reduce U.S. oil consumption to meet the immediate crisis. Nixon proposed a fifty-mile-per-hour national speed limit, suspension of industrial conversions from coal to oil (previously undertaken to meet environmental regulations), reduced airline flights, and accelerated the licensing of nuclear plants. He also announced Project Independence, a plan to achieve energy self-sufficiency by 1980. On November 25, 1973, Nixon announced additional measures including forbidding gasoline sales on Sunday and ornamental lighting except during Christmas.[165]

According to Nixon's first energy policy director, John Love, the administration's strategy was "to allocate the reduced quantities of gasoline to the retail level and force a reduction in demand by permitting customers to wait in lines . . . at stations."[166] These gas lines took an immediate toll on Nixon's popularity. Together, adverse public reaction to the unfolding Watergate scandal, gas shortages, and higher gas prices drove Nixon's Gallup Poll approval rating down to 27 percent.[167] During the embargo, the Organization of the Petroleum Exporting Countries (OPEC) raised its benchmark price from $4 per

barrel ($15.51 in 2000 dollars) to $12 ($46.54 in 2000 dollars). Inflation dur-
ing the Johnson and Nixon years had depreciated the value of the dollars
OPEC producers received for their exports by 37 percent, and OPEC producers now exploited supply disruptions to recoup these losses and increase
their real incomes.

Largely because of Nixon's cynical manipulation of the levers of economic
policy to create the impression that the economy was doing better than it
actually was when he sought re-election (maintaining the appearance of low
inflation and high prosperity), the recession that ran from November 1973 to
March 1975 was the worst economic downturn the nation suffered since
World War II. A new term, "stagflation" (concurrent inflation and recession)
entered the language. In April 1974, OPEC lifted its embargo. The supply
problem receded, but higher oil prices still burdened the U.S. economy.[168]
Inflation soared to 12.3 percent. The unemployment rate, which was 5.5 percent when Nixon left office in August 1974, climbed to a peak of 9.0 percent
in May 1975. Ironically, all Nixon's tampering with the economy left him
without the one resource he needed in order to remain in office in the wake of
the Watergate revelations—sustained public support.

Jimmy Carter

The Great Inflation that Lyndon Johnson had ignited and Richard Nixon
had stoked grew into a roaring fire during Jimmy Carter's presidency. When
Carter assumed office, he believed the two major problems confronting the
United States were inadequate energy supplies and a stagnant economy.
While he won congressional approval for two major energy laws, the contradictions inherent in his proposals and the compromises he made to secure
their passage made for an incoherent and economically irrational energy policy. The economic stimulus package, which he also saw enacted, proved both
unnecessary and ineffective.

Inflation, however, became Carter's undoing both economically and politically. Although Milton Friedman's assertion that "inflation is always and

everywhere a monetary phenomenon" is almost universally accepted today, what caused inflation was still disputed during the 1970s. Over the medium and long term, monetary policy determines price level, while fiscal and regulatory policies affect the real economic growth. To control inflation, however, Carter rejected monetary restraint in favor of the Keynesian tools of federal spending restraint, higher federal taxes, and voluntary wage and price guidelines. Fearing that higher interest rates would cause a recession, Carter proved unwilling to support a stringent monetary policy long enough to allow the Federal Reserve to squeeze out inflation and dampen inflationary expectations. As a result, the gains made against inflation during the Ford administration were reversed. Inflation rose from 5.8 percent in 1976 (Ford's last year in office) to 12.5 percent in 1980, the year Carter retired from the presidency.

In early 1977, Carter proposed an economic stimulus package consisting of a $50 tax rebate, $900 million in corporate tax reductions, and additional spending on public works. After securing the reluctant support of Democratic leaders, Carter abruptly withdrew his rebate proposal on April 14, 1977, without congressional consultation.[169] Congress eventually did enact a $20 billion stimulus package without the tax rebate, but Carter's sudden and unexplained reversal in strategy alienated many Democrats. Carter then proposed a tax reform package—eliminating the partial exclusion for capital gains and various business deductions, and replacing the personal exemption with a tax credit—in late 1977.[170] Congress rejected virtually all of his proposals and instead increased the capital gains exclusion in 1978.[171]

Carter moved aggressively on energy policy in 1977. During the brutal winter of 1976–1977, an artificial shortage of natural gas caused by federal price controls had forced schools and factories in many states to close.[172] Carter directed his energy adviser, James Schlesinger, to develop a comprehensive energy plan for increasing domestic production and decreasing imports. In a televised address on April 18, 1977, Carter proclaimed this approach to be "the moral equivalent of war."[173] Carter thought it unconscionable that oil and natural gas companies made additional profits from selling existing supplies as prices rose. Rather than deregulate the prices of all domestic supplies of oil and natural gas, Carter proposed a cumbersome regulatory structure to maintain price controls on old production, while deregulating prices on new production. Carter feared that higher energy prices would sap consumer spending and drive the U.S. economy back into a recession. He might have reconciled his energy and social equity goals by compensating consumers through an across-the-board income tax reduction and higher entitlement payments to low-income households. But believing that increasing federal budget deficits caused inflation, Carter ruled out this option.

Carter favored new regulations mandating specific energy-saving technologies, regardless of their costs and benefits, rather than relying on higher prices to entice firms to develop inexpensive means of reducing energy consumption. To help Carter enact his energy proposals, Speaker Tip O'Neill assembled a special House committee to mark it up. The House passed Carter's plan largely intact on August 5, 1977.[174] The Senate gutted its key provisions and, despite the president's personal intervention, pared back regulatory recommendations, deregulated interstate natural gas prices, and scaled back Carter's tax recommendations.[175]

On July 5, 1979, Carter unexpectedly cancelled a planned television address on energy policy and spent the next several days conferring with business, labor, government, academic, and religious leaders at Camp David (see chapter 4). When he emerged from his consultations, Carter, in his long-awaited address, presented a number of specific energy recommendations. They included: (1) cutting oil imports by one-half by 1990; (2) deregulating domestic oil prices; (3) imposing a 60 percent "windfall profits" tax on oil companies; (4) establishing an Energy Security Corporation to subsidize research into synthetic fuels; (5) creating an Energy Mobilization Board to override federal, state, and local environmental and land use laws that might block energy development; and (6) authorizing gasoline rationing. By May 1980, Congress approved Carter's recommendations on domestic oil price deregulation, windfall profits, and the Energy Security Corporation, and it authorized $88 billion in subsidies for synthetic fuels over ten years.[176]

In 1978, polls found that inflation had replaced unemployment as the public's major concern. When Arthur Burns's term as Federal Reserve chairman expired on January 31, 1978, instead of appointing a prominent monetary economist dedicated to ending inflation to this post, Carter settled upon former Textron Chairman and Chief Executive Officer G. William Miller. The new chairman did not understand monetary economics and lacked the stature in the financial community to have credibility during a crisis. Rather than restrain monetary growth, the Federal Reserve continued to maintain an accommodative policy to prevent a recession and rising unemployment.

As inflation surged, the foreign exchange value of the U.S. dollar declined rapidly. In January 1978, Secretary of the Treasury Michael Blumenthal tried to stabilize the dollar by using $25 billion in foreign currency to buy dollars.[177] This helped, but only temporarily. On April 11, 1978, at Blumenthal's urging, Carter proposed limiting federal pay raises to 5.5 percent as an anti-inflation measure—a step that was both poorly received and totally ineffective. Inflation rose to 9.0 percent in 1978. In a televised address on October 24, Carter announced Phase II of his anti-inflation program: voluntary guidelines limiting wage increases to 7 percent and limiting the federal budget deficit to no more than $30 billion in fiscal year 1979. He claimed these measures would limit inflation to 6.5 percent in 1979.[178]

To Carter's dismay, inflation accelerated during the first half of 1979. As a part of his cabinet reshuffle, Carter moved Chairman Miller from the Federal Reserve to the Treasury Department in July 1979. Carter then elevated the highly respected president of the Federal Reserve Bank of New York, Paul Volcker, to chairman. Volcker's selection won wide praise on Capitol Hill, on Wall Street, and in foreign capitals. No stranger to monetary economics, Volcker understood that central banks can eliminate inflation through their capacity to control the money supply. He was willing to increase interest rates and endure temporarily higher unemployment in order to break inflation, and had the fortitude to withstand pressure to ease monetary policy prematurely, before inflationary expectations subsided.

While attending International Monetary Fund (IMF) and World Bank annual meetings in Belgrade in October 1979, Volcker grew fearful that the foreign exchange value of the dollar was about to collapse. He abruptly returned and convened an emergency meeting of the Open Market Committee of the Federal Reserve. Afterward, Volcker announced that the Federal Reserve would increase the discount rate and adopt new procedures to target the growth of the money supply rather than interest rates.[179] In November 1979, economic adviser Alfred E. Kahn told Carter, "our present anti-inflation program has failed." Inflation accelerated to 13.3 percent during 1979. Yet the only policy option that Kahn offered Carter was imposing credit controls.[180]

In January 1980, the annualized inflation rate rose to 18 percent. Both interest rates and the unemployment rate were rising. A recession began in January and remained through July. On March 14, Carter announced yet another plan: (1) balancing the federal budget by fiscal year 1981, (2) increasing the federal gas tax by ten cents per gallon, and (3) imposing emergency controls on loans to consumers. Carter's promise to balance the budget was hollow in that he did not itemize any cuts but pledged not to reduce any entitlements. Congress immediately rejected the gas tax hike.[181] After a brief drop in inflation and interest rates in the second quarter, inflation, unemployment, and interest rates were headed up again in the third quarter. In 1980, the annualized inflation rate was 12.5 percent.

While most of what Carter attempted with regard to the economy failed, he did achieve some modest successes. At Kahn's urging, Carter came out in favor of price and product deregulation in a number of industries that Franklin Delano Roosevelt had brought under federal regulation during the New Deal. With Carter's support, Congress enacted the Airline Deregulation Act (October 24, 1978), the Staggers Rail Act (October 14, 1980), and the Motor Carrier Act of 1980. All were intended to increase competition in the transportation sector.[182] On March 31, 1980, Carter signed the Depository Institutions Deregulation and Monetary Control Act, which phased out the deposit interest rate regulations on banks and thrift institutions that FDR had imposed. Carter's deregulation policies stand as the only measures he put in place regarding the economy that proved beneficial over time.

Ronald Reagan

Ronald Reagan was the most economically successful president in the last third of the twentieth century. Unlike his four predecessors, Reagan was willing to endure the short-term pain of a monetary-induced recession in order to quell inflation. He reduced marginal income tax rates and expanded upon the deregulation initiative Carter began. Reagan looked upon these measures as ways to release the creative and entrepreneurial impulses of the American people, which had been blocked from achieving their full potential by the disincentives of high taxes and excessive regulations. He launched important international initiatives—the Free Trade Agreement with Canada and the Uruguay Round of multilateral negotiations—that would deeply integrate the United States into a global economy over the next two decades. In all, Reagan's politics helped produce an eight-year expansion of the American economy and paved the way for an unprecedented eighteen years of growth.

Reagan's economic policies were shaped, at least in part, by what he had studied in school. He majored in economics at Eureka College before Keynesian economics became popular among academics, and he left familiar with the foundations of neoclassical theory. During his years in Hollywood, Reagan, drawing on his own experience, concluded that high taxes discouraged work and that lower taxes carried with them incentives for greater productivity. When he ran for president in 1980, Reagan proposed cutting individual income tax rates by 30 percent over three years and accelerating tax depreciation schedules for business investment. During the summer of 1981, Congress modified Reagan's proposal by cutting individual income tax rates by 25 percent over four years. Among other things, it also reduced the maximum capital gains tax rate to 20 percent, expanded tax deductions for retirement savings plans, and indexed tax brackets for inflation. It also substantially reduced windfall profits taxes. Reagan signed the Economic Recovery Tax Act (ERTA) into law on August 13, 1981.

In 1982 and 1984, Congress rescinded some of ERTA's provisions relating to business but left most of its other provisions intact. While Reagan had proposed making the first 10 percent rate cut retroactive to January 1, 1981, ERTA's first 5 percent rate cut took effect on October 1, 1981. Thus, the effective rate cut for 1981 was only 1.25 percent. Since indexation did not become effective until 1985, bracket creep prevented individual taxpayers from receiving a real income tax reduction until January 1, 1983, about the time economic expansion began.

In 1984, Reagan instructed Secretary of the Treasury Donald Regan to prepare a comprehensive tax reform package that, unlike ERTA, would be simple and revenue neutral (i.e., deep rate reductions would be offset by reductions in tax deductions and credits). The resulting Tax Reform Act of 1986 slashed the maximum individual income tax rate from 50 percent to 28 percent and the maximum corporate income tax rate from 46 percent to 35 percent.

The Reagan administration's approach to inflation also broke with recent precedent. To combat the recession of the first half of 1980, Carter's last year in office, the Federal Reserve accelerated the growth of the money supply to lower interest rates—but abruptly reversed course by decelerating the growth of the money supply and raising interest rates in September 1980. Monetary policy was substantially tightened in May 1981 and again in February 1982 even though a recession had begun in August 1981. Unlike Johnson, Nixon, Ford, and Carter, who pressed Federal Reserve chairmen for accommodative policies, Reagan gave Volcker a free hand. He was willing to endure the recession in order to end the Great Inflation even though he knew that unemployment would rise and that his opinion ratings would drop. In a February 1982 press conference, Reagan proclaimed, "I want to make clear today that neither this administration nor the Federal Reserve will allow a return to the fiscal and monetary policies of the past that have created the current conditions. . . . I have confidence in the announced policies of the Federal Reserve Board. . . . The administration will always support the political independence of the Federal Reserve Board." Inflation, which had been 12.5 percent in 1980, fell to 8.9 percent in 1981 and 3.8 percent in 1982. Interest rates also declined.

Politically, Reagan paid a steep price for taking this stand. His party lost twenty-six seats in the House of Representatives in the 1982 elections. Commentators speculated about another failed presidency and predicted the end of "Reaganonomics." They did not know it at the time, but that very month, the United States would embark on a peacetime boom without historical precedent. As real GDP growth surged to 7.2 percent in 1984, unemployment fell quickly from a peak of 10.8 percent in December 1982 to 7.3 percent two years later, and it continued falling. "They aren't calling it Reaganomics anymore," Reagan proclaimed.[183]

Despite occasional lapses, Reagan also boldly pushed for deeper integration of the United States with the world economy and against protectionist policies. This approach came to be known as "globalization." In 1982, the administration began pushing the other signatories of GATT to launch multilateral trade talks with the broader goals of (1) removing non-tariff trade barriers, (2) substantially reducing tariffs on agricultural goods and limiting agricultural subsidies, (3) creating a framework for liberalizing trade in services, (4) protecting intellectual property rights, and (5) establishing a settlement mechanism for trade disputes. Many trading partners mistakenly feared that the United States might turn toward protectionism without a new round of talks; consequently, the United States and 115 other countries launched the Uruguay Round in Punta del Este on September 20, 1986. Although negotiations continued for seven years and spanned two other administrations, Reagan's priorities continued to set the agenda for the most comprehensive trade liberalization pact ever signed—the Uruguay Round Agreements—and the largest tax cut in world history.

Reagan also pursued bilateral and regional trade liberalization. He first experimented with a limited Free Trade Agreement (FTA) with Israel in 1984 and then negotiated a comprehensive Free Trade Agreement with Canada in 1987. The Canada FTA became the precedent for negotiating FTAs with Mexico, Chile, Singapore, Australia, five Central American republics, the Dominican Republic, Colombia, Peru, Panama, and South Korea in subsequent administrations.

During his presidency and afterward, many criticized Reagan's "tolerance," to use Arthur M. Schlesinger's word, of large federal budget deficits and an increased federal debt. While Reagan had promised to balance the budget in his 1980 campaign, he had also stated that if forced to choose between increased defense spending and deficits, he would accept deficits in order to fund a military build-up. Critics predicted that large budget deficits would cause interest rates to rise and crowd out private investment, rendering economic expansion unsustainable. Contrary to this conventional wisdom of the era, interest rates fell dramatically as inflation expectations subsided in spite of high budget deficits. The liberalization of controls on cross-border investments—known as "capital controls"—prevented crowding-out.

Before 1973, capital controls had largely prevented individuals and firms in one country from making portfolio investments in other countries, limiting the market for Treasury debt securities largely to U.S. savers. By 1980, however, capital liberalization opened this market to savers around the world. At the same time, ERTA had dramatically increased the after-tax return on investments in America relative to investments in other countries. Consequently, foreign savings flooded into U.S. financial markets. The annual net inflow of foreign investment in U.S. assets increased from $62 billion (equal to 2.2 percent of GDP) in 1980 to $247 billion (equal to 4.8 percent of GDP) in 1988.

Through empirical studies, economists have found that temporary increases in budget deficits associated with recessions or wars do not have significant effects on interest rates, while increases in budget deficits associated with structural imbalances between outlays and receipts modestly increase real long-term interest rates. (Notionally, economists divide interest rates into three components: (1) the real interest rate that reflects underlying supply and demand factors in credit markets, (2) the inflation premium that reflects inflationary expectations, and (3) the risk premium that is specific to a particular bond or loan.) An empirical study published in 2003 by the Federal Reserve found that a permanent increase in federal budget deficits equal to 1 percent of GDP boosted real long-term interest rates by about 0.25 percent.[184] Reagan's budget deficits did not retard the expansion that began in November 1982 through higher interest rates, as many critics had predicted, for two reasons. First, the falling inflation rate gradually reduced the inflation premium, partially offsetting any increase in real interest rates due to budget deficits. Second, a large part of the increase in budget deficits during Reagan's first term was associated with the recession, and the structural budget deficit (which affects real long-term interest rates) fell during his second term. The budget deficit peaked in fiscal year 1983 at $207.8 billion (6.0 percent of GDP) and then gradually fell to $152.6 billion (2.8 percent of GDP) in fiscal year 1989. Reagan's last budget deficit was only slightly above the average—1.6 percent of GDP—of all budget deficits since World War II.

Federal debt rose from $789 billion (25.8 percent of GDP) on September 30, 1981, to $2.191 trillion (40.6 percent of GDP) on September 30, 1989.

However, federal debt as a percent of GDP at the end of Reagan's presidency remained well below its peak of 106.2 percent at the end of World War II. While not fully understood during Reagan's presidency, it is now clear that his military build-up was a form of economic warfare on the Soviet Union. Reagan viewed this surge of federal spending as akin to the spike in defense outlays that had occurred during the Civil War and both World Wars, and further that defense outlays could be safely reduced after the Cold War was won. Indeed, the fall of the Soviet Union allowed his successors George H. W. Bush and Bill Clinton to significantly reduce defense outlays and bring the federal budget back into balance.

Reagan's policies contributed to an enormous economic boom. Real GDP grew by an average 3.6 percent a year from 1981 to 1988, and the U.S. economy produced 16 million new jobs. When he left office, the unemployment rate was 5.4 percent. All income groups shared in the overall prosperity.[185] Reagan's policies found many imitators throughout the world. In the decades since he left office, global competition helped cause many countries to slash individual and corporate tax rates.

Many critics have blamed Reagan's tax policy for the growth in the income disparity between the poor and the well-to-do during his time in office. However, recent economic research suggests that tax policy had little to do with this trend. In a 2007 research report for the Joint Economic Committee, Robert P. O'Quinn found that income inequality had already begun to increase in the mid-1970s and that it continued to increase under subsequent administrations that increased taxes (George H. W. Bush and Bill Clinton) and under an administration that lowered them (George W. Bush).[186] In an empirical study published in 2003, David H. Autor, Frank Levy, and Richard J. Murnane found that skill-biased technological change was the major cause of this trend toward greater income inequality in the United States over the last quarter century.[187] As the real cost of acquiring information technology has plummeted, businesses have substituted computers and computer-driven machinery for workers performing routine tasks. Simultaneously, computerization enhances the marginal productivity of highly skilled, college-educated workers performing nonroutine tasks, increasing the demand for such labor relative to other types of labor, and, as a result, driving up their compensation relative to other workers. In 2007, economists at the IMF found that skill-biased technologically is increasing income inequality in many economies around the world, including China and India.[188] Over time, analysts came to realize that the most effective way to reduce disparities in income between high and low earners in a changing economy that places a premium on the acquisition of skills was through improved education and training. It was therefore no accident that each of his three immediate successors awarded education a high priority. Each declared his attention to be an "education president."

Bill Clinton

When Bill Clinton ran for president in 1992, he promised to "focus on the economy like a laser beam."[189] In office, he compiled a record in this area that was above average but hardly great. Although the recession that began in July 1990 ended in March 1991, President George H. W. Bush did not benefit politically from the recovery. The reasons include Bush's incompetence when it came to public relations; his disdain for the "vision thing"; his casual breaking of his 1988 "no new taxes" pledge; and his perceived preoccupation with international affairs. Ironically, the very success that Reagan and Bush had achieved in overseeing the peaceful dissolution of the Soviet empire enabled an Arkansas governor with virtually no experience in defense and international affairs to emerge as a serious presidential candidate.

For the Democratic Party, which had repeatedly lost presidential elections after nominating candidates who promised a return to Great Society liberalism, Clinton, through his reputation as a centrist and as an innovator at the state level, seemed the perfect choice. A southerner, Clinton had the capacity to return to the Democratic column states in his region that had increasingly trended Republican. Clinton appealed to self-proclaimed "Reagan Democrats" by promising to pay attention to the concerns of those who "work hard and play by the rules."[190] He proposed shedding the party of its reputation for high taxation and spending and softness on crime.

If Clinton needed any reminding of the major issue on voters' minds, a sign a campaign worker posted in his headquarters served that purpose: "It's the economy, stupid." Clinton promised to reduce the federal budget deficit, cut taxes for middle-income households, create more jobs, increase U.S. competitiveness through education and training, and invest in modernizing America's physical infrastructure. He explicitly ruled out raising taxes on the middle class to pay for his proposed programs. In a three-way race against the sitting president and a third-party candidate running as a deficit hawk—businessman Ross Perot—Clinton won with 43 percent of the popular vote and an Electoral College victory of 370 to Bush's 168.

Clinton's most significant achievement was balancing the federal budget. When Clinton took office during fiscal year 1993, the deficit stood at $255.0 billion (equal to 3.9 percent of GDP). When he left office in fiscal year 2001, the budget had a surplus of $128.2 billion (equal to 1.3 percent of GDP). Many factors contributed to this turnaround. First, Clinton assembled the most market-oriented economic team since Kennedy's. It included former Chairman of the Senate Finance Committee Lloyd Bentsen, who became Clinton's first secretary of the treasury; former House Budget Committee Chairman Leon Panetta, who became director of the Office of Management and Budget and later chief of staff to the president; and former Goldman-Sachs executive Robert Rubin, who became the chairman of the Council on Economic Policy and replaced Bentsen as Secretary of the Treasury.

These advisers, along with Federal Reserve Chairman Alan Greenspan, pressed Clinton to make passage of a "credible deficit reduction plan" his highest priority during his first year in office.[191] In 1993, financial markets expected that large budget deficits would continue indefinitely into the future. This expectation kept real long-term interest rates higher than necessary. Clinton's team reasoned that a credible deficit reduction plan would lower long-term interest rates. By reducing financing costs, lower long-term interest rates would encourage households to purchase homes and invest in the stock market, and stimulate businesses to invest in productive structures, equipment, and software.

On February 17, 1993, Clinton laid out his deficit reduction plan before Congress. Clinton had to use all of his considerable political gifts and persuasive powers to move his proposals through a Democratic Congress. The House passed the Omnibus Budget Reconciliation Act of 1993 (OBRA 1993) by one vote.[192] Vice President Al Gore cast the tie-breaking vote in its favor in the Senate. Not a single Republican voted for Clinton's program in either the Senate or the House primarily because of its tax-raising provisions and the virtual exclusion of the minority party from the negotiations. Clinton's package (1) increased the maximum individual income tax rate from 31 to 39.6 percent, (2) hiked the maximum corporate income tax rate from 34 to 35 percent, (3) repealed the earnings cap on the Medicare portion of federal payroll taxes, (4) jumped the taxable portion of Social Security benefits, (5) increased the gas tax by 4.3 cents per gallon, and (6) limited tax deductions for higher-income households. Upon Clinton's recommendation, Congress used some of the additional revenues to expand the Earned Income Tax Credit entitlement program, initially a Reagan idea, for lower-income workers.

Almost all of the spending reductions that Clinton and the Democratic Congress made during his first two years in office came through defense cuts. Real outlays for defense fell by an average of 5.0 percent a year, and real outlays for domestic discretionary programs and entitlements rose by an average of 1.9 percent a year and 3.0 percent a year, respectively. By fiscal year 1995, the federal budget deficit had fallen, but only to $164.0 billion (equal to 2.2 percent of GDP). Although some GOP leaders had predicted that OBRA 1993's passage would plunge the country into recession, the economic recovery that had begun in March 1991 continued.

In his first two years in office, Clinton won congressional approval for Reagan-inspired trade liberalizations. Reagan had proposed the concept that became the North American Free Trade Agreement (NAFTA) when he announced his candidacy for president in late 1979. Before leaving office, President George H. W. Bush and his Canadian and Mexican counterparts signed NAFTA and submitted it to their respective legislatures for ratification. Clinton, perhaps fearful of antagonizing organized labor, had been ambivalent about NAFTA during his campaign. As president, he embraced it. After negotiating two side agreements to the treaty, one on the environment and the other on labor standards, Clinton sought congressional approval for NAFTA. Although a majority of House Democrats opposed NAFTA (102 to 156), NAFTA passed the House with a 234-to-200 vote on November 17, 1993, because of strong Republican support (132 to 43). The Senate approved it by a 73-to-26 vote two days later.

Representative Mickey Cantor subsequently completed the multilateral trade liberalization negotiations Reagan had commenced in 1986. Threats of Senate filibusters delayed final ratification of the Uruguay Round Agreements (URA) until after the 1994 elections. The lame-duck Congress approved URA by a vote of 288 to 146 in the House and 68 to 32 in the Senate. This vote was the high-water mark for international trade and investment liberalization during the Clinton administration.

In December 1994, Clinton convened the first Summit of the Americas in Miami. Thirty-four countries sent representatives. The leaders pledged to begin negotiations to create a Free Trade Area of the Americas pact, based on NAFTA, by 2002. The leaders of the United States, Canada, and Mexico also pledged to begin negotiations to expand NAFTA to include Chile. In the absence of presidential Trade Promotion Authority (TPA), which had lapsed in April 1994 and remained mired in political deadlock, both of these negotiations floundered. With the United States out of action, Canada and Mexico negotiated separate bilateral FTAs with Chile. After George W. Bush secured TPA, the United States and Chile finally signed a Free Trade Agreement on September 3, 2003.

Whatever goodwill Clinton had earned with congressional Republicans, business leaders, and the public through his skillful handling of trade liberalization evaporated during his ill-fated attempt to enact universal health insurance. Clinton had delegated this issue to First Lady Hillary Rodham Clinton. Largely in secret, she and a team of advisers devised a costly, complex, and excessively bureaucratic program that failed to gain public support. It languished in Congress after prolonged and strident debates. Partly because of the manner in which the Clintons approached the health care issue, the political landscape in Washington changed dramatically after the 1994 election, when the Republicans won control of both houses of Congress for the first time in forty years.

Egged on by outside supporters and congressional backbenchers, who believed the Republicans had a mandate to slash government spending, House Speaker Newt Gingrich and Senate Majority Leader Robert Dole pushed through a budget reconciliation plan of their own. As Clinton had during the health care debacle, the Republicans overreached by pressing ahead without building the necessary public support. Clinton's successive vetoes of Republican budgets produced two government shutdowns of nonessential services from November 14 to November 19, 1995, and from December 16, 1995, to January 6, 1996. In an attempt to appear reasonable while galvanizing his own base of supporters, Clinton maintained that he would sign any reasonable budget, even one that included tax cuts, providing that it contained no major cuts in spending on education, the environment, Social Security, and Medicare. He mentioned these four program areas often enough to have made them his mantra. Clinton's masterful use of the bully pulpit (which he employed to present the Republican Congress as radical and callous), Republican blunders, the public empathy, and the eloquence Clinton displayed in the aftermath of the Oklahoma City bombing helped reverse his political fortunes. His approval ratings rose while those of Congress fell.

Counting on the threat of a Treasury debt default to force Clinton to sign the Republicans' reconciliation bill, Gingrich severely underestimated the ability of the Treasury to pay interest for an extended time by manipulating the Exchange Stabilization Fund and various trust funds. Moreover, Gingrich committed a major public relations faux pas of his own that made him and his party appear vindictive and petty. After he returned to Washington from the funeral of assassinated Israeli leader Yitzhak Rabin, Gingrich complained about having to exit from the rear of Air Force One, while Clinton and his party had left from the front. Democrats and the media castigated him a "crybaby."[193] Clinton and the Republicans agreed to a continuing resolution that froze most discretionary spending for the rest of the fiscal year. While Clinton clearly won this political battle, the resulting budget stalemate produced a significant but largely ignored policy victory for congressional Republicans. Real outlays for domestic discretionary programs fell by an average of 0.6 percent a year over the next three fiscal years.

In the area of welfare reform, Clinton also scored a public relations victory, but conceded another policy win to the Republicans. During the 1992 campaign, Clinton promised to "end welfare as we know it."[194] During his first two years in office, Clinton had experimented with waivers of federal regulations to allow states to experiment with various reforms of the Aid to Families with Dependent Children (AFDC) entitlement program, which FDR had established under the Social Security Act. In the "Contract with America" unfurled during the 1994 Congressional elections, Republican candidates for the House pledged to support legislation that sought to reduce welfare outlays and discourage out-of-wedlock births. The Republican Congress subsequently passed, and Clinton twice vetoed, bills that reformed welfare along these lines.

Unlike the budget fight the previous winter, in which Clinton won the public relations battle, this time, Republicans enjoyed considerable public support for their welfare reform proposals. On August 22, in the midst of his re-election campaign, Clinton reversed himself and signed the Personal Responsibility and Work Opportunity Reconciliation Act of 1996, which abolished two entitlements, AFDC and the Job Opportunities and Basic Skills Training program, and replaced them with a block grant, known as Temporary Assistance to Needy Families, to the states. The act also imposed minimum work and other requirements on beneficiaries and limited lifetime benefits to sixty months.

In taking this step, Clinton demonstrated his mastery of triangulation—holding one's electoral base intact while embracing, in part, policies associated with the opposing political party. Clinton's standing as a centrist was re-established when three officials in his administration, who were associated with the liberal wing of the Democratic Party, resigned in protest over Clinton's agreeing to a maximum eligibility for welfare of five years. Senator Daniel Patrick Moynihan—who had advised Nixon on welfare policy and once denounced a system in which the government, after promising to solve the poverty problem, added millions to the ranks of the underclass—opposed the bill. He warned of children joining the ranks of the homeless, "trying to get a little warmth by sleeping on subway grates."[195] Just as Republican predictions about Clinton's tax hikes throwing the economy into recession never came to pass, Democratic warnings of welfare reform's imminent failure proved equally alarmist. Ten years after the bill's passage, Clinton noted with pride that welfare rolls had plummeted from 12.2 million in 1996 to 4.5 million in 2006, and that 60 percent of single heads of households, once on welfare, had found work.[196]

After his re-election, Clinton approved most of the Republican-sponsored tax reduction measures that he had vetoed eighteen months earlier. The Taxpayer Relief Act of 1997 reduced the maximum tax rate on capital gains from 28 to 20 percent, instituted a $500 per child tax credit for middle-income families, and increased the estate tax exemption to $1 million. Despite these tax reductions, spending restraint and growing tax revenues from a booming economy moved the federal budget into surplus for the first time since fiscal year 1969. In fiscal year 1998, the federal government ran a surplus of $69.3 billion (equal to 0.8 percent of GDP).

Once the federal budget moved into surplus, the fiscal restraint that both Clinton and Congress had demonstrated began to wither. Without a deficit, policy makers felt less able to resist constituent demands for lower taxes and for increased spending. To block additional tax reductions, Clinton devised a brilliant public relations gambit. In his 1998 State of the Union Address, delivered at the very moment the Monica Lewinsky scandal was breaking, Clinton challenged Congress to "save Social Security first." In essence, he proposed that the budget surpluses should accumulate until a bipartisan consensus emerged to restructure Social Security and Medicare. To the extent that it achieved Clinton's overall objective of blocking tax reductions, the gambit worked. However, Clinton never presented a plan to rework Social Security or Medicare. Nor did he seriously sit down with congressional Republicans to bring about the very bipartisan consensus he spoke of.

Alan Greenspan, in his memoirs, records that Clinton aides told him that the president never intended to pursue Social Security or Medicare reform. By failing to do so, Clinton forfeited his chance to achieve presidential greatness. The symbolism, let alone the reality, of a Democratic president enacting major structural changes in programs that Franklin Delano Roosevelt and Lyndon Johnson signed into law would have been the domestic equivalent of Nixon's casting aside a pillar of American foreign policy—long sacrosanct to conservatives—when he visited the People's Republic of China. Had he pressed the case, Clinton might also have been able to draw upon the bipartisan cooperation through which he had balanced the budget and reformed welfare to transform American educational enterprise as a means of enhancing U.S. competitiveness in an increasingly global economy.

Instead, during his last two years in office, Clinton was forced to use his considerable political skills to fend off Republican attempts to impeach and remove him from office. Future historians may well record that he stayed away from entitlement and education reform in order to keep liberal Democrats at his side as he struggled to remain in office throughout the Monica Lewinsky episode.

As Clinton increasingly came to depend on his restless liberal base, which never warmed to his free trade and budgetary policies, he began to take the concerns of environmental and labor organizations into greater account in subsequent trade negotiations. As a result, he failed to achieve one of his major goals, a new round of multilateral trade negotiations during the World Trade Organization (WTO) Ministerial Conference in Seattle in 1999. Clinton's instructions to his trade representative, Charlene Barshefsky—to insist on the inclusion of environmental and labor standards and the exclusion of any serious reduction in agricultural subsidies—provided trade ministers from developing countries with little incentive to go along with a new round. Had he succeeded, Clinton, like his role model, John F. Kennedy, would have a trade round named for him. Had Clinton not allowed his personal peccadilloes to intrude upon his presidency, he might have retained the political independence necessary to become one of the country's few transformational presidents. While he achieved many successes in office, including an average real GDP growth rate of 3.6 percent a year, Clinton was not that kind of president.

6

PRESERVING AND
EXTENDING LIBERTY

*T*his chapter focuses on how well the nation's presidents advanced the principal mission of the country they led. As Margaret Thatcher said about the United States, "No other nation has been built upon an idea—the idea of liberty." Preserving the liberty of their fellow citizens, extending liberty to people who had historically been denied it, and providing hope to people elsewhere in the world who yearn for it are among the president's responsibilities. The good news is that most presidents performed this function well. The bad news is that too many presidents who traditionally rank near the top in presidential ratings surveys came up short in this most important area.

How ought "liberty" be defined? For the purposes of this work, the term "liberty" connotes the protection and advancement of freedoms that the nation's framers proclaimed to be the rights of *all* Americans and assigned government the task of securing. Presidents will be assessed in the pages that follow, not solely according to contemporary attitudes about which policies proved correct over time and which proved wrong, but also in relation to the continuum of prevailing public opinion in their times.

For example, Franklin Delano Roosevelt's decision to order the internment of Japanese American citizens and permanent residents during World War II is today universally condemned across the broad spectrum of American political opinion. While Roosevelt's action enjoyed wide popular support at the time he took it, it also aroused opposition in important—if not sufficiently numerous— quarters. FBI Director J. Edgar Hoover, for instance, opposed Roosevelt's action—thinking it unfair and unwarranted—and made his views clear. Had FDR wanted to ignore public and political pressures to sign this order, he could well have done so without suffering major political ramifications. Similarly, going back further in time, Woodrow Wilson's acquiescence to demands of his cabinet that the federal government introduce racial segregation into its hiring and management procedures enjoyed far greater support in 1913 than it would today. Yet the criticism Wilson received from within his progressive governing coalition when he acted on those requests suggests that he, too, could just as easily have dismissed the proposal out of hand and suffered few, if any, lasting political consequences.

Presidents will *not* be evaluated in this chapter according to how they handled several modern-day social issues around which no consensus has yet formed across the political spectrum. Prior to the Civil War, people held diverging views about the nature and the morality of slavery and whether it should be allowed to spread. It took a civil war to produce a consensus about it, although not necessarily one to which all sides subscribed voluntarily. Public opinion today remains similarly divided about a host of issues that have come to the fore in recent decades: abortion, same-sex marriage, gun control, stem cell research, the death penalty, drug legalization, and many more. In each instance, each side's assertion of its rights under the Constitution to certain liberties has been countered by its opposition's insistence that granting them would undermine others' rights. The lack of consensus on these issues and the relatively few presidents who have been in office since these issues have been seriously debated at the national level make meaningful comparisons exceedingly difficult to make as of this writing.

In terms of advancing liberty, fourteen presidents compiled exemplary records, while eight came up wanting. Although presidential performance has not been bad overall, one hopes that future presidents will improve upon it.

**THREE PRESIDENTS
RECEIVE A SCORE OF 5:**

Abraham Lincoln

Ulysses S. Grant

Lyndon B. Johnson

**ELEVEN PRESIDENTS
RECEIVE A SCORE OF 4:**

George Washington

James Madison

Zachary Taylor

Benjamin Harrison

Warren G. Harding

Calvin Coolidge

Franklin D. Roosevelt

Harry S Truman

Dwight D. Eisenhower

John F. Kennedy

Ronald Reagan

**NINE PRESIDENTS
RECEIVE A SCORE OF 3:**

Thomas Jefferson

James Monroe

John Quincy Adams

Chester A. Arthur

Theodore Roosevelt

Gerald Ford

Jimmy Carter

George H. W. Bush

Bill Clinton

**EIGHT PRESIDENTS
RECEIVE A SCORE OF 2:**

John Adams

James K. Polk

Grover Cleveland

William McKinley

William H. Taft

Woodrow Wilson

Herbert Hoover

Richard Nixon

**EIGHT PRESIDENTS
RECEIVE A SCORE OF 1:**

Andrew Jackson

Martin Van Buren

John Tyler

Millard Fillmore

Franklin Pierce

James Buchanan

Andrew Johnson

Rutherford B. Hayes

(W. H. Harrison, J. A. Garfield, and G. W. Bush were not evaluated.)

The Founding Presidents

Any examination of how well the presidents fared in preserving and extending liberty would have to begin with the first four—all of whom were among the nation's founders. George Washington, John Adams, Thomas Jefferson, and James Madison played a direct role in winning American independence and in shaping the new nation's government structures. They also, through word and deed, set the standards against which American progress in preserving and extending freedom can be measured. Though judged by the standards of modern times—and, in some instance, even in theirs—all can be said to come up short, all four deserve credit for launching the American experiment in self-governance and for keeping it afloat at times when it faced serious internal divisions and foreign threats to its security and survival.

George Washington, as he does on most such lists, scores first among the founding presidents. Congress approved the Bill of Rights early in his administration and Washington used his influence to assure that the necessary number of states ratified it. Its passage must be considered one of his paragon domestic achievements. In suppressing the Whisky Rebellion Washington struck a major blow for the rule of law and republican government. That goal achieved, he was generous in his pardoning practices. Washington also merits a place of honor for breaking with the conventions of his times in freeing his slaves at his death and for making what was essentially a private action a public lesson in civic virtue. (He did all this, of course, after he had left the presidency.)

John Adams, the only founding president not to have owned slaves, took the lead in banning slavery in Massachusetts before he became president. In office, he succeeded in averting a potentially devastating war with France. His acquiescence to—and vigorous enforcement of—the Alien and Sedition Acts, which were aimed primarily at political opponents and critics, earn him a low grade.

His successor, Thomas Jefferson, deserves to be marked down on similar grounds. Jefferson, who rightly decried Adams's prosecution of political opponents as a "reign of witches" during the embargo crisis, incarcerated an even greater number of dissenters than had Adams.[1] Jefferson does deserve some credit for attempting to spread the liberty he envisioned for his fellow citizens across a continent, thereby rendering it more secure. He warrants demerits for failing to resolve the ambivalence he felt about slavery and for not recognizing how the empire of liberty as he envisioned it undermined the principles of human equality he articulated to the world in 1776. Abraham Lincoln had it right when he said, "All honor to Jefferson," who introduced "into a merely revolutionary document, an abstract truth applicable to all men and at all times."[2] If Jefferson stopped short of extending the promise he had made to all Americans, many of his successors did not. Their path would have been even more arduous had he not at least pointed the way.

James Madison, for all his demonstrated incompetence in so many areas as president, nonetheless warrants a place of distinction on any honor roll of presidents who preserved and extended liberty. He jeopardized the nation's security when he embarked on a war he lacked the wherewithal to wage. Yet, unlike Adams and Jefferson, he remained faithful to the Bill of Rights he helped to ratify. At a time when the nation's very existence was in greater peril than at any other juncture in American history, with the exception of the Civil War, none were tried by their government for treason or sedition. Publications that criticized Madison and his policies were left unmolested.

Andrew Jackson

Historians often depict the rise of "Jacksonian democracy" as a good thing. The term connotes the expansion of the franchise to include most white males and the accompanying transfer of power from a small, wealthy elite to a leadership class more "representative" of the population. Jacksonian democracy inevitably brought to the fore a new kind of politician. Historian Richard Hofstadter rightly described the type as "a caterer to mass sentiment."[3] Although the Jacksonians came to power by virtue of their ability to compile majorities at the ballot box, they proved just as capable of undermining liberty as the less representative class they displaced. Having deftly exploited the liberalization of voting requirements and mastered the mass-marketing techniques of their era, they were often able to govern in the absence of constraints. Tyranny of the majority, at times, replaced what the Jacksonians regarded as tyranny of the minority. When Jackson and his cohorts controlled both the executive and legislative branches, and the president was able to assert control over his party, they felt free to take the constitution into their own hands. Often, they operated without challenge. In this context, the speech Lincoln delivered to the Young Men's

Lyceum in Springfield, Illinois, while a twenty-eight-year-old state legislator in 1838, can be seen as a call to resist threats unrestrained majorities posed to liberty.

Jackson's ascension to the presidency resulted from a combination of factors: his popularity as the hero of the Battle of New Orleans, his personal charisma, and, most of all, changes in state election laws that resulted in the selection of presidential electors by popular vote and the removal of property qualifications for voting. Accounts of Jackson's inauguration told of backwoodsmen and other members of the great unwashed from the frontier making a shambles of White House furnishings as they celebrated Old Hickory's coming to power. Jefferson—whose disciple Jackson claimed to be because of their shared advocacy of strong states rights, a limited central government, and a strict constructionist interpretation of the Constitution— would not have looked kindly on such a scene. Jackson's guests were hardly the kind of crowd that had been motivated by appeals to reason. Having observed Jackson when he was a United States senator, Jefferson considered him a "dangerous man" who showed "very little respect for laws or constitutions."[4] Even if these were not the words Jefferson actually used, as one historian has opined, as president Jackson certainly behaved in the manner Jefferson might have anticipated. In no case was this more apparent than in Jackson's treatment of Native Americans.[5]

In the farewell address he issued in 1837, Jackson cited his destruction of the Second Bank of the United States, his suppression of South Carolina's attempt to nullify federal law, and his removal of Native American tribes to areas west of the Mississippi River as the accomplishments of his administration of which he was most proud.[6] Each of Jackson's predecessors had sent American armed forces—sometimes under Jackson's command—to protect settlers against Native American raids. Washington and Jefferson hoped that if Native Americans adopted American agricultural practices and ceased their "wandering ways," they would be able to live side by side with their white neighbors.[7] Hoping to incorporate Native Americans into his "empire of liberty," Jefferson sent Christian missionaries to convert them and entice them to adopt white ways.

Whatever the feasibility of Jefferson's approach, Jackson was less open to assimilation, even where it succeeded. When he became president in 1829, five "civilized" tribes—the Choctaw, Chickasaw, Cherokee, Creek, and Seminole—claimed lands in Southern states. Many resided in Georgia or on lands that Georgia ceded to the federal government when Jefferson was president. The federal government, in turn, granted the Native Americans title to them. The tribes engaged in both hunting and agriculture and made various attempts to accommodate to white Christian society. The Cherokee developed a written language, converted to Christianity in increased frequency, and governed themselves according to a written constitution. In the manner of the self-made Jackson, some adopted the ways of Southern planters, which included owning black slaves.[8]

After the Revolutionary War, Georgia's state government had opened its interior lands to white settlers through a series of lotteries. As the southern and central thirds of Georgia were settled, state leaders cast their eyes on the Cherokee properties in the northern third of Georgia as possible sites for new white settlements. Jackson had polled particularly well among such settlers, who sought to better themselves by bringing undeveloped lands into agricultural production. Interest in taking these lands from the Cherokee accelerated when gold was discovered in their vicinity in 1828, immediately prior to Jackson's election. Whites launched terrorist attacks upon the Cherokee to drive them out. With the arrival of a sympathetic administration in Washington, D.C., the state of Georgia passed a law revoking the Cherokee title to the land and began to prepare it for disbursement.

In his first annual message to Congress, Jackson asked that unincorporated lands west of the Mississippi be designated for Native Americans then living in the southeast. Although he described his proposal as voluntary, Jackson, citing states rights, declared that he was helpless to protect the Cherokee (presumably from the attacks of white settlers). The president, who would boast that he successfully stood down South Carolina over a tariff dispute, cast himself in this instance as a helpless bystander when it came to enforcing federal treaty obligations to Native Americans in the face of a state government's opposition. After a prolonged debate, Congress passed the Indian Removal Act in 1830. Northern Democrats, representing Quakers in Pennsylvania and a group of legislators opposed to Jackson's policies, who soon coalesced into the Whig Party, voted against it. The Choctaws and Chickasaws, choosing not to resist, relocated to what is today the state of Oklahoma. When the Creeks refused to depart, Jackson sent the army to enforce what he had termed a "voluntary" measure. The Seminoles, after a long armistice, resumed hostilities against settlers in the Florida territory. The Fox and the Sac, having already been forced westward, began moving east. In transit, they commenced the Black Hawk War.

In a demonstration of just how "domesticated" and "Jeffersonian" the Cherokee had become, they took their case to the federal courts. In *Cherokee Nation v. Georgia*, Chief Justice John Marshall, on behalf of a majority of the Supreme Court, stated that a member of a tribal nation could not sue a sovereign state. In *Worcester v. Georgia*, the Court found that state law did not extend to lands in the possession of a "distinct community."[9] While Jackson may never have said, "John Marshall has made his decision, now let him enforce it," he might as well have. He did nothing to deter Georgia officials and residents from continually harassing the Cherokee or to protect their victims. One group of Cherokee accepted Jackson's terms and agreed to relocate to Oklahoma. Another, practicing its own form of Jacksonian democracy, decided in a referendum to stay on the land to which they claimed title under previous treaties with the United States.

In 1834, Jackson secured passage of the Indian Intercourse Act, which set aside additional western lands for Native Americans to inhabit and carried assurances of permanent federal protection. As he signed the measure, Jackson set a deadline for the Cherokee to depart. During the administration of his designated successor, Martin Van Buren, with Jackson looking on approvingly from the Hermitage, the U.S. Army forcibly removed the Cherokee and escorted them west. Robert Remini's description of what ensued reads more like an account of what transpired a century later under a totalitarian regime in Central Europe than it does the actions of an administration that saw itself as extending democratic principles:

Efficient Georgia militiamen had rounded up over seventeen thousand Cherokees. These bewildered Indians, homeless, destitute, hungry, could hardly understand what had happened to them. They were herded into a concentration camp. Many sickened and died. In June the first contingent of about a thousand Indians was taken to steamboats and sent down the Tennessee River on the initial leg of the westward trip, a journey the Cherokees came to call the "Trail of Tears." They were boxed like animals into cars drawn by two railroad locomotives. Again there were many deaths because of the oppressive heat and the cramped conditions in the railroad cars. The Cherokees walked the last leg of the "Trail of Tears" until they reached their final destination beyond the western border of Arkansas. In all it was an eight-hundred-mile journey.[10]

In all, sixty thousand Native Americans traveled the Trail of Tears. About a quarter of the Cherokee nation perished en route.[11]

Jackson maintained, as do some of his biographers, that his removal policy was—if not in the best interests of Native Americans—inevitable. Arthur M. Schlesinger Jr., in his Pulitzer Prize–winning book, *The Age of Jackson*, did not consider the incident significant enough to make mention of it. Other scholars, echoing Jackson, regard the policy to which he referred as Indian removal as the unpreventable result of relentless white demands for Native American land. Remini reminds readers that Jackson's opponent in the 1832 election, Henry Clay, held no higher opinion of Native Americans than did Old Hickory. In support of this view, he cites Clay's comment, while in Adams's cabinet, that the disappearance of Native Americans "would be no great loss to the world."[12] Yet whatever Clay's personal prejudices, it does not follow that had he been president instead of Jackson in the 1830s, Clay would have pursued the same policies. Evidence suggests the contrary.

For openers, Clay opposed the Indian Removal Act. John Sergeant, Clay's vice-presidential running mate in 1832, provided legal counsel to the Cherokee. Theodore Frelinghuysen, who would run for vice president on Clay's ticket in 1844, led the Senate opposition to the Removal Act.[13] Whig

Congressman Davy Crockett, who under Jackson's command waged battle against many Native American tribes, lamented the prospect of a "once powerful people being driven from their land." He voted against the measure, thereby severing his remaining political and personal relations with Jackson.[14]

When it came to preserving and expanding freedom, Jackson came up short. His views on racial equality and slavery were no more advanced than his attitude toward Native Americans. Unlike other slaveholders who served as president, Jackson never voiced the slightest moral reservations about slavery as an institution and had no qualms about extending it. The bravery that African American soldiers, both slave and free, and other nonwhite combatants had shown under his command during the Battle of New Orleans did not persuade him—as it had Washington, and would Lincoln, Grant, and Theodore Roosevelt—that such soldiers, having proven themselves as worthy in battle as others, might merit the right to enjoy the same liberties as other civilians afterwards.

Jackson's nonchalant acceptance of slavery, his advocacy of a strong union, and his expansionist yearnings invite the conclusion that he would have been open to a continental union with slavery permitted in much, if not most, newly acquired territories. His political disciples suggested that the matter be decided not by Congress but by "popular sovereignty" (popular majorities in the affected territories). Jackson showed his own hand when he switched allegiances from his steadfast ally and successor, Martin Van Buren, to his Tennessee protégé James K. Polk ("Young Hickory") in the run-up to the 1844 Democratic National Convention. Fearful that the admission of Texas as a slave state would exacerbate sectional tensions, Van Buren had opposed annexing the lone star republic, while Polk favored it. Territory and power always mattered more to Jackson and Polk than human rights. A remark Lincoln made to a colleague would have been lost not only on Jackson but on other practitioners of Jacksonian democracy: "You think slavery is *right* and ought to be extended, while we think it *wrong* and ought to be restricted. That, I suppose, is the rub."[15]

James K. Polk

How James K. Polk, through the extraordinary competence he demonstrated in achieving his objectives, set the United States on the path to civil war was discussed in chapter 4. When it came to extending the full freedoms of Jacksonian democracy to aspiring slaveholders and other white males and restricting them to nonwhites, Polk proved himself worthy of being considered Jackson's heir. Polk's assertion that he paid little heed to the interests of slaveholders as he fashioned his expansionist policies must rank among the greatest falsehoods any U.S. president ever uttered. It was not for naught that colleagues termed him "Polk the mendatious." If shortsightedness should be added to the list of his failings, duplicity certainly should.

Early in his tenure, Polk moved away from his party's "54°40' or fight" position in settling the Oregon boundary dispute with Great Britain. Holding to his original position would have assured the admission of several additional free states to the union. As the war he launched against Mexico began to wind down, Polk proposed extending the Missouri Compromise line, at 36°30' north latitude, to the Pacific Ocean. This would have extended slavery considerably, and well into present-day California. Polk, an advocate of manifest destiny, drew a line on his territorial designs for the U.S. when he opposed annexing all of Mexico, a move several congressional leaders advocated. Through the Treaty of Guadalupe Hidalgo, Polk annexed only sparsely populated portions of Mexico south of the 36°30' line—a violation of his 1844 campaign promise to add new territories both north and south of the line.

Polk did this not because of concern for the Mexican people, but because he did not want to extend citizenship to a large number of Roman Catholics, who shared their church's opposition to slavery. The prospect of extending citizenship to large numbers of people who held such beliefs, in Polk's eyes, raised the possibility of slavery being banned from much of the territory he had acquired. Polk's vision for his country proved harmful over time, igniting the fuse that would set off civil war. Regrettably, he possessed the administrative and political skills necessary to impose it.

Zachary Taylor

Historian David M. Potter referred to the death of Zachary Taylor, sixteen months into his presidency, as "one of those extraneous events which . . . alter the course of history."[16] Unlike other imponderables that surround the deaths of other presidents in office—such as whether FDR would have waged the Cold War and what Kennedy would have done about Vietnam—how Taylor would have handled issues he left behind is easier to surmise. Before he died on July 9, 1850, Taylor supported the admission of California into the Union as a free state, was prepared to do the same with regard to New Mexico, and indicated his opposition to the harsh fugitive slave law that became part of the Compromise of 1850.

Taylor took these stands in full knowledge that admitting new free states would permanently alter the political balance in Congress and in the Electoral College and that, in time, Congress and the states could pass a constitutional amendment abolishing slavery where it already existed. Such a course, had the nation followed it, would have spared the lives of the 620,000 Americans who died in the Civil War, the maiming of hundreds of thousands of others, and a century's legacy of sectional bitterness and racial injustice. It would have taken a very determined president to have pulled this off. Taylor, at the time of his death, was showing every sign of evolving into such a president.

If his three successors sought to placate or appease would-be secessionists, Taylor all but welcomed the opportunity to stand them down. Taylor told their principal spokesmen that he would personally lead the army to suppress their movement and would "hang" persons "taken in rebellion . . . with less reluctance than he had deserters and spies in Mexico," where he had commanded American forces during the U.S.-Mexico War.[17] A Southerner and a slaveholder, Taylor emerged from his forty years of service in the U.S. Army a strong unionist. Had he lived to complete his term, Taylor might have been able to draw upon his personal standing to bring to the fore sufficient numbers of Southern moderates to hold the "fire-eaters" at bay. He did live long enough to denounce South Carolina's John C. Calhoun and Mississippi's Jefferson Davis—Taylor's former son-in-law—as "chief conspirators" against national unity.[18]

The Whigs settled upon Taylor as their presidential nominee in 1848 because of the popularity he enjoyed in all parts of the country. Taylor was a war hero, a Southern planter, a slave holder, and a firm unionist. Running on the Free Soil ticket, former President Martin Van Buren pulled enough antislavery Democrats away from Lewis Cass, the implementer of Jackson's Indian Removal policy, to enable Taylor to carry the pivotal state of New York. (He won the presidency with 47 percent of the popular vote.) As a candidate, Taylor proved a better politician than his handlers expected. On controversial issues such as the tariff, he waffled. When asked his stance toward slavery in the territories, Taylor, donning the garb of an orthodox Whig, suggested that he would sign whatever measures Congress sent him. A year before he entered the race, Taylor predicted that he would win the presidency with the votes of "Whigs, Democrats, and native voters."[19] As president, he retained in office Democrats who expressed a willingness to work with him and rallied to his side both Free Soilers and "conscience Whigs" (Northerners opposed to slavery and its extension).

With this coalition in place, Taylor might well have killed secessionist agitation in its cradle. Had he failed and a civil war erupted in 1850 rather than in 1860, a slaveholding commander in chief might have held more states in the Union than would the Republican president from Illinois who was elected a decade later. An experienced soldier, Taylor might also have had better luck in his selection of generals than would Lincoln.[20] Lincoln described Taylor's capacity to inspire and rally his forces as a "dogged incapacity to understand that defeat was possible."[21] William Seward, who worked with both Taylor and Lincoln, found Taylor as willing to "try conclusions with [the secessionists] as General Jackson was with the nullifiers."[22] Had he lived long enough to do so, Taylor might have spared his nation a series of presidents who were more calculating than courageous.

Millard Fillmore

In the late 1950s, *Mad Magazine* published a series of satiric articles about the man it dubbed the nation's "most obscure" president, Millard Fillmore. It proclaimed the installation of the first White House bathtub as his most memorable achievement. Unfortunately for posterity, while Fillmore remains obscure, he was hardly insignificant. In any discussion of the extension and preservation of liberty, he merits inclusion among the nation's worst presidents.

Whig party bosses had added Fillmore—a New Yorker and former chair of the House Ways and Means Committee—to Taylor's ticket in order to balance competing political factions within the pivotal state of New York. Fillmore's backers' primary objective had been to deprive New York party chieftain Thurlow Weed and former Governor William Seward of influence in a Taylor administration. Fillmore and his supporters had been critical of Seward's cultivation of immigrants and Catholics and for his opposition to extending slavery into the territories. With Fillmore kicked upstairs (and out of New York), Weed used his influence in the state legislature to elevate Seward to the U.S. Senate. There, Seward exercised control of federal patronage destined for New York. Before long, President Taylor was relying more on Seward's counsel than on Fillmore's.

Upon Taylor's death, Fillmore replaced the deceased president's entire cabinet and most of his appointees. Through his designation of Daniel Webster as secretary of state, Fillmore signaled his preference for Northern "cotton Whigs" (those willing to placate would-be secessionists) over "conscience Whigs" (those seeking to limit slavery). Fillmore next championed the Compromise of 1850. Fillmore played a critical role in securing passage of the Compromise of 1850 by pressing significant numbers of Northern legislators, opposed to it, to abstain from voting.[23] His public characterization of this package of bills as the "final settlement" to the country's sectional conflict proved to be one of the shortest-lived presidential predictions in history.[24] Fillmore's rigorous enforcement of the fugitive slave law split his party in his native northeast. Harriet Beecher Stowe's publication of *Uncle Tom's Cabin* during his term subsequently drew national attention to the draconian law Fillmore had approved. (With ample justification, Lincoln dubbed Stowe the "little woman who started the big war."[25])

Fillmore's wife was said to have warned him that signing the fugitive slave law would end his political career. His action indeed doomed whatever chance he had of securing the 1852 Whig presidential nomination.

Fillmore performed one additional disservice to his country. As a means of drawing off votes from the newly constituted Republican Party—which sought to restrict the spread of slavery—Fillmore ran for president on the Know-Nothing ticket in 1856. His platform called for reduced immigration, a longer naturalization process, and official discrimination against Catholics.

Two years later, while seeking a seat in the U.S. Senate, Abraham Lincoln made clear where he believed such a program would lead the country: "As a nation," he said, "we began by declaring that 'all men are created equal.' We now practically read it, 'All men are created equal, except Negroes.' When the Know-Nothings get control, it will read, 'All men are created equal except Negroes, and foreigners, and Catholics.'" Upon the thirteenth president's death, the *New York Times* wrote that Fillmore's "misfortune" was "to see in slavery a political and not a moral question."[26] He was not the last to make this mistake.

Franklin Pierce and James Buchanan

Flaws in both of these men's character were addressed in chapter 2. Pierce proved as wanting in courage and conviction as Fillmore, and Buchanan proved as cynical and as obtuse. Northern critics derided all three for being "doughfaces," Northern politicians who willfully did Southerners' bidding.

Abraham Lincoln

The Great Emancipator's major contributions to the extension of liberty have been assessed in previous chapters. In addition to ending slavery on the North American continent, Lincoln took a multitude of other actions, large and small, that conveyed his empathy with the downtrodden and the fundamental fairness in which he applied the power of government. The one negative legacy he left was his selection of his second vice president.

Andrew Johnson's unexpected succession to the presidency had severe and enduring negative consequences.

Andrew Johnson

Of all the presidents, Andrew Johnson has taken the deepest plunge in surveys assessing presidential greatness. In polls Arthur M. Schlesinger Sr. conducted in 1948 and 1962, Johnson placed among the average presidents.[27] He has been ranked a failure in every ensuing survey. This change resulted not from the discovery of new information about Johnson's intentions and actions as president but from a shift in attitudes on the part of his evaluators about the correctness of those actions. This has been especially true in regard to Johnson's views on race and his disinclination to protect the rights, liberties, and safety of emancipated slaves.

With the official end of Reconstruction in 1877, Southern states, recently re-admitted to the Union with their residents' full citizenship rights restored, were left free to manage their internal affairs. Gone was the omnipresent threat of federal intervention to enforce the Thirteenth, Fourteenth, and Fifteenth Amendments and accompanying legislation. With sectional healing and reconciliation occupying a central role in civic culture in the North as well as the South, the federal government awarded the plight of former slaves less and less of a priority. As part of the attempt to create a new national narrative, works of history began to appear that glorified the "Lost Cause" and castigated those responsible for Reconstruction. Authors of this genre held that after the Civil War—which Southern sympathizers now called the "War between the States"—greedy Northern carpetbaggers and treacherous local scalawags plundered the region, leaving the bulk of its white population impoverished. This corrupt gang, having seized power with the support of Radical Republicans in Congress, retained it, this storyline held, through their ability to manipulate former slaves, to whom they had extended the franchise. Works from this perspective held up Andrew Johnson as a hero for his efforts to thwart all of this.

Such writings also depicted the Ku Klux Klan of the 1860s and 1870s not as terrorists who intimidated the freedmen and their Republican allies from exercising their right to vote, but as preservers of property rights and protectors of Southern white women. Both, this interpretation held, had been put at risk by the presence of millions of unsupervised blacks living in freedom in the defeated states, where they sometimes comprised a majority of the population. According to this school of thought, the disenfranchisement of Southern blacks that accompanied the end of Reconstruction, and the imposition of racial segregation, which followed in due course, were important milestones in the restoration of Southern white "liberties." This view gained credence throughout academe. Its principal perpetuator was William Archibald Dunning of Columbia University.[28]

During the first six decades of the twentieth century, the "Dunning School" of Reconstruction remained the dominant one. Dunning disciples brought forth several biographies, plays, and films that cast Andrew Johnson as a martyr to the Southern cause. Although challenges to Dunning's thesis occasionally appeared, such as W. E. B. Du Bois's *Black Reconstruction*, none acquired sufficient sway over mainstream historians to temper Dunning's account. In popular culture, Dunning's views found their way into novels such as Thomas Dixon's *The Clansman*; silent films such as D. W. Griffith's *The Birth of a Nation* (which had been based on Dixon's work); and both the book and movie versions of Margaret Mitchell's *Gone with the Wind*.

Dunning and his students wrote the history that generations of historians and presidents read.[29] In those accounts, Andrew Johnson came across as a courageous president who fought for the independence of his office as well as for benign and beneficent Reconstruction policies. This view held sway until quite recently. In his Pulitzer Prize–winning book, *Profiles in Courage*, John F. Kennedy devoted a chapter to Senator Edmond Ross, who cast the deciding vote in the Senate that prevented Johnson's removal from office. Preparing to run for president at the time this book appeared, Kennedy espoused the then-prevalent view of Johnson's presidency among historians.[30] *Profiles in Courage* would be among the last books to cast Johnson in a favorable light. Sources Kennedy cited for his chapter on Ross and others were of a decidedly Dunning cast.[31] Ironically, as president, Kennedy, through his efforts to enact civil rights legislation, would indirectly and inadvertently help cause historians to alter their views about Andrew Johnson.

Those who pick up Kennedy's account today might agree that Ross demonstrated great courage in withstanding public and political pressure to oust Johnson from office. They might share Johnson's view that the law he disobeyed—the episode that triggered his impeachment—was unconstitutional, as the Supreme Court later held. They might also share Ross's view that disagreement with a president's policies does not constitute grounds for impeachment. All but the most unreconstructed Confederate sympathizer, however, would conclude that the policies Johnson advocated were not in the best long-term interests of the United States. For his rigorous pursuit of them, Johnson should be held to account.

Like Jackson and Lincoln, Andrew Johnson began life in the humblest of circumstances. Born in December 1808, a little more than a month before Lincoln, Johnson was the son of a landless North Carolina laborer and a seamstress. Apprenticed to a tailor when he was fifteen, Johnson ran away, took up residence in Greenville, Tennessee, and opened his own tailor shop. At the age of twenty, he was elected an alderman. He subsequently served as mayor of Greenville, state representative, Congressman, governor of Tennessee, and U.S. Senator. A Jacksonian Democrat, Johnson, like his hero, firmly believed in both states rights and a strong Union. As a campaigner and public orator, Johnson proved particularly apt on the stump.

As a politician, Johnson made improving the lot of poor Southern whites his primary concern. While in the state legislature, as a means of reducing the influence of wealthy slaveholders, Johnson sought to end the practice of counting slaves as three-fifths of a white person in apportioning Congressional seats.[32] (He advocated not counting these designated "nonpersons" at all.) As he pressed his views, Johnson displayed an orneriness that impeded his effectiveness. President James K. Polk, to whom Johnson was politically allied, found Johnson as a Congressman "vindictive and perverse in his temper and conduct."[33] A member of Johnson's cabinet later remarked that Johnson had "no confidants" and "sought none."[34]

With the Union dissolving in 1861, Johnson became the sole U.S. Senator from a state that had seceded not to resign his seat. With the fall of Nashville, Lincoln named Johnson military governor of Tennessee. Johnson promptly shut down anti-Union newspapers, dismissed anti-Union officeholders, seized the Bank of Tennessee and railroads, and arrested political opponents. "Treason must be made odious and traitors punished," Johnson stated repeatedly.[35] To entice pro-Union, but not necessarily antislavery, Democrats to vote for Lincoln in 1864, Lincoln's managers, with the president no idle bystander, selected Johnson as Lincoln's running mate in 1864. The two ran not as Republicans but as nominees of the makeshift National Union ticket. After Johnson succeeded to the presidency upon Lincoln's assassination, differences surfaced between this pro-Union Democrat and Republicans who had embraced him on grounds of political expediency.

In their approach to Reconstruction, Lincoln and Johnson both maintained that because secession was not constitutional, rebel states had technically never left the Union. Unlike the congressional Radical Republicans, neither regarded the Southern states as conquered territory. They were prepared to allow the rebellious states to elect state governments and to send representatives to Congress once 10 percent of eligible voters in 1860 had sworn allegiance to the Union. Johnson wanted newly constituted state legislatures to renounce secession, ratify the Thirteenth Amendment, and repudiate the debt of the former Confederate state government as prerequisites for their readmission to the Union. He expressed the hope that they would bar high-ranking Confederate officials and military officers from holding public office, but did not make this a condition of restoring constitutional rights to their residents.

Lincoln and Johnson differed, however, in the degree to which they were prepared to press the newly reconstructed states to extend civil and voting rights to former slaves. In his letter to Louisiana's military governor and in his last public speech, Lincoln said that he hoped that the franchise would be extended to blacks who had some education or who had fought for the Union. Judging from the manner in which he had steadily moved towards full and permanent emancipation, it is reasonable to assume that Lincoln would have prodded states he allowed back into the Union to proceed in this fashion. Radical Republicans, who later did battle with Johnson, felt that Lincoln's plans were too lenient. In 1864, they enacted the Wade-Davis bill, which required a majority—not a mere 10 percent—of eligible voters to swear allegiance to the Union before a state could be readmitted. After Lincoln pocket vetoed it, they admonished the still-to-be-re-elected president to respect the "legislative authority of the people."[36] Had he survived, Lincoln might have maneuvered himself into a centrist position between the Radicals and the former Confederates. Johnson lacked either the political sagacity or the personal inclination to try.

As Lincoln's vice president, Johnson had played no role in shaping Lincoln's Reconstruction proposals. Once president, he sought to close the door to the freedmen that Lincoln had left ajar. The Ten Percent plan he circulated among military governors in the unreconstructed states made no mention of allowing recently emancipated slaves to vote. Although Johnson had once spoken, as had the Radicals, of dividing up the great plantations and parceling the smaller plots out to "honest, industrious men," he intended poor Southern whites and not blacks as recipients.[37] As president, he did not pursue this plan.

In the period between Lincoln's assassination in April 1865 and the time Congress reconvened in December, Johnson exercised a free hand over Reconstruction policy. "No other single individual contributed more to the shaping of the contours of reconstruction policy," wrote historian Brooks Simpson.[38] In those critical eight months, Johnson delayed by a century the granting of full citizenship rights to blacks and prolonged the time it would take for the South to catch up to the North in economic development. In the words of Radical Senator Charles Sumner, Johnson "flung away" the opportunity to reshape American society on terms consistent with the aims of the war.[39] When he took office, the defeated South—with Union forces omnipresent—was at its most vulnerable point. Johnson had it within his power to extend the full rights of citizenship to all within his native region. No less an authority than Robert E. Lee believed that Virginians would have looked upon extending the franchise to the freedmen as but a result of the war.[40]

Had Johnson done so, he would have spared the nation a century of continued sectional strife and African Americans a century of continued second-class citizenship, degradation, and worse. Had he acted to hasten the economic development of the region, Johnson might also have improved the lot of the poor Southern whites for whom he insisted he cared so deeply. Instead, Johnson provided erstwhile Confederates with reason to believe that political and social relations in the South—as they existed prior to the war—would resume, as before.

Shortly after taking office, Johnson recognized four reconstructed state governments according to the terms of his Ten Percent plan. On May 29, 1865, he issued a Proclamation of Amnesty and Reconstruction. It required owners of property in excess of $20,000 to request pardons on a case-by-case basis. Since most Southern planters fell into this category, some have surmised that Johnson inserted this measure as a means of humiliating his former political opponents in the South. While the proclamation left open the possibility of black property owners being allowed to vote, it left to the states the decision of whether to grant them the franchise. Johnson did not press the matter. He ignored protests that he was putting ballots in the hands of former rebels and leaving many who had fought for the Union at the mercy of their former enemies.[41] One Tennessee unionist, taking a view similar to Lee's, advised Johnson that if he acted promptly, Southerners would accept extension of the franchise to former slaves.[42]

When state legislatures began to enact Black Codes, Johnson voiced no protests. Under these measures, blacks who ventured out in public had to show proof of employment in order to avoid stiff fines or possible imprisonment. To reporters and members of Congress, Johnson expressed doubt that the freedmen could tend to their own affairs unsupervised.[43] Many former slaves accepted work from their former employers at subsistence wages. In many places, peonage had replaced slavery. Johnson furthered the process along when he stripped the Freedmen's Bureau of its powers to train former slaves for gainful occupations. He simultaneously stepped up the pace at which he pardoned plantation owners, hastening their eventual return to power.

Johnson also did not object when Southern states, disregarding his advice, sent former Confederate officials and military officers to Congress. The Republican Congress, however, refused to seat them. Angered at Johnson's conduct during its absence, Congress then formed a Joint Committee to oversee

Reconstruction and passed a bill extending the life of the Freedman's Bureau and another to counter the Black Codes. Johnson vetoed both measures. In language reminiscent of that Jackson used when he vetoed the bill renewing the charter of the Second Bank, Johnson declared the Freedmen's Bureau unconstitutional because the Constitution had not authorized Congress to perform functions that the bureau performed. He also objected to the absence of a similar bureau to assist Southern whites. In his veto of the civil rights measure, Johnson proclaimed the act a violation of states' rights. Congress overrode him in both instances. Thus began a four-year tug of war, with each branch of government seeking to impose its own Reconstruction policies and to force the other to accept it.

The standoff produced a constitutional crisis that Johnson might easily have averted. The most obvious way for him to do so would have entered into an alliance with centrists in both parties as a means of fending off the Radicals. While one can easily envision Lincoln's bringing different political blocs together, Johnson rendered such a convergence of common interests impossible through his two vetoes. Centrists like Lyman Trumbull considered the Freedmen's Bureau and the civil rights bill the bare minimum they needed in order to satisfy their constituents that the aims of the war had been achieved. With neither of the bills Johnson had vetoed making any mention of extending the franchise to the freedmen, Johnson could easily have found common ground with centrist Republicans who had sided with Lincoln in his occasional tiff with Radicals such as Thaddeus Stevens and Charles Sumner. Had they remained behind him, they along with Northern Democrats could have sustained Johnson in his quest to allow the states to decide the suffrage question. Through his two vetoes, however, Johnson pushed such centrists into the Radical camp—at least on policy. (Several would later join with Ross, voting to acquit Johnson during his impeachment trial.)

Johnson's rift with Congress widened when he actively opposed the Fourteenth Amendment after it passed both houses of Congress. He sought and failed to persuade the legislature in his native Tennessee to block its ratification. With the yet-to-be-ratified amendment very much on the minds of voters during the 1866 congressional and state elections, Johnson embarked on a national tour to help elect sufficient numbers of Democrats who opposed it. His "swing around the circle" tour proved as disastrous to his objectives as it had been daring. Johnson came across as coarse, mean, and angry. He denounced legislators by name and traded insults with hecklers.

The new Congress, firmly under Radical control, divided the ten Southern states still technically out of the Union into five military districts. It placed a general at the head of each district and tasked the commander with registering voters and drafting state constitutions, guaranteeing universal suffrage to males—regardless of their race. When Johnson vetoed the Radicals' plan, Congress, not surprisingly, overrode him. In the heat of the controversy, Johnson failed to notice that the generals had not only registered 703,000 freedmen, but also registered 627,000 Southern whites, many of them poor.[44] To prevent Johnson from obstructing its Reconstruction plans, Congress forbade the president from using his powers as commander in chief to issue orders to the district generals without the concurrence of the commander of the army, Ulysses S. Grant. Congress next passed the Tenure of Office Act, which forbade the president from removing officials the Senate had confirmed without its approval.[45] Declaring the measure unconstitutional, Johnson vetoed it. Again, Congress overrode him. Johnson's attempt to remove Secretary of War Edwin Stanton from office, in direct violation of this statute, triggered his impeachment.

By pressing the formal powers of his office to the extent that he had, Johnson provoked Congress to assert its own institutional prerogatives. Stalemate and institutional paralysis resulted. That squandered the opportunity to bind up the nation's war wounds in a way consistent with the aims of the side that had won. What the United States most needed in 1865 was a president with the political dexterity, vision, and compassion necessary to complete the work of the Civil War. At the outset of that war, Lincoln and Johnson were both strong unionists. Each in his own way mustered the courage and resolve necessary to meet the challenges before them (Lincoln as president-elect and as commander in chief, Johnson as senator and military governor). As president and as a politician, Lincoln grew in office. In relating to his fellow politicians, he knew when to be flexible, when to be firm, and when to be subtle. Johnson, while he could also be tough, proved more obstinate than courageous. He preferred to govern less through persuasion and more through formal authority. In contrast to his predecessor, Johnson shrank rather than grew in office. And the nation he led suffered the consequences.

Ulysses S. Grant

As he approached the bar of history, Ulysses S. Grant started out with three strikes against him. First, as the man who waged "total war" against the Confederacy, he understandably received the animus of those who felt its effects. Stories of Yankee cruelty as Union forces brought the ravages of war to Southern cities and towns passed through the generations. Feelings hardened with the passage of time. Second, with the Dunning view of Reconstruction on the ascent and Jim Crow laws tightening their grip by the turn of the twentieth century, Grant's historical reputation, largely because he tried to protect the rights of former slaves, as Jean Edward Smith aptly stated, became one of the casualties of white supremacy.[46] (Grant was the last president before Dwight D. Eisenhower to send federal troops to the South to protect the right of blacks to vote.)

One would have expected, however, that Grant's reputation would rise once the Dunning view of Reconstruction gave way. His consistent ranking among presidential failures in most surveys, however, attests to the staying power of opinions disseminated by the third group of Grant detractors—political reformers. In the words of historian William Hesseltine, this group "stuffed the ballot boxes of history" against Grant.[47] Their ranks included essayists Henry Adams and Charles Francis Adams Jr.; *Nation* editor E. L. Godwin; and former abolitionist and future mugwump Carl Schurz. These detractors awarded higher priority to civil service reform, tariff reduction, and "good government" than they did to the civil rights of African Americans in the South and elsewhere. Having borne witness to how corrupt political machines such as that of New York's "Boss Tweed" came to power (by manipulating immigrant votes and plundering public treasuries), they regarded Radical Reconstruction little more than a means through which Northern political bosses might perpetuate their power southward, with blacks substituting for immigrants.

Feeling a kinship with the upper stratum of educated Southern whites, these reformers believed that "better elements" in both North and South should govern. They pressed for systemic changes that would enable them and people like themselves to take their natural place in society. Political reformers, who pressed for literacy tests and property requirements as pre-conditions for voting in the North, could hardly be expected to look favorably upon proposals to allow uneducated and landless emancipated slaves to vote in the South. "Universal suffrage," Charles Francis Adams Jr. declared, "can only mean . . . the government of ignorance and vice—it means . . . a Celtic proletariat on the Atlantic Coast, an African proletariat on the shores of the Gulf, and a Chinese proletariat on the Pacific."[48] Neither the Know-Nothings of the 1850s nor the Ku Klux Klans of the nineteenth and twentieth centuries could have said it any better. In addition to increasing their own sway at the ballot box by diminishing the number of votes cast by the "lower orders," reformers sought to enhance their influence over policy through civil service reform. In an age when the number of males holding college degrees was miniscule, this group stood to benefit in inverse proportion whenever government positions were filled through competitive examination rather than political patronage.

Simply put, Grant was not this crowd's kind of guy. He had sided with the Radicals in their attempt to unearth Johnson's Reconstruction policies. Some of those very Radicals were closely affiliated with Northern political machines the reformers despised. Closely aligned with the congressional Radicals and Northern political machines were many Southern state Reconstruction governments. In 1868, Grant had been the leading choice of these three groups for president. Contributing to his 52.7 percent victory in the popular vote had been the more than 700,000 African American voters in Southern states.[49] (Carrying several Southern states, largely with the help of these voters, Grant prevailed over New York Governor Horatio Seymour in the Electoral College 214 to 80.) By the time his successor left office, the number of African American voters in the South had dwindled to a pittance. Not surprisingly, another important element in Grant's winning coalition was Civil War veterans organized by the Grand Army of the Republic.

As president, Grant remained steadfast to those who had helped elect him (especially to Northern party stalwarts and Southern blacks). Henry Adams's caustic declaration that "the progress of evolution from President Washington to President Grant was alone evidence enough to upset Darwin" should be read with Adams's disdain for these very people in mind.[50] Unable to gain entry into Grant's administration and unable to defeat him for re-election in 1872, reformers set out to discredit him by magnifying the scandals that erupted during Grant's time in office and by belittling his achievements, which included multiple efforts to assist recently emancipated slaves.

When compared to scandals of more recent vintage, those that transpired under Grant were of short duration, inflicted no long-term damage on governmental institutions, did not involve Grant personally, and did not encroach upon the civil liberties of other Americans. All had as their common cause the personal greed of the individuals who perpetuated them. Some came to light through the efforts of other Grant appointees. One of these, the Credit Mobilier scandal, took place before Grant took office and exclusively involved members of the legislative branch rather than the executive.

Grant, it must be said, did himself few favors by peopling his administration as carelessly as he had and by the manner in which he responded when troubles beset his appointees. After the death of his former military aide and most trusted presidential adviser, John Rawlins, during his first year in office, Grant had no one around him with sufficient standing in his eyes to present him with an unvarnished account of what was truly transpiring in his administration. Nor did he have anyone in his inner circle with an eye toward appearances. Some criticize Grant for allowing Secretary of War William W. Belknap to resign after the House of Representatives impeached him for taking kickbacks from traders at Indian posts and before the Senate could try him. Belknap, once out of office, still faced criminal prosecution, and Grant did not pardon him. Unpersuaded that his personal assistant Orville Babcock had participated in the "Whiskey Ring" that had defrauded the government of millions of dollars in excise taxes, Grant testified in the subordinate's favor. Critics charged that this action on the president's part made a mockery of his very public admonition to his attorney general to "let no guilty man escape."[51] As Truman and Reagan might attest, public relations blunders, misplaced trust in aides, and even misdoings of aides do not, in and of themselves, make for a failed presidency. One would not, however, discern this from most accounts of Grant's presidency.

At the outset of his administration, Grant took on the laudable but contradictory goals of restoring sectional harmony while remaining true to principles that Lincoln had articulated and Johnson had abandoned. "Let us have peace," Grant penned in accepting the 1868 Republican presidential nomination. Even before he took office, however, Grant found such sentiments incompatible with his other aim of not surrendering the "results of the war." [52] The platform on which he ran committed his administration to universal male suffrage, a pledge Grant took seriously.

As a candidate and after his election, Grant actively pressed for ratification of the Fifteenth Amendment, which became part of the Constitution during his first year in office. To enforce the provisions of both the Fourteenth and Fifteenth Amendments and accompanying legislation, Grant also pressed for and approved legislation that established the Department of Justice, replete with a unified system of prosecutors and a solicitor general to argue cases for the government in court. Grant's approach to assuring blacks in the South the franchise contrasted sharply with that of Johnson. Assured that Johnson would not enforce edicts the Radicals in Congress had enacted, white vigilantes used terrorism and other forms of intimidation to keep likely Republican voters in the South away from the polls. In 1866, Confederate military veterans and scions of wealthy planters formed the Ku Klux Klan (KKK) to spearhead such activities, which they directed against southern blacks and their white allies.

With Grant's enthusiastic support, Congress passed the Enforcement Acts, which outlawed the use of bribery, intimidation, and force to impede or obstruct voting. The measures provided for the prosecution of violators in federal courts. Upon requests from state governors, Grant sent federal troops to support state militias that policed elections. In 1871, he asked Congress to pass legislation to enable him to suppress the KKK. The statute he signed authorized the president to suspend *habeas corpus*. Owing to his vigorous enforcement of the measure, Southern politicians and some Northern headline writers dubbed Grant "Kaiser Ulysses."[53] With Grant declaring the Klan's activities nothing short of rebellion, federal troops arrested hundreds of persons. Thousands fled, fearing arrest. After Attorney General Amos T. Akerman released ringleaders in exchange for information, he brought the worst offenders to trial, often before all-black juries.[54] In the face of often brutal intimidation of witnesses and jurors, federal officials won six hundred convictions.[55]

Most accounts conclude that Grant had, through these actions, effectively broken the Klan's back. Advising Grant to continue taking a hard line, Akerman suggested that those who resorted to terrorism "take a kindness on the part of the government as evidence of timidity, and hence are emboldened to lawlessness by it."[56] No sooner had Grant and Akerman won this battle against their hooded foes, Grant—giving in to pressure from railroad lobbyists, who complained of excessive interference in their affairs—replaced Akerman as attorney general.

Most students of Grant's presidency have not found evidence that changes in attorneys general in any way slowed down or impeded Grant's efforts to protect freedmen's rights. Federal interventions and prosecutions continued unabated under Akerman's successors.[57]

In addition to using the military and the courts to protect the rights of African Americans, Grant sought to better their station by providing them with means to exercise economic leverage over their former masters. In the years preceding Grant's election as president, U.S. officials had expressed interest in annexing the island republic of Santo Domingo. Its strategic location rendered it suitable for a naval base and coaling station for American vessels in the Caribbean. Grant reasoned that, were the United States to acquire the territory, blacks might use their option of relocating as a means of persuading their employers to "raise their wages and improve their living conditions as in order to retain their labor."[58] Whatever the merits of his proposal, the clumsy manner through which Grant sought its ratification virtually assured its doom.

First, Grant circumvented official channels when he sent his personal aide Orville Babcock to open talks with the island's rulers. (Babcock was rumored to own land on the island that would appreciate if the proposition went forward.[59]) Second, Grant did little to build support for his idea in the Senate, which would have had to approve any treaty Grant's team brought back. Grant took personal offense when Senate Foreign Relations Committee Chairman (and leading Radical Republican) Charles Sumner objected to the acquisition. Unable to persuade Sumner to change his tune, Grant grew vindictive. To remain in his good graces, Senate Stalwarts stripped Sumner of his committee chairmanship.[60] The quarrel did little to advance Grant's goal. (Grant's forces by themselves proved unable to muster the necessary two-thirds vote necessary to approve the treaties.)

Grant's attempt to annex Santo Domingo produced some previously unimaginable alliances. In favor of Grant's proposal stood African American spokesman Frederick Douglass, Senator Hiram Revels, and Representative James Rainey—two of the first blacks to serve in Congress—and most party Stalwarts. Sumner, one of the preeminent defenders of African American civil rights, found himself in the company of reformers and avowed racists who were alarmed at the prospect of new state governments with blacks at their helm. In the *Nation*, E. L. Godwin voiced doubt that "ignorant Catholic Negroes" could become American citizens.[61]

As his presidency progressed, Grant, in the words of the *New York Times*, vacillated between "boldness and moderation" in protecting the freedmen's civil rights.[62] His actions were more the result of circumstance than inclination. With the army reduced to a fraction of what it had been at the height of the war, Grant did not have at his disposal sufficient troops to suppress a sustained rebellion. He suspected that repeated federal interventions would lead the public to conclude that reconstructed state governments lacked the necessary local support to survive on their own. Weighing equally on his mind was the realization that, in the North, support for his policies had begun to weaken, thanks in no small part to reformist and Democratic criticisms and the rising salience of economic issues. Still, Grant never wavered from his commitment to uphold what he regarded as the rightful results of the war. In the aftermath of his impressive re-election—he won with 56 percent of the vote—Grant had a suggestion for those who professed to be "tired" of racial politics, or who pressed him to tend to other matters: "Treat the Negro as a citizen and a voter, as he is and must remain, and soon parties will be divided not on the color line, but on principle. Then we shall have no complaint of sectional interference."[63]

Aware that the president's options were limited, white supremacists, as Akerman had predicted, resorted to violence with increasing frequency. In 1873, with two factions claiming to be the legitimate state government of Louisiana, Grant sent troops to install the government the courts had declared elected. Critics in all sections of the country denounced Grant as an "American Caesar." In retaliation for his intrusion, the faction Grant had removed from power murdered scores of blacks, many of them elected officials. Months later, when the ousted Democratic state administration attempted a coup d'état against the elected government, Grant empowered General Philip Sheridan to maintain order. The president voiced increasing impatience at the prevailing double standard of those who denounced Sheridan (primarily Democrats and "reformers" in both parties), but looked the other way as "barbarous individuals," who had assassinated black elected officials, escaped the reach of justice.[64]

In the fall of 1874, with the Democratic Party of Mississippi resolved to take control of the state's government "peacefully if we can, forcibly if we must," Grant uncharacteristically hesitated. "The whole public are tired out with these annual, autumnal outbreaks in the South, and there is so much unwholesome lying in regard to the cause and extent of these breaches of the peace that the great majority are ready now to condemn any interference on the part of the Government," he wrote Attorney General Edwards Pierrepont.[65] With Democrats and reformers making federal intervention in the South a major issue in the upcoming Ohio state elections, Grant decided to hold back until he was confident that Republicans retained control of this pivotal Northern state. A Democrat victory there, he feared, would be interpreted across the country as a repudiation of his Reconstruction policies.

Reassured that Ohio would remain in friendly hands, Grant ordered Pierrepoint to send federal troops into Mississippi. They arrived too late, however, to exert much influence. The politics of intimidation had worked. With a "Redeemer" government now in place in Mississippi, only three southern states remained under Republican rule. "I should have intervened. I believed it was a mistake at the time," Grant told black state representative John Lynch afterward. "If I made a mistake," he explained, "it was one of the head and not of the heart."[66] The president, correctly and with appropriate bitterness, voicing his frustration, opined that when white Southerners spoke of having their rights "respected," what they really wanted was "the right to kill Negroes and Republicans without fear of punishment and without loss of caste or reputation."[67]

After the Democrats, buoyed by the Panic of 1873, took control of the House of Representatives in 1874, Democrats and reformers of all sections and parties began attaching riders to bills, barring the use of federal troops in police elections in the South without the expressed consent of Congress. Grant demanded, but did not receive, additional force legislation from Congress. Such legislation would have granted him powers similar to those he had used against the KKK years earlier. Congress did enact the Civil Rights Act of 1875. The measure contained a clause banning racial discrimination in public accommodations, similar to the ones contained in the Civil Rights Act enacted ninety years later and the Fair Housing Act of 1968. Grant's successors declined to enforce it, and the Supreme Court struck it down in 1883.[68]

Grant remains the sole president to apologize in his farewell message for his personal and policy failings. "It was my fortune, or misfortune, to be called to the office of Chief Executive without any previous training," Grant began. "Under such circumstances it is but reasonable to suppose that errors of judgment must have occurred." "Mistakes have been made," he continued, coining a phrase many a subsequent public official would repeat, perhaps unaware of its source. Grant then eloquently summarized what the state of the nation was at the time he took office and how he attempted to change it for the better. Picking up the story after Lincoln's assassination, he wrote:

> The intervening time to my first inauguration was filled up with wran-
> glings between Congress and the new Executive as to the best mode of
> "reconstruction," or to speak plainly, as to whether the control of the

Government should be immediately thrown into the hands of those who had so recently and so persistently tried to destroy it or whether the victors should continue to have an equal voice with them in this control. Reconstruction, as finally agreed upon means this and only this, except that the late slave was enfranchised, giving an increase, as was supposed, to the Union-loving and Union supporting votes. If free in the full sense of the word, they would not disappoint this expectation. Hence, at the beginning of my first administration the work of reconstruction, much embarrassed by the long delay, virtually commenced.

Mistakes and all, the old soldier had done his duty. He deserves better on the pages of history.

Rutherford B. Hayes

During the 1876 presidential campaign, President Grant's last attorney general, Alfonso Taft, wrote Republican nominee Rutherford B. Hayes a disturbing letter. "It is a fixed and desperate purpose of the Democratic Party in the south that the Negroes shall not vote, and murder is a common means of intimidation to prevent them," Taft said.[69] When it appeared that Hayes had lost the election to Democrat Samuel Tilden, Hayes lamented what might become of the "poor colored men of the South" should the Democrats return to power. He surmised they might suffer a fate worse than slavery.[70] That the outcome he so feared came closer to reality under a Hayes rather than under a Tilden administration remains one of the ironies of presidential history.

Although Tilden won the popular vote by more than two hundred thousand votes, disputed tallies in South Carolina, Mississippi, and Florida cast a cloud over the Electoral College. (Had the black turnout been what it had been in the previous two elections, Hayes would easily have prevailed.) The Republican Senate and the Democratic House appointed a bipartisan commission of fifteen members to decide the election. With the group poised to return an 8 to 7 party-line vote in favor of Hayes, party leaders convened offstage and brokered a deal. Democrats agreed not to interfere with Hayes's ascension to the presidency, while Republicans pledged that Hayes would withdraw remaining federal troops in the south and that his cabinet would include a southerner. There was also talk of a federal subsidy for construction of a southern transcontinental railroad.

The Hayes family, Republican patronage dispensers, and southern Redeemers were not the only ones pleased with the results. Reformers who had so disparaged Grant could hardly contain their glee. "The Negro will disappear from the field of national politics. Henceforth, the nation, as a nation, will have nothing to do with him," the *Nation* happily predicted.[71] Historian Eric Foner called the arrangement that made Hayes president "a decisive retreat from the idea, born during the Civil War, of a powerful national state protecting the fundamental rights of American citizens."[72] Yet in survey after survey, Foner's colleagues consistently rate Hayes an average president. If what Foner says is true, how many presidents could have been worse? "To think that Hayes could go back on us when we had to wade through blood to help place him where he is now," said one of the freedmen.[73]

As secretary of state, Hayes appointed William M. Evarts, Andrew Johnson's former attorney general and principal defender during the impeachment trial. Reformer Carl Schurz, who had condemned Grant for sending troops to protect blacks, became Hayes's secretary of the interior and functioned as the administration's point man for civil service reform. In setting policy toward the south, Hayes consulted Lucius Lamar, one of the architects of the alleged coup that had toppled the last Republican reconstruction state administration in Mississippi.[74] Every bit Schurz's equal in educational attainment and reformist sentiment, Lamar later served as secretary of the interior under Democrat Grover Cleveland. (Schurz, his predecessor, crossed party lines to support Cleveland in 1884.)

In his inaugural address, Hayes—like Grant before him—endorsed two contradictory goals. He vowed to protect the constitutional rights of all Americans and also to "restore honest and efficient local government" in the southern states. As Hayes made good on his promise to withdraw remaining federal troops from the south, which then numbered around three hundred, Bourbon

Democrats in whom Hayes entrusted the future of the freedmen efficiently, if not always honestly, deprived their Republican constituents of their newly attained voting rights. They did so in ways that minimized protests or outbreaks of violence that might provoke northern calls for renewed intervention. Democratic-controlled state legislatures enacted "grandfather clauses," which stated that in order to vote, one's grandfather had to have been eligible to vote. Literacy tests proved another favored device to hold down black registration and turnout. Hayes, some say, inadvertently inspired the use of literacy tests as a prerequisite for voting when he proposed linking universal education and universal suffrage. The prospect of federal funds being used to teach blacks to read, some scholars argue, lay at the root of Democratic opposition to the use of federal funds for education for the rest of the nineteenth century and well beyond.[75]

After the 1878 congressional and state elections, Hayes admitted in private that his experiment in entrusting southern whites to protect the civil rights of blacks had failed.[76] He made some anemic moves to show his concern for a significant part of his constituency that was steadily losing its freedoms every day of his presidency. As Democratic Congresses repealed civil rights laws, Hayes exercised his veto. He made no effort, however, to enforce the statutes he helped retain on the books. A bitter Benjamin Wade, one of the initial Radical Republicans, observed that Hayes had been faithless to the very men who had risked their lives to vote for him. Without black votes, Wade pointed out, Hayes would never have risen to the post from which to acquiesce to the denial of their rights.[77] Rayford W. Logan recorded that "white supremacy was more securely entrenched in the south" when Hayes left the White House than when he entered it.[78] By such standards, Grant, the scandal-ridden Stalwart, made a far superior president than did Hayes, the scandal-free reformer. The day may be approaching when surveys of presidential greatness reflect that.

Benjamin Harrison

Many Americans know little about Benjamin Harrison and even less about what he did to protect and extend liberty. Having served as a brigadier general in the Union army, Harrison supported President Ulysses S. Grant's efforts to protect the voting rights of the freedmen. "We entered into an obligation solemn as a covenant with our God to save these people from the dastardly outrages that their rebel masters are committing upon them," Harrison said early in his career.[79]

Unlike Hayes, Harrison refused "to purchase the presidency by a compact of silence" on voting rights.[80] He was acutely aware that the reason Grover Cleveland pulled ahead of him by 90,728 in the popular vote in 1888 was because southern state governments had aggressively suppressed the black turnout. (Harrison prevailed in the Electoral College, 233 to 168.) Again, unlike Hayes, Harrison, as a candidate and as president, refused to forsake his black supporters, even if this created the impression that he put partisan concerns ahead of sectional reconciliation. He reminded his fellow Republicans that the generous veterans' pension bill he had sponsored might have survived Cleveland's veto had "black friends of the Union soldier had their fair representation in Congress."[81] Even if others did not, Harrison remained mindful of the implicit threat in the Fifteenth Amendment that states that did not carry out its voting rights provisions stood to see the number of representatives allotted to them lowered.

As president, Harrison backed two ill-fated measures to protect the civil rights of blacks. One, introduced by Massachusetts Representative Henry Cabot Lodge, would have required federal supervision of congressional elections. Harrison took a direct role in drafting this bill. He sought the advice of black leaders in his native Indiana and, in an effort to pass it, drew upon friendships he had made on Capitol Hill during his time as a senator. Harrison called for passage of Lodge's bill in his annual message. As would so many bills like it in later years, it cleared the House (on a party-line vote) but succumbed to a Senate filibuster led by southern Democrats.

Harrison also sought to assist blacks through federal expenditures on education. Three times prior to his becoming president, the Senate passed bills introduced by Senator Henry Blair of New Hampshire that would have provided federal aid to public schools. While in the Senate, Harrison had sponsored an amendment to assure that states did not discriminate against blacks in disbursing these funds. (If federal funds were fairly distributed, southern Democrats feared, blacks would soon be able to pass the literacy tests state governments had imposed as a means of circumventing the Fifteenth Amendment.) After the Afro-American League endorsed the Blair bill in January 1890, opposition among Democrats and reform-oriented Republicans solidified against the proposal. As president, Harrison tried to revive the bill in Congress, but he failed.

Unable to secure blacks their right to the franchise under the Constitution and unable to provide them with tools with which to surmount state-imposed restrictions, Harrison sought before leaving office to assure their physical safety. In his last annual message, he became the first president to call for a federal antilynching law. "To my mind," Frederick Douglass said of Harrison, "we never had a better president."[82]

Theodore Roosevelt

As a soldier, sportsman, explorer, and politician, Theodore Roosevelt came into contact with people from all backgrounds and walks of life. Most of the time, he judged them by their individual merits. Lessons Roosevelt learned about human behavior did not always prevent him from voicing certain racial theories. Nor did they disabuse him of opinions he held about nonwhites being inferior to whites and certain ethnic groups being inferior to Anglo-Saxons. When it came to protecting and extending liberty, Roosevelt acted, as he did in other matters, on impulse and instinct. Early in his presidency, he articulated his concept of the "square deal" in remarks he made to black soldiers standing guard at Lincoln's tomb. "A man who is good enough to shed his blood for the country is good enough to be given a 'square deal' afterward," Roosevelt said. "More than that no man was entitled to, and less than that, no man shall have."[83]

As president, Roosevelt used the symbolic powers of his office to reduce racial prejudice and provide opportunities for African Americans to advance. Like Lincoln, Grant, and Harrison, Roosevelt decried lynching as a direct assault on civilization. "No man can take part in the torture of a human being without having the nature of his own moral nature permanently lowered," he said in his annual message in 1906.[84]

Shortly after becoming president, Roosevelt startled social circles in the north and in the south when he became the first president to invite a prominent African American leader to dine with him at the White House. Upon learning that the president had invited educator Booker T. Washington to his table, Senator Ben "Pitchfork" Tillman of South Carolina declared that Roosevelt's action would necessitate the killing of one thousand members of Washington's race in the south before they "learned their place again."[85] So intense was the criticism that Roosevelt, who had described his hosting of Washington as "a splendid recognition of the essential character of presidential office," conceded to social arbiters that he had committed an "indiscretion."[86] Writer Mark Twain advised him that the president was not as free as an ordinary citizen to dine with whomever he pleased.[87] While Roosevelt continued to receive African Americans in the White House, he received them only in business settings.

In making appointments, Roosevelt followed the practice of his Republican predecessors of naming African Americans to federal posts in recognition of their service to the party. Most came with the endorsement of Booker T. Washington, who headed the Tuskegee Institute. These appointments advanced several goals of both the appointees and their presidential patrons. In parts of the south where blacks could not vote, federal appointees, and their families and supporters, often constituted all that remained of the Republican Party. At national nominating conventions, blacks in southern delegations often played pivotal roles in deciding presidential nominees. African Americans, who could vote in other parts of the country, paid attention to presidential appointments of blacks to various posts. Those in southern states looked upon such appointees in their regions as one means through which they too might attain greater opportunities.

Roosevelt did not have an easy time making such appointments. When he announced his intention to reappoint Minnie Cox postmistress of Indianola, Mississippi, her white neighbors ran her out of town. Refusing to replace her,

Roosevelt ordered the post office closed. With Cox remaining on the federal payroll, residents of Indianola had to travel miles to pick up their mail. In time, Roosevelt allowed the post office to reopen and under different management.

When he learned of Roosevelt's intention to appoint black physician William Crum as customs collector for Charleston, South Carolina, Senator Tillman declared, "We still have guns and ropes in the South . . . and know how to use them."[88] Roosevelt repeatedly named Crum to the post as a recess appointment. (Crum obtained Senate confirmation late in Roosevelt's tenure, only to be replaced by Roosevelt's successor, William Howard Taft, who named a white southern Democrat-turned-Republican to the post.) Roosevelt maintained that he had remained steadfast to his African American designees because he wanted to "keep open the door of opportunity."[89] Sometimes he would say "hope" in place of "opportunity."

Having grown up during Reconstruction and shown some sympathies for reformers who denounced Radical Reconstruction, Roosevelt was willing to offend local sensibilities only up to a point. He did not send federal troops or U.S. marshals to Mississippi to protect Cox or to enable her to perform her duties. He also remained hands-off when it came to enforcing voting rights. His characterization of his approach serves as a useful guide in assessing not only him but his successors: "To acquiesce in this state of things because it is not possible at this time to attempt to change it without doing damage is one thing," he said. "It's quite another to do anything which will seem formally to approve it."[90]

Roosevelt named blacks to prominent posts in the north, as well as in the south. When word leaked that he intended to name a black assistant U.S. attorney in Boston, Columbia University students debated the proposition that Roosevelt's "policy of appointing Negroes to offices in states where sentiments is opposed to it is unwise."[91] William Henry Lewis, the son of slaves, was a perfect example of the kind of person Roosevelt wanted to install in federal posts. Lewis's father had fought in the Union Army. Lewis was among the first blacks to gain admission to Amherst College, where he became an All American football player. Under the rules then in operation, Lewis continued to play football after he enrolled at Harvard Law School.

Roosevelt saw Lewis play, befriended him, and invited the star athlete to his home. Lewis won election to several local and state posts before Roosevelt tapped him for U.S. attorney. (Taft would subsequently designate Lewis assistant attorney general of the United States, the highest federal post held by a black person up to that time.)

Late in his presidency, Roosevelt, through an indulgence of pride and stubbornness, added a stain to his reputation that continues to mar his legacy with regard to the expansion and protection of liberty. In the summer of 1906, residents of Brownsville, Texas, reported that a group of black soldiers had gone on a shooting spree. One person was reported killed and another wounded. When interrogated, none of the soldiers confessed to the crimes. Nor, when ordered to do so, did any reveal the identities of the perpetrators. Roosevelt approved an army recommendation that all the soldiers—numbering 170 in three units, including six Medal of Honor recipients—be dishonorably discharged. After conducting an investigation, an erstwhile Roosevelt ally, Senator Joseph Foraker, questioned Roosevelt's assertion that the soldiers had entered into a "conspiracy of silence."[92] Foraker also criticized Roosevelt's dismissal of the accused units without allowing them their day in court.

In response, Roosevelt began a campaign to discredit Foraker. He charged that Wall Street, angered over his trust-busting activities, had enticed Foraker to attack him.[93] When Booker T. Washington wrote Roosevelt on behalf of the soldiers' rights to face their accusers, the president suggested that his friend lacked the information, to which he as commander-in-chief had been privileged, to be able to judge his actions.[94] At the annual Gridiron Dinner, a night traditionally set aside for presidential and journalistic frivolity, Roosevelt, departing from both custom and character, launched a personal attack upon Foraker, who responded in kind.

Roosevelt's public bluster was a failed attempt to conceal private pangs of guilt. When novelist Owen Wister asked Roosevelt why he had not ordered a court of enquiry for at least the unit officers, Roosevelt blurted out, "Because I listened to the War Department, and I shouldn't."[95] He made no mention of the Brownsville episode in his memoirs. Nor did he ever admit he might have made a mistake in this instance. Having allowed himself to make this decision in haste, and too proud to admit he was in the wrong, innocent people suffered. In his handling of this incident, Roosevelt fell short of a promise he had made to himself when he became president. "I have not been able to think of any solution of the terrible problem offered by the presence of the Negro in this continent," he confided, " but of one thing I am sure, and that is that in as much as he is here and can neither be killed nor driven away, the only wise and honorable and Christian thing is to treat each black man and each white man strictly on his merits as a man. . . . it may be that I am wrong, . . . but if I am, then all my thoughts and all beliefs are wrong, and my whole way of looking at life is wrong."[96]

Woodrow Wilson

Upon learning of Woodrow Wilson's death, U.S. Senator Claude Augustus Swanson proclaimed the recently deceased president "A true Virginia gentleman."[97] To him the term connoted courtliness and a projected sense of dignity—traits commonly associated with Robert E. Lee. When he was eleven years old, Wilson stood "momentarily" at Robert E. Lee's side when the former general visited Augusta, Georgia. He would never forget the awe that had come over him as he looked up at the face of the man most people in his region regarded as a demigod.[98]

When applied to race relations, the term "Virginia gentleman" also connoted the paternalism and condescension that educated, upper-class whites exhibited toward blacks. While Wilson had little use for the more virulent and violent forms of racism that lower-class whites practiced at the time he was growing up, he remained a man of his region and his era. "The only place in the world, where nothing has to be explained to me is the South," he would say.[99] Through a combination of his own racial attitudes, his willingness to act on them, and the influence southern Democrats exerted over his administration, Wilson set back the aspirations and hopes of African Americans by more than a generation.

In his best-selling, multivolume *A History of the American People* (1902) and his shorter *Division and Reunion* (1909), Wilson popularized William

Archibald Dunning's views on Reconstruction. He praised the Ku Klux Klan of the 1860s and 1870s for achieving through "intimidation" what they could not obtain through the ballot box or the courts.[100] What it sought, of course, was the right of southern whites to run local affairs for their benefit, while relegating blacks to the sidelines, stripped of rights and protections they had been granted by war, constitutional amendments, and legislation. While president of Princeton University, Wilson discouraged African Americans from seeking admission, and none were admitted while he remained on the scene.[101] Throughout his life, his taste in humor ran to "darkey" jokes, common to his native region.[102]

A month into Wilson's presidency, Postmaster General Albert S. Burleson, a Texan, complained at a cabinet meeting about friction between white and black workers in his department. Wilson approved Burleson's proposal that all government departments be segregated along racial lines. Others in the heavily southern cabinet, including Navy Secretary Josephus Daniels and Treasury Secretary William Gibbs McAdoo, were supportive. By some accounts, Wilson acted on behalf of his first wife, Ellen Axson Wilson, who, after visiting the Bureau of Engraving and Printing, expressed outrage to her husband that blacks and whites worked side by side.[103] At the same time, Wilson began replacing black Republicans his predecessors had named to federal posts with white Democrats. He made brief attempts to appoint some African American Democrats but ceased when the Democratic majority in the Senate balked at confirming them.[104] (He declined to follow Roosevelt's precedent of naming some African Americans as recess appointments.) By the middle of Wilson's first term, the Civil Service began requiring that applicants for federal positions supply a photograph with their applications.[105]

Had Wilson resisted this creeping segregation, he would have found ample support among his fellow progressives—of both parties—and in parts of the business community. Both the prominent banker Jacob Schiff and the Sears-Roebuck magnate Julius Rosenwald objected to the imposition of segregation within the federal government.[106] Frank Cobb, editor of the *New York World* and a key Wilson supporter, proclaimed Wilson-styled segregation "small, mean, and petty" and demanded that the president "set his heel upon" this form of "Jim Crow government."[107]

Wilson recanted on a promise he had made as a candidate to appoint a commission to assess the status of blacks in the United States. The National Association for the Advancement of Colored People (NAACP), frustrated by the slow pace of Wilson's Republican predecessors when it came to protecting the rights of African Americans, had endorsed Wilson for president in 1912. Rosenwald and others had offered to finance such a commission as a private entity, obviating the need to seek congressional approval and appropriations. Wilson tossed the idea aside, insisting that the mere designation of such a commission carried the appearance of an "indictment."[108] With lynchings on the rise—they would average between fifty and ninety each year Wilson served as president—such an indictment would have been warranted.

At a meeting with black leaders, Wilson proclaimed segregation beneficial to their race. He took umbrage when Monroe Trotter, founder of the black newspaper the *Boston Guardian*, reminded the president that segregation had not been federal policy during the fifty years that had passed since Emancipation. Taking offense that Trotter had taken issue with him, Wilson suggested that if the group wished to meet with him again, it would have to find someone other than Trotter to act as its spokesman. After the meeting, Wilson suggested to the *New York Times* that blacks who had voted for him in the expectation that he would embrace nondiscriminatory policies should rectify their mistake in the next election.[109]

Wilson's unpleasant exchange with Trotter remained on his mind a year later when Wilson became embroiled in a controversy surrounding D. W. Griffith's silent motion picture *The Birth of a Nation*. Based on the novel *The Clansman* by Thomas Dixon, the film brought the Dunning view of Reconstruction to the silver screen. Interspaced among the scenes were captions that quoted verbatim from Wilson's writings. In response to Dixon's request, the president held a private showing of Griffith's production at the White House. After viewing the film—in the presence of family, government officials, and personal friends—Wilson was said to have declared it history "written with lightning." He was reported to have added that his one regret was that it was "all so terribly true."[110] Church groups, black leaders, and Civil War veterans picketed theaters in protest of the film's depiction of blacks and of

Reconstruction. Violence erupted in many cities. In Boston, Trotter was in the forefront of efforts to have the film banned. When northern Democrats and clergy objected to the president's purported endorsement of the film, Wilson confided to his aide Joe Tumulty that he would gladly disavow the film if he could do it in such a way that he did not appear to be giving in to "that unspeakable fellow . . ." (he had mispronounced or forgotten Trotter's name).[111] Tumulty then spread word that Wilson agreed with the movie's critics.

During his presidency, Wilson had several opportunities to use the visibility and prestige of his office to calm racial tensions. Sometimes, he exacerbated them. During his time in office, tens of thousands of blacks relocated from the rural south in pursuit of jobs in the industrial north. As the Great Migration continued unabated, so too did outbreaks of violence against these nonwhite newcomers. When whites went on a killing spree against blacks in East St. Louis in 1916, Wilson, running for re-election, accused Republicans of "colonizing" the city by importing blacks to pad voting roles.[112] He remained silent when similar violence against blacks erupted in Memphis, Waco, Philadelphia, Chicago, Omaha, and elsewhere.

When rioters, some affiliated with the International Workers of the World (IWW), mounted sustained assaults against blacks throughout the Midwest the following year, Wilson ignored calls by black leaders, local officials, and voices within his own Justice Department to maintain order and protect black victims. In response to IWW appeals for support, former president Theodore Roosevelt informed an IWW official that he was willing to hear complaints that factory owners had hired nonunion black workers to replace striking whites, but that he could not sanction violence as a means of resolving grievances. Roosevelt agreed to meet with union officials, but only after the "murderers had been brought to justice."[113] In response to the East St. Louis riots, Representative Leonidis Dyer, picking up on a recommendation that President Harrison made a generation earlier, introduced the first of what would be several bills to make lynching a federal crime.[114] Wilson showed no interest in the Dyer bill, and it stalled in the Democratic Congress.

On July 28, 1917, three months after the United States entered World War I, approximately eight thousand blacks marched in silence down New York's

Fifth Avenue to demand an end to racial discrimination and violence. Citing wartime censorship provisions, a police officer removed a sign from one marcher that depicted a black person on bended knees before Wilson, appealing to him to bring democracy to America before carrying it to Europe.[115] One year later, Wilson, for the first time, issued a proclamation condemning lynching and mob violence.[116] Historian Kendrick A. Clements attributed Wilson's belated action to his fears that unrest in the black community, should it become manifest, would disrupt the war effort.[117]

As Wilson waged what he termed a war to "make the world safe for democracy," he presided over racially segregated armed forces. Most of the 350,000 blacks who served in uniform worked as laborers, stevedores, and cooks, and answered to white commanders. Veterans hospitals, which sprang up during and after Wilson's presidency, were segregated.

In the period when Wilson was still struggling to keep the United States out of the war in Europe, he voiced fears that American entry into the conflict would take a severe toll on civil liberties at home. "To fight you must be brutal and ruthless," he told an editor, "and the spirit of ruthless brutality will enter into every fiber of our national life, infecting Congress, the courts, the policeman on the beat, and the man in the street."[118] Once the United States had joined in the hostilities, Wilson allowed his appointees to make his prophesy a reality. Congress enacted, with Wilson's support, the Espionage Act of 1917, the Alien Act of 1918, and the Sedition Act of 1918. Wilson entrusted their enforcement to people he knew would act on their own prejudices. Postmaster General Burleson, who had made his department safe for segregation, retained aides to screen more than 125,000 pieces of daily mail for leftist literature. While Wilson would occasionally voice displeasure that Burleson had confiscated journals the president knew not to be seditious, he allowed his subordinate to continue on as before.[119]

Attorney General A. Mitchell Palmer, jolted by a bomb anarchists had sent to his home, arrested and deported thousands, often solely on the basis of hearsay. (These were called the "Palmer Raids.") Whether on purpose or otherwise, "anti-Hun" propaganda that George Creel's Committee on Public Safety produced for dissemination abroad made its way into state laws at home in the form of government-sanctioned discrimination against German Americans. Informed by a local resident that the White House retained a German-born laborer, Wilson replied that he would "rather the blamed place should be blown up than persecute innocent people."[120] These noble sentiments notwithstanding, anti-German hysteria swept the country during the war. After the armistice, it was quickly succeeded by an "anti-Red" panic. Wilson did little to blunt either.

Wilson's failure to protect the liberties of his fellow citizens at home—or to take into account sentiments of certain minority groups—contributed, in part, to his failure to attain American participation in his beloved League of Nations. Trotter and other black leaders Wilson had turned away followed him to the Paris Peace Conference, demanding that he make good on his war declaration pledge to allow "those who submit to authority" to "have a voice in their own government."[121] Wilson used his influence at the Paris Peace Conference to block a Japanese-initiated amendment on racial equality.[122] The last thing he wanted was to have the League of Nations he brought into being probe into the hiring and employment practices of the American government, let alone into the social arrangements in his beloved South. Not surprisingly, Trotter denounced Wilson's move. Eager to give a hearing to anyone opposed to the treaty Wilson brought home, the president's primary nemesis, Senator Henry Cabot Lodge, allowed Trotter to denounce Wilson's creation before the Senate Foreign Affairs Committee. Trotter decried its failure to assure racial justice within all nations who joined the League.[123] German Americans, many of whom had voted for Wilson in 1916 because of his party's boast that Wilson had kept the United States out of war, wondered aloud why he acquiesced to a "vindictive" peace, of the kind he had pledged to prevent. Irish Americans and Italian Americans gave voice to slights they believed the treaty had shown their ancestral homelands by inflating the size of Republican Warren G. Harding's presidential victory in 1920.[124]

On occasion during his presidency, Wilson did act to protect and expand the liberty of some of his fellow Americans. Mostly, these actions were symbolic in nature. After Wilson was elected president, Protestant fundamentalists and prohibitionists sought to prevent him from naming his principal, aide Joseph

Tumulty, as his executive secretary. Taking a break from denouncing blacks and Jews, populist Democratic Senator Tom Watson of Georgia warned that Tumulty, given such a berth in the executive office, would share state secrets with the Vatican.[125] Standing by the appointment, Wilson confided to a friend that his only reservation about his choice was not Tumulty's Catholicism but his aide's inability to see beyond his native Hudson County, New Jersey.[126]

During his fourth year in office, Wilson nominated Boston lawyer Louis D. Brandeis to the U.S. Supreme Court. In the face of criticism that became increasingly anti-Semitic in tone, Wilson pressed Senate Democrats to confirm his nominee. Despite opposition from both of Brandeis's home state senators, the American Bar Association, the president of Harvard University and the dean of its law school, former President William Howard Taft, and many others, Brandeis won confirmation by a vote of 47 to 22, with one Democrat voting no and three Republicans voting yes. "I never signed any commission with such satisfaction," Wilson wrote at the end of what had been a four-month controversy.[127]

Wilson was a latecomer to women's suffrage. His first and second wives, both strong-willed and educated women, had opposed granting women the vote. Before the United States entered the war, Wilson argued that extending the franchise to women was a matter best decided by the states. In the face of suffragette picketers in front of the White House daily, intermittent arrests, and skirmishes outside his window, Wilson endorsed women's suffrage in January 1918 as a necessary war measure. Thereafter, he pressed for passage of what became the Nineteenth Amendment in 1920. Evidence suggests that he came around at the behest of his three daughters, who lobbied him intensely.

Like Cleveland, and Taft before him, Wilson opposed efforts to impose literacy requirements for new immigrants. He opposed discriminatory immigration quotas aimed at reducing the number of people allowed in from central, southern, and eastern Europe. Like Theodore Roosevelt, however, Wilson, in deference to West Coast sentiment, voiced no objections to reducing the number of immigrants from Asia.

Finally, while Wilson is primarily remembered for his failure to attain American entry into the League of Nations, he did make the United States a beacon of hope for oppressed peoples throughout the world, both in his time and since. Several nations received their first glimmer of freedom as a result of his efforts during and after the First World War. Wilson made clear that when the United States goes to war, it does so not in pursuit of territory but to uphold its ideals, to protect the weak, and to establish conditions conducive to the spread of democracy. He was the first president to give force to the term "human rights" and to make their advancement a goal of foreign policy and a standard against which the United States evaluated other nations.

After 1917, every time American policy makers have debated whether and under what circumstances to send troops abroad, impose economic sanctions, intervene in foreign conflicts, enforce international decrees, or engage in public diplomacy, one side would either proclaim itself "Wilsonian" or have the term thrust upon it. Wilson's spirit inspired American forces during the Second World War as well as during the First. It could be found in western and eastern Europe, in Asia, throughout the former Soviet Union and its satellites, in Bosnia, in Kosovo, in Afghanistan, and in the Middle East. Whether realized or not, and however Wilson may have drifted from his own vision and that of his country, his reminding the world of the universal promise contained in his nation's founding documents ignited hopes throughout the world that self-government and respect for liberty need not remain exclusively American preserves. That is part of his legacy too.

Warren G. Harding

Historians have not been kind to Warren G. Harding. He routinely places at or near the bottom in surveys of presidential greatness, whatever the ideological makeup of the jurors. For years, his sole roommate in the failure category was Grant. Pierce, Buchanan, A. Johnson, and Nixon subsequently joined them. Most people know little about Harding, save for the tidbits they happened to have picked up about scandals that came to light after Harding died and about his exceedingly messy private life.[128] Another thing for which Harding remains famous is the garbled vocabulary and his famous pledge to return the country to "normalcy."[129] What the slogan really conveyed was a rest from anything that reminded voters of Wilson and Roosevelt.

After years of frenetic domestic reform followed by a world war, Harding offered the nation a breather. In both style and substance, he was as different from Wilson as was humanly possible. If Wilson could, as David Lloyd-George noted, "put into words the unspoken hopes, desires, and purposes of millions," Harding preferred platitudes. If Wilson spent hours alone in his study, Harding enjoyed his card games and liquor. If Wilson was aloof and arrogant, Harding was approachable and affable. If Wilson tried to push blacks and their concerns off to the side, Harding offered victims of racial prejudice promises of succor. This latter aspect of Harding's presidency has been drowned out by all the reports and wisecracks about the graft and sex that characterized his administration.

Several times during his front porch campaign, Harding received delegations of African Americans and listened to their concerns. "If the United States cannot prevent segregation in its own service, we are not in any sense a democracy," he told them.[130] Upon taking office, Harding asked Attorney General Harry M. Daugherty to investigate complaints that peonage was on the rise in several southern states. A month later, Daugherty, whom historians remember primarily as head of the "Ohio Gang" that brought Harding to power, informed the NAACP that their suspicions had been confirmed, Harding's Justice Department initiated prosecutions in three states.[131] Acting on another front, Harding began to increase the number of blacks serving as presidential appointees. Letters went out from the White House to department heads soliciting names of suitable appointees.[132] In a special message to Congress, Harding embraced proposals that Wilson had rejected, including the commission to assess the status of blacks in American society and Representative Dyer's antilynching proposal. The president's endorsement of the measure brought increased attention to lynching as an issue. With Harding's support, the NAACP and religious organizations mounted a spirited campaign on behalf of the Dyer bill. It passed the House in 1922 but succumbed to a Democratic filibuster in the Senate.

During a speech in Birmingham, Alabama, before a segregated audience in October 1921, Harding called for an end to Jim Crow and to the disenfranchisement of blacks. "We cannot go on, as we have gone on for more than half a century, with one section of our population . . . set off from real contribution to solving national issues, because of a division on race lines," he said.[133] From a podium in a park named in honor of his predecessor, Harding told his listeners to "let the black man vote when he is fit to vote; prohibit the white man voting when he is unfit to vote."[134] While hardly a clarion call for federal intervention in state election procedures and practices, Harding had done more to challenge local norms than had any of his recent predecessors.

Blacks in his (segregated) audience smiled approvingly. Sensing that he had made less of an impression on whites who had turned out to hear him, Harding pointed his finger in their direction and told them, "Whether you like it or not, unless our democracy is a lie, you must stand for that equality." Press accounts noted that at this juncture, the blacks in the assembly cheered. In an effort to be conciliatory, Harding noted that as a result of the Great Migration, the nation's "race problem" had become national in scope. He said that the increased presence of blacks in other sections of the country had caused many to modify previously held views. The president then called for "larger charity on all sides" as well as for "a beginning of understanding."[135]

Harding died before he could follow up on his remarks with concrete policies. It is unknown whether Harding could have pressed the Democratic leader Senator Oscar Underwood of Alabama, with whom Harding enjoyed a close relationship, to allow the Dyer bill to pass the Senate. (Perhaps he and Underwood, two former Senate insiders, might have been able to come to some understanding about Dyer's bill over a card game.) Wilson's former critic, Monroe Trotter, believed that Harding did not award the antilynching bill a high enough priority. As evidence, Trotter cited the president's limiting the special session of Congress that he called to legislation restructuring the Merchant Marine.[136]

If he did not make amends for all the slights Wilson had inflicted on blacks, Harding acted to heal other wounds left over from Wilson's era. Early in his term, he informed Daugherty that he wanted Socialist leader Eugene V. Debs, convicted in 1918 under the Sedition Act, released from prison. (Debs was serving a ten-year sentence for speaking out against the war.) Wilson's attorney general A. Mitchell Palmer had recommended that Wilson pardon Debs before leaving office. With the war over, the sixty-five-year-old Debs was not a threat to anyone, Palmer maintained.[137] Sensing an opportunity to heal some of the domestic divisions that had been a by-product of the war, as well as to reap some goodwill in unexpected quarters, Harding not only commuted Debs's sentence but also invited the former prisoner to visit with him at the White House. "Mr. Harding appears to me to be a kind gentleman; one whom I believe possesses human impulses," Debs remarked as he departed.[138] History might some day agree.

Calvin Coolidge

If most historians have presented Warren G. Harding as an incompetent and a reprobate, too many have cast Calvin Coolidge as a nonentity. More people can probably recite Dorothy Parker's response to reports of Coolidge's death ("How can they tell?") than can relate anything of substance about him. Even though he never said, "The business of America is business," textbooks and books of quotations nevertheless claim that he did.[139] Many who have attempted to come to terms with Coolidge presented him a tool of the rich and sometimes as the unwitting architect of the Great Depression. Others have painted him as a dolt, or even as a clown. (Visitor: "I have a bet that I could not get more than two words out of you." Coolidge: "You lose." Hostess: "Mr. President, you obviously do not enjoy these dinners. Why do you attend so many?" Coolidge: "A man's got to eat somewhere.") Contemporaneous observers including Will Rogers, who liked to impersonate him, found Coolidge's wit compelling. (Visitor: "Mr. President, are you related to the Coolidges of *Boston*?" Coolidge: "*They* say no.")

Behind the terseness, which won Coolidge the nickname "Silent Cal," stood an exceedingly crafty and successful professional politician. If Coolidge had a motto that captured his attitude toward life and public affairs, it was "do the day's work."[140] As governor of Massachusetts, Coolidge became a national figure by doing just that. (Such was the title of a speech he delivered upon his election as president of the Massachusetts State Senate in January 1914.) When the Boston police walked off their jobs in a labor dispute, he sent the

National Guard to protect the city's citizens. "There is no right to strike against the public safety by anybody, anywhere, any time," he wired American Federation of Labor President Samuel Gompers.[141] A year later, Coolidge was vice president.

While climbing the political ladder from alderman to president, Coolidge considered responding to citizens' concerns to be doing his day's work. During his years of service in the Massachusetts legislature, Coolidge came to know Monroe Trotter and other Boston-based civil rights activists. His acquaintance with William Henry Lewis, an African American who had held several prominent posts under Theodore Roosevelt and Taft, extended back to the time he and Coolidge were both undergraduates at Amherst. Coolidge helped reduce racial tensions during the controversy that arose after the film *The Birth of the Nation* opened at Boston's Tremont Theater on April 10, 1915. Fights erupted inside the theater and out on the streets. Trotter, Lewis, and two thousand others marched to the Massachusetts State House to protest the screening of the film. Democratic Governor David Walsh promised them redress. Soon the lower house of the Massachusetts legislature passed a bill to establish a three-member censorship board empowered to shut down—by majority vote—performances it deemed incendiary.

Those opposed to the measure tried to block it in the Senate by voting to return it to committee. By custom, Coolidge, then serving as Senate president, did not vote on legislation. On this occasion, however, he instructed the clerk to call his name. Coolidge's vote brought the resolution to a tie. This stopped attempts to recommit the bill, thereby clearing it for passage on the floor. Coolidge's action did not go unnoticed. "Opponents of 'Birth of the Nation' Win," declared a headline in the *Boston Post*.[142] The *Boston Globe* reported that "only the action of [Senate] President Coolidge . . . prevented a reconsideration of the vote."[143] True to his wont, Coolidge had given no indication of what he intended to do prior to the vote. Nor did he comment on his action afterward. He had done the day's work.

In accepting the Republican vice presidential nomination in 1920, Coolidge pledged that the Harding administration would work to end lynching and provide equality of opportunity for all Americans.[144] After he succeeded to the presidency in 1923, Coolidge called for the enactment of a federal antilynching law in each of his six State of the Union addresses. While Coolidge did not make mention by name of what he often referred to as a "foul crime" in one of these speeches, listeners knew what he had in mind when he proclaimed that African Americans "should be protected from all violence and supported in the peaceful enjoyment of the fruits of their labor."[145]

Coolidge, the notoriously frugal New Englander, increased funding every year for federal programs that provided education and training to African Americans. His files show extensive correspondence between the White House and the Departments of Agriculture and Labor about these programs. As had Hayes, Harrison, and Harding, Coolidge advocated a federal department of education and a greater role for the federal government in furthering the education of blacks, specifically. He showed particular interest in Howard University, the last surviving remnant of the Freedmen's Bureau, and recommended hefty increases to its budget.

Coolidge also continued Harding's practice of referring complaints about civil rights violations to the Justice Department, but left it to his cabinet secretaries to decide how—or whether—to remove the vestiges of Wilson's segregation from their departments. A recent biographer has, with some justification, categorized Coolidge's undertakings on behalf of blacks as "halting and impartial."[146] While it is certainly true that when it came to involving himself in controversy Coolidge did not go looking for trouble, it is also the case that when he was presented with evidence of certain abuses, Coolidge took action. In 1924, his executive secretary ordered an immediate investigation of reports the White House received about a Jim Crow station operating on government property opposite the Key Bridge in Washington, D.C. After Trotter wired the vacationing Coolidge that "four colored examiners" had been assigned space apart from their white colleagues in the Department of the Interior, the president's top aide wired the head of the bureau: "The President directs you to revoke such segregation at once."[147]

At the same time, Coolidge did not follow the advice of those recommending that he issue an executive order to desegregate the entire federal government. In his personal relations and conduct, Coolidge showed himself free of the prejudices of his era. When a secret service agent referred to the president's valet as a "fine, colored gentleman," Coolidge corrected him: "Brooks isn't a colored gentleman," he said, "he's just a gentleman."[148] The respect Coolidge showed for his black associates and constituents in private as well as in public contrasted sharply with that which Wilson demonstrated.

As vice president, Coolidge dedicated a hospital for African American veterans at the Tuskegee Institute. He took the occasion as an opportunity to call for greater tolerance:

> Those who stir up animosities, those who create any kind of hatred and enmity are not ministering to the public welfare. We have come out of the war with a desire and a determination to live at peace in all the world. Out of a common suffering and a common sacrifice there came a new meaning to our common citizenship. Our greatest need is to live in harmony, in friendship, and in good-will, not seeking an advantage over each other but all trying to serve each other.[149]

Shortly after taking office, Coolidge received word from African American leaders that an avowed racist, sympathetic to the KKK, had been put in charge of the hospital he had dedicated. "Our women are insulted and our sick neglected," one letter said.[150] Having resigned itself to the reality of a segregated military and Veterans Administration, the NAACP requested that all black staff be retained to tend to black patients. Shortly thereafter, C. Bascom Slemp, a former Virginia congressman whom Coolidge had recently retained as his executive secretary, provided William Henry Lewis with the names of 248 black employees and 12 white employees at the hospital and assured him that the whites would be replaced as soon as possible. In addition to seeking to resolve the matter, Slemp may also have wanted to shore up his own standing with the president. In a letter to Slemp about another matter, Lewis had made mention of Slemp's having voted against the Dyer antilynching bill.[151]

Some students of Coolidge's presidency have taken him to task for his failure to speak out forcefully against the KKK.[152] Several of Coolidge's contemporaries, William Henry Lewis among them, held this view at the time. (Lewis endorsed Democrat John W. Davis for president in 1924 because Davis had denounced the Klan by name, while Coolidge had not.) The second Ku Klux Klan came into being in 1915. It took its inspiration from the earlier organization of the same name that Grant had destroyed in 1871. Its formation can be traced to two events that occurred in 1915: the lynching of Jewish businessman Leo Frank in Georgia and the release of *The Birth of a Nation*. While the first Klan directed violence almost exclusively toward African Americans, the second, in what historian Robert Ferrell has called the "great bigotry merger," broadened its universe of victims to include Catholics and Jews.[153] Claiming a membership of up to five million, the second Klan peaked in membership during the 1920s. Not just a southern phenomenon, it exerted considerable influence in Indiana, Maine, Oklahoma, Oregon, and elsewhere.

In 1924, the Klan had enough sway at the Democratic National Convention to prevent New York Governor Alfred E. Smith, a Catholic, from obtaining the party's presidential nomination. While Coolidge made no specific mention of the Klan during his campaign, he did appear before assemblages of its potential victims. In a speech before the Holy Name Society, a Catholic organization, Coolidge spoke of "ordered liberty." In the footsteps of Lincoln, he referred to the "better angels" of the nature of American society.[154] Emmet Scott, secretary-treasurer of Howard University, wrote Coolidge in praise of the president's speech. In his letter, which he published in black periodicals throughout the 1924 campaign, Scott made references to a "hooded order" that sought to deny blacks their basic rights as citizens. He assured Coolidge that African Americans were aware of his "distinguished services in behalf of their race."

Coolidge reminded a citizen who protested the Republican Party's decision to nominate an African American man for Congress that, in the recent world war, "500,000 colored men and boys were called up under the draft" and that "not one of them sought to evade it." Echoing Theodore Roosevelt, he wrote that the "door of hope . . . of opportunity" would not be "shut on any man . . . purely upon the grounds of race and color."[155] Coolidge then made this correspondence public.

The summer after Coolidge's re-election, forty thousand Klan members paraded past the White House. The vacationing Coolidge kept silent. On October 6, 1925, he delivered a major address on tolerance before the recently formed American Legion at its convention in Omaha. His choice of venue was as significant as his message. The Klan had brought considerable violence and chaos upon Omaha and upon Nebraska's state government two years earlier. Members of the lower house of the legislature, boasting of their Klan affiliations after being evicted from the statehouse, sought to reconvene in a federal facility. Coolidge, through Slemp, denied them access. Responding to the news, a newspaper ran a large picture of the president on its front page above a two-word caption in large letters: "He Intervenes."[156]

Standing before the legionnaires, Coolidge stated that during the recent war, "no man's patriotism was impugned or service questioned because of his racial origin, his political opinion, or his religious convictions." He called for an immediate "demobilization of racial antagonisms, fears, hatreds, suspicions."[157] (In its tone, it bore a close resemblance to one Dwight D. Eisenhower delivered in 1954 at the height of McCarthyism, when he admonished his listeners not to join the "book burners." This was discussed in chapter 3.)

From the vantage point of the twenty-first century, Coolidge might well have done more to preserve and extend liberty, especially at home. He could have been more venturesome and less cautious when it came to righting numerous wrongs. Known to harbor objections to restrictive immigration quotas based on national origins, Coolidge nonetheless signed them into law. And while Coolidge ended the mistreatment black soldiers received at a segregated veterans hospital, it would not be until after another world war and the coming to power of another "accidental president," Harry S Truman, that the armed forces of the United States and the Veterans Administration would be ordered integrated. When it came to making good on promises contained in the nation's founding documents, Coolidge—while not a Truman or an LBJ, let alone a Lincoln—towered above Jackson, Wilson, and Hoover. What

Coolidge was not, as John M. Barry, Amity Shlaes, and other recent commentators have noted, was the fool so many have made him out to be in the pages of history.[158]

Herbert Hoover

Herbert Hoover did not intend to set back progress his fellow citizens had made in enjoying the full benefits of liberty that had been their birthright under the Constitution. To the contrary, he acted to further it at home and abroad before becoming president. Hoover had spoken out against the Palmer Raids. After Polish soldiers executed thirty-seven Jewish civilians at the end of World War I, he threatened to withhold American food shipments to Poland in the absence of assurances that such incidents would not be repeated.[159] Much as he subscribed to the prevailing racial prejudices of his day, Hoover believed that blacks could advance through education and training. As secretary of commerce, Hoover ordered his department desegregated, thereby tearing down at least one reminder of Wilson's harmful legacy.[160] He closely followed the work of commissions that advised Harding and Coolidge about the status of blacks. As president, Hoover boosted federal appropriations to Howard University to upgrade its professional schools.

Whatever his intentions, however, the manner in which Hoover governed worked to reverse advances blacks had made under his predecessors. His failures resulted in part from his belief that all social problems could be solved if organizations operated according to the principles of scientific management.[161] Hoover was, as John M. Barry proclaimed him, a "brilliant fool."[162] He regarded himself as a disinterested and impartial expert. He believed that once organizations adopted scientific procedures, people would behave as his theories predicted and that outcomes could be anticipated, if not controlled. Unfortunately, Hoover was often blind to how people actually behaved.

Some of Hoover's limitations came to the surface in 1927 after Coolidge sent him, in his capacity as secretary of commerce, to the Mississippi Delta to coordinate relief efforts after the Mississippi River overflowed its banks.

Although Hoover did an extraordinary job in coordinating food distribution and rescue efforts, he failed to consider that local elites would use the aid he made available to re-inforce prevailing norms of social control. Evidence of exploitation was abundant. Had Hoover looked up from his papers long enough to notice, he might have observed local officials giving federal relief to whites at no cost while they charged blacks heavily for it. Those too poor to pay were forced into servitude. State officials, designated at Hoover's urging to provide refugees with food and shelter and to check the spread of disease, began forcing blacks to work as peons, repairing breeches in the levees. National Guardsmen, often on orders of governors, randomly corralled blacks, herding businessmen, professionals, sharecroppers, and tradesmen alike onto trucks and driving them wherever their labor was needed.[163]

While the Great Engineer neither planned nor approved of such forced labor camps, he had empowered those who did. Ambitious for the presidency, he ignored what went awry or remained hidden from view, preferring to bask in the glory of what was otherwise hailed as another example of his extraordinary administrative capabilities. Hoover's work in the Delta, trumpeted by the brigade of public relations people he had brought along with him, boosted his already considerable popularity. Party regulars, however, remained wary of him. Their hostility was rooted in no small part to Hoover's penchant for scientific management, which he deemed a more preferable way of distributing government largesse than through patronage, and his open contempt for the politics they practiced.

Looking beyond the party machines for support in his run for the White House, Hoover entered into alliances with southern whites hailing from regions where the Grand Old Party (GOP) had been historically weak. Over the years, coalitions of machine politicians, blacks, and aging Civil War luminaries had been able to block attempts to substitute lily-white delegations for biracial ones from southern states. This all changed with the ascendancy of Hoover the reformer.

In the election of 1928, Hoover carried five states of the old Confederacy: Virginia, Tennessee, North Carolina, Texas, and Florida. Not surprisingly, the Great Engineer chalked this up to his personal popularity rather than to the aversion many Protestant voters in the region had to the Catholicism of Democratic presidential nominee Governor Alfred E. Smith of New York. While Hoover continued to appoint blacks to federal posts, he tried to balance these appointments with others that would enhance his appeal to southern whites. Hoover's most dramatic attempt to cater to southern whites was his nomination of John J. Parker, a North Carolinian, to the U.S. Supreme Court. When Parker ran for governor of his state in 1920, he had argued that blacks not be allowed to vote on the grounds that their past participation in the democratic process had incited racial prejudice.[164] The NAACP waged an aggressive campaign to reject Parker's nomination, and the Senate, which the Republicans controlled 56 to 39 with one Independent, rejected Parker in a 41-to-39 vote. Seventeen Republicans and the Independent joined twenty-three Democrats to defeat the nomination.

The Parker nomination and the Great Depression began the withering of ties between the GOP and its once dependable African American supporters. While blacks, voting in northern states, largely stuck with Hoover in 1932, it would not be long before they heeded the advice of Robert Vann, publisher of the *Pittsburgh Courier*, and turned "Lincoln's picture to the wall."[165]

Franklin D. Roosevelt

Franklin Delano Roosevelt merits a place of honor among the nation's presidents for all he did to rid the planet of the twin scourges of Nazi Germany and a militaristic Japanese empire. Few presidents faced as serious a threat to the survival of liberty as did Roosevelt. He met the challenges that came his way head on and mobilized the nation's industrial might, economic power, and morale to wage and win the most monumental military effort in American history. Roosevelt nobly defended freedom in what John F. Kennedy termed "its hour of maximum danger."[166] He was among the first Americans to recognize the threat Adolf Hitler posed to the survival of democracy and free institutions. Prior to the Japanese attack on Pearl Harbor, Roosevelt worked feverishly within the limits of public opinion and congressional authorization, and sometimes beyond them, to help the

United Kingdom and other nations resist continued assaults and to beef up American defenses so that the United States would be better able to wage war when it eventually came.

Whatever his successes as a commander in chief and military strategist, however, Roosevelt did considerably less than he might have, especially given the overwhelming popularity he enjoyed during much of his presidency, to extend and preserve liberty in other areas. Whereas many of Roosevelt's Republican predecessors (Grant, Harrison, T. Roosevelt, Harding, and Coolidge) had all supported federal legislation to outlaw lynching, FDR kept silent. Democratic Senators Edward Costigan and Robert F. Wagner, picking up where Republican Representative Leonidis Dyer had left off, introduced an antilynching bill shortly after FDR's inauguration. Unwilling to antagonize white voters in the south and segregationists they elected to represent them in Washington, FDR refused to support it.

Roosevelt also resisted adding antidiscrimination provisions to federal legislation in order to placate southern Democrats, who chaired key committees and might hold his program hostage if he interfered with the way they ran things back home. Because large portions of federal relief were funneled through state and local governments, blacks in southern states had access to these funds only through the sufferance of southern officials who continued to deny them their civil rights. Roosevelt's hallmark domestic achievement, the Social Security Act of 1935, expressly exempted domestics and agricultural workers, many of whom were African American. Although the Servicemen's Readjustment Act of 1944, commonly known as the GI Bill, did not discriminate directly in its distribution of college tuition monies on the basis of race, many colleges and universities did discriminate in their admissions policies—indirectly denying these education benefits to many black veterans.[167] (Federal funds provided under the act flowed unabated to institutions that refused blacks—many of them veterans—admission.) The story was a similar one with regard to mortgages funded under the legislation.

In 1941, FDR issued Executive Order 8802, which forbade discrimination in government hiring and throughout the defense industry. He also appointed the Fair Employment Practices Committee. He took both steps reluctantly. His purpose was to preempt public protests being planned by civil rights organizations and labor unions. At Roosevelt's personal request, A. Philip Randolph called off a march on Washington he had planned in order to draw attention to discriminatory hiring practices in government and throughout the defense industry. Two decades later, the march would take place in support of civil rights legislation. After Randolph cancelled the march, Roosevelt did not return to the subject of racial discrimination again.

In 1942, Roosevelt famously signed Executive Order 9066, which compelled U.S. citizens and permanent residents of Japanese ancestry to take up residence in internment camps.[168] Under the order, 120,000 persons—62 percent of them American citizens—were forced to abandon their homes, farms, and businesses. Unlike the smaller numbers of German or Italian Americans who were also interned, Japanese Americans were rounded up and detained as a group, rather than as individuals suspected of providing aid and comfort to the enemy. Director of the FBI J. Edgar Hoover objected to Roosevelt's order, stating he saw no security risks grave enough to warrant such discrimination against an entire group of citizens. In 1980, a commission appointed by Congress concluded that the internments had been motivated more by racism than by military necessity, and in 1988, President Ronald Reagan proclaimed FDR's internment policy as a "grave wrong" and signed legislation awarding loyal Japanese Americans who had been interned, or their heirs, restitutions.

Some historians criticize FDR for his slowness to acknowledge the Holocaust and for his failure to make the rescue of European Jews a major aim of the war once the United States had entered it. Roosevelt maintained that the best way to combat and end what was transpiring in Hitler's death camps was for the United States to win the war at the earliest possible moment.[169] The truism of that statement should not absolve Roosevelt for the conscious decisions he made or allowed others to make not to allow into the United States, both before and during the war, more who sought to escape Hitler's persecution than he did.[170]

In early 1939, one thousand Jewish passengers on the S.S. *St. Louis* remained for days docked in Havana, Cuba. The Cuban government refused to allow them to disembark as they waited for permission to enter the United States. In the absence of a positive reply from the U.S. government, the ship returned to Europe. That same year, Roosevelt refused to support the Wagner-Rogers bill, which would have admitted twenty thousand Jewish children under the age of fourteen to the United States. On his watch, the bill died.[171] In contrast, Roosevelt and Congress actively endorsed legislation that allowed for the admission of children from war-torn Britain into the United States to wait out the war. There was also the matter of foot-dragging by Roosevelt appointees (especially Breckenridge Long) at the State Department in issuing visas. As a result, the already restrictive quotas for southern and eastern Europe went unmet before and during the war. In taking the stance he did toward these issues, Roosevelt allowed the politics and the prejudices of those in his orbit, as well as some of his own, to guide him. (He had come under fire from anti-Semitic groups for the high number of Jews he had appointed to government posts. Prior to the United States's entry into World War II, aviator-hero Charles Lindbergh voiced what was well within mainstream opinion when he singled out British and Jewish interests as the only ones who stood to gain from American participation in the war.)

How FDR would have responded to increased Soviet aggression at the end of World War II and its refusal to abide by agreements it had made at Yalta prior to the war's end remains among the most intriguing and unanswered questions in American history. It is understandable why, at a time when the United States was allied with the U.S.S.R. in the midst of a world war, that Roosevelt kept silent about atrocities the Soviet Union committed inside and outside its borders. Less so is Roosevelt's failure to comment on crimes Joseph Stalin committed prior to the war. It is inconceivable that Stalinist purges and gulags escaped his attention. Equally troubling is the inattention and lack of concern Roosevelt paid to warnings that Stalin ordered agents to infiltrate the highest reaches of the American government.

Harry S Truman

In protecting and expanding liberty, Harry S Truman surpassed all of his Democratic predecessors and several of his Republican ones. In the immediate aftermath of World War II, the KKK increased the number of atrocities it committed against African Americans. It especially targeted as its victims African American war veterans. A good many were beaten and lynched by local terrorists, who enjoyed the protection of local authorities. Walter White, Chief Secretary of the NAACP, took his concerns about these increased outbreaks of racially motivated criminal acts to the new president. As John McCain and Mark Salter noted, Truman "was not a man to ignore a shocked conscience or let actions so vile to his sound moral code go unanswered."[172]

He asked Attorney General Tom Clark to investigate what became of many of the cases that had come to the White House's attention. Not surprisingly, Clark found that all-white juries were unwilling to convict other whites for assaults against blacks. By executive order, Truman named a commission to investigate the full extent of civil rights violations and to recommend remedies. In the first speech any American president delivered before the NAACP since its founding in 1911, Truman proposed federal antilynching legislation, the abolition of poll taxes, and an end to discrimination in the workplace. The president threw the full weight of his office behind the commission report, *To Secure These Rights*. Truman asked Congress to enact the measures that he had already endorsed in his NAACP appearance, as well as proposals to desegregate interstate transportation, protect voting rights, establish a civil rights division within the Justice Department, and remove racial barriers to immigration.

More than a year before White had alerted him to the KKK atrocities, Truman, in one of his first acts as president, had asked Congress to make permanent the Fair Employment Practices Committee that FDR had established. Although the bill succumbed to a Senate filibuster, Truman ignited what would be a long national debate over civil rights that Roosevelt had so tried to avoid. Soon, Truman issued Executive Order 9981, which desegregated the armed forces and the civil service.[173]

Truman pursued all these actions even though he shared some of the prejudices against blacks, Jews, Catholics, and other minorities that many of his contemporaries held and voiced. Truman was known to use the "N-word" in casual conversation, wrote disparagingly of Jews after visits to New York City, and maintained that the Vatican would dictate policy should a Catholic be elected president.[174] Truman, however, believed that his responsibility under the Constitution trumped his personal biases. Just to be on the safe side with his neighbors (and with some of his relatives), he cautioned his listeners not to mistake his embrace of equality before the law as an endorsement of social equality. Like his hero Andrew Jackson, Truman formed most of his opinions on the basis of personal experience and prejudices rather than political philosophy. Fortunately for his minority constituents, most of Truman's prior experiences with minority groups had been positive.

Informed by a KKK official that he would have to pledge not to hire Catholics if he expected the organization's backing when he ran for local office in the 1920s, Truman demanded the return of his $10 initiation fee. During World War I, Truman had commanded Battery D, a battalion heavily comprised of Irish Catholics. Every time he ran for public office, Truman did so with the support of the men who called him "Captain Harry," but without the KKK's endorsement.[175] Like several other presidents who served in the military, Truman found war to be a great equalizer. He accepted his responsibilities as commander in chief with the utmost seriousness, especially its implicit contract of mutual responsibilities and obligations between the commander in chief and those who served under him in the armed forces. "My stomach turned over when I learned that Negro soldiers, just back from overseas, were being dumped out of army trucks in Mississippi and beaten," he wrote a friend.[176]

His embrace of civil rights cost Truman considerable support in the south, a region that was still heavily Democratic. In protest of Truman's support of a strong civil rights plank in the 1948 Democratic platform, entire delegations walked out of the convention. In the hope of depriving Truman of sufficient numbers of Democratic votes in order to throw the election into the House of Representatives—where southern bargaining power might be enhanced—South Carolina Governor Strom Thurmond ran for president on the newly formed States Rights Party ticket. Reminded that the civil rights provision to which he objected was similar to those contained in previous platforms on which Roosevelt had run with Thurmond's support, the governor replied, "I agree, but Truman really *means* it."[177] Truman's stand may have cost him support in other parts of the country as well; Gallup reported that only 7 percent of the public supported his agenda on civil rights.[178] Not surprisingly, little of it passed while he was president.

Early in Truman's presidency, it fell to him to decide what would become of persons displaced by the war overseas, many of whom were Jewish survivors of Hitler's death camps who had no place to go. After an academic, whom Truman had sent overseas to investigate the treatment of displaced persons, reported back that they were faring no better under the Allies than they had under their oppressors, Truman ordered immediate improvements. Overriding opposition from his most trusted adviser, Secretary of State George C. Marshall, a few years later Truman extended diplomatic recognition to the State of Israel moments after it declared its existence. In making this decision, Truman was, in part, influenced by his association with his former business partner, Eddie Jacobson, who acted as a broker between him and Zionist leaders.[179] Because of the courage and tenacity Truman displayed during his presidency, dreams of freedom became closer to reality for millions both at home and abroad.

Dwight D. Eisenhower

One year into Dwight D. Eisenhower's presidency, the Supreme Court declared segregation of public schools unconstitutional under the equal protection clause in the Fourteenth Amendment. After the court issued its *Brown v. Board of Education* decision, Eisenhower said little, other than that he considered the court's ruling the law of the land and that he would enforce it. Some interpreted his failure to issue a strong endorsement of the ruling as evidence that he disagreed with it and might not be aggressive in enforcing it. The president's behavior was consistent with how he conceived of the powers of his office. Eisenhower believed the president should enforce all Supreme Court decisions. He also thought a president could elicit greater compliance with a controversial decision if he did not appear as an advocate for either side. "If the day comes when we can obey the orders of our courts *only when we personally approve of them*, the end of the American system, as we know it, will not be far off," he wrote.[180] In his subsequent writings and actions, however, Eisenhower made clear that he agreed with the *Brown* decision.[181]

Behind the scenes, Eisenhower used the *Brown* decision as leverage to bring about peaceful integration. He summoned the three members of the commission that ran the District of Columbia and ordered them to commence the desegregation of the city's schools immediately. By the end of Eisenhower's first term, with his support, the last vestiges of segregation had been dismantled in the national capital and within the federal government. Discrimination in government employment and in contracting was banned.[182] Eisenhower used his well-developed bureaucratic skills and organizational competence to eliminate what remained of discrimination in the U.S. armed forces.

Eisenhower's brand of leadership put a premium on forbearance and restraint. Hoping that others might follow their example, he singled out for praise individuals and school districts that had successfully and peacefully dismantled segregation. He urged opponents of school integration to voice their objections only through peaceful and legal means. Having spent time in southern states earlier in his life, Eisenhower feared that, unless and until attitudes changed, white parents would remove their children from public schools rather than allow them to attend integrated ones.[183] Eisenhower would have preferred that the Supreme Court not begin its assault on segregation with something as emotional to parents as their children's education. Nevertheless, once the court had acted, Eisenhower was intent on supporting it.

Three years after the court handed down its *Brown* ruling, Eisenhower sent the 101st Airborne Division to escort nine black students into Central High School in Little Rock, Arkansas, after an unruly mob had denied them entrance. Governor Orval Faubus ordered the National Guard to prevent the nine students from entering. He then withdrew the troops, leaving the students at the mercy of the mob. Eisenhower publicly justified his intervention not in the name of integration but by the need to quell an insurrection. If Ike did not, as critics charged, seek to use the bully pulpit to *preach* the virtues of integration, he was prepared to use his powers as commander in chief to enforce the Supreme Court's order. Like the general he was, Eisenhower instructed the Justice Department and the Pentagon to send sufficient forces to Little Rock to assure that they could carry out their mission. He sent one thousand soldiers. By sundown on the day Eisenhower intervened, the mission had been completed with a minimum of disruption. Eisenhower's action made him the first president since Ulysses S. Grant to send federal troops to the south to enforce the civil rights of African Americans.

That same year, Eisenhower also became the first president since Grant to send a civil rights bill to Congress. Historians and journalists have heaped mountains of praise upon Senate Democratic Majority Leader Lyndon Johnson for the deft manner in which he steered the 1957 bill to passage by offering an amendment that essentially rendered it ineffective (see chapter 3).[184] Surprisingly, they have awarded Eisenhower little praise for introducing a much stronger version of the bill than the one Congress passed and for fighting to enact it hard as he did.[185] Eisenhower's persistence kept the measure alive and produced some rather unusual alliances, such as the one between conservative Republican Senate leader William F. Knowland and liberal Democratic Senator Paul Douglas. Civil rights historian Taylor Branch noted that when it came to civil and voting rights, Eisenhower and the civil rights leadership were of one mind. "With his right to vote assured, the American Negro could use it to secure his other rights," Eisenhower insisted.[186] (As president, Johnson would take this identical position less than a decade later.)

Incensed by Ike's bill, Truman's former tormentor, Senator Strom Thurmond of South Carolina, spoke against Eisenhower's proposal for thirty-six hours, setting a new record for filibusters. Johnson's controversial provision allowing for jury trials of election officials accused of violating the statute raised the ire of the civil rights establishment. Diplomat Ralph Bunche, baseball great Jackie Robinson, and A. Philip Randolph urged a veto. Vice President Richard Nixon termed the Johnson provision "a vote against the right to vote."[187] In his memoirs, Ike bitterly complained about Democrats who put aside their professed interest in the underdog and went along with Johnson's maneuver.[188] Aware of the symbolic importance of his signing the first civil rights bill in nearly a century, Eisenhower approved the weakened measure.[189] The act established both the Civil Rights Commission and the Civil Rights Division in the Justice Department, which

Truman had initially requested. Ike then proposed and shepherded through another civil rights bill in 1960 that provided for federal poll inspectors.

John F. Kennedy

Civil rights was not high on John F. Kennedy's agenda at the outset of his presidency. Nor had he shown much passion for the issue as a senator. In the words of his trusted adviser Theodore C. Sorensen, Kennedy "simply did not give much thought to the subject," and he did not have any "background or association or activity in race relations."[190] When he made a stab at the 1956 Democratic vice-presidential nomination, Kennedy received considerable southern support. Afterward, he joked that he would be singing "Dixie" for the rest of his life.[191] In the run-up to the 1960 Democratic Convention, many regarded Kennedy as the south's favorite northern contender. Southern officeholders, as well as the civil rights leadership, had made note of Kennedy's vote in support of Lyndon Johnson's amendment that watered down the 1957 civil rights bill.

As the presidential nominee, Kennedy employed the conventional Democratic strategy of marshalling heavy turnouts among southern whites and northern union workers, Catholics, and blacks—important components of his party's base. To endear himself to black voters, Kennedy said that racial discrimination in housing could be removed by a "stroke of a pen" and that as president he would ban it in this fashion. His campaign made certain that news of the telephone call Kennedy made to Coretta Scott King, Martin Luther King Jr.'s wife—expressing concern over her husband's arrest on trumped-up charges—was discreetly leaked to key civil rights leaders and the black press.

Kennedy disappointed the civil rights leadership when he announced that he would not be introducing civil rights legislation during his first year in office.[192] His record on appointments was decidedly mixed. Kennedy named a record number of blacks to federal posts and appointed several avowed segregationists to judgeships in jurisdictions where civil rights organizations had major cases pending. Kennedy and his team made symbolic gestures to demonstrate their opposition to segregation.

Initially, Kennedy regarded demands for increased enforcement of civil rights provisions and new protections more as problems to be managed than as major priorities. Inspired by the clarion call to service that he had issued in his inaugural address, hundreds and eventually thousands of young Freedom Riders journeyed south to assure—through peaceful confrontations and eventually court orders—compliance with a Supreme Court decision that had banned segregation on interstate buses. Administration officials worked to protect demonstrators from violent attacks along their route.

In his endeavor to enforce a court order compelling the University of Mississippi to admit black military veteran James Meredith, Kennedy followed Eisenhower's Little Rock precedent. He did so, however, with a smaller show of force, which met with greater resistance. About a third of the ill-equipped five hundred federal marshals Kennedy ordered to the scene suffered injuries at the hand of brick and bottle throwing mobs. Two bystanders were killed. The crisis ebbed only after Kennedy federalized the Mississippi National Guard, which was already on the scene, and sent federal troops to back them up.

Kennedy began to show greater concern for both the issue of civil rights and the safety of demonstrators after the Rev. Martin Luther King Jr. led an epochal march on Birmingham, Alabama. Dating back at least to his time in the navy, Kennedy admired people who demonstrated great physical and other forms of courage. On May 2, 1963, scenes of the vicious dogs Sheriff "Bull" Connor turned on young demonstrators appeared on front pages of newspapers and flashed on television sets across the country. One particular photo of a dog poised to bite into a young man in the abdomen caught Kennedy's eye. He was reported to have been sickened and repulsed by what he had seen.

In June 1963, Alabama Governor George C. Wallace sought to block with his person two African American students a court had ordered admitted to the University of Alabama from enrolling. By the time Wallace took his place in what he termed the "schoolhouse door," he found that the Kennedy administration had out-organized him. Kennedy aides had persuaded trustees, state officials, and faculty to come out in favor of desegregation. At his behest, nearly one hundred corporations in the area agreed to hire African

Americans. Kennedy again federalized the National Guard. In the event they were needed, troops at Fort Benning were poised to be helicoptered in. Wallace backed down.

That evening, in a national address, Kennedy became the first modern president to describe civil rights as a moral issue. "It is as old as the scriptures and as clear as the constitution," he said. "The heart of the question is whether . . . we are going to treat our fellow Americans as we want to be treated."[193] After reciting a series of indignities blacks suffered, Kennedy asked his audience who among them would be content to stand in their place, and who among them would be content with the counsels of patience and delay. He promised to send major legislation to Congress within a week. Initially wary when informed that a quarter of a million demonstrators would be marching on Washington in support of the bill, Kennedy's administration urged its organizers to have speakers tone down their rhetoric. Impressed by the proceedings, Kennedy received a delegation of the march's organizers.

In the weeks following his submission of what would become the Civil Rights Act of 1964, Kennedy worked with key committees and especially with the Republican leadership of both houses of Congress to clear its way to passage. The civil rights bill was further along to passage than the rest of Kennedy's program at the time of his assassination. Lyndon Johnson may have driven a tougher bargain with some holdouts, issued greater threats, and increased the pressure by proclaiming the bill a memorial to his slain predecessor. But by the time he left for Dallas, Kennedy had done much of the heavy lifting. In the words of historian John N. Giglio, "Kennedy's efforts, not his death, had contributed most to its passage."[194]

Lyndon B. Johnson

Lyndon Johnson's successful efforts to pass the Civil Rights Act of 1964 and the Voting Rights Act of 1965 and the effects they had on the country were discussed in detail in chapter 3.

Richard Nixon

Had the cover-up of what Nixon's attorney general John Mitchell termed the "White House horrors" succeeded, the liberty that all Americans enjoy as their birthright, including protections under the Bill of Rights, the separation of powers, and checks and balances as set out in the Constitution, might have been severely compromised. Former special prosecutor Kenneth Starr has suggested that, in bowing to the Supreme Court's order that he surrender incriminating evidence (those famous tapes) to investigators, Nixon too recognized the sanctity of the rule of law.[195] In view of all that had transpired prior to Nixon's resignation and all he and his aides had done to precipitate a constitutional crisis, readers will be forgiven for not listing Nixon's final actions as president among his finest hours.

The cynicism and *realpolitik* that Nixon and Secretary of State Kissinger practiced on the world stage led them to be too tolerant of military juntas and too wary of elective governments in developing countries in which U.S. policies were not popular. They were also too jittery about criticizing how their negotiating partners, particularly the Soviet Union and the People's Republic of China, treated dissenters, minorities, and people of faith within their borders.

As a congressman, senator, and vice president, Nixon had established a reputation as a moderate on civil rights. In his race against John F. Kennedy in 1960, he carried approximately one-third of the votes cast by African Americans. In presenting himself as a centrist alternative to the more liberal Nelson A. Rockefeller and the more conservative Ronald Reagan, Nixon won the 1968 Republican nomination after convincing southern delegates that he would be less aggressive in enforcing civil rights measures than would Rockefeller or the Democrats. In exchange for the support of leaders such as Senator Strom Thurmond, who had switched allegiances to the GOP, President Nixon made a series of commitments, including a promise to appoint more conservative judges and go slowly when it came to desegregating schools. Thus was born the "southern strategy," through which Nixon would effect a realignment of the parties by adding to the Republican column votes of southern whites, who had habitually voted Democratic.

Among the ironies of Nixon's presidency was that it was he who offici-
ated over the final dismantling of segregation in the American south. Early
in his administration, Nixon set out to achieve full implementation of the
Brown v. Board of Education decision. Working through Secretary of Labor George P. Shultz, Nixon's advisers set up biracial panels in each affected state to devise and implement plans to desegregate. In public, Nixon
generally shied away from taking credit for his achievement. In private, and
occasionally in public, he signaled to his southern supporters that the cost
of their noncooperation would entail more court orders, which he would
enforce.

One Nixon aide described his boss's strategy as keeping "liberal writers"
convinced that he was doing what the Supreme Court required and his "conservative supporters" convinced that he was not doing any *more* than it
required.[196] Nixon's efforts in this area might properly be regarded as the domestic equivalent of his historic, precedent-shattering visit to China. In both
instances, he achieved his primary goal of achieving what his Democratic
predecessors had not.

Gerald R. Ford

Gerald Ford's efforts to resettle Vietnamese refugees in the United States
and elsewhere after the fall of Saigon were noted in chapter 2. At the time of the
signing of the Helsinki Accords, a priority of Ford's, human rights activists and
many conservatives belittled them as a Soviet victory because they conceded to
the "inviolability" of existing European borders. In the late stages of the Cold
War, however, the accords, through the lip service they awarded the right to
peaceful dissent, proved a major boon to democratic elements behind what
was still considered an Iron Curtain. Dissidents with the courage to speak out
cited official protections the Helsinki Accords promised them. Because of their
skills in attracting media attention and Western support, these dissidents, in
the long run, proved more successful in achieving their aims than had their
predecessors who had attempted armed revolt decades earlier.

Jimmy Carter

As a presidential candidate, Carter pledged to put human rights at the head of his international policy concerns. Unlike his predecessors, he did not hesitate to criticize governments allied with the United States against the Soviet Union if they denied basic human rights to their own citizens. Carter withdrew support from Nicaraguan dictator Anastasio Somoza and imposed sanctions on several Third World nations to prod them into holding elections. However, Carter proved inconsistent in his execution of his own policy, and, like his predecessors, he allowed strategic and other considerations to set his human rights priorities. (His failings were discussed in chapter 4.)

Ronald Reagan

Historians will long debate the degree to which Ronald Reagan caused or hastened the demise of the Soviet Union. With that peaceful but transformative event, fears of the world ending through a nuclear exchange between the United States and its major world rival ceased. Reagan's role in bringing this about and the by-products it wrought, which included the extension of liberty and democracy to millions of people long considered captive to tyranny, was hardly inconsequential. If the former leaders of what was truly an evil empire can be believed, it was Reagan's determination and willingness to spend them into the ground that forced a change in Soviet policy and strategy. For achieving that, Reagan ranks with Lincoln and FDR as one of three presidents who brought down what had indeed been monstrous evils.

On the domestic front, Reagan's record of extending liberty was more mixed, and a historical consensus has yet to emerge as to which of his actions were truly liberating, which were necessary, and which were unwise or short-sighted. In reducing marginal income tax rates, Reagan, as had Kennedy before him, empowered more individuals to take control over their destinies. More new and small businesses were founded during his time in office than ever before in the nation's history and more Americans owned shares of stock in private companies.

With regard to race relations and other human rights concerns, the insensitivity Reagan unintentionally displayed, plus the obtuseness of his staff, marred what might otherwise be regarded as a commendable record. Supporters of civil rights took offense when, as the Republican nominee for president, Reagan appeared on August 3, 1980, at the Neshoba County Fair and proclaimed his support for states' rights.[197] In the summer of 1964, in Philadelphia, Mississippi, a few miles from where Reagan had delivered his remarks, members of the KKK had brutally murdered three civil rights workers, Andrew Goodman, James Chaney, and Michael Schwerner, with the apparent complicity of the local police. Reagan's critics and Democratic officials have charged ever since that Reagan's choice of venue and the message he delivered, if not symptomatic of racism or callousness on Reagan's part, were at least an attempt either to appeal for support from racists or to signal to them that his administration would not vigorously uphold the civil rights of minorities or aggressively prosecute those who violated them.

Reagan and his supporters had ample reason to decry what he regarded as false and hypocritical charges. Throughout his life, Reagan had abhorred and denounced all forms of racism. Among his early memories was his father forbidding him from viewing D. W. Griffith's *The Birth of a Nation* because of its racist themes.[198] When black players on his football team at Eureka College were denied access to a hotel, Reagan took them to his parents' home to spend the night.[199] As a sports announcer, Reagan advocated the integration of major league baseball.[200] After a California cemetery refused to bury the body of a decorated Japanese American soldier who had fallen in combat, Reagan, then an Army captain, said at a unity gathering in the Santa Anna Bowl that "the blood that has soaked into the sand is all one color."[201] As president, Reagan, contrary to the advice of some key advisers, signed legislation that provided for payments to Japanese Americans who had been interred and to their heirs and conveyed an apology.[202] In his remarks, Reagan termed the wartime internment of these civilians "a great wrong."[203] Reagan had been on record as favoring Harry Truman's civil rights policies as well as the Navy's decision to drop its ban on Japanese Americans. He resigned from a country club in Hollywood when he found out that it did not welcome Jewish members.[204]

As a conservative spokesman, and as a governor, Reagan was indeed an advocate of states' rights. But he hardly favored them as a pretext for depriving African Americans civil rights. Nor did he seek common ground with segregationists, who did. Reagan had been sympathetic to the Sagebrush Rebellion, a movement that advocated transferring the administration of federal lands in thirteen western states from the Bureau of Land Management to state agencies. The "rebels" justified their claim in the name of states' rights.[205] As California's governor, Reagan had come to dislike federal intrusion, regulations, and "land grabs." When he spoke of "states' rights," Reagan meant a return to what he regarded as the historic role states played in managing the natural resources within their borders and in administering and setting education and other domestic policies. He did not seek to apply the principle as a means of stripping any American of his or her civil rights. While no racist, Reagan, at the same time, in the words of a biographer, "never supported the use of federal power to provide blacks with civil rights systematically denied to them."[206]

As an astute politician, however, Reagan should have been aware of how people on both sides of the civil rights debate would read into his visit to Neshoba and his failure to refer to its recent past history while he was there. Yet, if the visit had been planned to convey the message Reagan's critics charged, it hardly squared with his well-publicized visits to urban settings, where he decried the failures of liberalism to attract jobs and investment to areas where some of the poorest Americans lived. His stop in the South Bronx, where he announced his support for urban enterprise zones, for instance, attracted considerable attention. Reagan and his handlers did appreciate how the candidate's appearance with the father of Polish Solidarity leader Lech Walesa at Liberty State Park in Jersey City, with the Statue of Liberty as a backdrop, might well be received among Polish Americans. According to Lou Cannon, the only thing Reagan's visit to Neshoba did for his campaign was cost him the support of some suburban moderates.[207]

After he became president, Reagan and the civil rights community would have their differences over public policy. Although Reagan maintained that the

Voting Rights Act of 1965 had been unnecessary, he approved its renewal. After initially opposing the establishment of a legal holiday to honor Dr. Martin Luther King Jr., Reagan signed the measure into law. Another question on which he reversed himself concerned the tax exemption of Bob Jones University. Reagan's three predecessors favored depriving the religious-based institution in Greenville, South Carolina, such an exemption because it officially prohibited interracial dating. Unaware of the thinking that guided previous presidents on the case, Reagan initially saw it as an instance of the federal government seeking to regulate religion. He changed his mind after attending a meeting that presidential adviser Michael Deaver arranged between Reagan and African Americans serving in his administration.[208]

In addition to dustups such as these, Reagan and his detractors had some genuine philosophical differences. Consensus has yet to form over Reagan's expressed reservations about the advisability and utility of programs such as affirmative action were wise or accurate. What one camp saw as the broadening of rights and opportunities the other believed led to additional unfairness and perpetuation of stereotyping. In recent years, elected leaders and public intellectuals suggested moving away from a system that places emphasis on race to one that emphasizes social class. During his presidency, Bill Clinton suggested that the system needed to be "mended" rather than "ended." During the 2008 presidential primaries, Barack Obama, a candidate for the Democratic nomination, suggested that his daughters not be awarded additional consideration under such programs on the grounds that they were not disadvantaged.

Late in Reagan's term, his advisers showed the same tin ear they had earlier revealed during the Neshoba incident. To commemorate the fortieth anniversary of V-E day and postwar American friendship with West Germany that followed, Reagan agreed to visit a German military cemetery outside of Bitburg. When this cemetery was discovered to contain the graves of forty-nine Waffen-SS soldiers, Jewish organizations, Holocaust survivors, American veterans organizations, members of Congress, and the media demanded that the president cancel his visit. As a show of support for Chancellor Helmut Kohl, who had honored Reagan's request to station Pershing II missiles in his country, Reagan refused to cancel his appearance. His stand was identical to the one he took when an aide tried to persuade him to back away from his Neshoba appearance in 1980. An actor, Reagan insisted, should always appear once his billing has been announced.[209] Instead, Reagan added to his itinerary a stop at the Bergen-Belsen death camp. After a quick stroll through the Bitburg cemetery in silence, Reagan delivered one of the most moving addresses of his career at Bergen-Belsen. His closing words were:

> Everywhere here are memories—pulling us, touching us, making us understand that they can never be erased. Such memories take us where God intended His children to go—toward learning, toward healing, and, above all, toward redemption. They beckon us through the endless stretches of our heart to the knowing commitment that the life of each individual can change the world and make it better.
>
> We're all witnesses; we share the glistening hope that rests in every human soul. Hope leads us, if we're prepared to trust it, toward what our President Lincoln called the better angels of our nature. And then, rising above all this cruelty, out of this tragic and nightmarish time, beyond the anguish, the pain and the suffering for all time, we can and must pledge: Never again.[210]

Jack Kemp was right to have called Ronald Reagan the "last lion of the Twentieth Century."

7

DEFENSE, NATIONAL SECURITY, AND FOREIGN POLICY

*P*residents have multiple policy options and fewer constraints in the international arena than in domestic policy. Consequently, any evaluation of their performance in this area poses many challenges. Some of the most successful presidents achieved their international objectives without resorting to war. When that proved impossible, they provided the leadership that enabled the United States to prevail in a necessary or inevitable war. The less successful presidents reacted to international events more than they shaped them. Some blundered into wars and other foreign entanglements that did little to enhance American security or advance American interests. Such successes and failures are not all that difficult to assess. More difficult to evaluate on their own terms are two other groups of presidents: those who managed to avoid wars that did not need to be fought and those who opted for wars of choice that they executed brilliantly.

Some presidents articulated the role they wished the United States to play in the world as part of the overall vision they advanced in their campaigns. Others, whose realm of experience had exclusively been in domestic policy and who hoped to concentrate their focus on that arena, had to make their way as circumstances demanded. How well presidents implemented or developed the stance they took toward defense and national security matters is another way to assess their performance. Presidents whose records in these areas were assessed in prior chapters will not have their successes or failures revisited here.

Presidents who achieved major international policy goals without resorting to war include George Washington, John Adams, Thomas Jefferson, James Monroe, Theodore Roosevelt, Harry S Truman, Dwight D. Eisenhower, John F. Kennedy, and Ronald Reagan. Those who prevailed in a war after failing to avert it through other means were Abraham Lincoln, Woodrow Wilson, and Franklin D. Roosevelt. Presidents who either allowed themselves to be tossed about by events or pursued policies that proved harmful to the nation's interests include Thomas Jefferson, James Madison, Jimmy Carter, and Lyndon Johnson. It is too early to determine on which of these lists to place George W. Bush. As of this writing, it is difficult to see, when assessing the war in Iraq, how future historians could include him among that handful of presidents who executed wars of choice brilliantly: James K. Polk, Abraham Lincoln, William McKinley, and George H. W. Bush. If events on the ground go better than what was anticipated during much of his time in office, historians of the future may well regard it as others have the Korean conflict: costly and poorly executed, but worthwhile. If this comes to pass, on the pages of history Bush may be seen in the same way as to Harry Truman, as he himself has suggested.

For their handling of the nation's international and defense policies:

EIGHT PRESIDENTS RECEIVE A SCORE OF 5:

George Washington
James Monroe
James K. Polk
Abraham Lincoln
William McKinley
Theodore Roosevelt
Franklin D. Roosevelt
Ronald Reagan

SIX PRESIDENTS RECEIVE A SCORE OF 4:

John Adams
Woodrow Wilson
Harry S Truman
Dwight D. Eisenhower
John F. Kennedy
George H. W. Bush

NINETEEN PRESIDENTS RECEIVE A SCORE OF 3:

Thomas Jefferson

John Quincy Adams

Andrew Jackson

Martin Van Buren

John Tyler

Millard Fillmore

Zachary Taylor

Franklin Pierce

James Buchanan

Andrew Johnson

Ulysses S. Grant

Rutherford B. Hayes

Chester A. Arthur

Grover Cleveland

Benjamin Harrison

William H. Taft

Richard Nixon

Gerald Ford

Bill Clinton

THREE PRESIDENTS RECEIVE A SCORE OF 2:

Warren G. Harding

Calvin Coolidge

Herbert Hoover

THREE PRESIDENTS RECEIVE THE FAILING SCORE OF 1:

James Madison

Lyndon B. Johnson

Jimmy Carter

(W. H. Harrison, J. A. Garfield, and G. W. Bush were not evaluated.)

George Washington

Washington's highest priority as president was preserving the internal cohesion and the independence of a young and fragile country. This, he knew, meant maintaining a friendly distance from three European powers that remained a presence in North America and in the Caribbean basin: France, Great Britain, and Spain. War against any of them might result in the recolonization of the United States. On the other hand, a close alliance with any of them, as a means of fending off the others, might turn the United States into a vassal of its more powerful ally. While commander in chief of the Continental Army, Washington hinted at his future approach to international policy. Although he was grateful for the financial and military support France provided the American colonies in their struggle for independence, he remained wary that the new nation might grow too close to its benefactor. "The nation which indulges toward another an habitual hatred, or habitual animosity, is in some degree a slave," he warned in his presidential farewell address.[1]

During his second term in office, Washington feared that strong public sentiment in favor of France might draw the United States into war with Great Britain. When hostilities broke out between revolutionary France and the monarchies of Europe in 1793, Washington issued the Proclamation of Neutrality. This document asserted that the United States would remain "friendly and impartial" with both belligerents. Washington was aware that his proclamation contravened the Treaty of Alliance of 1778, which required the United States to aid France during a war if the French government so requested.

To force Washington's hand—or at least to circumvent his policy—the French government sent Edmond-Charles Genêt as its ambassador to the United States to recruit American volunteers and privateers to harass British ships in the Atlantic and Caribbean. Initially, Genêt received a warm welcome. Democratic-Republican societies (organized by Jefferson and Madison) held receptions in his honor. As secretary of state, Thomas Jefferson had been sympathetic to France. He urged Genêt to take his country's case to Congress.[2] Fearful that an open break between the two branches over the French aid question would spark violence on American streets, Washington demanded Genêt's recall. He wound up offering him asylum after the Jacobins came to power.

In 1793 and 1794, the British navy tested Washington's patience when it captured 350 American merchant ships in the Caribbean. Rather than accede to Jeffersonian demands for war, Washington sent Chief Justice John Jay to London to negotiate a peaceful settlement of Anglo-American differences. In addition to trade restrictions it had placed on American goods and the disregard it showed American shipping rights, other American grievances against the crown included Britain's retention of forts in the Northwest Territory in violation of the Treaty of Paris and Britain's continued instigation of Native American attacks upon American settlers. In a precursor to the disastrous policy Jefferson would pursue as president, the House of Representatives passed an embargo on all trade with Great Britain.

Jay returned with a treaty that resolved some but not all of the disputes between the countries. The British government agreed to evacuate its remaining forts and to compensate American merchants for captured ships and cargo. It dropped its opposition to American trading in the West Indies, with the proviso that the United States restrict the size of its ships and reduce its exports of cotton and other agricultural goods that competed with similar commodities produced in British colonies in the region. The two nations agreed on the parameters of the Canadian boundary and agreed to settle by arbitration any remaining disputes over debts incurred prior to the Revolutionary War. A professed abolitionist, Jay had not, as Jeffersonians had demanded, pressed the British government on compensation to slaveholders, whose "property" British soldiers had set free or encouraged to flee during the war.

Under the treaty, the British government retained the right to seize cargo on vessels of neutral ships bound for enemy ports and to impress sailors it suspected of desertion. These provisions, along with the treaty's failure to end all trade restrictions or provide for the compensation of slaveholders, led Democratic-Republicans to oppose the treaty's ratification. Jay mordantly joked that he could walk through every state by night with his path illuminated by his burning effigies. Having resigned from Washington's cabinet, Jefferson, now in opposition, proclaimed, "Acquiescence to insult is not the way to escape war."[3] Drawing upon Washington's popularity, Hamilton, acting as both the president's agent and the leader of the Federalist Party, steered the treaty through the Senate in a 20-to-10 vote, after stripping out some trade restrictions.

As leader of the Jeffersonian majority in the House of Representatives, Madison demanded that the House be privy to all correspondence between Jay and his British counterparts. He argued that, because the treaty contained spending provisions and that the Constitution mandated that all appropriations bills originate in the House, it had a right to see the documents. Washington, drawing upon his personal prestige, cast himself as even more of a strict constructionist than the Jeffersonians. He reminded them that the Constitution awarded the House no role in ratifying treaties. By withholding of the information Madison requested, Washington established the principle of executive privilege. When the House subsequently sought to render the treaty meaningless by blocking appropriations to fund its provisions, Washington aggressively lobbied Congress for the funds. The critical appropriation passed the House by three votes.[4]

Washington fought as hard as he did for the Jay Treaty because he did not believe that the United States was sufficiently strong militarily to win a second war against the world's strongest power. He estimated that the United States would need at least twenty years to develop that capability. In the meantime, he was willing to settle for whatever concessions he could extract from the British. That the United States came as close as it did to losing its second war with the United Kingdom, which it commenced in 1812, underscored the soundness of Washington's policy.

John Adams

Angered that the United States had granted what the French government regarded as preferential trade status to its enemy, Great Britain, under the Jay Treaty, the French navy began to seize American merchant ships bound for British ports. President John Adams sent a delegation to Paris to resolve differences between the two nations. When French Foreign Minister Charles Maurice de Talleyrand-Périgord refused to receive the Americans until bribes had been paid, war fever rose in the United States. Jeffersonians in Congress, convinced that Adams had deliberately presented the French in a poor light, demanded to see the evidence against Tallyrand. After Adams released information that exonerated his administration, he found himself in the awkward position of fending off demands within his own Federalist Party for war with France with the opposition lending him tepid and skeptical support.

Though troubled by the bribery revelations, Jefferson, now vice president, continued to advocate France's case. Jefferson even advised the French government not to make concessions to Adams in advance of the next presidential election, which Jefferson expected to win. With the French growing increasingly belligerent, Adams began bolstering the nation's defenses. At his urging, Congress authorized the construction of twelve frigates for the navy and an army of up to fifty thousand. During the next three years, the young nation's fledgling navy proved effective in fending off French privateers and warships. These naval successes strengthened Adams's hand at the negotiating table.

Had Adams been more competent as a party leader and shown more of a flair for public relations, his administration would be primarily remembered for avoiding an unnecessary war with the world's second strongest power. Instead, it is best known for the internal divisions and mounting partisanship that erupted on its watch and the disregard it showed for the civil liberties of its critics. Adams had been elected president in a highly partisan contest with Jefferson. Aware that he lacked Washington's stature, Adams, as a means of improving his standing within his party, retained Washington's entire cabinet. He soon discovered that most of those he had reappointed awarded their loyalties not to him but to former Secretary of the Treasury Alexander Hamilton, Adams's archrival within his party. The haughty and moralistic Adams proclaimed Hamilton nothing more than the "bastard brat of a Scotch peddler."[5] Hamilton returned the compliment many times over.

Ex-president Washington let it be known that he could be pressed into service should his country require it. With war clouds looming, Adams decided to put his predecessor at the head of a provisional army. When the time came for him to serve, the former president, obviously at Hamilton's behest, made his services conditional on Adams appointing Hamilton as Washington's second in command. With Washington delaying his return to the field, Hamilton raised an army. Hamilton's dramatic return to the national stage encouraged his followers in Congress to increase their demands that Adams request a declaration of war against France.

Hostile to standing armies in principle, Jefferson feared that Hamilton would use war with France as a pretext for suspending civil liberties at home. Jefferson's suspicions were borne out when Congress passed four laws, known collectively as the Alien and Sedition Acts of 1778. The Naturalization Act increased from five to fourteen years the time that foreign-born residents had to wait before applying for citizenship. The Alien Friends Act permitted the president to deport any resident alien deemed "dangerous to the peace and safety of the United States." The Alien Enemies Act, the only one of these four laws still in effect, allows the president to deport or intern any resident aliens whose country is at war with the United States. The Sedition Act allowed for the fining and imprisonment of anyone who criticized the government, its policies, or its officers.

In enforcing the Alien and Sedition Acts, Adams's administration seemed more interested in persecuting political opponents than in protecting national security. Opposition newspapers were suppressed, their editors placed in jail, as was at least one congressman. Jefferson, not without reason, complained that a "reign of witches" infected the country.[6] He and Madison secretly drafted resolutions, which passed the Kentucky and Virginia legislatures, declaring the Sedition Act unconstitutional and hinting that it might not be enforced within these states. In response, Hamilton threatened to lead his army into Virginia to enforce the act and suppress any rebellion. Rioting ensued in two Pennsylvania counties when federal authorities attempted to collect a property tax that Congress had enacted to pay for the armed forces.

While the country's politics became increasingly polarized and both sides threatened violence, Adams all but devolved into a bystander. After an eight-month absence from the capital, he belatedly defused tensions between federal authorities and Virginia officials, pardoned the Pennsylvania rebels, and sent a peace delegation to Napoleon's court. On the eve of the 1800 election, France agreed to cease harassing American ships, but not to compensate Americans for property previously seized. As had Washington before him, Adams jumped at a less than perfect agreement that prevented a war he was not certain the young United States could win. In doing so, he spared his country what he would later call the "guilt of an unnecessary war."[7]

Thomas Jefferson

Thomas Jefferson's acquisition of the Louisiana Territory, which virtually doubled the territory of the fledgling United States, and the peaceful manner in which he obtained it rank among the most extraordinary achievements in American history. To achieve this end, Jefferson cast aside, at least temporarily, one of the basic tenets on which he campaigned for the presidency. That he had the capacity to do this made his accomplishment all the more remarkable. Unfortunately, because Jefferson failed to be as flexible in his approach to other international developments, he met with fewer triumphs as he attempted to enhance American security.

Holding four mutually exclusive objectives simultaneously—low taxes, balanced budgets, minimal defense outlays, and a refusal to accede to blackmail from foreign powers—Jefferson frequently painted the U.S. government into corners. Before Jefferson dismantled most of the navy that Adams had bequeathed him, he used it to win an astounding military victory against the Barbary pirates. As he pressed forward on his promise to reduce defense outlays, Jefferson failed to consider how this action rendered meaningless the moral pronouncements he made in the international arena without the power to back them up.

Jefferson's blindness to this reality doomed the attempt he made to entice the warring French and British to respect the rights of neutrals on the high seas when he placed an embargo on trade with those nations. Rather than achieve its ends, the measure helped produce the first presidentially induced recession in U.S. history. It was not by accident that he excluded from the list of accomplishments he requested be engraved on his tombstone—his authorship of the Declaration of Independence and Statute of Virginia for Religious Freedom, and his founding of the University of Virginia—any mention of his presidency, which ended on a most sour note.

James Madison

If Jefferson demonstrated limited ideological flexibility during his presidency, James Madison exhibited none. Throughout the negotiations that produced the Louisiana Purchase, Jefferson assigned no role to Madison, his secretary of state, other than the drafting of arguments in support of the president's action. Once president, Madison refused to countenance even the *appearance* of any deviation from ideological purity. This, combined with his poor judgment in making appointments, nearly ended the American experiment in self-government and independence.

Madison's decision to wage a second war against Great Britain in 1812 was probably the worst national security mistake any president ever made. Believing Congress to be the preeminent branch of the government, he acquiesced to congressional demands for war without first securing the financial and military means to wage it. His financial difficulties stemmed from his having allowed the national bank he had once opposed to go out of business. The country's state of military unpreparedness resulted from Jefferson and Madison's opposition to standing armies.

That the United States survived the folly known to history as the War of 1812 resulted more from Commodore Oliver Perry's victory in the Battle of Lake Erie (facilitated by fortuitous weather conditions), Major George Armistead's steadfast defense of Fort McHenry, and the British disinclination to continue hostilities than from any action of Madison's. Andrew Jackson's victory in the Battle of New Orleans—although it occurred two weeks after the Treaty of Ghent had been signed and the war had officially ended—demonstrated to the world the resolve of the young nation to retain its independence.

James Monroe

In the international arena, James Monroe proved more successful than his two Democratic-Republican predecessors in attaining his objectives. He did so without resorting either to self-defeating economic sanctions or to war. After General Andrew Jackson, perhaps exceeding orders, attacked Spanish forces on a mission intended to repel Native American attacks on new settlers, Spain ceded Florida to the United States. In exchange, Monroe agreed to settle outstanding American debts with Spain. Through deft negotiations, Monroe also extended the boundaries of the Louisiana Purchase. As Spain's grip on the Western Hemisphere loosened, Monroe extended diplomatic recognition to the emerging Latin American republics.

In the doctrine that carries his name, Monroe warned European powers against further colonization in the Americas. Since the United States was still a minor power on the world stage, Monroe recognized that he needed a means other than rhetoric and an emerging but still weak U.S. navy to enforce his edict. Aware that Britain had reasons of its own for wanting to prevent European rivals from acquiring footholds in the Western Hemisphere, Monroe played this situation to his advantage. He eschewed a formal alliance, which his secretary of state, John Quincy Adams, warned would give the appearance of coming in "as a cock-boat in the wake of the British man-of-war."[8] Monroe relied on British self-interest to give his doctrine meaning. Sheltered by the British navy, the United States turned its attention to its internal development, unimpeded by the threat of invasion or foreign distractions.

James K. Polk

James K. Polk was the first president to take office determined to wage a war of choice. He was also the first to manipulate his country into war under a false pretext.[9] Through a combination of bluff and brawn, Polk had masterfully resolved the Oregon–British Columbia boundary dispute with the United Kingdom.[10] With this matter resolved, peacefully, Polk turned his attention to acquiring territory from Mexico. And when the Mexicans rejected his offer to purchase California, Polk resolved to get it by other means.

Relying on deceit and chicanery, he ordered troops to march south, maneuvered Congress into recognizing that a state of war existed and financing a war he was not certain it wanted. Polk fabricated intelligence, withheld vital information from Congress, preempted debate on war policy, and gambled that members of Congress would not cut funds to troops in the field despite many of its members' misgivings about the causes and aims of the war. With these manipulations, Polk set a dangerous precedent for what some of his less competent successors attempted in successive centuries. The manner in which Polk executed the U.S.-Mexico War and succeeded in attaining his goals merits a place of distinction among the nation's war presidents. His success in attaining his territorial ambitions, however, set the United States on a path toward civil war. As was argued in earlier chapters, Polk's failure to anticipate the harmful long-range consequences of his victory and to temper his actions accordingly should cause historians to lower their overall evaluation of his presidency.

Abraham Lincoln

Although the major issues of his presidency were domestic in nature, Abraham Lincoln made the difficult task of keeping the United States a single country somewhat easier through his shrewd handling of international affairs and his subtleness as a diplomat. Regarding his actions on the international stage as means of furthering his domestic objectives, Lincoln brought to bear in this arena all the political skills that served him so well elsewhere. On April 19, 1861, seven days after Confederate forces fired on Fort Sumter, Lincoln proclaimed a blockade of southern ports to prevent the rebellious states from exporting cotton and importing arms, ammunition, and other manufactured goods. As Lincoln's allies and adversaries both recognized, the issuance of a blockade entailed some legal risks.

Most of the world considered blockades instruments of war that one independent nation imposed on another. Lincoln maintained that the conflict in which the United States was engaged was not such a war, but rather an internal rebellion. He recognized, however, that some might see his imposition of a blockade as tacit recognition that the southern states had, in fact, become a separate nation. When Representative Thaddeus Stevens advised Lincoln that, by his logic, the United States had blockaded itself, Lincoln assumed the role of the bumbling backwoodsman that he knew many considered him to be. Ceding Stevens's point, Lincoln said that he did not have much experience as a lawyer with the "law of nations," but, now that he had declared the blockade, "we must get along as well as we can."[11] He would have it both ways.

Later that year, Lincoln faced his most formidable foreign challenge. Captain Charles D. Wilkes, commander of the U.S.S. *San Jacinto*, stopped the

British vessel *Trent* off the coast of Cuba and seized two Confederate agents bound for Europe. With the public and much of the press hailing Wilkes as a hero, Lincoln and Secretary of State William Seward contemplated how best to respond to British protests and threats of war. As tensions mounted, Lincoln used Senate Foreign Affairs Committee Chairman Charles Sumner, whose international contacts exceeded his own, as his back channel to gauge public and official sentiment in Britain. Unwilling to have two wars on his hands at a time, Lincoln tried to assuage British sentiments by volunteering that Wilkes had not acted on presidential orders. He offered to submit the matter to arbitration.

In the face of a British ultimatum threatening war unless the two prisoners were released, Lincoln, backing down, reverted to an argument that most Americans, familiar with their recent history, would have recognized. Upon the advice of the U.S. ambassador to the Court of St. James, Charles Francis Adams, Lincoln ordered the Confederate agents freed on the grounds that their capture had violated the right of neutral nations to freedom of the seas. His argument cast Britain in a role the United States had played as a neutral in the run-up to the War of 1812, and saw its rights violated by warring belligerents. With the confederates released, the British government tensions eased. Lincoln had averted a second and simultaneous military conflict.

As the Civil War progressed, Lincoln's primary international policy goal remained preventing France and the United Kingdom from extending diplomatic recognition to the Confederate States of America. Future Prime Minister William E. Gladstone had proclaimed that, through military victories, Jefferson Davis had made a nation of the Confederacy. Aware that public opinion in both European countries ran against slavery, Lincoln saw the efficacy in using emancipation as a propaganda tool to prevent them from extending full diplomatic recognition to the seceded states. By delaying his issuance of the preliminary Emancipation Proclamation until after the Union victory at the Battle of Antietam in September 1862, Lincoln provided anti-slavery forces in the British Parliament with ammunition to help block their government from recognizing the Confederacy. He followed up by sending prominent Americans abroad to make the Union's case. Lincoln also wrote to foreign audiences that he believed would be sympathetic to his goals. In his letter to workers in Manchester and London, Lincoln warned of the danger slavery posed to free labor.

When the Russian navy docked ships in the harbors of New York and San Francisco during the winter of 1861–1862, Lincoln held a reception in honor of these foreign guests. Ordered by their government out of Baltic ports so that they could be free to engage in combat should the Crimean War resume, Lincoln seized upon the presence of these Russian visitors as an opportunity to signal to the British and French governments that he had other cards to play on their continent in the event they made life more difficult for him and his. When Napoleon III intervened in Mexico in December 1861, in obvious violation of the Monroe Doctrine, Lincoln pretended not to notice. His one-war-at-a-time strategy prevailed all the way through Appomattox. (How Theodore Roosevelt, Woodrow Wilson, and Franklin D. Roosevelt approached national security and international affairs has been discussed in previous chapters.)

Harry S Truman

"Tell him that if he wants to break up the Democratic Party in the middle of a war, that is his responsibility," an exasperated Franklin D. Roosevelt blurted out when he heard that Senator Harry S Truman was hesitant to run for vice president in 1944.[12] Party leaders had insisted that Roosevelt replace incumbent Vice President Henry Wallace as his running mate. They considered Wallace a drag on the ticket, too unreliable politically, and too leftward leaning. Suspecting that Roosevelt was in poor health, these power brokers recognized that the Democratic convention was probably be nominating two presidents rather than one. Party leaders knew Truman, regarded him as one of their own, and thought him up to the job. They persuaded Roosevelt to accept him.

In wooing Truman, Roosevelt knew precisely which buttons to push. The Democratic Party meant everything to Harry Truman. After his haberdashery failed, the Pendergast political machine of Kansas City, Missouri, put Truman on its ticket for county office. Truman had been an honest figurehead behind whom Tom Pendergast performed and hid his corrupt practices. Likewise, the machine supported Truman for U.S. senator in 1934 to keep federal patronage flowing to Pendergast's organization rather than to its St. Louis rival. In the Senate, Truman voted down the line for whatever Roosevelt wanted. He even supported the president's ill-fated attempt to pack the Supreme Court. Breaking ranks with other midwestern Democrats, Truman also backed FDR's plans to supply the United Kingdom with arms and munitions to fend off a Nazi invasion. Roosevelt knew that Truman could not abide the thought that party stalwarts would hold him responsible should the Democrats be defeated in 1944.

Yet the two men had never been close. Their temperaments and social backgrounds were too different for them ever to have become friends. Truman had a reputation as a straight shooter and loyal soldier. The more devious Roosevelt was not known to impart his loyalties to anyone but himself. In spite of the support Truman had shown him, Roosevelt tilted toward Truman's opponent in the 1940 senatorial primary. As a result of the bosses' successful brokering, however, they were thrust on the same team in 1944. "Well, if that's the situation, I'll have to say 'yes.' But why the hell didn't he tell me in the first place?" Truman asked, having been assured that Roosevelt *really* wanted him.[13]

Although Truman was not widely known to most Americans when he joined Roosevelt's ticket in 1944, he had, through a combination of hard work and party loyalty, become a Senate insider with a solid reputation. Truman performed his most notable achievement in the Senate when he chaired a special committee to investigate defense contracting. Truman's committee was credited with saving the government $15 billion. A poll of Washington correspondents published in *Look* magazine rated Truman one of the ten people in Washington most valuable to the war effort. *Time* placed him on its cover.[14]

While Truman did not desire to be president, he had confidence in his ability to succeed once in the job. As political scientist Richard E. Neustadt, who as a young man worked in Truman's White House, observed, Truman built his image of the office out of his perceptions as a politician, as a Democrat, and from what he had read about presidents that he admired.[15] To Truman, the president was the person in charge of the government, who made important decisions, built a record for his party, and spoke for the entire nation.[16] Among his predecessors, Truman especially admired Andrew Jackson, James K. Polk, Andrew Johnson, and Woodrow Wilson. Whatever their failings, all came to office with specific objectives in mind and pursued them vigorously.

When Truman learned of Roosevelt's death, the new president told reporters that he had felt as though "the house, the stars, and all the planets" had fallen on him.[17] Perhaps he did. But he had been aware of Roosevelt's declining health. After he had had lunch with the president weeks before he died, Truman observed that Roosevelt lacked sufficient strength to stir his coffee. Once president, Truman employed the no-nonsense operating style that had served him so well in the Senate. He asked Roosevelt's aides what plans his predecessor developed with regard to the war and is aftermath. Truman was amazed to learn that Roosevelt preferred improvisation to planning. Roosevelt had not even bothered to brief his vice president on work to develop the atomic bomb. Truman ordered atomic bombs dropped on Hiroshima on August 6, 1945, and on Nagasaki three days later. For the rest of his days, Truman maintained that his actions shortened the war and saved millions of American and Japanese lives that would have been lost had the United States invaded Japan.[18]

Left to make his own way as World War II wound down, Truman followed his instincts. Initially, he misjudged Joseph Stalin and Soviet intentions toward the European continent. After conferring with the Soviet dictator at Potsdam, Truman said that Stalin reminded him of Pendergast. Truman initially considered Stalin both "honest" and "smart as hell."[19] He felt betrayed, however, when Stalin's subsequent actions revealed that he would not abide by commitments he had made to hold democratic elections in Eastern European countries in which the Soviet army remained after the war.

After the British government announced that it could not defend Greece and Turkey beyond March 1947, Truman enunciated the doctrine that took his name. He proclaimed that the United States would "support free peoples who are resisting attempts of subjugation by armed minorities or by outside pressure."[20] With those words, he committed more than $400 million in military assistance to Greece and Turkey. This action became the first of many that Truman took during his presidency to implement the containment strategy that State Department official George F. Kennan advanced as an alternative to both war and appeasement. Its primary objective was to prevent the spread of communism to countries not already under Soviet control.

Yet to some critics, then as well as now, the open-ended commitment that the United States made to resist communist aggression—as well as the president's silence on the kinds of governments that the United States would defend in the name of anticommunism—set the United States on a course that ultimately led it into the quagmire known as the "war in Vietnam." Indeed, Secretary of State Dean Acheson's warning about rotten apples poisoning entire barrels appeared to anticipate the "domino theory" subsequent administrations evoked in support of the commitment of American troops to thwart the advance of communism. Truman's willingness to allow European countries to reassert colonial rule over Asian territories that U.S. forces had liberated from Japanese rule may have set the United States on this path. Truman indeed appeared less sensitive to the democratic and nationalistic aspirations of the people of Asia than Roosevelt had been.[21] He also floundered at first in designing a consistent policy in Europe. While the people of Greece and Turkey constituted independent nations at the time Truman spoke and were technically "free" in the sense that they were not under communist rule—at the time he came to their aid—neither Greece nor Turkey was a functioning democracy on a par with those in western Europe. Whatever its inherent difficulties, ambiguities, and contradictions, the Truman Doctrine achieved its stated purpose largely because of the president's resolve.

Three months after he issued this doctrine, Truman unfurled his European Recovery Program, commonly known as the "Marshall Plan." Through it, the United States demonstrated to war-weary Europeans what it was *for* (market economies, free elections, international trade and investment, European integration, democratic principles, and high living standards) as opposed to what it was against (the spread of communism). In a commencement address at Harvard University, Marshall declared that the program was directed against no specific country or doctrine "but against hunger, poverty, desperation, and fear."[22] If Kennan's ideas gave force to the Truman Doctrine, columnist Walter Lippmann provided the intellectual fervor necessary to build support for the Marshall Plan. After surveying the devastation across Europe, Lippmann wrote that the scale of what was needed was enormous and that the United States needed to embark on a postwar equivalent of the Lend-Lease program.[23]

In his efforts to implement the Marshall Plan, Truman displayed a political mastery almost unique in the history of the presidency. With Republicans in control of both Houses of Congress, and Truman's domestic problems mounting, few fully expected him to win the 1948 election. Suspecting that a Republican Congress would balk at a monumental undertaking that carried the name of a Democratic president, Truman took care to name the proposal in honor of George C. Marshall. He then used his friendly back-channel relations with his former Senate colleague, Senate Foreign Relations Committee chairman Arthur H. Vandenberg, to forge a bipartisan foreign policy.

Picking up, as if on cue, the suggestion in Marshall's speech that the impetus for assistance should come from Europe, British Foreign Secretary Ernest Bevin organized Europe's response in the form of what Neustadt termed a "bill of particulars."[24] In a calculated risk, Truman and Marshall offered assistance not only to noncommunist democracies but also to the Soviet Union and its satellites. Stalin's rejection of such assistance provided the United States with one of its first propaganda victories in what was fast becoming the Cold War. Truman convened a special session of Congress in November 1947 and requested $560 million in emergency aid for Europe. One month later, Congress allotted $17 billion (equal to 7.0 percent of U.S. GDP in 1947) for a program that Winston Churchill rightly called "a turning point in the history of the world."[25]

Also in 1947, Truman secured passage of the National Security Act, which combined the separate Departments of the Navy and War into a Department of Defense, made the Army Air Corps into a separate service—the

Air Force—and established both the National Security Council and the Central Intelligence Agency. On June 24, 1948, when the Soviets imposed a blockade on Berlin to starve the western half of the city into submission, Truman organized an unprecedented airlift that kept West Berlin functioning. The Soviets lifted the blockade on May 11, 1949. The resolve that Truman demonstrated during the airlift cemented the bonds between the American and German peoples that endure to this day. That same year, Truman joined the heads of twelve other governments in signing the treaty that established the North Atlantic Treaty Organization (NATO). For the next half century, NATO served as the bulwark of the Western defense that preserved peace and freedom in Western Europe.

While Truman the politician railed against the "Do Nothing [80th] Congress" for thwarting his domestic initiatives, Truman the statesman achieved his most important and enduring legacies, all of which were in defense and international policy, through partnerships he forged with some of the very Republicans he found so recalcitrant when it came to civil rights, housing, and health insurance for the elderly. Truman took care during the 1948 presidential campaign—one of the most hard-fought presidential campaigns in history—to limit his attacks on Republicans to domestic matters.

Once returned to office, with the Cold War spreading from Europe to Asia, Truman compiled a decidedly more mixed record. On June 25, 1950, troops from the communist Democratic People's Republic of Korea in the northern half of the Korean peninsula crossed the 38th parallel, invading its noncommunist neighbor, the Republic of Korea. The United Nations Security Council passed a resolution condemning the invasion, demanding the withdrawal of invading forces, and calling upon U.N. members to assist South Korea. The resolution enabled Truman to order American ground forces, then stationed in Japan under the command of General Douglas MacArthur, into South Korea. Truman defined their mission as a "police action" intended to enforce a United Nations resolution.

His decision to forgo asking Congress for a formal declaration of war against North Korea set a precedent his successors would repeatedly follow.[26] Some historians cite this decision as a significant step toward the rise of an "imperial" presidency. Truman opted to commit American troops in this fashion partially as a means of demonstrating that the newly constituted United Nations, unlike its predecessor, the League of Nations, could successfully repel aggression against a member state through collective military action.[27] However, given that the United States supplied more than four-fifths of non-Korean troops and that all U.N. forces served under an American commander, the argument that Americans were in Asia merely to enforce a U.N. resolution was practically fiction.

With the benefit of hindsight, Truman's decision to defend South Korea appears to have been in the long-term interests of the United States. It signaled to the Soviet Union that the United States and its allies would resist further communist aggression with force, if necessary. South Korea emerged from the conflict as a strong military ally and trading partner for the United States. Nevertheless, Truman and his advisers demonstrated less competence in applying the containment policy in Asia than they had in Europe, where the United States suffered no military casualties and had applied multiple means of resisting aggression.

Secretary of State Dean Acheson's omission of South Korea from a list of countries that the United States would defend militarily may have led the Soviet Union and the People's Republic of China to conclude that the United States would not resist if North Korea moved against its neighbor. It certainly left the administration in the embarrassing position of having to explain why the United States was willing to suffer high casualties to defend a country the administration had not previously declared strategically important to American interests. Moreover, the survival of an independent South Korea was tangential at best to the administration's primary objective—deterring Soviet aggression in Europe.[28]

In September 1950, MacArthur effected an amphibious assault at Inchon, forcing enemy troops back into North Korea. Buoyed by this development, the United Nations, accepting language that Truman officials supplied, appeared to change the objectives of the war. On October 7, 1950, the United Nations reiterated the war's aim as the establishment of a unified, independent, and democratic Korea.[29] (The initial resolution had limited the war's objectives to the restoration of South Korea's territorial integrity south of the 38th parallel.) MacArthur assured Truman that communist China would not intervene if American forces crossed into North Korea. Ignoring back-channel communications he had received to the contrary, Truman authorized MacArthur to advance. As he approached the Chinese border, MacArthur appeared to have destroyed North Korea's capacity to wage war. At that juncture, tens of thousands of Chinese troops crossed into North Korea, initially pinning down MacArthur's forces near the Yalu River. Although MacArthur staged a successful retreat across the 38th parallel, American public opinion, having been led to expect victory along the terms outlined in the latest U.N. pronouncement, turned against Truman.

Undeterred, MacArthur pressed Washington to persue an all-out victory. He recommended a naval blockade of China, an invasion of mainland China by nationalist forces that Chiang Kai-shek commanded on Taiwan, bombing of Chinese factories, and deploying additional American troops to reinvade North Korea. General Omar Bradley counseled that MacArthur's plan would produce "the wrong war, at the wrong place, at the wrong time, with the wrong enemy."[30] Coming to believe that escalating the war in Korea would weaken American strength in Europe, and fearing that the Korean conflict could escalate into a nuclear exchange with the Soviet Union, Truman reverted to his prior position.[31] He again defined the military objective as a return to the status quo before North Korean troops had invaded South Korea.

When MacArthur continued to make his case in the media and in letters to key members of Congress, Truman relieved the general of his command. Public opinion ran heavily in MacArthur's favor. A year before he left office, Truman scored the lowest approval ratings in the history of the Gallup Poll, pulling a mere 22 percent. As MacArthur's replacement stabilized matters on the ground, Truman, acting through intermediaries, commenced negotiations with the enemy. North Korea's demand that the United States forcibly repatriate prisoners of war against their will proved a major stumbling block. Truman held his ground, knowing that his decision meant that more American soldiers would lose their lives as the talks dragged on. In all, 54,246 Americans died in the Korean war.

Months after succeeding Truman as president, Eisenhower negotiated the armistice that ended the Korean war. Eisenhower's credible threat to use certain nuclear weapons if peace negotiations remained stalled helped persuade both China and the Soviet Union to press for an end to the conflict. The power struggle in the Kremlin that began with Stalin's death on March 5, 1953, also played a role in ending the conflict. Both China and the Soviet Union pressed North Korea's leader, Kim Il-sung, to agree to an armistice. (Other of Eisenhower's foreign policy achievements are discussed in Chapter 4.) In the end, while Truman made many mistakes in his Asia strategy, few could have anticipated the demands of his times. As a friend of the author expressed it, "Harry never had five minutes to catch his breath all the time he was president." Most of the time, he acted wisely. Substituting Henry A. Wallace with Harry S Truman ranks among the greatest decisions Franklin Delano Roosevelt ever made.

John F. Kennedy

Defense and international affairs remained John F. Kennedy's primary concern throughout his political career. Kennedy had developed a keen interest in these subjects at an early age. From his college years on, he had observed at close range many notable world events. With the exceptions of the two Roosevelts and Eisenhower, Kennedy entered the presidency better versed in international affairs than had any previous twentieth-century president. Kennedy's achievements in international policy are as notable for what he managed to avoid as what he initiated in how the United States managed the Cold War.

An avid reader since his youth, Kennedy paid particular attention to biography and to American, British, and world history. After FDR appointed his father Joseph P. Kennedy Sr. U.S. Ambassador to the Court of St. James in 1938, young Kennedy gained entry into a circle of people of his generation whose parents constituted Europe's ruling elite. Many of them entered public service in their respective countries around the same time that Kennedy did.

Several who stayed in contact with him would serve as valuable back channels, go-betweens, and informal advisers. While at Harvard, Kennedy toured Europe and kept a journal of his observations. He noted the regimentation in Hitler's Germany and the grimness prevalent in Stalin's Soviet Union. As Germany began to dismantle what had been the independent nation of Czechoslovakia, Kennedy's father sent him on a fact-finding trip to Prague.

For several months, Kennedy served as his father's private secretary. For a brief time, he functioned in a similar capacity for his father's counterpart in Paris, Ambassador William Bullitt. In addition to handling routine administrative affairs, Kennedy assisted American survivors of an ocean liner that had been torpedoed off the coast of Glasgow in the opening days of World War II. In his senior thesis, Kennedy sought to explain the origins of Britain's appeasement policy toward Nazi Germany. He attributed it to the failure of the British public to recognize the nature of the threat that Nazism and German aggression posed to their security. Kennedy would always retain his interest in the circumstances that led some politicians to follow public opinion and others to defy it. This would be the theme of a book he published two decades later, *Profiles in Courage*.

Kennedy's father, Joseph P. Kennedy Sr., had been a strong advocate of appeasement. By posing the question of his inquiry as he had, John F. Kennedy was able to avoid criticizing his father, without being tagged as an apologist for the elder Kennedy's views. The political and diplomatic skills Kennedy would display later in his career were already evident at this earlier stage of his life. With the help of family friends including *Time* publisher Henry Luce and *New York Times* reporter Arthur Krock, Kennedy turned the thesis into the best-selling book *Why England Slept*. Appearing at the height of the debate that was then underway in the United States over whether and how heavily the nation should upgrade its own defense capabilities, the book received considerable attention.

Kennedy's interest in international affairs only increased after World War II. Released from the navy after demonstrating heroism when he rescued members of his crew after a Japanese destroyer sliced in half the PT boat he commanded, Kennedy, through family ties, arranged to cover as a reporter the United Nations Conference in San Francisco in 1945 and the

British elections later that year. He voiced optimism about prospects for peace but made mention of the "belligerent attitude" policy makers detected among the Soviets.[32] Elected to the House of Representatives in 1946, Kennedy steadfastly supported Truman's containment policies. Kennedy criticized Roosevelt for having allowed much of Eastern Europe to fall into the Soviet sphere of influence. He also chided Truman for acquiescing to the communists' victory in the Chinese civil war in 1949.[33] Elected to the Senate in 1952, Kennedy secured a seat on the Foreign Affairs Committee five years later.

In a speech he delivered in 1957, Kennedy, breaking with the conventional wisdom of the times, urged that the United States support Algeria in its struggle for independence against France.[34] Earlier, he had criticized France for attempting to restore colonial rule in Southeast Asia after World War II. Kennedy argued that the United States should recognize the legitimate national aspirations of people in the Third World. If Kennedy was less willing than were Eisenhower and his secretary of state John Foster Dulles to regard nonaligned as allies of the Soviets, he was equally prone, as historian Hugh Brogan observed, to regard most conflicts in the developing world as part of the worldwide struggle between the United States and Soviet Union.[35] By the time Kennedy declared his candidacy for president, he had developed a reputation as one of the Senate's most ardent Cold Warriors.

In presenting himself as a worthy successor to a popular administration that suffered a series of public relations setbacks—the Cuban Revolution of 1959, the U-2 crisis of 1960, and the failed summit of 1960—he positioned himself to the right of his opponent, incumbent Vice President Richard Nixon. Kennedy charged that Eisenhower had allowed a "missile gap" to develop, leaving American defense capabilities on the verge of falling behind those of the Soviet Union. He attacked the outgoing administration for tolerating the establishment of a communist regime ninety miles from American shores and for not doing enough to help Fidel Castro's opponents in and outside Cuba to topple him.[36] Once president, Kennedy would reap a bitter harvest from expectations he had set through his campaign rhetoric that his administration would be more assertive toward the Soviet Union than had Eisenhower's.

Nearly four months into his term, Kennedy approved a CIA plan to help fewer than two thousand American-trained Cuban exiles invade their homeland and depose Castro. The invasion's chief planner, CIA officer Richard Bissell Jr., assured Kennedy that its execution would trigger uprisings on the island and that the rebels could retreat into the mountains, if necessary. From there they could, as had Castro before them, mount a guerilla insurrection, he suggested. Contrary to Bissell's assurances, Kennedy soon realized that the CIA plan would fail without the introduction of substantial U.S. ground forces and air cover. Kennedy directed the CIA to go to exceptional lengths to assure that the American role in this operation remained secret. To accommodate his insistence that U.S. participation would be both covert and limited, the CIA moved the invasion site miles away from the the the spot at which it was initially to have taken place. This change meant that invaders would have to travel across eighty miles of swampland before they reached the mountains.

Increased activity throughout the Caribbean basin, tips from dual agents, and leaks alerted Castro to the upcoming assault. As the exiles hit the beaches at the Bay of Pigs, 20,000 troops loyal to Castro were lying in wait. After rebel invaders, operating old B-26s launched from Nicaragua, destroyed half of Castro's air force, Kennedy still refused to acknowledge that the United States had been involved in the clandestine operation even though the invasion and its American sponsorship was now public knowledge. He cancelled a second air strike, refused to provide air fighter cover to the invading guerilla forces, and blocked the introduction of U.S. ground forces. (In so doing, he ignored Nixon's advice that he "find a proper legal cover" and "go in."[37])

In the aftermath of the Bay of Pigs fiasco, Kennedy won plaudits from the public and the press when he accepted the blame for what had ensued. "I'm the responsible officer of the government," he somberly declared at a press conference.[38] When his Gallup Poll approval rating shot up to 83 percent, Kennedy sardonically expressed surprise. "It's just like Eisenhower; the worse I do, the more popular I get," he told an aide.[39] While Eisenhower publicly voiced support for his successor, he privately labeled Kennedy's handling of the Bay of Pigs affair a "profile in timidity and indecision."[40] Foreign leaders took a similar view. Interpreting Kennedy's failure to complete what he had begun as a sign of weakness, Soviet Premier Nikita Khrushchev, at a summit with Kennedy six weeks later in Vienna, repeated an old threat to sign a treaty with East Germany, thereby establishing that communist government's sovereignty over the entire city of Berlin.

With Cold War tensions mounting, Kennedy requested an additional $3 billion increase in defense spending and an additional $350 million for civil defense, beefed up military recruitment, and called up reserves. In spite of Secretary of Defense Robert S. McNamara's admission early in Kennedy's term that there had, in fact, been no missile gap, the Soviets began adding to their nuclear and other arsenals. Kennedy responded in kind. The Berlin crisis of 1961 accelerated tensions. In a televised address, Kennedy reiterated American resolve to maintain land and air access to Berlin, retain a military presence there, and keep West Berlin a free city. In an action reminiscent of Acheson's failure a dozen years earlier to include South Korea on a list of nations the United States would defend, Kennedy did not include in his demands the free movement of people between Berlin's eastern and the western sectors. An adviser to Berlin Mayor Willie Brandt called this omission an invitation to the Soviets to do as they wished with East Berlin.[41] Within weeks of his address, the Soviets began building the Berlin Wall. "It's not a very nice solution, but a wall is a hell of a lot better than a war," Kennedy told aides.[42]

After the Bay of Pigs, the Kennedy administration increased its efforts to rid itself and the Western Hemisphere of Fidel Castro. In concert with American underworld figures such as Sam Giancana, eager to resume gambling operations in a "liberated" Cuba, the CIA repeatedly sought to assassinate the Cuban leader. As part of Operation Mongoose, which Kennedy approved, the agency spent an estimated $50 million and engaged four hundred Americans and two thousand Cubans to wage a secret war against Cuba by disrupting its economy through sabotage. On occasion, Kennedy's personal indiscretions intersected with his administration's clandestine operations, leaving the president exposed to possible blackmail or worse.[43] Aware of the extent of American efforts to eliminate him, Castro pestered his patrons in Moscow to protect the Marxist revolution in Cuba.

On October 14, 1962, CIA reconnaissance revealed that the Soviet Union had placed intermediate-range missiles on the island of Cuba. If activated and fired, the weapons could reach most American population centers. Kennedy called together a select group of key cabinet members and subordinates of varying rank and title to advise him. In appointing this Executive Committee, Kennedy attempted to compensate for the faulty intelligence he had received during the run-up to the Bay of Pigs crisis and the failure of government agencies, such as the CIA and the Joint Chiefs of Staff, to share information and fully consult with one another in advance of his taking action.

At its first meeting on October 16, 1962, the "Ex-Comm" ruled out acquiescing to the installation of the missiles. Attorney General Robert F. Kennedy said afterward that had he done nothing to remove the missiles, the president would most certainly have been impeached.[44] Even if the introduction of missiles so close to American shores did not, as the Kennedy brothers believed, alter the strategic balance between the two countries, the missiles' very presence exerted an inestimable psychological effect upon the American public and would be interpreted throughout the world as a setback to American objectives and prestige. All assembled agreed that their removal was in the nation's immediate interest.

Some favored immediate air strikes to take out the missiles as a precursor to an American invasion. Others demurred, citing the number of Soviet and Cuban lives that would be immediately lost and the likelihood that Khrushchev would retaliate by moving against Western interests elsewhere, probably in Berlin, or by firing the remaining missiles upon the United States. Years later, declassified Soviet archives revealed that the Soviet Union had stationed in Cuba a total of forty-three thousand troops, rather than the ten thousand the CIA had estimated, and that Moscow had sent tactical as well as strategic nuclear warheads to Cuba.[45] These tactical nuclear warheads would almost certainly have been used against American ground forces if the United States had invaded the island.

Kennedy proposed a blockade. In order to make it sound less provocative or warlike, he proclaimed his measure a "quarantine." American naval personnel would "visit and search" approaching ships for military supplies that would render the missiles operational.[46] In his speech to the nation on October 22, Kennedy warned that he would regard any missile fired from Cuba as an attack by the Soviet Union against the United States. He called for their immediate removal under U.N. supervision. To enlist the support of world opinion, Kennedy stressed the "sudden and secretive" nature of the Soviets' actions.[47] The next day, U.N. Ambassador Adlai E. Stevenson presented the U.N. General Assembly with photographs of the missiles as well as construction and other activities on the island the Soviets had supervised.

Prior to the crisis, Kennedy had carefully read Barbara Tuchman's *The Guns of August*, an account of how the decision of European leaders to begin mobilizing their armed forces escalated uncontrollably, through automatic triggers, into World War I. To prevent a similar automatic and unintended escalation that might lead to a more catastrophic war, Kennedy had the attorney general ride roughshod over all involved agencies and had McNamara monitor the armed forces closely so that hostilities could commence only upon presidential orders. Khrushchev had clearly miscalculated both how world opinion would react to the missile installation and the extent of Kennedy's resolve. After Kennedy announced the quarantine, the Soviet leader ordered six Soviet ships bound for the quarantined waters turned back. With the quarantine appearing to accomplish its aim, Kennedy still had to decide how to get the missiles removed. Intelligence estimates varied as to whether any, some, or all were already operational.

As he proceeded, Kennedy took into account the pressures on his adversary as well as the constituencies Khrushchev needed to satisfy in the Kremlin. He took care to avoid provoking Khrushchev and to allow the Soviet leader a way to back down without suffering a loss of face. When Khrushchev, through a back channel (which ran from the Kremlin to the KGB station chief in the Soviet Embassy in Washington to American Broadcasting Corporation diplomatic correspondent John Scali to Robert Kennedy), floated the idea of removing the missiles in exchange for an American pledge not to invade Cuba, Kennedy signaled his agreement. When Khrushchev offered the same terms in an emotional letter in which he warned against the two nations engaging in mutual annihilation, Kennedy formally accepted them.

In so doing, Kennedy ignored a second communication from Khrushchev, which had been widely broadcast throughout the communist world. The second letter included the demand that Kennedy remove missiles the United States maintained in Turkey, near the Soviet border. Kennedy passed word back that he would dismantle these missiles at a later date. To have agreed to such an exchange before the Soviets had removed the missiles from Cuba, Kennedy reasoned, would have given the impression that he had rewarded the Soviets for their misadventure. This would have weakened his standing both at home and abroad. (The deal Kennedy made with regard to the missiles in Turkey remained secret for many years.)

Kennedy used the high standing he enjoyed in the United States and throughout the world in the aftermath of the missile crisis to reduce tensions between the superpowers. His principal achievement in this arena was the Limited Nuclear Test Ban Treaty of 1963. While the treaty allowed for continued testing underground, it forbade such tests in the atmosphere, on the ground, under water, and in space. The treaty promised to reduce health hazards that nuclear fallout posed to civilian populations. Kennedy had repeatedly pressed for a more comprehensive ban on nuclear tests. Objecting to American inspections of its installations, the Soviets had long been opposed. In the first of what would prove several agreements, however, the Soviets decided to meet the Americans part of the way. Kennedy's test ban treaty set the precedent for the Treaty of Non-Proliferation of Nuclear Weapons (1969), the Anti-Ballistic Missile Treaty and the first Strategic Arms Limitations Treaty (both in 1972), and the Comprehensive Nuclear Test Ban Treaty (1996), measures his successors negotiated.

Kennedy articulated how he envisioned relations between the two superpowers might proceed in the commencement speech he delivered at American University on June 10, 1963:

> Let us not be blind to our differences—but let us also direct attention to our common interests, and to the means by which differences can be resolved. And if we cannot end now our differences, at least we can help make the world safe for diversity. For, in the final analysis, our most basic

common link is that we all inhabit this small planet. We all breathe the same air. We all cherish our children's future. And we are all mortal.[48]

The competence that Kennedy demonstrated through his handling of the Cuban Missile Crisis deservedly remains a textbook model of effective crisis management and conflict resolution. The caution with which he responded to threatening situations would continue to guide future presidents as they made decisions in a short time and in possession of inadequate, if not faulty, intelligence. Kennedy, Khrushchev, and their successors abided by the informal agreement the two superpowers reached in October 1962 not to allow themselves to drift into a situation in which the two superpowers risked a direct nuclear exchange. In other arenas, competition between the United States and the Soviet Union continued unabated, including in outer space.

In the vision that Kennedy advanced at American University can be found the seeds of the détente policies that Richard Nixon made his trademark in subsequent Soviet-American relations, and also in the approach that Ronald Reagan employed in his "trust but verify" efforts to bring the Cold War to an end. If Kennedy had held the line, Reagan pushed through it—not with invading armies or nuclear weapons, but with superior ideas, a stronger economy, and enhanced military capabilities.

(The foreign policy achievements and failures of Lyndon Johnson, Richard Nixon, Gerald Ford, Jimmy Carter, and Ronald Reagan were addressed in previous chapters.)

George H. W. Bush

Had George H. W. Bush, rather than Ronald Reagan, defeated Jimmy Carter in 1980, it is a safe bet that the Soviet Union would have survived into the twenty-first century. It all gets back to the "vision thing." A creature of the foreign policy establishment, Bush would have found it exceedingly difficult to free himself from the conventional wisdom that characterized Soviet experts and the arms control community in his time. It took a visionary like Reagan to realize that an accelerated arms race would bankrupt the Soviet

Union and compel its leaders to sue for peace. With the Soviet Union crumbling as he spoke, Bush—in what was termed the "chicken Kiev" speech—urged populations in Ukraine and the Baltic states to suppress their yearning for independence. Through his failure to recognize the inevitable dissolution of the Soviet Union and Yugoslavia, Bush bequeathed to his successor a series of challenges (ethnic cleansing and others) that might have been averted, had the forty-first president, and the so-called realists who advised him, followed a different strategy.

Bush's success in helping negotiate a free, unified Germany that became fully integrated to the West through its entry into and active participation in the European Union and NATO, and his efforts to assure the peaceful disintegration of the Soviet Union—once he recognized its inevitability—rank among his major and lasting achievements as president. After Iraq invaded the kingdom of Kuwait, Bush preserved Kuwait's independence through his brilliant execution of Operation Desert Storm. His masterful use of multiple international contacts he had made during previous service in diplomatic and intelligence posts created the appearance and the reality of a truly multinational endeavor to enforce a U.N. resolution. But the military victory Bush obtained, which allowed Saddam Hussein to remain in power, assured that the United States would continue to engage with Saddam militarily. Furthermore, Bush did little to press the liberated Kuwait or the kingdom of Saudi Arabia, which requested American arms and troops to defend it, to improve their human rights records, adopt democratic institutions, or reduce their support for Islamic extremists.

Bill Clinton

If there were such a thing as the international equivalent to school uniforms and other bite-sized measures that characterized his domestic agenda, Bill Clinton would go to the head of the pack of presidents. After a disastrous attempt at nation building in Somalia (to which his predecessor had committed American troops to maintain order and end atrocities), resulting in the bodies of dead American soldiers being dragged through the streets, and a confusing and ill-defined intervention in Haiti, Clinton brought an end to the ethnic cleansing in the former Yugoslavia, first in Bosnia, and later in Kosovo. He also had their perpetrators tried for war crimes in the International Court of Justice at The Hague.

Standing down congressional and other critics, who argued that the United States had no discernible interests in the region, Clinton ordered repeated air strikes and sent ground troops as peacekeepers to the area despite his weakened political position in the face of scandal and impeachment proceedings. With his political capital diminishing as Clinton struggled to stay in office at the height of the Monica Lewinsky affair, Clinton obtained political cover from two inflluential Republican senators, both war heroes, Majority Leader Bob Dole and John McCain. In the midst of the unfolding crisis in Kosovo, Hollywood released the film *Wag the Dog*. Its title became a metaphor for a president commencing a war in a small, distant country as a means of diverting attention from a sexual scandal at home.

Clinton forged and maintained good relations with Boris Yeltsin, president of the first democratically elected government in Russia's history. He shepherded new democracies in Central and Eastern Europe, once part of the Soviet bloc, into NATO. He became the first American president to use his good offices to broker a peaceful end to the "Troubles" in Northern Ireland. Clinton's determination and willingness to risk short-term strains with the United Kingdom earned him the trust of both Catholics and Protestants in the six counties of Northern Ireland, the Republic of Ireland, and elsewhere. By his own admission, Clinton might have done more to end the genocide that ensued in Rwanda while he was president.

Overestimating both his powers as a negotiator and the intentions of Palestinian leader Yasser Arafat, Clinton failed to achieve his goal of bringing an end to the Israeli-Palestinian conflict. Clinton might have come closer to attaining his objectives had he appeared less fixated on winning the Nobel Peace Prize. The first president to visit Africa, and one of the first to recognize India's strategic importance to the long-term interests of the United States, Clinton helped hasten a warming of relations between the United States and the world's largest democracy. (His efforts on behalf of NAFTA and other free-trade initiatives were discussed in chapter 5.)

The forty-second president's score would be considerably higher had he responded more forcefully to terrorist attacks against American targets throughout the world, warned his fellow citizens more than he did about the threat al-Qaeda posed to their security, and better fortified his country to withstand attacks. Few would consider Clinton's responses to the bombings of the Khobar Towers in Saudi Arabia (in which nineteen U.S. military personnel were killed), the attacks on two American embassies in Africa (which killed hundreds), and the attack on the U.S.S. *Cole* (in which seventeen sailors were killed) in Yemen to be sufficient. Moreover, the substantial cuts Clinton made in the defense budget, as he increased spending in other areas, may have left the United States more vulnerable to these kind of attacks.

George W. Bush

Whatever history will say about George W. Bush's decision to launch a preventive war of choice in Iraq, based on intelligence reports that Saddam Hussein had developed weapons of mass destruction, no one will argue that the world was a safer place and the Iraqi people better off with Saddam in power. Bush's toppling of the Taliban government in Afghanistan and Saddam's regime in Iraq resulted in millions of people enjoying greater freedom from fear and, if not as of this writing, the full blessings of democracy.

History will also make note of the significant humanitarian assistance Bush provided the poorest countries of the world and of the attention he paid to the continent of Africa. It may question the excessive patience Bush showed with the Pakistani government's slow pace in facilitating the capture of Osama Bin Laden, especially after the president declared nations of the world allied with the United States or with the terrorists. It can be expected that history will be critical of Bush for failing to make the United States less dependent on oil from the Middle East.

Bush's presidency was definitely an important and a transformational one. Whether at the end of his eight years in office the nation was more or less secure and confident in its place in the world cannot as yet be known.

8

WHAT DOES
IT ALL MEAN?

*N*ow that each of the nation's presidents—save William Henry Harrison and James A. Garfield, who died early into their terms, and George W. Bush, who was still in office when this book was written—has been assigned scores, the obvious question that comes to mind is, what characteristics should voters seek while deciding among presidential aspirants? Which candidates are likely to have successful presidencies, and which may prove disastrous? The best dozen presidents shared many common traits. So did the dozen or so worst of the lot. At various points during their lives, these were on view to anyone who cared to inspect them. If properly assessed, they can be more predictive of presidential performance than can candidates' achievements in their pre-presidential careers or the programmatic promises they make as presidential candidates.

What to Look for in Presidential Candidates

SCOUT OUT A SENSE OF PURPOSE. Nearly all presidents who earned a rating of great or near great articulated specific goals that they wanted to achieve as president. George Washington wanted to make the

American experiment in independence and self-government succeed. Abraham Lincoln sought to restrict the spread of slavery and put the institution on the road to extinction. Dwight D. Eisenhower aimed to maintain a bipartisan consensus for the containment policies toward the Soviet Union. Ronald Reagan wished to accelerate economic growth by reducing taxes, regulations, and inflation, and to end the Cold War both peacefully and on terms favorable to the West.

With the exception of Franklin Delano Roosevelt, none of the great or near great presidents aspired to the presidency from an early age. Then again, none of the other great or near-great presidents had as stellar a presidential role model within their families as FDR found in his fifth cousin, Theodore Roosevelt. The first President Roosevelt, as a soldier, adventurer, and statesman, dominated the news while the second was coming of age. At a time when FDR's peers were contemplating their career options, young Franklin proclaimed that he intended to be assistant secretary of the navy, governor of New York, and president—just like Theodore. While neither Roosevelt entered the presidency with firm ideas about how they would handle domestic matters, both had a clear sense of what they wanted to do in the international arena, even if these concerns were less pressing than domestic ones at the time they took office.

FDR ranks high for his early recognition of the threat that Adolf Hitler and Nazism posed to the world and for the skillful leadership he provided during World War II. However, FDR fares less well when his character, economic experimentation, and human rights policies are considered. In all but the last, FDR ranks beneath his famous relative. While both Roosevelts prided themselves for being innovators as they approached the severe economic crises of their day, Theodore Roosevelt, as would John F. Kennedy and Ronald Reagan, generally made wise economic decisions and stuck with policies he put in place. In contrast, Franklin Roosevelt, like Jimmy Carter and Richard Nixon, sometimes made poor economic decisions and vacillated between contradictory policies.

EXAMINE HOW THEY MET ADVERSITY. Like many of their fellow citizens, most successful presidents overcame adversities that came their way at certain points in their lives. The nature of those hardships varied, as did the manner in which they responded to them. All of the great and near great presidents emerged from conflicts and disappointments they encountered stronger and more resilient than they had been before. That is what made their previous ordeals transformative. All regarded these adversities as learning experiences, however painful. None emerged from such setbacks regarding themselves as victims. None were known to complain or whine— at least out loud or in public—about their private misfortunes.

Washington emerged from the French and Indian War a celebrated hero for the bravery he had shown in battle and for risking his life to save others in service to the crown. Yet his status as a colonial blocked him from receiving an officer's commission in the British army. By reorienting his life's goals, and by remaking his character, Washington won the esteem of his fellow Americans. They put him in command of the Continental Army and made him the nation's first president. Resentful that his father had hired him out to neighbors and kept his earnings, Lincoln set out to make his own way in the world. He developed a sense of empathy through personal adversity. Once president, he became an instrument in the freeing of an entire people. Theodore Roosevelt developed his capacity for leadership in the Dakota Badlands, where he had gone to drown his grief after experiencing a dual family tragedy. While Franklin D. Roosevelt did not realize it at the time, his struggle to overcome polio proved but a dress rehearsal for battles he would wage against the Great Depression, Hitler, Mussolini, and Tojo.

Dwight and Mamie Eisenhower saw their first-born child succumb to scarlet fever at the age of three. While Dwight, the future general and president, appeared to have overcome his loss, he remained mindful of the empty place in his life. Each year, on the deceased child's birthday, Ike sent Mamie flowers. In his later years, on a return visit to the American cemetery at Normandy, Eisenhower spoke to reporter Walter Cronkite about the sacrifices war had inflicted on parents of the fallen. He noted the joy he took in his grandchildren and lamented that the war had denied parents, who had lost a child in battle, the opportunity to become grandparents. Such sentiments, perhaps sparked by occasional musings about what pleasures his deceased son might have brought him, sharpened Ike's sense of responsibility for other people's children, whom he sent into battle. His hope that he would not have to do so again shaped his defense and international policies.

Expecting his older brother to fulfill his father's political ambitions for the family, John F. Kennedy had planned to lead a leisurely, quiet life as a teacher, writer, or diplomat. After his brother Joseph P. Kennedy Jr. died in combat during World War II, and he encountered his own brush with death, JFK radically changed his ambitions. Through a combination of family pressures and an awakened sense of calling, Kennedy, at the age of twenty-nine, threw himself into a career for which his brother had been preparing to enter for years. In making his father's ambitions his own, Kennedy became the conscious vehicle through which millions who shared his Irish Catholic heritage sought to realize theirs.

Ronald Reagan rose above a disrupted childhood, a failed marriage, and a fading acting career to win what one biographer termed the "role of a lifetime." Having embarked on a new career when most of his contemporaries were winding theirs down, Reagan reverted to another role that he had played earlier in life, that of lifeguard. This time, he would stand guard over the free world and extend its boundaries. Having surmounted his humble origins, Reagan tried to help others expand their horizons by reducing the burdens of high inflation and high taxation. In contrast to these examples, Herbert Hoover never failed at anything until after he had become president. The nation might have been better served at the outbreak of the Great Depression if he had.

LOOK FOR BROAD LIFE EXPERIENCES. Most great and near great presidents had multiple occupations, not all of them in politics, before becoming president. Through the depth and breath of their experiences, successful presidents learned how to relate to people in all walks of life. Washington did this as a soldier, as a Virginia burgess, and as a business entrepreneur. Lincoln did it while swapping stories with neighbors as a storekeeper and postmaster in New Salem and as he rode circuit from courthouse to courthouse across Illinois. He once advised fellow politicians to use language that ordinary people could understand. Ulysses S. Grant, the failed tanner, and Harry S Truman, the failed haberdasher, learned similar lessons. Theodore Roosevelt came to measure a person's worth through the school of hard knocks he attended on the Dakota plains. He employed this lesson while organizing what became the Rough Riders and while assembling his administration.

Washington, Taylor, Grant, McKinley, T. Roosevelt, Truman, Eisenhower, and Kennedy found military service to be a great equalizer. Of all the soldiers-turned-presidents, Jackson stands alone in not allowing the valor and bravery he witnessed on the field to cause him to set aside racial, class, and other prejudices. Although Coolidge and Truman were professional politicians for most of their lives, both had started at the bottom. By knocking on doors for votes and listening to constituents, they developed the common sense, pragmatism, self-discipline, and high personal ethical standards they set for themselves. By instinct and temperament, FDR remained the "country squire" from Hyde Park. Yet he felt most at home and at ease in the company of others with disabilities at Warm Springs. Reagan never tired of reminding audiences that he was the only president ever to have headed a labor union. This experience sharpened his negotiating skills.

PROBE FOR A NATURAL CURIOSITY. Great or near great presidents remained curious all their lives about the world around them and about the causes of the problems they were called upon to solve. If these presidents did not display this trait in their approach to every issue, they certainly brought it to bear on matters on which they hoped to make their mark. Aware that tobacco farming depleted the soil, Washington experimented with substitute crops beginning in the 1760s. He diversified in other ways and grew prosperous selling grain, livestock, and dried fish, and distilling whiskey. Not as well versed in political philosophy and economic theory as his younger advisers (Alexander Hamilton, Thomas Jefferson, and James Madison), Washington, by the time Hamilton presented him with a dynamic plan to build a strong national economic infrastructure, was predisposed by his own life experience to recognize its potential.

With the Union army deficient in its generalship in the early stages of the Civil War, Lincoln taught himself military strategy by pouring over books he borrowed from the Library of Congress. The holder of a patent, Lincoln took an interest in how scientific knowledge and technological improvements might be harnessed to improve American living standards. He made maximum use of the technological instructions available and built on it. Despite having earned a C in introductory economics, Kennedy confounded advisers with the sophistication of his inquiries.[1] Years before his election as president, Reagan toured "Fort Know," the U.S. nuclear laboratory at Los Alamos. Dissatisfied that the only options available to the president in the event of a nuclear attack were annihilation or capitulation, Reagan started down the intellectual path that led him to the Strategic Defense Initiative.

Rare was the topic about which Thomas Jefferson, Theodore Roosevelt, and Bill Clinton were not conversant. Jefferson harmed his legacy through his unwillingness at a critical time in his presidency to free himself from rigid ideological constraints. Clinton might have ranked higher than he does had he brought to bear in pursuit of policies the organizational skills and self-discipline he exerted to attain and retain his office.[2] In the hall of presidents, Theodore Roosevelt was, in the words of playwright Robert Bolt, a "man for all seasons."

SEEK A WELL-DEVELOPED SENSE OF INTEGRITY. When Washington, Truman, and Eisenhower evoked executive privilege and the separation of powers as their reasons for withholding information from Congress and outside investigators, none suspected, let alone charged, that their true purpose was to cover up criminal conduct. Such were the strengths of their respective characters and reputations. With the passage of time, most analysts regard Gerald Ford's pardoning of Richard Nixon, Washington's sparing insurgents who had plotted the Whiskey Rebellion, and Lincoln's stopping executions of young soldiers accused of desertion to be in the national interest. Historians will long contrast these actions with Bill Clinton's pardoning relatives, friends of relatives, and in-laws, and, at the request of donors, Marc Rich, a commodities trader, indicted in

1983 for tax evasion and illegal trading with Iran who had fled the United States to avoid prosecution.

While capable of extraordinary flexibility as a politician, Lincoln, as a state legislator, as a congressman, and as president, let his constituents know precisely where his views diverged from theirs. Theodore Roosevelt warned his audiences to be wary of "weasel words." (What would he have thought of successors who spoke of reforming welfare "as we know it" or not raising taxes on the middle class "to pay for my programs"?) As Reagan recognized, transformative presidents presented their case in "bold colors" rather than in "pastels."[3]

In his selective prosecution of millionaires, his ventures into class warfare, and his scapegoating of his predecessor (long after he had defeated Hoover at the polls), Franklin D. Roosevelt was one of the few great or near-great presidents who allowed personal vindictiveness to influence his actions as president. Kennedy did this too, allowing his brother the attorney general to intimidate steel executives and purportedly ordering repeated audits of Richard Nixon's tax returns, actions that may also have come at the initiation of the attorney general rather than the president. On the policy side, JFK could be as vindictive as his brother. Upon the resolution of the Cuban Missile Crisis, Kennedy leaked that his U.N. ambassador, Adlai Stevenson, had advised acquiescence to Soviet demands. Earlier in his presidency, Kennedy froze Chester Bowles out of his administration for having vigorously objected to what became the Bay of Pigs invasion.[4]

CRAVE HUMILITY. Although confident in their abilities, successful presidents held their egos in check. None lost the sense that they had been elected to govern in the interests of others. They selected the best people available, including, on occasion, former rivals and members of the opposition party. Lincoln put into his cabinet four men who had competed against him for the 1860 Republican presidential nomination. Washington, Truman, and Reagan surrounded themselves with experienced, knowledgeable advisers whose intellect and experience were often superior to theirs. All great and near great presidents understood that they would receive the credit for the achievements of their subordinates. For this reason, they strove to find outstanding ones.

After a falling-out with aide-de-camp Alexander Hamilton during the Revolutionary War, General George Washington, aware of the upstart's intellectual and leadership capabilities, gave Hamilton his own military command and delegated to him major responsibilities. Later on, Washington entrusted Hamilton with the most important job in the cabinet.

Early in the Civil War, Lincoln said that he would be willing to hold the horse of (the conceited and egotistical) General George McClellan if that would help bring victory to the Union cause. (After McClellan failed to pursue the Army of Northern Virginia after the Battle of Antietam, Lincoln later replaced him.) Believing General George C. Marshall to be the greatest living American, Truman relied on Marshall's prestige to entice a Republican Congress to enact the successful plan that bore the general's name. Aware of his inattention to detail and his limitations as an administrator, Reagan retained James Baker, who had twice worked to deny Reagan the presidency, as his chief of staff.[5] "There is no limit to what you can accomplish as long as you don't mind who gets the credit," said a sign on Reagan's desk.

What to Avoid in Presidential Candidates

In many respects, the characteristics the nation's worst presidents shared were the opposite of those that the best presented. They do not make for a pretty picture.

WATCH OUT FOR CYNICISM AND COMPLACENCY. Many of the least successful presidents, except Hoover, entered politics at an early age and caught the presidential bug soon after their political careers began. After waging many campaigns for different offices, the least successful presidents became cynical about the motives of other officeholders and contemptuous of voters. This may account for their cavalier attitudes toward ethical, if not legal, "niceties." Some became so jaundiced en route to the White House that they assumed nothing they encountered was new or different from what they had come across in the past. Their "been there, done that" attitudes quickly turned into hubris. With the exception of Hoover and Carter, the unsuccessful presidents conveyed the impression that they could pull a fast one on an unsuspecting public, the media, or Congress. Some actually did.

STAY AWAY FROM WHINERS. Many if not most failed presidents saw themselves as victims. They wasted valuable time indulging in self-pity, usually before underlings, reporters, and even the public. The "woe is me" club of presidents has a large membership. Jackson, Andrew Johnson, Lyndon Johnson, Nixon, and Clinton all belonged to it. The whiners divided the world in their minds into two camps: those who gave them unconditional loyalty (which they tested constantly), and those out to do them in. In their eyes, the latter group grew considerably in size as problems mounted during their presidencies. Centuries from now, historians will still be listening to Nixon's recorded ruminations and ventures into self-pity. Few of these presidents followed Eisenhower's advice about not losing one's temper except by intent.

KEEP AWAY FROM KNOW-IT-ALLS. Less successful presidents were often, but not always, some of the most intelligent. Many were indeed the brightest person in any room they entered. They also could not resist letting everyone else in their presence know it. Their belief in their superior intellect, experience, and expertise discouraged them from seeking outside advice. If they knew all the answers, why, they wondered, should they waste time ascertaining the views of others? They saw their staff and department heads more as implementers than as advisers. These yes-men and yes-women shared a common characteristic: their continued dependence on the president who appointed them. In contrast, successful presidents tended to name to high posts men and women who had compiled records of achievement and distinction prior to joining a presidential administration.

Jefferson, convinced that his principles were based on scientific truths, sometimes rendered policy decisions by assertion. Wilson, his biographers say, sought the advice of a council of one. Wilson and Carter exuded a certainty that they were doing the Lord's work. It was not for naught that Calvin Coolidge dubbed Herbert Hoover "Wonder Boy." Unsure of his objectives, and harboring doubts about his Vietnam policies, Lyndon Johnson claimed that outside critics lacked the information necessary to second-guess him. Inside his administration, which reporters and biographers likened in its latter days to the Alamo, Johnson ignored information that ran counter to his impulses and bullied dissenters into submission.

STEER CLEAR OF CANDIDATES WITH A NARROW FOCUS. If great or near great presidents were shaped by numerous experiences with people from all walks of life, the unsuccessful spent most of their adult lives in a single pursuit: politics. What they knew about voters came exclusively through campaigning, polls, and focus groups. No headhunter or college admissions officer would declare the two Johnsons, Van Buren, Fillmore, Pierce, Buchanan, or Nixon as well-rounded. All saw politics as an end rather than as a means. LBJ admitted that he read only that which he found immediately useful. He and others in this group formed friendships on the same basis.

Surprisingly, three presidents who achieved extraordinary successes outside of politics before they became president—Wilson, Hoover, and Carter—also proved three of the poorest politicians ever to serve as president. Having risen through the ranks of the academy, Wilson had not come into much daily contact, before he ran for governor, with many people who had not been to college. Upon Wilson's death, British Prime Minister David Lloyd George suggested to the *New York Times* that Wilson might have had an easier time of things had he been introduced into the rough-and-tumble of politics at an earlier stage of his life.[6] Having become one of the wealthiest men of his age through his meticulous attention to detail as a mining engineer, Hoover never learned how to cope with the uncertainties of politics. As president, he either ignored them or sought to remove them by applying scientific principles. As both a nuclear engineer and an agribusinessman, Carter proved a master at detail. As president, he became so mired in trivialities that he lost the overall perspective that a president needs to succeed.

BE LEERY OF UNRELENTING IDEOLOGUES. While the United States has had several presidents who enunciated deeply held beliefs over the direction public policy should take, it has had only a few committed ideologues. At other times and in other places, committed ideologues showed greater allegiance to their agenda than to the best interest of their countries. To hasten his advance to power in Russia, Lenin accepted the aid of Germany, a nation at war with his country, and agreed to a disadvantageous peace. "Better Hitler than Bloom," cried French fascists prior to the Nazi invasion. Fortunately, wiser and less fanatical heads with a greater interest in the welfare of the citizenry prevailed in the United States throughout most of its history. While there were a few exceptions to this, by and large, the American people have kept true fanatics out of the White House.

Grateful to France for the assistance it provided the United States during the Revolutionary War, and emotionally committed to the tenets of the French Enlightenment, Jefferson at first cast a blind eye toward the excesses of the French Revolution. He stubbornly clung to his opinion that it was essentially benign in character long after most of his contemporaries came to recognize the Reign of Terror for what it was. He gave it up only after he realized that he might not lead his party to power unless he broadened his perspective. Whatever successes Jefferson achieved as president he attained when he cut himself free from self-imposed ideological constraints. Likewise, he encountered his greatest failure when he persisted in policies he insisted would succeed when economic and political realities suggested the contrary. Lacking Jefferson's capacity to cut himself free from ideological tenets—at least on occasion—and his ability to attract able advisers, Madison took the nation he led to the brink of disaster. On his watch, enemy troops set fire to both the White House and the Capitol.

STAND GUARD AGAINST BEARERS OF GRUDGES. If successful presidents overcame hardships and emerged stronger for the experience, adversity left unsuccessful presidents filled with resentments that they nursed throughout their lives. For them, what was political was also personal. Often, they used the power of their high office to settle personal scores. Having overcome adversity as young men, Jackson and Nixon used presidential powers to strike back at enemies, both real and imagined. Jackson lashed out at people of privilege, bankers, moralists, British subjects, and Native Americans. Nixon bristled at the well born and well positioned, who had advanced, sometimes at his expense, through family connections and inherited wealth, rather than by what he regarded as superior merit, skills, and hard work.

Wilson preferred to forgo U.S. participation in his major achievement, the League of Nations, rather than cede a point to his political and intellectual rival, Henry Cabot Lodge. Prior to the outbreak of the Civil War, James Buchanan, through his feud with Stephen A. Douglas, destroyed the only remaining truly national institution in the country, the Democratic Party. Lyndon Johnson, Richard Nixon, and Jimmy Carter shared a common antipathy toward anything "Kennedy." While not the first president to have an enemies list, Nixon was the only one to pass its names along to posterity through tapes he ordered made and did not think he would have to surrender.

ESCHEW TENDENCIES TOWARD BALD ASSERTIONS OF POWER. Presidents who confused their personal interests, desires, or policy preferences with the best interests of the country and who pressed to have their way on everything, oblivious to formal and informal constraints inherent in the American political system, inflicted great harm on the nation, the presidency, and themselves. Believing they were adhering to the part of their oath that bound them to "faithfully execute the office of president," they sometimes gave short shrift to their pledge to "preserve, protect, and defend the Constitution of the United States." They gave the impression that aggrandizement of power was their true goal, which they justified in terms of strengthening the presidency. In a televised post-presidential interview, Nixon suggested as much when he said that if the president ordered something done, then it was not illegal. This spirit gave rise to the Watergate scandal and the constitutional crisis it produced.

Nixon was not the only president to make such an assertion. Jackson showed a contemptuous disregard for court decisions and other possible constraints on his office. Buchanan sought to bribe voters in a territorial election, and Andrew Johnson attempted to nullify the results of the Civil War, Congress and public opinion be damned. Lyndon Johnson had a tendency to confuse his office with his person. Presidents who sought to stretch the powers of their office by the mere assertion and the exercise of might wound up weakening rather than strengthening the presidency as an institution. They found that before long the pendulum swung against them and, sometimes, their immediate successors, as other branches and public opinion asserted powers of their own. Such has been the American way.

With the United States in its third century as a free and independent nation, its constitutional system of separation of powers and checks and balances demands that the president have the capacity to distinguish, as Harry Truman best expressed it, between the person holding the nation's highest office and the President of the United States. Voters can determine the country's future by asking themselves how current and prospective presidents might stack up against the standards set forth in this book. Below is a report card depicting how past presidents fared.

Ranking	President	Character	Vision	Competence	Economic Policy	Preserving and Extending Liberty	Defense, National Security, and Foreign Policy	Average Score	Year of Inauguration
1	Lincoln	5	5	5	5	5	5	5.00	1861
2	Washington	5	4	5	5	4	5	4.67	1789
3	Roosevelt, T.	4	5	5	5	3	5	4.50	1901
3	Reagan	5	5	3	5	4	5	4.50	1981
5	Eisenhower	5	3	5	4	4	4	4.17	1953
6	Roosevelt, F.	3	4	5	3	4	5	4.00	1933
7	Taylor	5	4	4	3	4	3	3.83	1849
7	Grant	4	5	3	3	5	3	3.83	1869
7	McKinley	5	3	4	4	2	5	3.83	1897
7	Truman	5	4	4	2	4	4	3.83	1945
7	Kennedy	3	4	4	4	4	4	3.83	1961
12	Coolidge	5	3	4	4	4	2	3.67	1923
13	Harrison, B.	5	3	3	3	4	3	3.50	1889
14	Adams, J.	5	3	3	3	2	4	3.33	1797
14	Jefferson	3	4	4	3	3	3	3.33	1801
14	Monroe	3	4	4	1	3	5	3.33	1817
14	Adams, J. Q.	5	3	3	3	3	3	3.33	1825
14	Wilson	3	4	3	4	2	4	3.33	1913
14	Bush, G. H. W.	5	2	3	3	3	4	3.33	1989
20	Polk	1	2	5	4	2	5	3.17	1849
20	Ford	5	2	3	3	3	3	3.17	1974
22	Taft	5	3	2	3	2	3	3.00	1909
22	Clinton	2	3	3	4	3	3	3.00	1993
24	Arthur	3	2	3	3	3	3	2.83	1882
24	Cleveland	5	2	3	2	2	3	2.83	1885
26	Harding	2	3	2	3	4	2	2.67	1921
27	Jackson	3	2	5	1	1	3	2.50	1829
27	Johnson, L.	2	3	2	2	5	1	2.50	1963
29	Madison	5	2	1	1	4	1	2.33	1809
29	Hayes	3	2	2	3	1	3	2.33	1877
29	Carter	5	2	2	1	3	1	2.33	1977
29	Bush, G. W.	3	2	1	2	3	3	2.33	2001
33	Van Buren	2	2	3	1	1	3	2.00	1837
33	Fillmore	2	1	2	3	1	3	2.00	1850
35	Tyler	2	1	2	2	1	3	1.83	1842
35	Hoover	4	1	1	1	2	2	1.83	1929
35	Nixon	1	2	2	1	2	3	1.83	1969
38	Pierce	1	1	1	3	1	3	1.67	1853
38	Johnson, A.	2	1	1	2	1	3	1.67	1865
40	Buchanan	1	1	1	2	1	3	1.50	1857

(W. H. Harrison, J. A. Garfield, and B. H. Obama were not evaluated.)

AFTERWORD

George W. Bush: An Early Assessment

$\mathcal{F}$orecasting how history will ultimately regard George W. Bush's presidency so soon after he left office is a fool's errand. As Bush noted, what future historians will write about him rests to a large degree on his successor. For example, Republican presidential candidate Dwight D. Eisenhower criticized outgoing Democratic president Harry Truman's handling of the Korean War and other matters during the 1952 campaign. Yet after his election, Eisenhower continued many of his predecessor's policies.[1] Had Ike abruptly withdrawn American troops from the Korean peninsula, Truman today might be faulted for waging a costly, wasteful, and unsuccessful war rather than hailed for maintaining an independent South Korea that would eventually become a vibrant democracy and a valuable trading partner and strategic ally of the United States.

As of this writing, under Barack Obama, American troops remain in Iraq and Afghanistan. Persons suspected of committing or planning terrorist acts are still in detention at Guantánamo Bay. Thus far, Obama has been as reticent as Bush to involve Congress in determining what U.S. policy toward these persons should be.[2] Obama continued Bush's policy of purchasing preferred stock of banks with taxpayer funds to shore up their capital. Obama expanded upon Bush's initiative to pump billions of taxpayer dollars into Chrysler and General Motors to keep these bankrupt automakers operating.

Obama kept in place two of Bush's signature domestic programs: his "No Child Left Behind" program, established by law in 2001, and the White House Office of Faith-Based and Community Initiatives. On immigration reform, both Bush and Obama favor a "pathway" to citizenship for persons residing in the United States illegally. Obama may retain at least some of Bush's 2001 and 2003 tax cuts, due to expire on December 31, 2010, for families with incomes of less than $200,000. Although Obama criticized Bush for affixing "signing statements" to laws that he approved, Obama said that he will continue Bush's practice of disregarding provisions of legislation he signs into law—should he deem them to be harmful to the national interest or inconsistent with his interpretation of his presidential powers.[3] Time will tell whether Obama will take as assertive a stance as did Bush in defense of the "inherent" powers of the presidency during wartime. Odds are high that Obama will.

One definitive conclusion can be drawn about Bush at this early date. He fulfilled his ambition to be a president of "consequence." However, evaluating Bush's presidency poses for scholars a dilemma not unlike that which confronts those who write about Jackson. While historians will acknowledge Bush's success in achieving several of his policy objectives, they will debate for some time whether Bush's policies were the right ones for the country at the time. Historians will also ask whether Bush would have achieved more of what he set out to do had he pursued his objectives in ways different from the ones he chose.

While history's verdict on the Bush presidency must await future jurors, who will have access to still classified papers and yet-to-be-published memoirs, some preliminary conclusions can already be drawn. Like his forty-two predecessors, Bush brought to the White House personal characteristics that shaped his presidency. Also like the others, Bush left a mark on America's economy, its safety, and its standing in the world and upon the course of liberty at home and abroad. The pages that follow provide a blueprint from which future writers may work.

Character

George W. Bush was born in New Haven, Connecticut, in 1946. As the eldest child of one of the nation's most politically active and socially prominent families, he spent the better part of his formative years seeking to follow in the footsteps of his highly successful father, the future forty-first president of the United States, George Herbert Walker Bush. George W. Bush was exceedingly loyal to his family, took pride in its heritage of public service, and saw his ascension to the presidency as part of his inheritance. Once in office, Bush worked to build upon and ultimately surpass his father's legacy.

At the same time, Bush sometimes behaved as if the best way to improve upon his father's legacy was to repudiate some of his father's policies. In some of these instances, the younger Bush went down a path different from the one the elder Bush took because situations the two men confronted were dissimilar. On other occasions, the son, eager to avoid repeating what he believed to have been his father's mistakes, deliberately did the opposite of what his father had done in what appeared to be similar circumstances. In all he attempted, George W. Bush was determined to chart his own course.

If the forty-first president broke his pledge not to raise taxes, rupturing his relationship with the conservative base of the Republican Party and jettisoning his re-election, the forty-third cut taxes and resisted raising them, whatever the condition of the economy. If the elder Bush considered religious convictions to be a private matter and appeared awkward discussing them, the younger Bush appeared quite at ease giving public testimony to his faith. If the first President Bush left Saddam Hussein in power at the end of Operation Desert Storm, the second President Bush rid the world of a tyrant he believed to be a dangerous menace.

The most cursory comparison of the presidential records of George H. W. Bush and George W. Bush invites the conclusion that George W. Bush wanted to exceed expectations that his family and others had placed on him and to best his father at a game in which the elder Bush had excelled, politics. The forty-third president gave the impression that he sought to avenge his father's defeat, while claiming as his birthright the nation's highest office.

When George W. Bush was two years old, his family moved to Midland, Texas. Like his father, Bush attended the Phillips Academy in Andover, Massachusetts. By the time he enrolled, Bush's family and teachers had concluded that "W" would fall short of his father's athletic and academic achievements. (One writer, who speculated that Bush had suffered from dyslexia or attention deficit/hyperactivity disorder during his childhood, saw Bush's fondness for the phrase "soft bigotry of low expectations" as evidence that he identified with children with learning disabilities.)[4] At Andover, Bush was known as a mischievous maverick. Friends dubbed him "the Lip."[5] He began a lifetime practice of addressing peers by nicknames, often derisive, he had assigned them. He also acquired what appeared to be an omnipresent smirk with which he greeted the world.

As president, Bush occasionally reverted to the quirky behavior he had displayed as an adolescent. At a ceremony welcoming Queen Elizabeth II to Washington, D.C., Bush cast an unexplained wink at his visitor. At a summit meeting, he gave what seemed an unwelcome back rub to German chancellor Angela Merkel. In accepting the presidential nomination of his party for the second time, Bush drew attention to the strut some detected in his gait. "In Texas, they call this walking," he said.

When an academic adviser, noting Bush's C average and middling test scores, suggested that he designate three choices of colleges, a defiant Bush listed Yale as his first, second, and third choices. With his grandfather, a U.S. senator and a Yale trustee, and his father, a onetime honor student, a former captain of the Yale baseball team, and member of the secret society Skull and Bones, George W. Bush knew that he would gain admission to Yale. The Yale that he attended, however, was a university undergoing a major transformation. "We were the last vestiges of the rich man's school," a Yale contemporary of Bush's remarked. During Bush's time there, each incoming class at Yale contained more public high school graduates and fewer legacies from places like Andover than the one that preceded it. "The son of an alumnus, who goes to a private preparatory school, now has less of a chance of getting in than some boy from P.S. 109," complained conservative columnist William F. Buckley Jr., who had attended Yale a generation ahead of Bush.[6]

Bush did not take too well to Yale's new meritocracy. He spent time at Delta Kappa Epsilon Fraternity and the secret society Skull and Bones. While at Yale, Bush volunteered in his father's unsuccessful campaign for the U.S. Senate in 1964. According to Bush family lore, the younger Bush was deeply hurt when Yale chaplain William Sloane Coffin told W that his father had been defeated by a better man, incumbent senator Ralph Yarborough.[7] The experience turned the younger Bush against liberal intellectuals, whom, he concluded, derided traditional American values and thought themselves superior to most Americans.

One of the greatest paradoxes of Bush's career was that this son of privilege would don the mantle of the populist, standing up for "ordinary Americans" against liberal intellectuals, not all that different from the ones he had encountered at Yale. Bush became an attitudinal conservative. He came to that philosophy through experience and emotion rather than through study.

After graduation from Yale in 1968, Bush floundered. He drifted in and out of jobs he had landed through family connections. He also drank excessively and engaged in rowdy behavior. After an altercation in which he challenged his father "to go *mano a mano*," Bush announced that he been admitted to Harvard Business School. He told his parents that he had applied to show them he could get in.[8] After obtaining his MBA from Harvard, Bush used his family ties to attract investors for several oil-related business ventures. Most lost money. One analyst contrasted Bush's impulsive "roll the dice" approach to the oil business to his father's methodical cultivation of experts who knew where oil was most likely to be found.[9] Bush's impulsiveness remained with him. After Bush had acquired the Texas Rangers, he announced that his baseball team would place less emphasis on statistics and more on the character of its players.[10]

Preferring to "get on with it," whatever the particular "it" was at any given time, Bush grew impatient with subordinates. He displayed little interest in learning how the companies and organizations that he managed actually worked or whether decisions he made were properly implemented. One economist, who enjoyed briefing Bush's vice president, Richard Cheney, said that he doubted Bush would have invited back anyone who dared take up his time with a ten-minute presentation.[11]

The image of Bush as "the decider" was evident early in his career. Bush took pride in his ability to size up people quickly, make decisions, and move on to other matters. During Bush's presidency, his tendency to "go with his gut" sometimes worked to his embarrassment. When he met Russian president Vladimir Putin for the first time on June 16, 2001, Bush proclaimed that he had seen the goodness of Putin's soul. On September 2, 2005, before he had seen and fully assessed the devastation Hurricane Katrina had wrought upon New Orleans and along Mississippi's Gulf Coast, Bush proclaimed that Federal Emergency Management Agency director Michael Brown ("Brownie") was doing "one heck of a job."

Bush valued brevity and consensus. He wanted his senior advisers to agree upon a certain course before meetings convened.[12] He detested prolonged discussions in the manner of Washington or Eisenhower, both alumni of prolonged "Councils of War" in which advisers strenuously debated different policy options before the president made his preference known.

Beginning in 1978, Bush underwent several style-changing and life-changing experiences. After losing a 1978 congressional race to a candidate who derided Bush's eastern elitist credentials and his Andover-Yale pedigree, W resolved never to "be out-Texaned again."[13] Aware that his father never completely shook the image of a transplanted "Yankee" in the Lone Star State, W set out to change his image. He reminded reporters that he had attended Jacinto Junior High School in Midland, while his father had gone to Greenwich Country Day School.[14] Bush consciously acquired mannerisms he considered common among "true Texans." By the time he became president, he had become in his own eyes the "real thing."

Bush's embrace of religion was another important part of his overall makeover. By all accounts, Bush's turn to religion at the age of forty gave him the self-discipline to quit drinking. He replaced what he had come to see as an unhealthy diversion with regularly scheduled regimens of vigorous physical exercise. Religion also brought out Bush's sense of empathy. Stories about his demonstrations of kindness and generosity toward wounded soldiers, surviving relatives of victims of terrorist attacks, and others abound. Bush did not behave as if he believed his personal religious beliefs were superior to those of others. He did not push his brand of religion on associates. Nor was he judgmental in his assessment of the morals and values of others.

At the same time, Bush's turn to religion did not alter all of his established behavioral patterns and attitudes. For example, he continued to use profanity in private. His embrace of the Christian faith had no effect on his actions with regard to pardons and computations. While on the campaign trail, to a reporter, he mimicked the pleas that a death row inmate had made to him on television to spare her life.[15] As president, Bush rejected twice as many pardon requests in his first seven years as Bill Clinton had rejected in eight years and five times as many as Ronald Reagan had rejected in eight years.[16] (Bush's refusal to pardon Lewis "Scooter" Libby, Cheney's chief of staff, for a perjury conviction, after first reducing his sentence to time already served, put a strain on relations between Bush and his vice president.)

As he reordered his life's priorities, Bush took a more active role in his father's political ascent. He kept a close eye on his father's chief political adviser, Lee Atwater, demanding to know why the family should trust the political operative. He lashed out at reporters he considered unfair to his father. During the re-election campaign, W became his father's "enforcer," firing his father's chief of staff, who had become a political liability. Family and friends surmised that W was channeling the anger and frustration that he had previously exhibited into a higher purpose, protecting his family's political interests.

Having seen the impact faith had exerted on his life, Bush came to believe that faith-based remedies could help redress social ills. As governor and as president, Bush favored using public funds for such purposes. Bush's faith informed his views on abortion. It may also have been the source of the extraordinary interest Bush took in programs intended to reduce disease and alleviate other forms of suffering in Africa. He was the single force behind the President's Emergency Plan for AIDS Relief, which funds treatment for millions of afflicted persons on that continent and cares for an even greater number of orphans and children. Bush's admonition that others "stop coming to Africa feeling guilty" and instead come "with love and feeling confident for its future" was hardly a sound bite.

Unlike John F. Kennedy, Bush failed to articulate what obligations a president, in the making of public policy, owed his fellow citizens who did not share his religious convictions. Kennedy, for instance, in opposition to his church, allowed federal officials responsible for administering foreign aid to disseminate information about birth control. Bush, like Reagan and his father, imposed "gag orders" on the subject of abortion in both domestic and foreign arenas. On the question of stem cell research, Bush tried to have it both ways. Consistent with his religious view, which held that destroying embryonic stem cells was, like abortion, a form of murder, Bush barred federal participation in embryonic stem cell research. Yet he left the door open for state governments and the private sector to engage in this activity.

By the time he ran for president, Bush had mastered the language of evangelical Protestantism sufficiently enough to deflect the demands that some of its more ardent practitioners made on him. When one cleric urged that he pledge not to appoint homosexuals to office, Bush replied that as a "sinner," he was not about to begin differentiating among sins.[17] Bush's answer, which helped him avert an unwanted controversy, gives testimony to both his canniness as a politician and his reluctance to cast judgment upon the private lives of those in his employ. While Bush's faith was genuine, he came to it, as he did his conservatism, more through experience than through reading and study. "He has absolutely zero interest in anything theological—nothing," remarked Doug Wead, who guided Bush into the world of Protestant evangelicalism.[18] As he had his acquired Texas mannerisms and his instinctual conservatism, Bush used his faith to project an identity he had carefully and self-consciously chosen. It became, as Bush said, part of his "shtick."[19] Bush wanted to be perceived as a "compassionate conservative," unleashing "armies of compassion" to administer social welfare programs and cut taxes to create a "prosperity with a purpose."

Bush's faith also reinforced his predisposition to perceive issues in terms of right and wrong and to decide matters quickly. One observer noted that it freed Bush from the kind of agonizing deliberations his father endured, thereby lightening the burdens of office.[20] Bush relied on his religious faith as a "first cut" to help him decide policy questions. About Bush, Bill Clinton said, "He does not know anything. He does not want to know anything. But, he's not dumb."[21]

Vision

When he ran for president, George W. Bush did not promise many things. Although terrorist attacks on U.S. interests abroad were increasing and a recession was on the horizon, the United States was at peace, and its economy appeared sound. While outgoing president Bill Clinton remained popular (Gallup had his approval rating at 57 percent prior to the election), voters were ready to move beyond the controversies, scandals, and partisan battles that characterized the Clinton era. Bush, a self-disciplined, religious family man from outside the world of Washington, seemed the perfect antidote to both Clinton and congressional Republicans, who had battled each other for six years. Bush's record as governor of Texas supported his claim that he could get people of different parties to work together to solve problems and that he would govern as a "compassionate conservative."

Bush proposed returning the federal budget surplus to citizens through tax cuts; improving education by raising standards and holding students, teachers, and schools more accountable; and using faith-based approaches to ameliorate social ills. As he had in Texas, Bush worked hard to add Hispanic Americans to his electoral and governing coalitions. (When he won reelection as governor, Bush won 49 percent of the votes Hispanic Americans cast. In his two campaigns for president, Bush polled 34 percent with this group in 2000 and 44 percent in 2004.[22] As a candidate, Bush ran better with this group than had most other Republicans.)

Bush's proposed tax cuts helped link him in voters' minds with another successful governor who became a much beloved and fondly remembered president, Ronald Reagan. Bush's "compassionate conservatism" moniker, like his father's advocacy of a "kinder and gentler America," was an attempt to differentiate him from the "social conservatives" that some voters, particularly outside of the South, found "strident." After years of divided government and partisan warfare, many voters welcomed the idea of a "uniter"—and not a "divider"—in the Oval Office.

On foreign policy, Bush said little. In a debate with his opponent, Vice President Al Gore, Bush criticized Clinton's readiness to commit troops in pursuit of abstract concepts such as "nation building." He expressed skepticism toward involving U.S. troops in conflicts in which he discerned no direct American interests. Bush promised a more "humble" foreign policy.

Once president, Bush, drawing upon his relatively high approval ratings (CNN reported it at 62 percent in April 2001), enacted his three top domestic priority items with relative ease. In partnership with Senator Edward M. Kennedy (D-MA) and Representative George Miller (D-CA), Bush secured passage of the "No Child Left Behind" Act of 2001, which he signed into law on January 8, 2002. By executive order, Bush established the White House Office of Faith-Based and Community Initiatives. He won easy passage of the Economic Growth and Tax Relief Reconciliation Act of 2001 (EGTRRA), which cut taxes by $1.35 trillion over ten years, and signed the measure into law on June 7, 2001. During the 2000 campaign and as the tax bill advanced through Congress, Bush made clear that he intended to use the tax code as a means of implementing his social agenda. (The reasons Bush's first tax bill did less to boost economic growth than many of his supporters expected will be discussed in a later section.)

During his second term, Bush proposed partial privatization of Social Security and an immigration reform plan, which included a "pathway to citizenship" and a "temporary guest worker" program. Having failed to prepare the country for either during his re-election campaign, Bush saw both measures stall.

As president, Bush often failed to differentiate between means and ends and between outcomes that resulted from individual effort and others that came as a result of government guarantees. In his second inaugural address, Bush praised three landmark pieces of legislation: the Homestead Act, the Social Security Act, and the GI Bill of Rights. Each, he said, increased the economic independence of all Americans. In linking the three together, Bush failed to distinguish what accounted for the success of each as well as how the different programs worked. The Homestead Act awarded tracts of land the government owned to people who would develop them through "sweat equity." Social Security is an entitlement program with compulsory participation. GI benefits are both forms of deferred compensation for those who served in the nation's armed forces and rewards for their sacrifices. In the next line of his speech, Bush similarly confused high standards in education (a means) and "an ownership society" (an end). "We will widen the ownership of homes and businesses, retirement savings and health insurance," he said, "preparing our people for the challenges of life in a free society."[23] Again, he was unclear whether the federal government's role was to establish fair rules for competition or ensure certain outcomes regardless of what that competition produces. As with his conservatism and his religious views, Bush's domestic vision came to him more through emotion and "gut instinct" and preference than through thought. He formed his opinions on foreign policy in the same manner.

Although Bush had articulated less of a foreign policy vision than a domestic one when he ran for president, he appeared to be moving toward one prior to the attacks of September 11, 2001. In his early months as president, Bush settled on a "go it alone" approach toward the rest of the world. He renounced American participation in the Kyoto Protocol, which places severe reductions in carbon emissions in developed countries. (Years before he took office, the U.S. Senate rejected American compliance by a unanimous vote.) Putting a strain on Russian-American relations, Bush summarily abrogated the Anti-Ballistic Missile Treaty, a cornerstone of American policy toward the Soviet Union since the Nixon era, in order to hasten development of a missile defense system in Europe.

Bush wavered when asked how the United States might react should Taiwan formally declare its independence from China. (For decades, the official U.S. line had been that Taiwan was a province of China, but that its disagreements with the mainland should be resolved peacefully.) Tensions between the United States and China rose and subsided after China downed an American military plane that strayed into its territory and Secretary of State Colin Powell negotiated the crew's release.

Bush's critics characterized his stance toward other countries as "American hegemony." Bush's supporters and adversaries alike came to regard his early actions as the first of what would be four "Bush Doctrines."[24] At their core was the underlying premise that the United States would act in its own interests as conditions warranted. Many of Bush's critics declared the various Bush Doctrines "unilateralist." In each of the ensuing doctrines he issued, Bush assigned a more expansive role for the United States in world affairs than he had in the one or ones that preceded it.

The second of Bush's doctrines, the "with us or against us" one, came in the aftermath of the attacks of 9-11. It drew no distinction between terrorists, who planned the 9-11 attacks, and those who harbored them. In the run-up to the invasion of Iraq he ordered, Bush proclaimed his third doctrine, that of "prevention." It sanctioned U.S. military action against any state that had developed weapons of mass destruction and appeared willing to use them against the United States or one of its allies. Interspersed with "prevention" was its rhetorical sister, "regime change." In his third iteration of the prevention doctrine, Bush advanced another argument in support of his decision to wage a "preventive" war in Iraq: bringing democracy to the Middle East. "It is presumptuous and insulting," he said, "to suggest that a whole region of the world—one-fifth of the humanity that is Muslim—is somehow untouched by the most basic aspirations of life. . . . In our desire to care for our children and give them a better life, we are the same. For these fundamental reasons, freedom and democracy will always and everywhere have greater appeal than the slogans of hatred and the tactics of terror."[25]

Finally, Bush enunciated in his second inaugural address his fourth doctrine, the eradication of tyranny from the planet and the spreading of democracy to all of its regions. "So it is the policy of the United States to seek and support the growth of democratic movements and institutions in every nation and culture, with the ultimate goal of ending tyranny in our world." Bush, as he made clear, did not intend to achieve this ambitious goal solely through armed conflict or the use of American troops. Yet as the U.S. forces became bogged down in Iraq simultaneously putting down an insurrection against its American occupiers, seeking to end armed conflict among rival religious factions, and working to build a stable government, Bush's policies lost congressional and public support. To many, the rising casualties and lack of discernible progress that followed the invasion of Iraq, which Bush had proclaimed a critical step in the spreading of democracy across the Middle East, appeared as harbingers of what lay ahead elsewhere. By the end of his presidency, Bush's declarations seemed as far away from their realization as did Wilson's 1917 pledge to "make the world safe for democracy."

Interestingly enough, as Bush worked his way through each of these doctrines, he never settled upon a readily identifiable name for the wars he waged. The Pentagon used the term "Operation Enduring Freedom" in referring to U.S. involvement in Afghanistan. "Operation Enduring Iraqi Freedom" followed. Such designations made no mention of the Taliban or of al-Qaeda. On the podium, Bush never appeared comfortable denouncing "Islamo-fascism," "radical Islamic fundamentalism," or any other label his neoconservative and other advisers urged him to tag on those who waged war against the United States. Instead, Bush talked about a "war against terrorism." This characterization was more a denunciation of al-Qaeda's tactics than its ideology. Bush's declaring war on terrorism would be analogous to Franklin D. Roosevelt's declaring war on sneak attacks and blitzkriegs rather than on Japanese militarism or German Nazism.

Like Woodrow Wilson, Franklin D. Roosevelt, and Lyndon B. Johnson before him, Bush came to office hoping to be a domestic reformer. Like they, he can claim some important victories in this arena. Unlike FDR, who could claim foreign policy and national security credentials prior to his election as president on which he could draw when waging and winning a major war became his primary objective, Bush had next to none. (All he could cite when running for president were contacts he established with governors of several Mexican states when he was governor of Texas.) Nor did Bush, as did Lincoln and FDR, adapt his strategy and tactics to accommodate changed conditions. By the time Bush showed a readiness to do so, it was only after the course he had been following seemed certain to end in disaster.

Like Wilson, Bush proved more effective when his party controlled Congress. Neither made much of an effort to grant his political opposition either a

symbolic or a meaningful role in policy making before or after it won control
of Congress. Like LBJ, Bush suffered from his failure to set clear goals for the
wars he waged and proved devoid of the competence necessary to attain those
he articulated.

Competence

In his early days as president, Bush tried hard to transcend whatever bitterness remained from the five-week dispute over which presidential candidate
won Florida's 27 electoral votes—and with them, the presidency—in 2000.
Declared the winner, Bush became the first person since Benjamin Harrison
to become president after losing the popular vote. (Al Gore outpolled Bush by
543,816 votes.)[26] Facing a House of Representatives of 221 Republicans and
212 Democrats and a tied Senate, Bush attempted to cultivate goodwill with
Democrats and liberals. He appeared before the Democratic congressional
winter retreat in Hershey, Pennsylvania, hosted the Congressional Black Caucus at the White House, invited the Kennedy family to a private screening of
the movie *Thirteen Days* (a depiction of JFK's handling of the 1962 Cuban
Missile Crisis), and named the Justice Department main building in honor of
former attorney general Robert F. Kennedy, among other gestures.

   With the exception of the brief partnership he forged with Senator Edward
Kennedy and Representative George Miller to pass the No Child Left Behind
Act of 2001, Bush made little progress in his attempt to build bipartisan support for his agenda. In part, this resulted from misperceptions that partisans
on both sides held of their opposites. In Texas, Bush, while governor, had
forged a productive relationship with Democratic lieutenant governor Bob
Bullock, believed by many to be the most powerful official in the state. Given
this track record, Bush may have come to Washington believing he might
replicate the working relationship he had enjoyed with Bullock and other
Texas Democrats with congressional Democrats. If such was indeed the case,
Bush failed to consider that Democratic congressional and other leaders in
Washington were decidedly more liberal than their Texas counterparts.

For their part, congressional Democrats may have assumed that, once in office, Bush, like his father before him, would willingly set aside much of what he had said during his campaign in exchange for harmonious relations with Congress. Such thinking ignored two essential differences between the two presidents and the circumstances that confronted each. The elder Bush had to govern with his party in the minority in both houses of Congress. His son saw his party in control of all of Congress. Moreover, George W. Bush was more ideologically driven than his father. He also took office believing that many of the accommodations his father had made to congressional Democrats in Congress had been mistakes.

Partisan feelings hardened on both ends of Pennsylvania Avenue at the very moment when Bush appeared to have easy going on Capitol Hill. (His tax cuts passed the House 240 to 154, with 28 Democrats and 1 independent in favor, and the Senate 58 to 33, with 12 Democrats and 46 Republicans in favor.) Ironically, the rise in partisan acrimony began with an ideological split, not between Democrats and Republicans but within the president's own party. It had as its origins the rather unconventional use Bush made of his vice president and his practice of deferring to his second in command on matters in which he believed his deputy was more experienced.

When George Bush selected Richard Cheney as his running mate, pundits were all but unanimous in their praise. The conventional wisdom held that, by reaching out to someone experienced in the ways of Washington, Bush had reassured skeptics about his lack of experience on the national and international stages. Less widely stated in public was that Cheney would add intellectual heft to Bush's ticket. Evidence in support of these hypotheses was plentiful. Where Bush had no experience in matters of national security, Cheney had served as secretary of defense under Bush's father. Where Bush had not served in Congress and enjoyed few relationships on Capitol Hill, Cheney had been elected as Wyoming's single member of the House six times. His peers elected him minority whip. If Bush was unfamiliar with the workings of the federal bureaucracy and impatient with its procedures and protocols, Cheney had served as chief of staff to President Gerald Ford. If Bush cast himself as an outsider, Cheney was the proverbial insider. To say that Cheney "knew his way around" would be one of the greatest understatements of American history.

According to Bush campaign lore and political "spin," Bush selected Cheney after being impressed at the diligence with which the former defense secretary had vetted other potential Bush running mates. Having briefly considered running for president, Cheney, who suffered several heart attacks, had long ago abandoned that objective. In Bush's mind, Cheney's lack of presidential ambitions left him free to do the president's bidding as an "honest broker."

Although Cheney lacked personal ambition, he was hardly bereft of policy goals and philosophical objectives he hoped to further. Most were compatible with Bush's, though the president would prove slow to comprehend fully the ramifications that might flow from their implementation. Over the next eight years, Cheney would use his proximity to the president to enact public policies he favored and to advance his conception of what powers the president enjoyed under the Constitution.

Early in their relationship, Bush said that Cheney was free to attend whatever meetings he chose and delve into issues and policies as he pleased. In making this decision, Bush apparently gave little consideration to how the vice president, an official elected to a four-year term and second in line to the presidency, might tower over staffers, who served at the president's pleasure, in such settings or whether his presence and participation would crowd out alternative or dissenting views. Nor was the new president particularly attentive to how a free agent, exercising vast powers in carrying out tasks Bush assigned him, might, by intent or otherwise, wall the president off from much of what was transpiring within his administration.

Bush might better have served his own personal and institutional interests by having someone, whose primary function was to protect him from the actions of others, act as the bearer of bad news and, when necessary, intervene on his behalf. Nancy Reagan did this for her husband. Robert Kennedy performed in a similar capacity for his brother. Having played this role for his father, Bush certainly appreciated the importance of this function. Perhaps he expected Cheney to exercise it. Karen Hughes, Bush's communications adviser of years standing, who might have ably performed this role, returned to

Texas early in Bush's presidency.[27] Bush's practice of staffing his administration at all levels with too few able and tested persons of independent standing and with too many hacks, cronies, and incompetents all but ensured that there would be few on the inside who felt secure enough in their standing with Bush to raise concerns. (Cheney, on the other hand, maneuvered with ease through persons he helped place throughout the administration.)[28]

Cheney, according to some Bush aides, had a "calming" effect on Bush.[29] He raised the president's comfort level by lessening Bush's load. If Bush preferred not to get into details and found budgets boring, Cheney was more than happy to take these matters on. While Bush was unacquainted with the folkways of Congress and with many of its members, Cheney picked up the slack. In a break with precedent, Cheney regularly attended the Senate Republican Conference and weekly luncheons of GOP senators.[30] As the Senate's presiding officer, he inherited an office on the Senate side of the Capitol. Cheney's former House colleagues provided him with another office off the House floor. From these two enclaves, Cheney worked congressional levers on behalf of the administration's program.

In the evenly divided Senate, five Republican moderates (Olympia Snowe and Susan Collins of Maine, Arlen Specter of Pennsylvania, Lincoln Chaffee of Rhode Island, and Jim Jeffords of Vermont) hoped to act as the balance of power between liberal Democrats and conservative Republicans. Cheney immediately dispelled them of such illusions. His conflict with them burst into the open when Bush, acting on Cheney's advice, rejected Jeffords's request to fund 70 percent of the costs of a federal mandate Congress placed on local schools with regard to special education spending. Jeffords responded by joining the Senate Democratic caucus. This, in effect, handed control of the chamber to the opposition political party. The prolonged controversy worked to Bush's disadvantage. Given Bush's willingness to spend so freely in other areas and the priority he awarded education, why he chose to draw a line at Jeffords's request remains puzzling. Deference to the advice of his number two is one possible answer.

In the aftermath of the attacks of 9-11, with the nation fully rallied around him, Bush made no attempt to bring Democrats into the war effort in dramatic or visible ways. Nor did he depart in the slightest degree from the partisan agenda he had pursued in his early months in office. Bush's stance contrasted sharply with that of Franklin D. Roosevelt. In 1940, prior to the entry of the United States into World War II, FDR appointed two prominent Republicans to positions of influence within his administration. He named Henry L. Stimson (Taft's secretary of war and Hoover's secretary of state) as secretary of war and Frank Knox (who had run for vice president in 1936 on the GOP ticket that opposed Roosevelt) as secretary of the navy. He subsequently sent Wendell Willkie, the man he had defeated in the 1940 election, as his personal representative to countries with which the United States became allied. Signaling that changed circumstances required a change in his approach to governing, FDR announced that "Dr. New Deal" had given way to "Dr. Win the War."

Bush made no comparable gestures to the Democrats. During his first six years in office, Bush preferred to operate primarily through partisan majorities. He named no Democrats of prominence to help oversee the war effort. Nor did he make the slightest adjustments to his agenda in order to establish national unity. Regaining control of Congress in 2007 after spending a dozen years in the minority, Democrats repaid Bush in kind. They upped their criticisms of his administration and its policies, convened multiple oversight hearings and investigations, and waged battle with him in the press and in the courts.

Bush came to pay a price in terms of lost support for his early and bold assertions of the inherent powers of his office in his capacity as commander in chief. Cheney entered the vice presidency convinced that, in response to the Watergate scandals, Congress had weakened the executive branch to the point that it had impeded its ability to protect the American people. Congress, in order to prevent repetitions of Nixon's practice of having intelligence agencies spy on American citizens, passed the Foreign Intelligence Surveillance Act. It required such entities to obtain warrants in advance of domestic surveillance and set up special courts to weigh the government's case for them. Congress also outlawed certain practices the CIA had routinely used while operating abroad. Convinced that these measures had rendered these agencies incapable of discharging their respective missions, Cheney sought to restore what he believed was the proper balance of power between the executive and legislative branches. Wherever possible, he preferred to have the executive act on his own rather than in collaboration with Congress.

On the first day of the Bush administration, a presidential underling reported that the president intended to leave the presidency "stronger than he found it."[31] While such statements are not unusual ones for new presidents to make, there is no reason to suspect that Bush, when he uttered them, had a clear idea of how he intended to strengthen the office he had inherited. As governor, he had spent little time musing about his executive powers, even though the Texas governorship was institutionally weak. In Austin, Bush concentrated on passing his program. Most likely, the man who saw himself primarily as the "decider" had, after his election, turned his thoughts more to policy initiatives than to the constitutional prerogatives of the presidency. As a candidate, Bush had not been prone to quote from the *Federalist Papers*, political treatises, or legal commentaries. Yet, to a man as determined to be a president of consequence as was Bush, the idea of a "stronger presidency" had to have had appeal. As he did with much else, Bush relied on those to whom he delegated important tasks to provide him with constitutional and legal rationales for what he attempted. And as he did in most matters, Bush acted on this advice.

Cheney, on the other hand, had very fixed ideas as to what constituted a "strong presidency." He and a team of lawyers at the White House and the Justice Department's Office of Legal Counsel advanced the theory of a "unitary executive." They argued that the president, by virtue of his powers as commander in chief, possessed under the Constitution inherent powers that, once asserted, lay beyond the reach of Congress and the courts.[32] In support of this argument, they cited Alexander Hamilton's argument, in Federalist Paper No. 70, that "energy in the executive" was essential in order to protect the community "against foreign attacks" and to provide efficient and effective administration of the laws. In support actions they subsequently took, they relied on two precedents: Lincoln's suspensions of *habeas corpus* during the Civil War and FDR's ordering that German nationals, who Hitler had sent to commit sabotage in the United States, be tried before secret military commissions.[33] Upon this advice, Bush unilaterally took a series of secret measures that sanctioned surveillance by intelligence agencies of telephone and other forms of communication inside the United States in the absence of warrants, as required by law; denied terrorist suspects, captured offshore and held at Guantánamo, "due process," either under the Geneva Convention or the U.S. Constitution; and sanctioned "enhanced interrogation techniques."

As he made these crucial decisions, Bush maintained that he did not need congressional authorization for any of these actions. Thus, he did not seek it. Nor did he seek to amend existing statutes in ways that would have given his actions the force of law in the event they were challenged. This failing, on his part, all but ensured subsequent court challenges, congressional reaction, increased criticism, and public skepticism. After the Supreme Court held in *Hamdan v. Rumsfeld* that the president needed to obtain congressional approval in order to establish military tribunals and that "enemy combatants" had access to U.S. courts in the event the president sought to deny them protections of the Geneva Convention's Common Article 3, Bush belatedly took his case to Congress. Ironically, Congress, in the Military Commissions Act it enacted in 2006, granted Bush most of the powers he had already invoked. It also sanctioned retroactively measures he had ordered.[34] Had Bush gone to Congress before the Supreme Court forced his hand, he might have spared his administration and the country much of the acrimony, controversy, and erosion of trust that had become commonplace by the end of his tenure.

Asserting his "inherent" powers as strenuously as he did, Bush went beyond one of the precedents his lawyers liked to cite. Lincoln, acting in his capacity as commander in chief, did indeed exercise powers the Constitution had either not granted the executive or appeared to have assigned Congress. He maintained, however, that the emergency measures he had taken when Congress was not in session were as temporary as they were extraordinary. Lincoln also asked Congress to approve retroactively all that he had done in its absence.[35] Bush and his team argued, in essence, that the inherent powers of the president as commander in chief, which Lincoln had maintained were exceptional, temporary, and permissible under certain circumstances, were routine and permanent.

The totality of controversies that involved Bush's assertion of his presidential authority inflicted irrefutable harm on his image and may well impact adversely on his standing in history. In at least one sense, he left the presidency weaker than he found it. Prior to *Hamdan v. Rumsfeld*, the courts had not limited the president's power to deny protections of the Geneva Convention or access to American courts to "enemy combatants." Bush's successors will have to live under these new constraints.

The ongoing battle over Bush's powers as commander in chief may have also hampered Bush's ability to achieve his international objectives. The paradox of an American president who lectured the world on the importance of spreading democracy and democratic institutions acting arbitrarily, sometimes in secret, often by impulse, and unaccountable to other branches of the government was not lost on Bush's critics, foreign and domestic. It is unlikely to escape the notice of historians.

As a candidate, Bush understood the importance of effective communications to successful campaigns. As president, he failed to appreciate the part public persuasion could play in building and maintaining support for the wars he chose to wage. This was not something Cheney could do for him. Nor was he much inclined to try. Asked his reaction to polls showing that two-thirds of Americans believed that the war in Iraq was not worth the costs, Cheney responded with the single word, "So?"[36]

Cheney's stance was, in part, understandable. He had not had to persuade key sectors of the public to follow his lead before. Unlike Bush, who defeated a popular incumbent Democrat to become governor, Cheney had encountered in Wyoming what was, at best, an anemic opposition. Why Bush did not use his natural talents on the stump on behalf of his national security policies as often or as effectively as he had on behalf of his election or his education and tax proposals remains a mystery.

Bush's ignorance about some of his administration's policies hampered his ability to explain or defend them to outsiders. "It seems to me that if somebody is talking to Al Qaeda, we want to know why," Bush remarked in defense of the warrantless domestic surveillance program his administration put into place. Yet, as one observer noted, the program Bush sanctioned cast a net well beyond this group of suspects.[37] So oblivious was Bush to the workings of this program or the dissension it caused within his own administration that it took the threat of mass resignations by attorneys at the Justice Department's Office of Legal Counsel and the director of the Federal Bureau of Investigation to get him to shut it down and seek congressional authorization for what he sought to do.[38]

While in office, Bush suffered the effects of his failure to think through the ramifications of what he said. At one press conference, he said that he regretted having used the words "bring it on," in which he appeared to have dared the enemy to attack U.S. forces. Often, he used words without defining what he meant by them, even though he and his advisers knew that they did not mean the same things across different cultures. One such word was "democracy." More than once, Bush appeared to mistake its forms (elections, written constitutions) for its substance (rule of law, protection of individual rights, and development of a civil society). One example of this confusion was Bush's insistence on holding elections in Iraq before negotiating a power-sharing arrangement between Shia and Sunni Arabs. (Statements from administration officials suggested that in the absence of Saddam Hussein, pluralism would instantaneously take hold.) In Gaza, Bush's insistence on holding elections may have facilitated the coming to power of Hamas, which, although committed to acts of terrorism, showed itself to be better organized and less corrupt than Fatah, the more moderate Palestinian political organization Hamas defeated.

Uninterested in detail, deficient in curiosity, and too willing to expect the best from underlings, Bush failed to supervise key subordinates with whom he entrusted the workings of his administration. After it had become clear that subduing Iraq would be a more arduous task than previously imagined, Bush failed to acknowledge the obvious. For a long time, Bush administration officials denied the existence of an insurrection. They attributed violence that Americans saw on television to isolated acts of "looters." Having gone in with an insufficient number of troops to occupy Iraq successfully, Bush refused for years to modify his strategy or his tactics.

Bush acted only after one prescient general pressed his arguments on his superiors hard enough to ensure that the debate extended beyond the walls of the Pentagon. It is impossible to imagine Bush, in the manner of Lincoln, spending hours poring over incoming communications, sending sentinels to the field to give him a fresh take on what transpired, countermanding generals' orders, or, when all else failed, attempting to teach himself military strategy. While Bush eventually approved the "surge" (an increase of 40,000 troops) that tipped the scales against the insurgency in Iraq by enhancing the sense of security of its population in certain locales, historians are likely to assign as much credit to its architect, General David Petraeus, for his persistence as they are to the president. They are all but certain to fault Bush for his stubbornness in clinging to the same policy in the face of years of failure. Obstinacy compounded by ignorance colored much of his presidency.

After Cheney brought army colonel Derek J. Harvey, a specialist on the region, to brief Bush on what had gone wrong following the American invasion of Iraq, Bush said that he did not understand why someone of Harvey's rank was briefing him. He inquired as to why Harvey thought he might be correct and Bush's advisers and generals wrong. Bush made clear that he did not wish to hear from the colonel again.[39] In the face of sustained reports that U.S. forces lacked sufficient body and vehicular armor and of relatives raising funds to provide the equipment, Bush, accepting Pentagon assertions that the needed materials were "in the pipeline," did not intervene. Congress eventually did.[40]

Bush remained equally as hands-off as stories circulated about alleged corruption, featherbedding, and abuses on the part of American-retained consultants, contractors, and per diem employees—many of them former Bush-Cheney campaign workers. As photographs of atrocities U.S. forces committed at Abu Ghraib circulated the globe, Bush stood by his secretary of defense, Donald Rumsfeld.

In an interview late in his presidency, Bush said that he had "no idea" why Paul Bremer, who headed the American-led Coalition Provisional Authority, disbanded the Iraqi army.[41] Some analysts consider that decision, along with Bremer's wide-scale purge of Baathists from Iraq's provisional government, as a factor that impeded the formation of a stable post-Saddam government. Yet Bush presented Bremer with the Presidential Medal of Freedom, as he has former CIA director George Tenet, who reportedly had assured the president that finding evidence that Saddam Hussein had weapons of mass destruction would be a "slam dunk."

Bush also made certain that people who dissented from the consensus that prevailed around him were ignored and replaced. Larry Lindsey, director of Bush's National Economic Policy Council, was dismissed after he publicly estimated that the costs of the war in Iraq would be $200 billion. (Official reports had it between $50 billion and $60 billion. By the end of 2008, its costs were about $600 billion.) General Eric Shinseki, army chief of staff, was eased out after he estimated that 500,000 troops would be necessary in order to occupy Iraq successfully. Secretary of Defense Donald Rumsfeld initially sent 130,000.

On the domestic front, Bush's management style also served him poorly. He and his team were caught unaware as Hurricane Katrina caused unprecedented havoc in New Orleans. The president, who claimed that the inherent powers of his office were unlimited, maintained through advisers that he lacked authority to "federalize" the Louisiana National Guard in the absence of the governor's request. Public squabbling among the federal, state, and local authorities hampered efforts to evacuate residents, provide emergency assistance, and maintain order. His legal team, always ready to cite precedent, seemed oblivious to Eisenhower's and Kennedy's federalizing the National Guard in the face of gubernatorial resistance to curb civil disturbances and enforce court orders to integrate educational institutions. Nor did they appear aware that Nixon sent the military to Mississippi in the aftermath of Hurricane Camille. These other presidents, like Bush, served after passage of the Posse Comitatus Act of 1878, which Bush's team cited in justification of his initial standoffishness. Bush, operating under the Insurrection Act of 1807 (which Jefferson had used to enforce the embargo), eventually sent 7,200 soldiers to the area, in addition to the 30,000 National Guardsmen already on the ground. Other federal efforts did not pick up substantially after Bush belatedly visited the region.

While president, Bush kept his distance from much of Washington, whose preeminent political fixtures exuded much of the liberal politics and social pretensions he disdained. This proved a major mistake. Bush lost opportunities to build personal relationships, upon which he might have been able to rely when unanticipated problems arose or when his political position deteriorated. Bush held fewer state dinners than his predecessors and regarded the ceremonial aspects of his office as unwelcome chores to be endured rather than as occasions to obtain information and push business along. A good mixer and a gracious host, when he wanted to be, Bush might have used his personal attributes more often to build support for his programs or goodwill for his administration. Disinclined to go sightseeing while abroad (another "waste of time"), Bush restricted his activities in foreign countries to official duties. He seemed not to appreciate how a U.S. president's going out of his way to visit a symbol of significance to a foreign population might raise his country's standing in their eyes. While in India, Eisenhower, for instance, journeyed hundreds of miles to stand before the Taj Mahal. The famous tomb never made it onto Bush's itinerary when he visited that country. The management style the country's first MBA president exhibited in office was a far stretch from what Bush would have been taught at Harvard Business School. The nation suffered greatly as a result of his failure to pay greater attention to what was said in class.

Economic Policy

On January 20, 2001, President George W. Bush inherited an economy that was weakening. A major contributing factor to this was the collapse of the high-tech stock bubble in the spring of 2000. Policy makers were slow to recognize in the winter of 2000–2001 that the economy was in decline. Indeed, the Congressional Budget Office and the Office of Management and Budget, as well as most private economists, were still forecasting moderate real GDP growth and large federal budget surpluses over the next decade.[42] During the 2000 campaign, Bush pressed for tax cuts as a means of returning the surplus to taxpayers. He had not embraced them as a means of stimulating economic growth. Nor did he and his team recognize the need to grow the economy at that juncture. As a candidate and later as president, Bush argued that the budget surplus was the "people's money" and not the government's and that they rather than bureaucrats in Washington knew better how to spend it.

Because business investment in structures, equipment, and software is the most volatile component of the U.S. economy, most economists maintain that the most effective way to stimulate economic growth and increase the number of jobs is to reduce disincentives to business investment. They argue that this might best be done by cutting corporate income taxes and tax rates, shortening tax-depreciation schedules, instituting an investment tax credit, reducing the tax rates on capital gains and dividends, and cutting marginal income tax rates on would-be investors.

The Economic Growth and Tax Relief Reconciliation Act of 2001, which Bush signed on June 7, 2001, contained only one of these growth-enhancing tax provisions: a reduction from 10 percent to 8 percent in the capital-gains tax rate for certain investments held for at least five years. Bush had not adjusted his tax plan to reflect the changed economic circumstances by reducing taxes on business investment. Nor did he delay implementing costly social policies he sought to advance through the tax code.

EGTRRA contained a tax rebate for 2001 and a gradual reduction in federal individual income tax rates through 2006. However, these rate reductions were phased in so slowly that they would not help the economy until at least 2004. EGTRRA increased the child tax credit from $500 to $1,000, reduced the "marriage penalty," increased the limits on precontributions to retirement accounts, and provided tax incentives for savings for educational expenses. Doubling the child tax credit and encouraging additional saving for education and retirement proved costly to the Treasury. Whatever the merits of these programs on policy grounds, their collective contribution to the growth of the economy was, at best, minimal. Bush, however, saw them both as long-term "investments" and the most tangible way of giving meaning to his brand of "compassionate conservatism." In private, as well as in public, Bush maintained that he wanted do more for the "single mom" who worked as a waitress while trying to raise two children on $25,000 a year. Most of his advisers, including his vice president, who were better versed in economics than Bush, maintained that growing the economy would do more to help such persons than would much of Bush's social agenda.[43]

Bush's EGTRRA differed in intention and result from President Kennedy's Revenue Act of 1962, which created the "investment tax credit"; President Lyndon B. Johnson's Revenue Act of 1964 (signed after Kennedy's death and more popularly known as the "Kennedy tax cuts"); and Reagan's Economy Recovery Tax Act of 1981. (See chapter 5.) Primarily intended to promote economic growth by reducing marginal income tax rates or by lowering the tax costs of new business investment, those prior measures succeeded in their objective. The more cluttered and complicated EGTRRA provided only a weak stimulus to the U.S. economy.

Unlike Kennedy and Reagan, Bush did not attempt to control the growth of federal spending. From fiscal year 2002 to fiscal year 2009, total real outlays rose by an average of 9.0 percent a year, the highest among all presidents since 1962. The average annual increases in real defense outlays, real domestic discretionary outlays, and real entitlement outlays were 8.8 percent, 4.3 percent, and 13.5 percent, respectively. Bush recorded the largest average annual increase in real defense outlays and the second-largest average annual increase in real entitlement outlays.

In 2003, Bush persuaded Congress to add a new prescription-drug benefit to Medicare, but did not insist that it be paid for either through a payroll-tax increase, higher insurance premiums paid by beneficiaries, or offsetting reductions in other benefits. Medicare's trustees project that the Hospital Insurance Trust Fund will run out of money by 2017. The Congressional Budget Office found that "if current laws do not change, federal spending on Medicare and Medicaid combined will grow from roughly 5 percent of GDP today to almost 10 percent by 2035 and to more than 17 percent by 2080."[44] By these lights, Bush's adding new benefits to a program that was encountering difficulty paying for existing benefits was nothing short of "fiscal malpractice."

Bush's unwillingness to control spending moved the federal budget from surplus into deficit. The recession that began in December 2007 pushed the federal budget even further into the red. During fiscal year 2001 when Bush took office, the federal budget surplus was 1.3 percent of the GDP. During fiscal year 2009 when Bush left office, the federal budget deficit was 10.0 percent of the GDP.

The March 2001 to November 2001 recession proved mild. The unemployment rate rose from 4.3 percent in March 2001 to only 5.5 percent in November 2001. However, real GDP growth remained sluggish, averaging 1.9 percent during the five quarters after the recession. Consequently, the unemployment rate continued to increase to a peak of 6.3 percent in June 2003. Because EGTRRA had been so poorly structured, however, the U.S. economy became overly dependent on the Federal Reserve keeping interest rates unusually low for too long a time. Because low long-term interest rates boost the housing sector, the Federal Reserve's failure to tighten credit in 2002 helped inflate the already developed U.S. housing bubble. This would have disastrous consequences for the U.S. economy in the second half of 2007 and 2008.

None of this was inevitable. Stanford University monetary economist and Bush's undersecretary of the treasury for international affairs from 2001 to 2005, John B. Taylor, had developed the "Taylor rule" to guide the Federal Reserve on how to adjust its target for the federal fund rate to maintain noninflationary economic growth. A comparison between the actual federal fund rate with the target federal fund rate implied by the Taylor rule allows the Federal Reserve to determine whether its monetary policy is too accommodative or too restrictive. Comparing actual data to the data from a Taylor rule–consistent simulation, Taylor found that the actual federal fund rate was significantly below the Taylor rule–consistent target federal fund rate from the second quarter of 2002 through the third quarter of 2006. Taylor concluded, "A higher federal funds rate path [consistent with the Taylor rule] would have avoided much of the housing boom."[45]

Bush could have affected the Federal Reserve's monetary policy through his appointments. On May 18, 2004, Bush renominated Alan Greenspan to serve as chairman of the Board of Governors of the Federal Reserve System until he was legally required to retire on January 31, 2006. For example, Bush could have appointed Taylor, who had been critical of Greenspan's policies, to the board if the president thought that the Federal Reserve's monetary policy was overly accommodative. Of the eight people Bush named to the Federal Reserve, only Ben Bernanke came with a background in monetary economics. Apparently, Bush was quite satisfied with Greenspan's inflation of the housing bubble.

The Jobs and Growth Tax Relief Reconciliation Act of 2003 (JGTRRA), which Bush signed on May 28, 2003, proved more beneficial to the U.S. economy than had EGTRRA. JGTRRA accelerated the marginal individual income tax reductions enacted in 2001, provided 50 percent expensing of business investment in equipment with the remainder depreciated over time, and cut the maximum tax rate on capital gains and dividends to 15 percent. Under JGTRRA, real GDP growth accelerated to an average of 3.1 percent from the second quarter of 2003 through the fourth quarter of 2006, and the unemployment rate fell to 4.4 percent in December 2006.

Ironically, in devising JGTRRA, the more effective of Bush's two tax cuts as far as economic growth is concerned, Bush exerted less influence. According to the chairman of Bush's Council of Economic Advisers, the president, by now convinced of the need to cut marginal tax rates on top earners in order to grow the economy, initially proposed eliminating all taxes on dividends to "make the tax code more fair."[46] He initially opposed cutting the tax rate on capital gains in order to avoid being criticized for "favoring the rich." According to one source, Vice President Richard Cheney worked behind the scenes to shape the final bill with House Ways and Means Committee chairman Bill Thomas (R-CA) to reduce but not eliminate the tax on dividends and use moneys saved by the change to cut capital-gains taxes, a proposal Bush had initially resisted.[47]

Advocating an "ownership society," Bush expanded the housing policies of his predecessor Bill Clinton. In 1994, President Bill Clinton declared, "More Americans should own their own homes." According to Department of Housing and Urban Affairs (HUD) documents, Clinton sought to "reduce down payment requirements and interest costs by making terms more flexible" and "increase the availability of alternative financing products in housing markets throughout the country." Using the Community Reinvestment Act of 1977, the Clinton administration pressed banks to lower their credit standards, reduce down-payment requirements, and promote highly unconventional alternatives to traditional fixed-rate fully amortizing residential mortgage loans. As a result, low-income and minority families that could not qualify for traditional loans under normal credit standards began to receive interest-only and negatively amortizing residential mortgage loans.[48]

Ignoring the implications for the safety and soundness of financial institutions and markets, President Bush put Clinton's housing policies into hyperdrive. Bush sought to "use the mighty muscle of the federal government" to increase the home-ownership rate among low-income and minority families. For three decades prior to 1995, the U.S. home-ownership rate hovered around 64 percent. Bush pushed it up to a peak of 69 percent in 2004, but at the cost of a global financial crisis and the resulting recession.

In 1992, President George H. W. Bush signed the Federal Housing Enterprises Financial Safety and Soundness Act of 1992. This act directed the secretary of housing and urban development to set affordable housing quotas for Fannie Mae and Freddie Mac. On October 31, 2000, Secretary of Housing and Urban Development, under President Clinton, Andrew Cuomo boosted the affordable housing quotas for 2001–2004.[49] Since Fannie Mae and Freddie Mac could not meet these higher quotas by purchasing conforming residential mortgage loans for securitization, they began to purchase AAA-rated portions of privately issued residential mortgage–backed securities containing subprime residential mortgage loans to meet these quotas. This regulatory-induced demand caused the explosive growth of subprime lending over the next six years. Bush could have rescinded the higher quotas. Instead, his second HUD secretary, Alphonso Jackson, boosted the affordable housing quotas for 2005–2008. Moreover, Bush pressed Congress to allocate $200 million per year to assist first-time buyers with down-payment and closing costs and to allow such buyers to qualify for government-insured mortgages without any down payments. As housing prices escalated, Bush pressed private lenders to extend bigger loans on generous terms to marginal home buyers. "Corporate America," Bush said, "has a responsibility to work to make America a more compassionate place."[50]

Bush grew concerned when Fannie Mae and Freddie Mac exploited implicit federal guarantees by borrowing huge sums at low interest rates to speculate on residential mortgage loans and residential mortgage–backed securities. He asked Congress to impose leverage limits on Fannie Mae and Freddie Mac and to strengthen their regulator, the Office of Federal Housing Enterprise Oversight. The House passed the necessary legislation. It cleared the Senate Banking Committee in a straight partisan vote on August 1, 2005, but the Democratic minority blocked it from floor consideration. Bush let the matter drop. "No one wanted to stop that [the housing bubble]," Glenn Hubbard, who chaired Bush's Council of Economic Advisers, recalled. "It would have conflicted with the president's own policies."[51]

Historically, banks have served as the main intermediaries between borrowers and savers by gathering deposits payable on demand and extending loans to families and nonfinancial businesses that cannot access credit markets directly by issuing corporate bonds or commercial paper. When depositors lose confidence in a bank, "runs" ensue. (A run occurs when depositors try to withdraw all of their deposits at once.) Because banks keep only small amounts of cash on hand, a run may cause a solvent bank to fail. Such runs can quickly spread. When many banks fail simultaneously, the total amount of credit contracts and a severe recession or even depression may occur.

To stabilize the bankcentric financial system, Congress created the Federal Reserve in 1913 to act as the "lender of last resort" to solvent but illiquid banks. Twenty years later, it established the Federal Deposit Insurance Corporation (FDIC) to protect families from losses because of bank failures.

During the past quarter century, an alternative financial system came into being that challenged the dominance of the banks. This system is based on securitization—the issuance of asset-backed securities collateralized by many loans bought from originators—and the purchase of these asset-backed securities by highly leveraged nondepository financial institutions, including independent investment banks, hedge funds, Fannie Mae, and Freddie Mac. This alternative financial system arose outside of prudential supervision by federal regulators and without access to the Federal Reserve's "discount window." By

2007, this alternative system had $12.7 trillion in assets. Collectively, banks had $13.5 trillion.

During the global financial crisis that began on August 9, 2007, when the international banking group BNP Paribas suspended withdrawals from three of its hedge funds that had investments in U.S. subprime mortgage–backed securities, the vulnerabilities of this alternative financial system became painfully obvious. At first, President Bush and Federal Reserve chairman Ben Bernanke thought that the financial crisis would harm a few mortgage banks that specialized in subprime mortgage loans and some hedge funds that had invested in subprime residential mortgage–backed securities, but would spare the rest of the economy. This optimistic view proved unfounded.

During the week of March 10–14, 2008, funding for Bear Stearns, an independent investment bank, evaporated. On Monday, March 17, 2008, the Federal Reserve, with the support of Secretary of the Treasury Henry Paulson, arranged for JPMorgan Chase to acquire Bear Stearns at a "fire-sale" price of $2 per share, later increased to $10 per share. Financial market conditions improved after this transaction, but began to deteriorate once again during the summer.

By fall, four major financial institutions were in deep trouble: Fannie Mae, Freddie Mac, Lehman Brothers, and the American Insurance Group (AIG). On September 7, 2008, Federal Housing Finance Agency director James B. Lockhart III found that Fannie Mae and Freddie Mac were insolvent and placed them into conservatorships. Secretary Paulson announced that the Treasury would provide each of these government-sponsored enterprises with up to $100 billion (later increased to $200 billion) of taxpayer funds to offset any losses that these government-sponsored enterprises incurred while they continued to operate.

During the week of September 8–12, 2008, funding for Lehman Brothers, another independent investment bank, evaporated. Despite a desperate search for a merger partner, the Federal Reserve and the Treasury were unable to arrange a "shotgun wedding" over the weekend. Lehman Brothers filed for bankruptcy on September 15, 2008. On the same day, Bank of America announced that it would acquire Merrill Lynch, another independent investment bank in deep financial trouble.

On September 16, 2008, funding for AIG evaporated, and its share price plummeted following a credit-rating downgrade. Among the financial institutions that had failed so far, AIG posed the greatest risk to the rest of the financial system. One of AIG's units, the AIG Financial Products Group, had sold $72 billion of credit-default swaps (CDSs) to major banks to insure their exposure to collateralized debt obligations, a complex form of asset-backed securities. CDSs function as a form of credit insurance in which the seller agrees to pay the buyer in the event of default on a referenced asset-backed security. By buying CDSs, banks can substitute the higher credit rating of the seller for the lower credit rating of the referenced asset-backed security. This substitution can reduce a bank's cost of capital for owning the referenced asset-backed security by as much as 80 percent. If the credit rating of a CDS seller falls below AA, CDS sellers must compensate CDS buyers by posting collateral of marketable securities with the CDS buyers.

As AIG's credit ratings fell in 2008, its collateral postings with CDS buyers increased from $2.9 billion on December 31, 2007, to $32.8 billion on September 31, 2008. Unable to raise funds or post more collateral, AIG threatened to file bankruptcy. Fearing that AIG's bankruptcy would trigger a chain failure of several major financial institutions, including Société Générale, Goldman Sachs, Deutsche Bank, UBS, Bank of Montreal, Wachovia, Barclays, Bank of America, and Dresdner Bank, the Federal Reserve extended an $85 billion emergency loan to AIG on September 16, 2008.

Stock markets around the world tumbled on Monday, September 15, 2008, and again on Wednesday, September 17. As a result, the Reserve Fund, a money-market mutual fund that had invested in Lehman Brothers' commercial paper, "broke the buck" (i.e., the market value of its assets was less than the market of its liabilities) and suspended conversions. This suspension ignited a run on all money-market mutual funds. By morning, there were $500 million of withdrawal orders in queue. To quell this run, the Federal Reserve extended more than $100 billion in emergency loans to money-market mutual funds, while the Treasury extended a government guarantee similar to FDIC coverage for deposits in banks to all money-market funds. These simultaneous actions ended the runs on money-market mutual funds.

Between September 17 and December 10, 2008, Chairman Bernanke directed the Federal Reserve to inject more than $1.3 trillion into the U.S. economy through regular or emergency loan facilities. Bernanke, who is the world's leading expert on the Great Depression, was determined not to repeat the Federal Reserve's mistakes of the 1930s. Bernanke aggressively used the Federal Reserve's emergency powers to provide emergency credit to banks and other financial institutions after credit markets seized up. In retrospect, Bernanke's decisive actions prevented a world financial meltdown.

On Saturday, September 20, 2008, Secretary Paulson proposed the Troubled Asset Relief Plan (TARP) to buy up to $700 billion of "toxic" assets from banks and other financial institutions. Stock markets continued to fall once it became clear that there was significant congressional and public opposition to the Paulson plan. In a televised address on Wednesday, September 24, 2008, President Bush pleaded in vain for the Paulson plan. Five days later, the House of Representatives defeated the Emergency Economic Stabilization Bill.

Financial conditions deteriorated rapidly, and credit markets became completely frozen. The House relented, and President Bush signed the Emergency Economic Stabilization Act on October 3, 2008. By this time, however, Secretary Paulson and Chairman Bernanke had become convinced that asset purchases would take too long to prevent an immediate financial collapse. During the week of October 6–10, 2008, the Dow Jones Industrial Average lost more than 22 percent of its value.

On October 14, 2008, Secretary Paulson announced a new strategy. The Treasury would use TARP funds to buy preferred shares in all major banks, regardless of their financial condition or need. That day, Paulson effectively ordered Bank of America, JPMorgan Chase, Wells Fargo, Citigroup, Merrill Lynch, Goldman Sachs, Morgan Stanley, Bank of New York–Mellon, and State Street to accept TARP funds through the Capital Purchase Program. Other banks would have one month to accept TARP funds on similar terms.

After Bernanke's $1.3 trillion liquidity injection, Paulson's decision to inject TARP funds directly into banks through preferred-share purchases was the second most important factor that stabilized financial markets. Paulson effectively "drew a line in the sand," saying those banks would survive.

The two other decisions that proved effective in ending the financial panic were the AIG "bailout" and the suspension of short sales in bank stocks. Unlike insurers, CDS sellers are not required to maintain actuarially adequate reserves to pay claims. Instead, CDS sellers hedge their risk through offsetting CDS purchases from other sellers, or short sales of a related stock. During late summer, AIG's financial problems triggered suspicions about the true condition of major banks and other financial institutions. Wanting to hedge their CDS risk exposure, banks, which had sold a majority of CDSs, sought to buy CDSs from other banks, boosting CDS prices. A number of quantitative hedge funds had developed investment models in which higher CDS prices for a company's debt securities triggered short sales of the same company's common stock. During the panic, hedging by banks that had sold CDSs and program trading by hedge funds simultaneously increased CDSs and drove down bank-share prices. Given the interconnectedness of all major banks through CDSs, this vicious cycle, if left unchecked, could have caused the failure of most large banks in the United States. The decisions to bail out AIG (and thereby make its CDS counterparties whole) and to suspend short sales in bank stock broke this cycle.

On the international front, Bush's economic record was, on balance, positive. President Bush supported the World Trade Organization in launching the Doha Development Round negotiations in November 2001. In 2002, Bush persuaded Congress to reinstate trade-promotion authority that had lapsed under President Bill Clinton in 1994. Before this authority lapsed again on June 30, 2007, Bush won congressional approval for free-trade agreements with Australia, Bahrain, Chile, Costa Rica, the Dominican Republic, El Salvador, Guatemala, Honduras, Morocco, Oman, Peru, and Singapore. The Bush administration also signed free-trade agreements with Colombia, Panama, and South Korea, but Congress refused to approve them before Bush left office.

After the Asian financial crisis of 1997–1998, the People's Republic of China intervened heavily in foreign exchange to suppress the appreciation of its currency, the renminbi, that might otherwise occur, in order to boost Chinese exports. Consequently, China accumulated $1.7 trillion of reserves, about two-thirds of which were invested in U.S. debt securities. This contributed to the U.S. housing bubble by artificially suppressing medium- and long-term U.S. interest rates. If not oblivious to this problem, Bush did little to address it.

In summary, Bush's second round of tax cuts in 2003 stimulated economic growth and brought the unemployment rate down. At the same time, the thrust of his overall economic policies contributed to the global financial crisis that began on August 9, 2007, in several ways. First, his poorly designed tax cuts in 2001 left the U.S. economy overly dependent on low interest rates. His acquiescence to the Federal Reserve's overly accommodative monetary policy from 2002 to 2006 fed the housing bubble. So too did his aggressive actions to increase home ownership that placed too low a priority on buyers' ability to meet mortgage payments. While Bush did try to rein in Fannie Mae and Freddie Mac, he was less alert to dangers that had become apparent in the alternative financial system.

The financial crisis triggered a recession that began in December 2007. By January 2009, the U.S. unemployment rate rose to 7.7 percent. On February 13, 2008, Bush signed the Economic Stimulus Act of 2008 that injected $152 billion into the U.S. economy, mainly through tax rebates to low- and middle-income families. As most economists predicted, Bush's poorly designed stimulus did not significantly boost either consumption or investment but merely added to the federal deficit. Overall, the effect of Bush's requesting or accepting massive increases in federal spending while at the same time cutting taxes produced mounting federal budget deficits, which weakened the overall health of the American economy. Bush deserves credit for sending Paulson to the Treasury and Bernanke to the Federal Reserve—and for standing by them as they acted to stabilize financial markets.

Preserving and Extending Liberty

Should Iraq and Afghanistan develop along the democratic lines that Bush hoped, history will credit the forty-third president with the liberation of at least 60 million people. Such outcomes, should they occur, however long delayed, will prove no small achievements.

History is certain to take a dim view of Bush's clumsy, misguided, arrogant, and even self-defeating assertions in pursuit of an all-powerful executive, accountable to no one, save the public only once every four years. It will be no exaggeration to say that he, egged on by his vice president and some legal advisers, turned routine requests for information into prolonged and disruptive controversies. These conflicts hardened feelings, aroused suspicion, eroded goodwill, and, on occasion, produced results different from and often contrary to what the administration hoped to achieve.

In spite of all the talk of Bush's supposed violations of civil liberties, these, like the reports of Mark Twain's premature demise, will prove to have been highly exaggerated. With the passage of time and the cooling of tempers, historians should note that, unlike Thomas Jefferson, Abraham Lincoln, and Woodrow Wilson, George W. Bush ordered no mass arrests of American citizens. Unlike John Adams and Wilson, Bush signed no alien or sedition acts. Nor did he press for or sign laws that allowed for round-ups of his critics or massive arrests and deportations.

Unlike Wilson, Bush did not allow his attorney general to embark on fear campaigns (modern-day equivalents of "Red Scares" and "Palmer Raids"). Nor did he sanction outright discrimination against and denials of constitutional protections of American citizens who were of the same ethnic background or religion as those who waged war against the United States. Unlike Franklin D. Roosevelt, Bush did not order the internment of thousands of American citizens and legal residents who were not suspected of having committed crimes and whose only common characteristic was a shared national or regional origin with those who perpetrated the attacks of 9-11.

Bush, setting an example for his fellow citizens, discouraged such blatant disregard of constitutional protections that the United States affords its citizens and those residing in its borders. Six days after the attacks of 9-11, Bush paid a visit to the Islamic Center of Washington, D.C., and proclaimed Islam a "religion of peace." Under Bush, and with government support and encouragement, enrollments in courses on the Arabic language and history of the Middle East dramatically increased. He and his administration resisted calls to "profile" travelers along racial and ethnic lines in screening for possible terrorists. He actively encouraged the inclusion of American Muslims in all aspects of American civil life. Bush's humanitarian undertakings in Africa, Indonesia, and elsewhere and his concern for the rights of women in the Muslim world and the emergence of democratic institutions throughout the developing world will not escape historians' notice.

Defense, National Security, and Foreign Policy

History's first clear and fair assessment of the most momentous decision Bush made as president, his ordering an American invasion of Iraq in 2002, will have to await the outcomes of still-unfolding events and the availability of yet-to-be-disclosed information. Of paramount importance will be the quality and thoroughness of the intelligence reports on which Bush acted that assessed the state of Saddam Hussein's building of weapons of mass destruction and the immediate threat they posed to the United States and its allies. Those seeking to make sense of Bush's actions at this early date fall into two camps: those who argue that the war in Iraq was unnecessary and faultily executed and those who believe it was necessary and faultily executed. Those taking either view will want to know why Bush launched the invasion of Iraq before he had concluded the military engagement he had previously ordered in Afghanistan. (How imminent did intelligence reports suggest Saddam Hussein's weapons of mass destruction program was?)

After the attacks of 9-11, Bush spoke for a united nation when he issued his ultimatum to the Taliban to turn over al-Qaeda operatives in Afghanistan to the United States or face the consequences. "Operation Enduring Freedom" (the name the Pentagon gave the invasion of Afghanistan) did not achieve all of the objectives Bush assigned it. It did not result in the capture of Osama bin Ladin, who, with his high command, was believed to have taken refuge beyond the Pakistani border, amid a cease-fire at the end of the battle of Tora Bora. Nor did it permanently destroy the enemy's capacity to inflict harm on Americans anyplace in the world. The Afghan incursion did remove the Taliban from power and succeed in transferring power to an elected government.

As they seek to make sense of Bush's actions in Afghanistan, historians will inevitably consider the merits of the policies Bush pursued toward its neighbor Pakistan. For most of Bush's time in office, his administration stood by Pakistani dictator Pervez Musharraf, as the U.S. government promised to bring democracy to Afghanistan, Iraq, and elsewhere. It repeatedly relied upon assurances that the Pakistani government was doing all within its power to help the United States capture Osama bin Ladin.

Yet as the military theater in Afghanistan began to take a backseat to the war in Iraq, the Taliban began to regroup. When Bush left office, it was reasserting control over large sections of the country beyond the reach of the central government. That government proved less successful and popular with the Afghan people than Bush and his team had anticipated. It was widely believed to be rife with corruption and tolerant of, if not dependent upon, the drug trade for its support and survival.

As a result of Bush's having waged two wars, without bringing either successfully to a conclusion on his watch, Bush's successor spent a good part of his first year in office weighing whether to follow, intensify, or reverse Bush's efforts. He opted to continue Bush's policies in Iraq, with the Bush-Petraeus "surge" continuing to work. On the advice of his military advisers, Obama deployed an additional 30,000 troops (10,000 less than his principal general publicly recommended) in support of a second surge in Afghanistan.

However history may fault Bush for his decision-making process and his handling of the war in Iraq for much of his time in office, it may also credit him for the courage he showed in pressing for Petraeus's surge in the face of almost unanimous opposition. Future president Barack Obama predicted in

2006 that the surge would fail and denied in 2007 that it was working. Future secretary of state Hillary Rodham Clinton said that accepting General David Petraeus's assessment that, as a result of the surge, American forces had begun to turn the tide in Iraq's Anbar province required a "willful suspension of disbelief."[52] The paid television advertisements MoveOn.org ran, with the phrase "General Petraeus or General Betray Us?," will long share a place—along with the "1964 Daisy ad," that presented presidential hopeful Barry Goldwater as an advocate of nuclear war—on any list of low points in the history of character assassination.

Whatever yet-to-be-released documents show about the intelligence reports available to Bush and others about the state of Saddam Hussein's weapons program, future policy makers and historians can be expected to ask themselves how they might have acted in Bush's stead based on the information that is already public. That Bush and his team, as well as their predecessors and several foreign governments, believed that Saddam Hussein had developed weapons of mass destruction and was prepared to use them is clear. That Saddam had once developed such weapons and had used them against his own people and other nations is beyond dispute. That Saddam acted in a manner that suggested he was as guilty as Bush surmised, carrying on a multiyear charade of admitting and expelling U.N. weapons inspectors and repeatedly violating "no-fly-zone" agreements, is also evident. That Bush and his team came to office determined to remove Saddam and "cherry-picked" intelligence in order to find a pretext for an invasion is a charge often asserted but remains to be proved.

Years hence, should Afghanistan and Iraq evolve into stable, vibrant democracies, Bush will be credited for helping transform the politics of their region and much of the world. As of this writing, that remains a tall order.

Bush will receive more immediate praise for the attention and resources he showered upon the African continent. (See previous section "Character.") Bush's swift, prompt, and competent delivery of American assistance to the people of Indonesia in the aftermath of the tsunami of 2004 greatly enhanced American standing in a nation with the largest Muslim population in the world. By refusing to be bound by what he considered a foolish consistency on the part of nonproliferation ideologues, Bush hastened a much-delayed warming of relations between the United States and India. In recognizing the obvious, that India had become a nuclear power, Bush justified the setting aside of sanctions that international agreements would have imposed upon it on the grounds that the world's largest democracy, because of its values, posed no threat to world peace.

By the standard Bush set in his State of the Union speech of 2002, in which he seemed unwilling to accept the existence of the "axis of evil," Bush fell short. At best, he bequeathed to his successor Afghanistan and Iraq as "works in progress" and an Iran and a North Korea hell-bent on becoming nuclear powers. If these countries succeeded in their objective, they could pose a more serious threat to the United States and its allies than Iraq ever did. Future historians will find it puzzling that Bush, after finding goodness in Vladimir Putin's "soul," did so little to improve his country's relations with Russia a decade after his father presided over the conclusion of the Cold War. They will also question why he seemed not to make China, which came to play an increasing role on the world stage during his presidency, a higher priority than he did.

Finally, while historians will for decades debate the soundness of Bush's actions, his reasons for making them, and his skills as an executive, they will note that Bush's defenders were correct in at least one respect: after September 11, 2001, for the rest of Bush's presidency, no further attacks upon Americans took place within the United States. That too will remain an important part of Bush's legacy.

ACKNOWLEDGMENTS

*W*riting books can be an arduous process. Many people, however, made the journey that led to this one not only pleasant but fun.

I want to begin by thanking my first editor at Basic Books (Perseus), Bill Frucht, for his dedication to this project and for the good cheer and generosity of spirit he brought to it from its outset. I express deep appreciation to my second editor at Basic Books (Perseus) Lara Heimert, her able assistants Brandon Proia and Ross Curley, project editor Melissa Veronesi, and copy editor Annette Wenda for their Herculean efforts on the paperback edition. I am equally appreciative of the meticulous attention Bill's colleagues at Basic Books showed to this project.

My agent, Alexander C. Hoyt, proved a rock of strength and support from the time this book was little more than a topic of conversation. Because of his deep knowledge of American history and his appreciation of the nuances and paradoxes that characterize so much of American politics, Alex doubled as a valuable colleague and critic. I deeply value his friendship.

A number of other friends, mentors, colleagues, fellow writers, and former students were kind enough to review all or part of this work as it went through several drafts. My friend Robert P. O'Quinn walked me through the complexities of the American economy and its ups and downs from the time of the nation's founding to the present. I also thank Robert for his helpful criticisms of all the chapters of this work. Several other cherished friends took time away from their own important work to help me improve upon mine. My deepest thanks go to Richard Brookhiser, Alexander I. Burns, John Dilulio, David

Grier, Harold Holzer, Walter Isaacson, Robert Kaufman, Thomas H. Kean Sr., Adam Klein, James M. McPherson, Andrew Malcolm, Alan Rosenthal, Ari Ruben, Frank Scaturro, and Vivek Viswanathan for their valuable insights.

The staffs of several research institutions and libraries provided valuable assistance to me in tracking down documents and furnishing me with information, often on the shortest of notice. Three cheers go to the able staffs of the Herbert C. Hoover, Franklin D. Roosevelt, John F. Kennedy, and Ronald Reagan Presidential Libraries, the Library of Congress, and Princeton University's Firestone Library.

Wallace Dailey, of the Theodore Roosevelt Collection at the Haughton Library of Harvard University, provided me with a draft of a speech Theodore Roosevelt delivered at the Groton School on May 24, 1904. David Donald, professor emeritus of Harvard University, kindly shared with me his reminiscences of President Kennedy's reactions to a talk the historian delivered on Reconstruction at the White House. Professor Samuel H. Williamson, President of MeasuringWorth.Com kindly granted me permission to cite data posted on www.measuringworth.com.

I would like to express my appreciation to Professor Robert George of Princeton University for inviting me to lecture once again on the American presidency at my alma mater in the fall of 2006 and to my students and colleagues at the Institute of Politics at Harvard University, the Annenberg School of Communication at the University of Pennsylvania, and the Elliott School of International Relations at George Washington University, on whom I tried out some of the ideas that appear in this work.

Finally, I would like to acknowledge my debt to several experts on the American presidency whose thinking heavily influenced my own. In writing this book, my thoughts often turned back to many delightful hours spent in their company contemplating what one of them termed "the mists of the American presidency." In a sense, this book and its author stand on the shoulders of the late "dean of presidential studies," Richard E. Neustadt; the late Woodrow Wilson scholar, Arthur S. Link; the late Emmet John Hughes; and Princeton University Professors Emeriti Fred I. Greenstein, James M. McPherson, and Paul E. Sigmund.

ECONOMIC
DATA SOURCES

BANKING Data on number of banks are from Series X 561–565. State Banks–Number of Banks and Assets and Liabilities: 1811 to 1830, Series 580–587. All Banks–Number of Banks and Principal Assets and Liabilities: 1834 to 1970, Series X 610–619. All Commercial Banks–Number of Banks and Total Assets by Federal Reserve Membership and Class: 1896 to 1970, Series X-634–655. National Banks–Number of Banks and Principal Assets and Liabilities: 1863 to 1970, Series X-656–677. Non-national Banks–Number of Banks and Principal Assets and Liabilities: 1863 to 1970 in *Historical Statistics of the United States: Colonial Times to 1970, Part 2* (Washington, D.C.: Government Printing Office, 1975), 1018, 1,019–20, 1,023, 1,024–26, 1,028–31. Data on bank suspensions are from Series X 741–755. Bank Suspensions–Number and Deposits of Suspended Banks 1864 to 1970.

ECONOMIC GROWTH Annual GDP data (since 1929) and quarterly GDP data since the first quarter of 1947 are from the U.S. Department of Commerce, Bureau of Economic Analysis, found at: http//www.bea.gov/national/index.htm#gdp. Annual GDP data from 1790 to 1928 are from Louis D. Johnston and Samuel H. Williamson, "The Annual Real and Nominal GDP for the United States, 1790–Present," Economic History Services (1 April 2006), http://eh.net/hmit/gdp.

FEDERAL BUDGET   Aggregate data since fiscal year 1900 and detailed data since fiscal year 1962 on federal outlays, federal receipts, federal budget surplus or deficit, and federal debt are from *Historical Tables, Budget of the United States Fiscal Year 2008* (Washington, D.C.: Government Printing Office, 2007). Aggregate data from fiscal year 1789 to fiscal year 1899 are from Series Y 335–338. Summary of Federal Government Finances–Administrative Budgets: 1789 to 1939, Series Y 352 in *Historical Statistics of the United States: Colonial Times to 1970, Part 2* (Washington, D.C.: Government Printing Office, 1975), 1,104. Detailed data from fiscal year 1789 to fiscal year 1961 are from Series Y 343–351. Federal Government Receipts by Source: 1940 to 1970; Series Y 352–357. Federal Government Receipts–Administrative Budgets: 1798 to 1939, Series Y 358–373. Internal Revenue Collections 1863 to 1970, Series Y 457–465. Outlays of the Federal Government: 1789 to 1970; Series 493–504. Public Debt of the Federal Government: 1791 to 1970 in *Historical Statistics of the United States, Part 2*, 1,105, 1,106, 1,107–8, 1,114–15, and 1,117–18.

HOUSEHOLD INCOME DATA   Annual data since 1967 is from the U.S. Department of Commerce, Bureau of the Census, http//www.census.gov/hhes/ www/income/histinc/inchhtoc.html.

INDUSTRIAL PRODUCTION   See http://www.federalreserve.gov/release/ 817. Industrial production monthly data since January 1921 are from the Board of Governors of the Federal Reserve System. Industrial production annual data from 1790 to 1915 are from Joseph H. Davis, "An Annual Index of U.S. Industrial Production, 1790–1915," *Quarterly Journal of Economics* (November 2004).

INTERNATIONAL TRANSACTIONS   Annual data since 1960 are from the U.S. Department of Commerce, Bureau of Economic Analysis, found at: http://www.bea.gov/international/index.htm#bop. Annual data prior to 1960 are from Series U 1–25. Balance of International Payments: 1790 to 1970, Series U 26–39. International Investment Position of the United States: 1843 to 1970, and Series U 187–200. Value of Export and Imports: 1790 to 1970 in *Historical Statistics of the United States, Part 2*, 864–68, 868–69, and 884–86.

INFLATION Consumer Price Index–Urban workers monthly data since January 1921 are from the U.S. Department of Labor, Bureau of Labor Statistics, found at: http://www.bis.gov/cpi/home.htm. Estimated annual data prior to 1921 are from Samuel H. Williamson, "Six Ways to Compute the Relative Value of a U.S. Dollar Amount, 1790–2006," measuringworth.com, 2007, http://www.measuringworth.com/uscompare/.

MANUFACTURING PRODUCTIVITY Annual data are from Series D 683–688. "Indexes of Employee Output (NBER): 1869 to 1969," in *Historical Statistics of the United States: Colonial Times to 1970, Part 1* (Washington, D.C.: Government Printing Office, 1975), 162.

MANUFACTURING WAGES Annual data are from Series D 802–810. Earnings and Hours of Production Workers in Manufacturing: 1909 to 1970 in *Historical Statistics of the United States, Part 1* (Washington, D.C.: Government Printing Office, 1975), 169.

POVERTY RATE Found at http://www.census.gov/hhes/www/poverty/histpov/hispovtb.htm. Annual data since 1967 are from the U.S. Department of Labor, Bureau of the Census.

UNEMPLOYMENT RATE See http://www.bis.gov/cps/home.htm. Civilian unemployment rate monthly data since January 1948 are from the U.S. Department of Labor, Bureau of Labor Statistics. Estimated civilian unemployment rate annual rate data from 1900 to 1947 are from Series D 1–10. Labor Force and Its Components: 1900 to 1947 in *Historical Statistics of the United States, Part 1*, 126.

NOTES

CHAPTER 1

1. Arthur M. Schlesinger Jr., "The Ultimate Approval Rating," *New York Times Magazine*, 15 December 1996, 46–51. Schlesinger followed up with an article of a more scholarly nature, "Rating the Presidents: Washington to Clinton," *Political Science Quarterly* (Summer 1997): 179–90.

2. For a discussion of what Clinton thought his place in history might be, see Dick Morris, *Behind the Oval Office: Getting Reelected Against all Odds* (Los Angeles: Renaissance Books, 1999), 305–8. PBS's *News Hour with Jim Lehrer* devoted much of one broadcast to this subject. Included was an interview with Clinton.

3. See Arthur M. Schlesinger Sr.'s "Historians Rate U.S. Presidents," *Life* (November 1948): 65–66, 68, 73–74, and "Our Presidents: A Rating by 75 Historians," *New York Times Magazine*, 29 July 1962, 12–13, 40–41, 43.

4. Representative Richard Henry Lee delivered this eulogy on 26 December 1799. Chief Justice John Marshall wrote it. See Matthew Spalding, "It's Still George Washington's Birthday (Not President's Day)," http://www.heritage.org/Research/Political Philosophy/wm426.cfm.

5. See Schlesinger Sr.'s "Our Presidents: A Rating by 75 Historians." The debate among historians with regard to Truman's place in history has centered around whether he increased world tensions or responded adequately to provocations as well as over his general competence. The preponderance of "new left" histories during the Vietnam era led conservative commentator William F. Buckley to suggest that Truman was being taken to task not for his "mistakes," but for his "virtues." See William F. Buckley Jr., "Harry Truman, RIP," 6 December 1972, reprinted in *Execution Eve* (New York: Putnam, 1973), 473–75. For more on Bush-Truman parallels made by Bush and others, see Michael Abramson, "Truman's Trials Resonate for Bush: President Battling Terrorism Has Shown Interest in Democrat's Strategies at Dawn of Cold War," *Washington Post*, 15 December 2006, A3.

6. http://politicalarithmetik.blogspot.com/2006/07/approval-at-new-low-for-president.html.

7. *USA Today*, 19 February 2007.

8. Schlesinger, "Rating the Presidents;" Calvin Coolidge, "Address before the American Society of Newspaper Editors, 17 January 1925, in *Foundations of the Republic* (New York: Charles Scribner's Sons, 1926), 185.

9. See Alvin S. Felzenberg, "Partisan Biases in Presidential Ratings: Ulysses, Woodrow, and Calvin . . . 'We Hardly Knew Ye,'" in *The Uses and Abuses of Presidential Ratings*, ed. Meena Bose and Mark Landis (New York: Nova Science Publishers, 2003), 43–51.

10. "400 Historians Denounce Impeachment: Case against Clinton Departs from Framers' Intent for Presidency, Letter Argues," *Washington Post*, 29 October 1998, 4.

11. Paul Simon had penned a book about Lincoln's pre-presidential career: *Lincoln's Preparation for Greatness: The Illinois Legislative Years* (Urbana: University of Illinois Press, 1990). Mario Cuomo, in collaboration with Harold Holzer, had edited a collection of Lincoln's writings: *Lincoln on Democracy* (New York: Harper Collins, 1990). He subsequently wrote *What Would Lincoln Do?*, an attempt to extrapolate from Lincoln's writings that he would have opposed the war in Iraq.

12. Schlesinger, "Rating the Presidents."

13. See, for example, C-SPAN's survey of historians and the Federalist Society/*Wall Street Journal* survey, both conducted in 2000, in Meena Bose and Mark Landis, eds., *The Uses and Abuses of Presidential Ratings* (New York: Nova Science Publishers, 2003).

14. Schlesinger, "Rating the Presidents."

15. Ibid.

16. Sean Wilentz, "The Worst President in History? One of America's Leading Historians Assesses George W. Bush," *Rolling Stone*, 21 April 2006.

17. Jay Tolson, "The Worst Presidents," *U.S. News & World Report,* 26 February 2007.

18. Quoted in Schlesinger, "Rating the Presidents."

19. Ibid.

20. Leading scholars who have attempted to account for different behaviors among the presidents have identified character as a primary determinant, even if they have defined it in dissimilar ways. James David Barber, in *The Presidential Character: Predicting Performance in the White House* (Englewood Cliffs, N. J.: Prentice Hall, 1992), saw this as the manner in which presidents defended or advanced their sense of self-esteem. He saw it as being shaped by their "world-views" (which resulted from their past experience, belief systems, and their view of human nature) and expressed through the political "styles" they adopted (rhetoric, interpersonal relations, and work habits).

21. Richard E. Neustadt, *Presidential Power* (New York: The Free Press, 1990), 29.

22. Ibid., 10.

CHAPTER 2

1. Gordon S. Wood, *Revolutionary Characters: What Made the Founders Different* (New York: Penguin Press, 2006) 42.

2. James Thomas Flexner, *Washington, the Indispensable Man* (Boston: Little Brown, 1974), 37.

3. Richard Brookhiser, *Founding Father: Rediscovering George Washington* (New York: The Free Press, 1996), 146.

4. William Sterne Randall, *George Washington: A Life* (New York: Owl Books, 1997), 268.

5. Brookhiser, *Founding Father*, 33.

6. It was on these grounds that the wife of the then-mayor of Philadelphia sought to persuade Washington to seek a second term. See Flexner, *Washington, the Indispensable Man*, 270–72.

7. Joseph J. Ellis, *His Excellency: George Washington* (New York: Vintage Books, 2005), 142.

8. Ibid., 144.

9. Brookhiser, *Founding Father*, 71.

10. Ibid., 127.

11. George Washington, Farewell Address, 1796, http://www.yale.edu/lawweb/avalon/washing.htm.

12. Brookhiser, *Founding Father*, 182.

13. Ibid., 183.

14. Ibid.

15. Wood, *Revolutionary Characters*, 63.

16. James M. McPherson, *Abraham Lincoln and the Second American Revolution* (New York: Oxford University Press, 1991), 89.

17. Richard Shenkman, *Presidential Ambition: How the Presidents Gained Power, Kept Power, and Got Things Done* (New York: Harper Collins, 1999), 138.

18. Ibid, 137, 148.

19. William C. Harris, *Lincoln's Rise to the Presidency* (Lawrence: University Press of Kansas, 2007), 9, and Doris Kearns Goodwin, *Team of Rivals: The Political Genius of Abraham Lincoln* (New York: Simon & Schuster, 2005), 49.

20. Goodwin, *Team of Rivals*, 53 and David Donald, *Lincoln* (New York: Simon & Schuster, 1995), 27–30.

21. Goodwin, *Team of Rivals*, 53.

22. Shenkman, *Presidential Ambition*, 123.

23. Richard C. Hofstadter, *The American Political Tradition and the Men Who Made It* (New York: Vintage, 1974), 138. As Hanks traveled only as far as St. Louis, if his recollection was accurate, Lincoln was reacting to other glimpses of slavery he had seen en route to New Orleans, or heard his kinsman tell him of his recollections of his visit to the slave market afterwards.

24. Harris, *Lincoln's Rise to the Presidency*, 62.

25. Shenkman, *Presidential Ambition*, 124.

26. Andrew Delbanco, ed., *The Portable Lincoln* (New York: Penguin Group, 1993), 19.

27. Ibid.

28. Goodwin, *Team of Rivals*, 91.

29. James M. McPherson, *This Mighty Scourge: Perspectives on the Civil War* (New York: Oxford University Press, 2007), 193.

30. Shenkman, *Presidential Ambition*, 124.

31. Ibid., 127.

32. Harris, *Lincoln's Rise to the Presidency*, 25, 333.

33. Shenkman, *Presidential Ambition*, 134

34. Abraham Lincoln, address to the Young Men's Lyceum of Springfield, Illinois, in Delbanco, *The Portable Lincoln*, 17–26.

35. See Shenkman, *Presidential Ambition*, chap. 7.

36. Hofstadter, *The American Political Tradition and the Men Who Made It*, 145.

37. Shenkman, *Presidential Ambition*, 163.

38. Harris, *Lincoln's Rise to the Presidency*, 145.

39. Ibid., 71.

40. Hofstadter, *The American Political Tradition and the Men Who Made It*, 122.

41. Ibid., 119.

42. Abraham Lincoln, Second Inaugural Address, cited in Delbanco, *The Portable Lincoln*, 320–22.

43. McPherson, *Abraham Lincoln and the Second American Revolution*, 89.

44. Michael Beschloss, *Presidential Courage: Brave Leaders and How They Changed America, 1789–1989* (New York: Simon & Schuster, 2007), 125.

45. Kathleen Dalton, *Theodore Roosevelt: A Strenuous Life* (Knopf: New York, 2002), 523.

46. The incident was the so-called Brownsville Affair, which is discussed at further length in chapter 6.

47. Dalton, *Theodore Roosevelt*, 523.

48. "Roosevelt on the Presidency," *New York Times*, 11 November 1932, 21.

49. Michael McGerr, "Theodore Roosevelt," in *The Reader's Companion to the American Presidency*, ed. Alan Brinkley and Davis Dyer (New York: Houghton Mifflin, 2000), 293–99.

50. Dalton, *Theodore Roosevelt*, 523.

51. Ibid.

52. Gerald Thompson, *Speaker's Treasury of Political Stories, Anecdotes and Humor* (New York: MJF Books, 1990), 64.

53. McGerr, 298.

54. McGerr, "Theodore Roosevelt," 299.

55. James Brough, *Princess Alice: A Biography of Alice Roosevelt Longwirth* (Boston: Little, Brown, 1995), 195.

56. Louis Auchincloss, *Theodore Roosevelt* (New York: Times Books, 2001), 15.

57. At a time when the nation was electing Civil War heroes to public office and the Grand Army of the Republic comprised one of the largest interest groups in the nation, Roosevelt's father's lack of military service was hardly advantageous to Roosevelt's political aspirations. Roosevelt may well have wondered whether his associates, many of whom were children of veterans, thought his father a coward. For a discussion of how Theodore Roosevelt Sr.'s lack of military service affected his family see Auchincloss, *Theodore Roosevelt*, 11.

58. Theodore Roosevelt, *An Autobiography* (New York: Charles Scribners Sons, 1929), 13.

59. Dalton, *Theodore Roosevelt*, 50.

60. Edmund Morris, *The Rise of Theodore Roosevelt* (New York: Coward, McGann and Geoghegan, 1979), 273.

61. William Roscoe Thayer, *Theodore Roosevelt* (Gossett and Dunlap: New York, 1919), 10.

62. Owen Wister, *Roosevelt, The Story of a Friendship* (New York: McMillan, 1930), 21.

63. Edmund Morris, *Theodore Rex* (New York: Random House, 2001), 81.

64. See John Morton Blum, *the Republican Roosevelt* (New York: Atheneum, 1968), chap. 5.

65. Hofstadter, *The American Political Tradition and the Men Who Made It*, 286.

66. McGerr, "Theodore Roosevelt," 297–98.

67. Ibid., 297.

68. Beschloss, *Presidential Courage*, 155.

69. George F. Will, "Gerald Ford's Perfect Pitch," *Washington Post*, 28 December 2006, A27.

70. James P. Pfiffner, *The Modern Presidency*, 3rd ed. (Boston: Bedford/St Martin's, 2000), 134.

71. Ford later wrote that his father had physically abused his mother. Gerald R. Ford, *A Time to Heal* (New York: Berkley Books, 1979), 42.

72. Ibid., 46.

73. Ibid., 47.

74. Douglas Brinkley, *Gerald R. Ford* (New York: Times Books, 2007), 14.

75. J. Y. Smith and Lou Cannon, "Gerald R. Ford, 93, Dies; Led in Watergate's Wake," *Washington Post*, 27 December 2007.

76. Yanek Mieczkowski, "Gerald Ford," in *The Reader's Companion to the American Presidency*, ed. Alan Brinkley and Davis Dyer (New York: Houghton Mifflin, 2000), 467.

77. Brinkley, *Gerald Ford*, 91.

78. Quang X. Pham, "Ford's Finest Legacy," *Washington Post*, 30 December 2006, A21.

79. For a fuller account of Wright's work and its effect on Reagan, see Jules Tygiel, *Ronald Reagan and the Triumph of American Conservatism* (New York: Pearson Longman, 2006), 1–2; Paul Kengor, *God and Ronald Reagan: A Spiritual Life* (New York: Regan Books, 2004), 17–26; and Ronald Reagan, *An American Life* (New York: Simon and Schuster, 1990), 32.

80. Kengor, *God and Ronald Reagan*, 19.

81. Reagan, *An American Life*, 33.

82. Ibid.

83. Tygiel, *Ronald Reagan and the Triumph of American Conservatism*, 5.

84. Anne Edwards, *Early Reagan: The Rise to Power* (New York: Morrow, 1987), 38.

85. Ibid., 62–63.

86. Tygiel, *Ronald Reagan and the Triumph of American Conservatism*, 9.

87. Ibid., 29.

88. Reagan, *An American Life*, 29.

89. David Abshire, *Saving the Reagan Presidency: Trust Is the Coin of the Realm* (College Station: Texas A&M Press, 2005), 208.

90. Kengor, *God and Ronald Reagan*, 36.

91. Tygiel, *Ronald Reagan and the Triumph of American Conservatism* 12.

92. Edwards, *Early Reagan*, 116.

93. Joseph J. Ellis, *American Sphinx: The Character of Thomas Jefferson* (New York: Vintage Books, 1998).

94. R. B. Bernstein, *Thomas Jefferson* (New York: Oxford University Press, 2003), 2.

95. Adrienne Koch and William Peden, *The Life and Selected Writings of Thomas Jefferson* (New York: Modern Library, 1944), 3.

96. Ibid.

97. Bernstein, *Thomas Jefferson*, 33.

98. Andrew Burstein, *The Inner Jefferson: Portrait of a Grieving Optimist* (Charlottesville: University of Virginia Press, 1995), 214.

99. Bernstein, *Thomas Jefferson*, 103.

100. Richard Brookhiser, *George Washington: Founding Father* (New York: The Free Press, 1996), 83.

101. Peter R. Henriques, *Realistic Visionary: A Portrait of George Washington* (Charlottesville: University of Virginia Press, 2006), 123.

102. Ibid., 115.

103. "It would give you a fever were I to name to you the apostates who have gone over to these heresies, men who were Samsons in the field and Solomons in the council, but who have had their head shaved by the English harlot" (Ibid., 117).

104 Ibid., 120.

105. Bernstein, *Thomas Jefferson*, 138.

106. Ibid., 169.

107. Shenkman, *Presidential Ambition*, 85.

108. Ibid., 84.

109. James M. McPherson, *Battle Cry of Freedom: The Civil War Era* (New York: Oxford University Press, 1988), 119.

110. Ibid., 120.

111. Joel H. Silbey, "Franklin Pierce," in *The Reader's Companion to the American Presidency*, ed. Alan Brinkley and Davis Dyer (Boston: Houghton Mifflin, 2000), 170.

112. Jean H. Baker, *James Buchanan* (New York: Times Books, 2004), 31.

113. John Seigenthaler, *James K. Polk* (New York: Times Books, 2003), 128–31.

114. Baker, *James Buchanan*, 78.

125. Shenkman, *Presidential Ambition*, 96.

126. Ibid., 99.

127. Ibid., 102.

128. Ibid., 110.

129. Ibid., 117.

120. Ibid., 107, and William E. Gienapp, "James Buchanan," in *A Reader's Companion the American Presidency*, ed. Alan Brinkley and David Dyer (Boston: Houghton Mifflin, 2000), 180.

121. Baker, *James Buchanan*, 81.

122. Ibid., 103, and Shenkman, *Presidential Ambition*, 117.

123. Baker, *James Buchanan*, 104.

124. Ibid., 151.

125. Owen Wister, *Roosevelt, The Story of a Friendship* (New York: Macmillan, 1930), 332.

126. Arthur S. Link, *Wilson: The Road to the White House* (Princeton: Princeton University Press, 1947), 1.

127. John Morton Blum, *Woodrow Wilson and the Politics of Morality* (Boston: Little, Brown, 1956), 6.

128. Ibid., 19.

129. Gary Scott Smith, *Faith and the Presidency* (New York: Oxford University Press, 2006), 165.

130. John Maynard Keynes, *Economic Consequences of the Peace* (New York: Harcourt, Brace and Howe, 1920), 42.

131. Thomas J. Knock, "Woodrow Wilson," in *A Reader's Companion the American Presidency*, ed. Alan Brinkley and David Dyer (Boston: Houghton Mifflin, 2000), 320.

132. Alexander L. George and Juliette L. George, *Woodrow Wilson and Colonel House, A Personality Study* (New York: Dover Publications, 1956), 8.

133. Such was the theme of George and George, *Woodrow Wilson and Colonel House, a Personality Study*.

134. Knock, "Woodrow Wilson," 319.

135. Ibid., 31.

136. George and George, *Woodrow Wilson and Colonel House, a Personality Study*, 38–39.

137. Ibid., 52.

138. Link, *Wilson*, 307.

139. See Patrick Devin, *Too Proud to Fight: Woodrow Wilson's Neutrality* (New York: Oxford University Press, 1975).

140. Woodrow Wilson, "Peace without Victory" speech, 22 January 1917, http://www.faithandfreedom.us/documents/20thcentury/wil_peacevictory.htm.

141. Woodrow Wilson, "War Message to Congress," 2 April 1917, http://wwi.lib.byu.edu/index.php/Wilson%27s_War_Message_to_Congress.

142. Mark Sullivan, *Our Times: 1900–1925*. Volume 5, *Over Here: 1914–1918* (New York: Scribner's, 1933), 542.

143. Blum, *Woodrow Wilson and the Politics of Morality*, 155.

144. Keynes, *Economic Consequences of the Peace*, 43.

145. Sullivan, *Our Times*. Volume 5, chapter 27, and Ibid., chapter 4.

146. David Lawrence, *The True Story of Woodrow Wilson* (New York: Doran, 1924), chapter 15.

147. Keynes, *Economic Consequences of the Peace*, 38.

148. The one time Wilson opted to go public, he did so in a clumsy attempt to persuade Italians to repudiate their government after he and his colleagues rejected demands that Italy be granted certain lands that had been part of the Austro-Hungarian Empire.

149. For a fuller account of the Lodge-Wilson dispute, see Thomas A. Bailey's, *Woodrow Wilson and the Lost Peace* (New York: Macmillan Company, 1944) and *Woodrow Wilson and the Great Betrayal* (New York: Macmillan Company, 1945); John Milton Cooper Jr., *Breaking the Heart of the World: Woodrow Wilson and the Fight for the League of Nations* (New York: Cambridge University Press, 2001); and Thomas J. Knock, *To End All Wars: Woodrow Wilson and the Quest for a New World Order* (New York: Oxford University Press, 1992).

150. George and George, *Woodrow Wilson and Colonel House*, 301.

151. See Edwin A. Weinstein, *Woodrow Wilson, A Medical and Psychological Biography* (Princeton: Princeton University Press, 1981).

152. Ibid., 279–80.

153. "Wilson: Great Man Says Lloyd-George," *Boston Globe,* 4 February 1924, 11.

154. Ibid., 301–2.

155. Ibid., 314.

156. Earl Mazo and Stephen Hess, *Nixon: A Political Portrait* (New York: Harper & Row, 1968), 11, and Bela Kornitzer, *The Real Nixon: An Intimate Biography* (New York: Rand McNally, 1960), 19. See also, Garry Wills, *Nixon Agonistes* (New York: Signet, 1970), 83.

157. Tom Wicker, *One of Us: Richard Nixon and the American Dream* (New York: Random House, 1991), 9.

158. Mazo and Hess, *Nixon*, 10.

159. Kornitzer, *The Real Nixon*, 19.

160. Richard Nixon, *Six Crises* (New York: Doubleday, 1962), 426.

161. Richard Nixon, "Farewell to White House Staff," 8 August 1974, www .shabbir.com/nonmatchbox/whithous.html.

162. Raymond Price, *With Nixon* (New York: Viking Press, 1977), 29. For another assessment of the "light" and "dark" sides of Nixon, see Jonathan Aitken, *Nixon: A Life* (Washington, D.C.: Regnery, 1994).

163. Wicker, *One of Us*, 9, and Mazo and Hess, *Nixon*, 18.

164. Nixon, *Six Crises*, and Wicker, *One of Us*, 9.

165. Wicker, *One of Us*, 47.

166. Hiss would serve a jail sentence not for espionage (the statute of limitations for that crime had expired) but for perjury. For the definitive account of the Hiss case, see Allen Weinstein's *Perjury: The Hiss-Chambers Case* (New York: Random House, 1978).

167. Nixon, *Six Crises*, chap. 1.

168. For various accounts of this race see Aitken, *Nixon*; Kornitzer, *The Real Nixon*; Irwin F. Gellman, *The Contender, Richard Nixon: The Congress Years, 1946–1952* (New York: The Free Press, 1999); Mazo and Hess, *Nixon*; and Greg Mitchell, *Tricky Dick and the Pink Lady* (New York: Random House, 1998).

169. Wicker, *One of Us*, 76.

170. Richard Nixon, "Checkers" speech, 23 September 1952, http://www.watergate .info/nixon/checkers-speech.shtml.

171. John F. Kennedy, Gridiron Dinner, 1958, cited in Bill Adler, ed., *The Complete Kennedy Wit* (New York: Citadel, 1967), 184.

172. Kennedy was in the hospital when the vote was taken. Nixon, as vice president, had not only presided over the Senate but had been tasked by Eisenhower to round up Republican votes against McCarthy.

173. Price, *With Nixon*, 39, and Benjamin C. Bradlee, *Conversations with Kennedy* (New York: Norton, 1975), 33.

174. Wicker, *One of Us*, 256–57, and Mazo and Hess, *Nixon*, 248–60.

175. Wicker, *One of Us*, 256.

176. Richard Nixon, *RN: The Memoirs of Richard Nixon* (New York: Grosset & Dunlap, 1978), 245.

177. Elizabeth Drew, *Richard M. Nixon* (New York: Times Books, 2007), 52.

178. Leonard Garment, *Crazy Rhythm: My Journey from Brooklyn, Jazz, and Wall Street to Nixon's White House, Watergate, and Beyond* (New York: Times Books, 1997), 163.

179. For a discussion of Nixon's policies, see Joan Hoff, in *Nixon Reconsidered* (New York: Basic Books, 1994).

180. Mark Shields, "The Last Liberal President," *Washington Post*, 4 August 1996, C7.

181. Richard Nixon, "Asia After Vietnam," *Foreign Affairs* 46:1 (1967): 111–25.

182. David Frost, *I Gave Them a Sword: Behind the Scenes of the Nixon Interviews* (New York: Morrow, 1978), 152. In his memoirs Nixon wrote that after losing his race for governor of California in 1962, he was subject to an extensive IRS audit and that after he became president, an official at the agency admitted that this action had been politically inspired. Nixon surmised that Robert Kennedy had initiated this action. See Nixon, *RN*, 247.

183. Nixon, "Farewell to White House Staff."

CHAPTER 3

1. Quoted in Steven Weisman, "Will Magic Prevail?" *New York Times Magazine*, 29 April 1984.

2. Hamilton's assessment of both Jefferson and Burr, and his prediction of how Jefferson would comport himself as president, proved prescient. In a letter to a leading Federalist, Hamilton denounced Jefferson's policy pronouncements as "tinctured with fanaticism." Most tellingly, Hamilton predicted that Jefferson, once in office, would not prove as hostile to executive authority or as admiring of the supremacy of the House of Representatives as he claimed while in opposition. The former treasury secretary anticipated that Jefferson would be more prone to "temporize" once in office. He concluded that Jefferson was not capable of "being corrupted." About the man who would mortally wound him in a duel, Hamilton wrote that Burr's "ambition without principle never was long under the guidance of good sense." See Richard B. Morris, *The Basic Ideas of Alexander Hamilton* (New York: Pocket Books, 1957), 407–9.

3. Alexander Hamilton, James, Madison, and John Jay, *The Federalist Papers* (New York: Bantam Books, 1982), 262.

4. Saul K. Padover, ed., *Thomas Jefferson on Democracy* (New York: D. Appleton-Century, 1939), 89.

5. Joseph Ellis, *American Sphinx: The Character of Thomas Jefferson* (New York: Vintage, 1996), 252.

6. Joyce Appleby, "Thomas Jefferson," in *The Reader's Companion to the American Presidency*, ed. Alan Brinkley and David Dyer (New York: Houghton Mifflin, 2000), 47.

7. R. B. Bernstein, *Thomas Jefferson* (New York: Oxford University Press, 2003), 145.

8. "The whole commerce between master and slave is a perpetual exercise of the most boisterous passions, the unremitting despotism on the one part, and degrading submissions on the other. Our children see this and learn to imitate it," Jefferson wrote in *Notes on the State of Virginia*. See Adrienne Koch and William Peden, eds., *The Life and Selected Writings of Thomas Jefferson* (New York: Modern Library, 1944), 277–79.

9. A man as fond of mathematical equations as Jefferson had to know that, except for the manner in which the framers treated slavery in apportioning Congressional seats and electoral votes, Jefferson might never have been elected president. Several scholars maintain that Adams would have won the election of 1800 if it hadn't been for the three-fifths clause. See Garry Wills, "Negro President," in *Jefferson and the Slave Power* (New York: Mariner Books, 2003), and Susan Dunn, *Jefferson's Second Revolution: The Election Crisis of 1800 and the Triumph of Republicanism* (Boston: Houghton Mifflin, 2004).

10. Ellis, *American Sphinx*, 247. In Lincoln's words, "by general law, life and limb must be protected, yet often a limb must be amputated to save a life; but a life is never wisely given to save a limb. I felt that measures otherwise unconstitutional might become lawful by becoming indispensable to the preservation of the Constitution through the preservation of the nation. Right or wrong, I assumed this ground and now avow it. I could not feel that to the best of my ability I had ever tried to preserve the Constitution if to save slavery or any minor matter I should permit the wreck of government, country, and Constitution all together." (Abraham Lincoln, "Letter to Albert G. Hodges," 4 April 1864, http://showcase.netins.net/web/creative/lincoln/speeches/hodges.htm).

11. Appleby, "Thomas Jefferson," 42.

12. See R. B. Bernstein, *Thomas Jefferson* (New York: Oxford University Press, 2003), 166. Jefferson's call for a 100,000-member militia exceeded (by 25,000) the number Lincoln would request after the firing upon Fort Sumter in 1861.

13. Ibid., 167.

14. See Leonard Levy, *Jefferson and Civil Liberties: The Darker Side* (Cambridge University Press, 1963).

15. Garry Wills, *James Madison* (New York: Times Books, 2002), 99.

16. Levy, *Jefferson and Civil Liberties*, 62.

17. Wills, *James Madison*, 61.

18. Lincoln, "Letter to Albert G. Hodges."

19. "Delbanco, *The Portable Lincoln*, 195–204.

20. James M. McPherson, *Drawn with the Sword: Reflections on the American Civil War* (New York: Oxford University Press, 1996), 199.

21. Delbanco, *The Portable Lincoln*, 195–204.

22. Ibid., 320–21.

23. Frederick Douglass, "Oration in Memory of Abraham Lincoln," 14 April 1876, http://teachingamericanhistory.org/library/index.asp?documentprint=39.

24. For further discussion of Lincoln's devotion to and enactment of Whig ideas, see McPherson, *Abraham Lincoln and the Second American Revolution*, 39–40, and Philip

Shaw Paludan, *The Presidency of Abraham Lincoln* (Lawrence: University Press of Kansas, 1994), chap. 5.

25. Stephen B. Oates, *With Malice toward None: The Life of Abraham Lincoln* (New York: Mentor Books, 1977), 412.

26. John Alexander Carroll and Odie B. Faulk, *Home of the Brave: A Patriot's Guide to American History* (New Rochelle, N.Y.: Arlington House, 1976), 285.

27. For a fuller discussion, see Louis L. Gould, *The Presidency of Theodore Roosevelt* (Lawrence: University Press of Kansas, 1991), chap. 2, 9.

28. Nathan Miller, *Theodore Roosevelt, A Life* (New York: Morrow, 1992), 337.

29. Theodore Roosevelt, *An Autobiography* (New York: Scribners, 1929), 550.

30. Ibid., 550.

31. Ibid., 548.

32. Ibid., 557.

33. John F. Kennedy, *Profiles in Courage* (New York: Harper & Row, 1956).

34. See Rowland Evans and Robert Novak, *Lyndon B. Johnson: The Exercise of Power, a Political Biography* (New York: New American Library, 1966), 127–40.

35. Doris Kearns Goodwin, *Lyndon Johnson and the American Dream* (New York: Harper & Row, 1976), 54.

36. As President Harding foresaw (noted in chapter 6), the southern states' refusal to move away from legally sanctioned segregation and racial discrimination as the twentieth century progressed imposed great economic costs on the American South. By denying education to African Americans and depriving them of access to certain jobs, state governments, in effect, confined a large proportion of their states' population to poverty. This assured that the region remained less economically competitive with the rest of the country. With the reawakening of the civil rights movement after World War II, some corporations, fearful of boycotts, work slow-downs, and adverse publicity, opted for other places as they expanded their operations. This widened the income gap between the south and other regions. Per capita income in the eleven states of the former Confederacy hovered at about 70 percent of the U.S. per capita income in the period between 1950 and 1963, when industries such as aerospace, electronics, and finance were growing rapidly. Following passage of the Civil Rights Act of 1964 and the Voting Rights Act of 1965, national and international firms, taking advantage of its lower cost of living, less restrictive labor practices, and universal use of air-conditioning, built new facilities in the southern states, and at an accelerated pace. By 1983, per capita income in the region had risen to 83 percent of the national average. By 2001, it had reached 87 percent. The growth in the region's population that resulted led to increased southern representation in both Congress and the Electoral College. This in turn enhanced the region's influence.

37. See Randall B. Woods, *LBJ: Architect of American Ambition* (New York: The Free Press, 2006), 62, and Goodwin, *Lyndon Johnson and the American Dream*, 65–66.

38. Evans and Novak, *Lyndon B. Johnson*, 120.

39. Strom Thurmond of South Carolina subsequently mounted a record-setting filibuster in excess of twenty-four hours.

40. Woods, *LBJ*, chaps. 17–19.

41. Ibid., 411.

42. Evans and Novak, *Lyndon B. Johnson*, 376.

43. John A. Andrew III, *Lyndon Johnson and the Great Society* (New York: Ivan R. Dee, 1998), 31.

44. Ibid., 35.

45. Evans and Novak, *Lyndon B. Johnson*, 497.

46. Ronald Reagan, "A Time for Choosing," speech delivered in support of Barry Goldwater for president, 27 October 1964, http://www.nationalcenter.org/Reagan Choosing1964.html.

47. Thomas W. Evans, *The Education of Ronald Reagan: The General Electric Years and the Untold Story of His Conversion to Conservatism* (New York: Columbia University Press, 2006), 6. After having defeated Reagan's challenge to his nomination by a mere 117 votes and delivering his acceptance speech, Ford invited Reagan to the podium in a gesture of party unity. In his convention closer, Reagan laid out in simple terms his own vision for the United States in the world. Although Reagan did not refer to his differences with Ford in these remarks, many a delegate departed the hall convinced that the convention had nominated the wrong man.

48. Ibid.

49. See Gary Scott Smith, *Faith and the Presidency: From George Washington to George W. Bush* (New York: Oxford University Press, 2006), 326.

50. Ibid. See also, Maureen Reagan, *First Father, First Daughter* (Boston: Little Brown, 1989), 64.

51. Paul Kengor, *God and Ronald Reagan: A Spiritual Life* (New York: Regan Books, 2004), 34.

52. Smith, *Faith and the Presidency*, 336.

53. Ibid, 231–32.

54. Ibid.

55. Joint Economic Committee of the 110th Congress of the United States, first session, June 2007, "Excess Burden of Federal Taxes Imposes higher Economic Cost," http://www.house.gov/jec/publications/110/rr110-8.pdf.

56. See Richard E. Neustadt's foreword to David Abshire, *Saving the Reagan Presidency: Trust Is the Coin of the Realm* (College Station: Texas A&M University Press, 2005), vii.

57. Lee Edwards, *The Essential Ronald Reagan* (New York: Rowman & Littlefield, 2005), 33.

58. *The Reagan Diaries,* ed. by Douglas Brinkley (New York: Harper Collins, 2007), 65.

59. Jules Tygiel, *Ronald Reagan and the Triumph of American Conservatism* (New York: Pearson Longman, 2006), 67.

60. Edwards, *The Essential Ronald Reagan*, 40.

61. For a more thorough assessment of Reagan's battles against communists within the motion picture industry, see Lou Cannon, *Governor Reagan* (New York: Public Affairs, 2003); Anne Edwards, *Early Reagan: The Rise to Power* (New York: Morrow, 1987); Peter Schweizer, *Reagan's War: The Epic Story of His Forty-Year Struggle and Final Triumph over Communism* (New York: Doubleday, 2002); and Edwards, *The Essential Ronald Reagan*.

62. Ibid.

63. Reagan to Gorbachev on Islamic revolution, 20 November 1985, memorandum of conversation, "Dinner Hosted by President and Mrs. Reagan," 8:00 to 10:00 P.M., Reagan papers. Also mentioned in Michael Beschloss, *Presidential Courage* (New York: Simon & Schuster, 2007), 326.

CHAPTER 4

1. Those interested in taking this up would do well to begin by reviewing the speech Lincoln delivered at the Lyceum at a time when Jacksonian democracy was coming into its own, as was discussed in chapter 2.

2. Walter Isaacson and Evan Thomas, *The Wise Men: Six Friends and the World They Made* (Boston: Faber and Faber, 1986).

3. James David Barber, *The Presidential Character: Predicting Performance in the White House* (Englewood Cliffs, N.J.: Prentice Hall, 1972), 290.

4. R. B. Bernstein, *Thomas Jefferson* (New York: Oxford University Press, 2003), 31.

5. Bernstein, *Thomas Jefferson*, 138–39.

6. Joyce Appleby, *Thomas Jefferson* (New York: Times Books, 2003), 48.

7. Joseph Ellis, *American Sphinx: The Character of Thomas Jefferson* (New York: Vintage, 1996), 228.

8. Bernstein, *Thomas Jefferson*, 147.

9. Appleby, *Thomas Jefferson*, 45.

10. Ellis, *American Sphinx*, 227.

11. For a fuller account of Lincoln's relations with his cabinet and its internal tensions, see Doris Kearns Goodwin, *Team of Rivals: The Political Genius of Abraham Lincoln* (New York: Simon & Schuster, 2005).

12. Goodwin, *Team of Rivals*, 174–75, 410–12.

13. "Simon Wolf at 84 Years: Lawyer, Philanthropist, Public Man and Friend of Many Presidents of the United States," *New York Times,* 23 October 1921, 85, and Simon Wolf, *The Presidents I Have Known: From 1860 to 1918* (Washington, D.C.: Press of B. S. Adams, 1918).

14. H. Jack Lang, ed., *The Wit and Wisdom of Abraham Lincoln as Reflected in His Briefer Letters and Speeches* (Cleveland: World Publishing Company, 1965), 208–9.

15. Ibid., 179.

16. John Stauffer, "Across the Great Divide," *Time,* 4 July 2005.

17. Frederick Douglass, "Oration in Memory of Abraham Lincoln," 14 April 1876, delivered at the unveiling of the Freedmen's Monument in Memory of Abraham Lincoln, Lincoln Park, Washington, D.D., http://teachingamericanhistory.org/library/index.asp?documentprint=39.

18. In 1908, in a mountainous region of the North Caucasus, a tribal chief asked Russian novelist Leo Tolstoy to tell him and his family about the ". . . greatest ruler of the world" who spoke with the "voice of thunder," "laughed like the sunrise," and whose "deeds were as strong as a rock," and who went by the name "Lincoln." Tolstoy was astonished that such "rude barbarians" were familiar with the growing Lincoln legend. See Goodwin, *Team of Rivals*, 747–48.

19. Richard C. Hofstadter, *The American Political Tradition and the Men Who Made It* (New York: Vintage, 1976), 41.

20. Holmes said this to his clerk, Donald Hiss—whose brother, Alger, Richard Nixon would help make famous. See Geoffrey C. Ward, *A First-Class Temperament: The Emergence of Franklin Roosevelt* (New York: Harper & Row, 1989), xiii.

21. Quoted in Philip Terzian, "Think Political Mudslinging Is Something New? Think Again," *Milwaukee Times Sentinel*, 5 September 2000.

22. Mark H. Leff, "Franklin D. Roosevelt," in *The Reader's Companion to the American Presidency*, ed. Alan Brinkley and Davis Dyer (New York: Houghton Mifflin, 2000), 374.

23. Franklin D. Roosevelt, Second Inaugural Address, January 20, 1937, http://www.bartleby.com/124/pres50.html.

24. Frances Perkins, *The Roosevelt I Knew* (New York: Viking, 1946), 9–14.

25. Robert A. Caro, *The Power Broker: Robert Moses and the Fall of New York* (New York: Vintage, 1975), chap. 16. On FDR during this period, see also Frances Perkins, *The Roosevelt I Knew*, chap. 1.

26. For accounts of Roosevelt at Warm Springs, see Ward, *A First-Class Temperament* along with Theo Lippman Jr., *The Squire of Warm Springs: FDR in Georgia, 1924–1945* (New York: Playboy Press, 1977) and Turnley Walker, *Roosevelt and the Warm Springs Story* (New York: A. A. Wyn, 1953).

27. Franklin D. Roosevelt, speech upon signing the Social Security Act, 14 August 1935, http://www.americanrhetoric.com/speeches/fdrsocialsecurityact.htm.

28. Hofstadter, *The American Political Tradition and the Men Who Made It.*

29. Emmet John Hughes, *The Living Presidency* (New York: Coward, McCann & Geoghegan, 1973), 190.

30. Franklin D. Roosevelt, "Fireside Chat," 29 December 1940, in John Grafton, ed. *Great Speeches: Franklin Delano Roosevelt* (Mineola, N.Y.: Dover Publiations, 1999).

31. Jean Edward Smith, *FDR* (New York: Random House, 2007), 419.

32. James MacGregor Burns, *Roosevelt: The Soldier of Freedom* (New York: Harcourt, Brace, Jovanovich, 1970), 422–24.

33. David Gergen, *Eyewitness to Power* (New York: Simon & Schuster, 2000), 201.

34. Hofstadter, *The American Political Tradition and the Men Who Made It*, 431.

35. Dwight D. Eisenhower, *Mandate for Change* (New York: Doubleday, 1963), 114.

36. John Lewis Gaddis, *Strategies of Containment: A Critical Reappraisal of American National Security Policy during the Cold War* (New York: Oxford University Press, 2005), 152.

37. Fred I. Greenstein, *The Presidential Difference: Leadership Style from FDR to Clinton* (New York: The Free Press, 1998), 52.

38. Matthew Brzezinski, *Red Moon Rising: Sputnik and the Hidden Rivalries that Ignited the Space Age* (New York: Times Books, 2007), 274.

39. Eisenhower, *Mandate for Change*, 274.

40. Peter Lyon, *Eisenhower: Portrait of a Hero* (Boston: Little, Brown, 1974), 854.

41. Greenstein, *The Presidential Difference*, 37.

42. Eisenhower, *Mandate for Change*, 60–61.

43. Ronald Reagan, "Farewell Address to the Nation," 11 January 1989, http://www.reaganfoundation.org/reagan/speeches/farewell.asp.

44. Anne Edwards, *Early Reagan: The Rise to Power* (New York: Morrow, 1987), 105.

45. David Gergen, *Eyewitness to Power: The Essence of Leadership, Nixon to Clinton* (New York: Simon & Schuster, 2000), 246.

46. Thomas W. Evans, *The Education of Ronald Reagan: The General Electric Years and the Untold Story of His Conversion to Conservatism* (New York: Columbia University Press, 2006), 9.

47. Lou Cannon, *Reagan,* (New York: Putnam, 1984), 253.

48. Gergen, *Eyewitness to Power,* 190.

49. John A. Farrell, *Tip O'Neill and the Democratic Century* (Boston: Little, Brown, 2001), 561.

50. Gergen, *Eyewitness to Power,* 197.

51. Ibid., 203.

52. Evans, *The Education of Ronald Reagan,* 200.

53. Michael Beschloss, *Presidential Courage: Brave Leaders and How They Changed America, 1789–1989* (New York: Simon & Schuster, 2007), 296.

54. Douglas Adair, "James Madison," in *The Lives of Eighteen from Princeton,* ed. William Thorp (Princeton, N.J.: Princeton University Press, 1946), 152.

55. Adrienne Koch, *Jefferson and Madison: The Great Collaboration* (New York: Alfred A. Knopf, 1950).

56. Ellis, *American Sphinx,* 249.

57. William A. DeGregorio, *The Complete Book of U.S. Presidents* (New York: Barricade Books, 1991), 69.

58. Ibid.

59. Ibid., 63.

60. Ibid., 77.

61. Drew R. McCoy, "James Madison," in *The Reader's Companion to the American Presidency,* ed. Alan Brinkley and David Dyer (New York: Houghton Mifflin, 2000), 63.

62. Ibid., 58.

63. Donald R. McCoy, *Calvin Coolidge: The Quiet President* (Lawrence: University Press of Kansas, 1988), 390.

64. For an account of Hoover's activities in the Mississippi Delta, see John M. Barry, *Rising Tide: The Great Mississippi Flood of 1927 and How It Changed America* (New York: Simon & Schuster, 1997), and Amity Shlaes, *The Forgotten Man: A New History of the Great Depression* (New York: HarperCollins, 2007), 15–16.

65. Robert Sobel, *Coolidge: An American Enigma* (Washington, D.C.: Regnery, 1998), 242.

66. Donald Kennedy, *Freedom from Fear* (New York: Oxford University Press, 1999), 43.

67. David Cannadine, *Mellon: An American Life* (New York: Alfred A. Knopf, 2006), 362.

68. While Hoover professed to admire intellectuals, who groped for "new shapes and forms for the world," he confessed that they got "on the nerves of the fellow who must keep the machinery of civilization operating in the meantime." That is certainly how he regarded intellectuals who presumed to advise policy makers, such as John Maynard

Keynes. See Herbert Hoover, *The Ordeal of Woodrow Wilson* (Baltimore: Johns Hopkins University Press, 1992), 234.

69. William A. Degregorio, *The Complete Book of U.S. Presidents* (New York: Wings Books, 1991), 476.

70. Hofstadter, *The American Political Tradition and the Men Who Made It*, 374.

71. Michael A. Stoff, "Herbert Hoover," in *The Reader's Companion to the American Presidency*, ed. Alan Brinkley and David Dyer (New York: Houghton Mifflin, 2000), 359.

72. Jura Koncius, "On Exhibit: Companions in Chief," *Washington Post*, 28 June 2007, H1.

73. Shlaes, *The Forgotten Man*, 28.

74. William E. Dodd, *Woodrow Wilson and His Work* (New York: Doubleday, 1920), 226.

75. Hofstadter, *The American Political Tradition and the Men Who Made It*, 369. Hoover was extremely proud of this designation. He included this quotation in his memoir of Woodrow Wilson.

76. Stoff, "Herbert Hoover," 359.

77. Cannadine, *Mellon*, 391.

78. Individual rates were reduced from a range of 1.125 to 25 percent to a range of 0.375 percent on taxable income over $4,000 ($40,000 in 2000 dollars) to 24 percent on taxable income above $100,000 ($1,005,254 in 2000 dollars), while the corporate rate fell from 12 to 11 percent. These reductions were temporary for tax year 1929, payable in 1930, and then expired.

79. Shlaes, *The Forgotten Man*, chap. 3.

80. Ibid.

81. Ibid.

82. Walter Bagehot, *Lombard Street: A Description of the Money Market* (Homewood, Ill.: R. D. Irwin, 1962 [1873]).

83. Milton Friedman and and Anna Jacobson Schwartz, *A Monetary History of the United States, 1867–1960* (Princeton, N.J.: Princeton University Press, 1963), 55.

84. Richard H. Timberlake, *Money Policy in the United States: An Intellectual and Institutional History* (Chicago: University of Chicago Press, 1993), 226.

85. Friedman and Schwartz, *A Monetary History of the United States, 1867–1960*, 24.

86. McKean, *The Boss* (New York: Russell and Russell, 1967), 226.

87. Shlaes, *The Forgotten Man*, 96.

88. Hoover wrote about his acquaintanceship with Keynes in *The Ordeal of Woodrow Wilson*.

89. Stoff, "Herbert Hoover," 363.

90. Joseph Alsop and Turner Catledge, *The 168 Days* (New York: Doubleday, 1938), 1.

91. Robert Dallek, "Lyndon B. Johnson," in *The Reader's Companion to the American Presidency*, ed. Alan Brinkley and David Dyer (New York: Houghton Mifflin, 2000), 439.

92. Roger H. Davidson, Walter J. Oleszek, and Frances E. Lee, *Congress and Its Members*, 11th ed. (Washington, D.C.: Congressional Quarterly, 2008), 309.

93. John A. Andrew III, *Lyndon Johnson and the Great Society* (Chicago: Ivan R. Dee, 1998), chap. 2.

94. Ibid., 43–44.

95. Doris Kearns Goodwin, *Lyndon Johnson and the American Dream* (New York: Harper & Row, 1976), 251.

96. Tim Weiner, *Legacy of Ashes: The History of the CIA* (New York: Doubleday, 2007), 239–42.

97. Greenstein, *The Presidential Difference*, 83.

98. Emmet John Hughes, quoted in Randall B. Woods, *LBJ: Architect of American Ambition* (New York: The Free Press, 2006), 620.

99. Greenstein, *The Presidential Difference*, 83.

100. Woods, *LBJ*, 597.

101. Dallek, "Lyndon B. Johnson," 440.

102. Woods, *LBJ*, 605.

103. Ibid., 608.

104. Farrell, *Tip O'Neill and the Democratic Century*, 440.

105. Quoted in Burton I. Kaufman and Scott Kaufman, *The Presidency of Jimmy Carter* (Lawrence: University Press of Kansas, 2006), 17.

106. Jimmy Carter, *Turning Point: A Candidate, a State, a Nation Come of Age* (New York: Times Books, 1992), 5.

107. Jimmy Carter, *Why Not the Best?* (Nashville: Broadman Press, 1975).

108. Ibid., 98.

109. Greenstein, *The Presidential Difference*, 131.

110. See Farrell, *Tip O'Neill*, especially chap. 19, and Steven Gillon, "Jimmy Carter," *The Reader's Companion to the American Presidency*, ed. Alan Brinkley and David Dyer (New York: Houghton Mifflin, 2000), 477–87.

111. For a discussion of Carter's relations with Congress, see Farrell, *Tip O'Neill*, chap. 19, 20, 22.

112. Greenstein, *The Presidential Difference*, 136.

113. Jimmy Carter, "Crises in Confidence Speech," 15 July 1979, http://www.american rhetoric.com/speeches/jimmycartercrisisofconfidence.htm.

Chapter 5

1. Gross domestic product (GDP) is the market value of goods and services produced by labor and property in the United States, regardless of the nationality of the producer. Nominal GDP is in current dollars. Real GDP is nominal GDP adjusted by the GDP deflator to eliminate the effects of price changes through time. In this book, real GDP is in 2000 dollars for historical comparisons.

2. Joseph Schumpeter, *Capitalism, Socialism and Democracy* (New York: Harper and Brother, 1942).

3. Forrest McDonald, *Alexander Hamilton: A Biography* (New York: Norton, 1979), 121.

4. Ibid., 119–20.

5. South Carolina and Massachusetts were unable to raise enough revenue to service their war debts; North Carolina, Rhode Island, and Virginia retired their war debts through "more or less fraudulent means"; and the other states struggled to meet their debt service. Ibid., 148.

6. Edward S. Kaplan, *The Bank of the United States and the American Economy* (Westport, Ct.: Greenwood Press, 1999), 14–16.

7. Ron Chernow, *Alexander Hamilton* (New York: Penguin, 2004), 29–33.

8. A funded government debt refers to a government that makes punctual payments of interest to its bondholders without retiring the principal.

9. McDonald, *Alexander Hamilton*, 215.

10. Ibid., 165–71.

11. Ibid., 197.

12. McDonald, *Alexander Hamilton*, 192–95, and Kaplan, *Bank of the United States and the American Economy*, 25–26.

13. McDonald, *Alexander Hamilton*, 202, and Kaplan, *Bank of the United States and the American Economy*, 24.

14. McDonald, *Alexander Hamilton*, 205–10, and Kaplan, *Bank of the United States and the American Economy*, 24–25.

15. In 1819, the U.S. Supreme Court affirmed Hamilton's reasoning in *McCulloch v. Maryland* (17 U.S. 316).

16. McDonald, *Alexander Hamilton*, 234.

17. Ibid., 232–36.

18. Douglas A. Irwin, "The Aftermath of Hamilton's 'Report on Manufacturers,'" National Bureau of Economic Research Working Paper 9943 (August 2003).

19. Calvin Coolidge, "Our Heritage from Hamilton," in *The Price of Freedom* (New York: Scribner's, 1924), 102.

20. Kaplan, *Bank of the United States and the American Economy*, 39–40.

21. Ibid., 41–42.

22. Richard Timberlake, *Monetary Policy in the United States: An Intellectual and Institutional History* (Chicago: University of Chicago Press, 1993), 14–18.

23. Kaplan, *Bank of the United States and the American Economy*, 38.

24. Ibid., 38.

25. Ibid., 38.

26. Robert V. Remini, *Henry Clay: Statesman for the Union* (New York: Norton, 1991), 137–44.

27. Kaplan, *Bank of the United States and the American Economy*, 49–55.

28. Ibid., 57–58.

29. Timberlake, *Monetary Policy in the United States*, 20–23.

30. Kaplan, *Bank of the United States and the American Economy*, 59–60.

31. Ibid., 68.

32. Ibid., 63.

33. Ibid., 73–75.

34. Richard C. Hofstadter, *The American Political Tradition and the Men Who Made It* (New York: Vintage. 1989), 61.

35. Ibid.

36. As a young military officer, Jackson risked disciplinary action by summarily ordering the execution of two British officers while on a military expedition to Spanish-controlled

Florida. He would cite the high number of British shareholders as one of his reasons for seeking to destroy the Second Bank of the United States.

37. Kaplan, *Bank of the United States and the American Economy*, 101–2, and Hofstadter, *The American Political Tradition and the Men Who Made It*, 68–69.

38. Kaplan, *Bank of the United States and the American Economy*, 101.

39. Hofstadter, *The American Political Tradition and the Men Who Made It*, 78.

40. Georgia, Louisiana, and New York switched from having their legislatures select presidential electors to having presidential electors determined by popular vote.

41. Hofstadter, *The American Political Tradition and the Men Who Made It*, 69–70.

42. "Methods of Electing Presidential Electors: 1788 to 1836," Series Y 1–26, and "Electoral and Popular Vote Cast for President, by Political Party: 1789 to 1968," Series Y 79–83, in *Historical Statistics of the United States: Colonial Times to 1970, Part 2* (Washington, D.C.: Government Printing Office, 1975), 1,071, 1,073–74.

43. Like Jackson, Senator Thomas Hart Benton (Missouri) was a "hard money" man who opposed all banks, thought bank notes inflationary, and insisted that only gold or silver should be used as money. Amos Kendell, editor of the *Argus of Western America*, a pro-Jackson publication, blamed the Second Bank for the Panic of 1819. Kentucky Representative Richard M. Johnson complained that the Bank did not circulate enough bank notes to relieve the mortgage debt burdens of farmers during periods of inflation. Approving of the bank as it was, Jackson's first secretary of the treasury, Samuel Ingham, persuaded Jackson to mute his opposition to it during his first year in office. Martin Van Buren (Jackson's first secretary of state and second vice president) and Roger Taney (Jackson's second attorney general, fourth secretary of the treasury, and appointee as chief justice) opposed the Bank mainly out of parochial interests. Wall Street financiers, who had funded Van Buren's political machine in New York State and would later support his presidential bid, wanted the Bank, headquartered in Philadelphia, abolished so that New York City would emerge as the financial capital of the country. Taney was a director of two state-chartered banks and an attorney for another that benefited from Jackson's order to remove Treasury deposits from the Bank. See Bray Hammond, *Banks and Politics in America from the Revolution to the Civil War* (Princeton, N.J.: Princeton University Press, 1957).

44. Andrew Jackson, "First Annual Message," 8 December 1829, http://www.presidency/ucsb.edu/ws/index.php.pid=29427.

45. Timberlake, *Monetary Policy in the United States*, 31; Kaplan, *The Bank of the United States and the American Economy*, 82–91, and Hammond, *Banks and Politics in America from the Revolution to the Civil War*, 323, and Robert V. Remini, *Andrew Jackson and the Bank War* (New York: Norton, 1967).

46. Kaplan, *The Bank of the United States and the American Economy*, 112–13.

47. Robert V. Remini, *Andrew Jackson and the Bank War*, 43.

48. Hofstadter, *The American Political Tradition and the Men Who Made It*, 79.

49. Kaplan, *Bank of the United States and the American Economy*, 124–26, and Timberlake, *Monetary Policy in the United States*, 41–42.

50. Robert Remini, *The Life of Andrew Jackson* (New York: Penguin, 1988), 234.

51. William A. DeGregorio, *The Complete Book of U.S. Presidents*, 3rd ed. (New York: Barricade Books, 1991), 118.

52. Timberlake, *Monetary Policy in the United States*, 43, and "Electoral and Popular Vote Cast for President, by Political Party: 1789 to 1968," Series Y 79–83.

53. Kaplan, *Bank of the United States and the American Economy*, 131. On May 20, 1833, Secretary of the Treasury Louis McLane opposed the removal, fearing that state-chartered banks would cause inflation through their unregulated note issues. On June 1, 1833, Jackson replaced McLane with William Duane. On September 23, 1833, Jackson fired Duane after he also refused to remove the Treasury deposits because he also felt "a change to local and irresponsible banks will tend to shake public confidence and promote doubt and mischief." Jackson replaced him with his subservient attorney general, Roger Taney (Kaplan, *Bank of the United States and the American Economy*, 129–31, and Timberlake, *Monetary Policy in the United States*, 43–46).

54. Kaplan, *Bank of the United States and the American Economy*, 132–34.

55. Sean Wilentz, *Andrew Jackson* (New York: Times Books, 2005), 108.

56. Gold was undervalued relative to silver at the mint price ratio of 1:15 compared to a market price ratio of 1:15.93. By decreasing the weight of gold in the dollar to 1.50g, the mint price ratio of gold to silver rose to 1:16 (Kaplan, *Bank of the United States and the American Economy*, 146).

57. Ibid., 153–54.

58. Timberlake, *Monetary Policy in the United States*, 51–64.

59. Kaplan, *Bank of the United States and the American Economy*, 154–55, Robert Sobel, *Panic on Wall Street: A Classic History of America's Financial Disasters and with a New Exploration of the Crash of 1987* (New York: Truman Talley Books, 1988), 46–48.

60. Peter L. Rousseau, "Jacksonian Monetary Policy, Species Flow, and the Panic of 1837," National Bureau of Economic Research Working Paper 7528 (February 2000), 30.

61. Sobel, *Panic on Wall Street*, 67–68.

62. Rousseau, "Jacksonian Monetary Policy, Species Flow, and the Panic of 1837," 1.

63. Kaplan, *Bank of the United States and the American Economy*, 156–57, and Sobel, *Panic on Wall Street*, 71–72.

64. Ibid., 156.

65. John Joseph Wallis, "What Caused the Crisis of 1839?" National Bureau of Economic Research Historical Paper 133 (April 2001), 18.

66. Joseph Wallis, Richard E. Sylla, and Arthur Grinath III, "Sovereign Debt and Repudiation: The Emerging Market Debt Crisis in the United States, 1839–1843," National Bureau of Economic Research Working Paper 10735 (September 2004), 1.

67. Ibid.

68. Richard Shenkman, *Presidential Ambition: How the Presidents Gained Power, Kept Power, and Got Things Done* (New York: HarperCollins, 1999), chap. 7.

69. Congress would not contest a president's right, without its consent, to remove an official from office whom the Senate had confirmed until the late 1860s, when it reached an impasse over Reconstruction policy with Jackson disciple President Andrew Johnson.

Years after the Senate failed to remove Johnson from office, the Supreme Court ruled the Tenure of Office Act that Johnson had violated was unconstitutional.

70. Philip Shaw Paludan, *The Presidency of Abraham Lincoln* (Lawrence: University Press of Kansas, 1994), chap. 5.

71. Ibid.

72. Quoted in James M. McPherson, *Abraham Lincoln and the Second American Revolution* (New York: Oxford University Press, 1991), 40. See also Leonard P. Curry, *Blueprint for Modern America: Nonmilitary Legislation of the First Civil War Congress* (Nashville: Vanderbilt University Press, 1968).

73. 156 U.S. 1 (1895).

74. The railroads were the Great Northern; the Northern Pacific; and the Chicago, Burlington, and Quincy.

75. Leslie L. Gould, *The Presidency of Theodore Roosevelt* (Lawrence: University Press of Kansas, 1981), 40, 49–53, 134.

76. Ibid., 51.

77. Ibid., 66–72.

78. Ibid., 149, 150–60, 164–65.

79. Ibid., 158, 164–69, 213–15.

80. Timberlake, *Monetary Policy in the United States*, 184, 254–55; Ron Chernow, *The House of Morgan: An American Banking Dynasty and the Rise of Modern Finance* (New York: Simon & Schuster, 1990), 121–28.

81. Timberlake, *Monetary Policy in the United States*, 186–94.

82. Gould, *The Presidency of Theodore Roosevelt*, 247–50; Timberlake, *Monetary Policy in the United States*, 251–52.

83. Gould, *The Presidency of Theodore Roosevelt*, 277–79; Timberlake, *Monetary Policy in the United States*, 214–19.

84. Woodrow Wilson, "First Inaugural Address," 4 March 1913, http://www.bartleby.com/124/pres44.html.

85. Kendrick A. Clements, *The Presidency of Woodrow Wilson* (Lawrence: University Press of Kansas, 1992), 37.

86. Ibid., 31–39.

87. The National Recovery Act would have extended collateralized loans to commercial banks based on their "real bills" (short term commercial and industrial loans used to produce and distribute goods and sevices). Timberlake, *Monetary Policy in the United States*, 217–19.

88. Chernow, *The House of Morgan*, 149–56.

89. Arthur S. Link, *Wilson: The New Freedom* (Princeton, N.J.: Princeton University Press, 1956), chap. 7.

90. Ibid.

91. Clements, *The Presidency of Woodrow Wilson*, 47–49.

92. Ibid., 49–51.

93. Ibid., 44, 81. The Republican Congress, elected in 1918, repealed the measure after World War I.

94. Ibid. The Supreme Court declared the statute unconstitutional in *Hamer v. Dagenhart*, 247 U.S. 251 (1918).

95. Timberlake, *Monetary Policy in the United States*, 258; Allan H. Meltzer, *A History of the Federal Reserve*, Volume 1, *1913–1951* (Chicago: University of Chicago Press, 2003), 84–90.

96. Laton McCartney, *The Teapot Dome Scandal: How Big Oil Bought the Harding White House and Tried to Steal the Country* (New York: Random House, 2008), 207.

97. Ferrell, *The Presidency of Calvin Coolidge*, 45–46.

98. For a fuller discussion of the question of whether Roosevelt was a radical or a conservative, who saved both capitalism and democracy, see James MacGregor Burns, *Roosevelt: The Lion and the Fox* (New York: Harcourt, Brace, 1956).

99. For the most recent account in this genre, see Amity Shlaes, *The Forgotten Man: A New History of the Great Depression* (New York: HarperCollins, 2007).

100. Doris Kearns Goodwin, *No Ordinary Time: Franklin and Eleanor Roosevelt, the Home Front in World War II* (New York: Simon & Schuster, 1994), 42–43, 107–9.

101. For a fuller exposition of this thesis, see Shlaes, *The Forgotten Man*.

102. Sweden, for instance, abandoned the gold exchange standard in 1931 in favor of a monetary policy of stabilizing domestic prices (similar to what the Federal Reserve pursued under Alan Greenspan) and government deficit spending until the economy recovered. In Sweden, real GDP exceeded its predepression level by 1934, and the Swedish unemployment rate fell below its predepression level by 1936. The United Kingdom and the Netherlands fully recovered by 1937.

103. Fred I. Greenstein, *The Presidential Difference: Leadership Style from FDR to Clinton* (New York: The Free Press, 2000), 24.

104. Of the remaining 5,430 banks, 3,398 were licensed to reopen later, after they were recapitalized, and 2,132 were permanently closed or merged with other banks (Milton Friedman and Anna Jacobson Schwartz, *A Monetary History of the United States, 1867–1960* [Princeton, N.J.: Princeton University Press, 1963], 421–28.)

105. Universal banks offer a wide spectrum of financial services including commercial banking, investment banking, and securities brokerage.

106. For a humorous account of how this resulted, see Hofstadter, *The American Political Tradition and the Men Who Made It*, 426.

107. George McJimsey, *The Presidency of Franklin Delano Roosevelt* (Lawrence: University Press of Kansas, 2000), 50–54; Meltzer, *A History of the Federal Reserve*, 443–50.

108. Meltzer, *A History of the Federal Reserve*, 456–63.

109. Ibid., 463–70.

110. McJimsey, *The Presidency of Franklin Delano Roosevelt*, 37.

111. Ibid., 100–105.

112. Michael R. Darby, "Three and a Half Million U.S. Employees Have Been Mislaid: An Explanation of Unemployment, 1934–1941," *Journal of Political Economy* 84, no. 1 (1976): 1–16.

113. Franklin D. Roosevelt, "Message to Congress on Unemployment Relief," 21 March 1933, http: www.presidenecy.ucsb.edu/wsindex.php?pid, and Franklin D.

Roosevelt, "Radio Address on Cooperation with Unemployment Census," 14 November 1937, http://www.presidency.ucsb.edu/wsindex.php?pid.

114. McJimsey, *The Presidency of Franklin Delano Roosevelt*, 43–48.

115. 295 U.S. 495 (1935).

116. Ibid.; McJimsey, *The Presidency of Franklin Delano Roosevelt*, 77, 67–82; Shlaes, *The Forgotten Man*, 214–45.

117. 297 U.S. 1 (1936).

118. McJimsey, *The Presidency of Franklin Delano Roosevelt*, 55–66.

119. David Cannadine, *Mellon: An American Life* (New York: Knopf, 2006), 509.

120. Shlaes, *The Forgotten Man*, 313.

121. McJimsey, *The Presidency of Franklin Delano Roosevelt*, x.

122. Franklin D. Roosevelt, "Statement upon Signing the Social Security Act," 14 August 1935, www.ssa.gov/history/fdrstmts.html.

123. Meltzer, *A History of the Federal Reserve*, 490–521; Timberlake, *Monetary Policy in the United States*, 288–96.

124. James N. Giglio, *The Presidency of John F. Kennedy* (Lawrence: University Press of Kansas, 1991), 131.

125. Ibid., 132-33.

126. Ibid.

127. Economist Walter Heller was impressed by the caliber of Kennedy's questions and with his extraordinary capacity to learn (ibid., 124). Kennedy would long remember suffering through the introductory course in economics at Harvard taught by instructor Russ Nixon. See Theodore C. Sorensen, *Kennedy* (New York: Harper & Row, 1965), 442, 487.

128. Giglio, *The Presidency of John F. Kennedy*, 136–37.

129. Ibid.

130. Ibid., 136.

131. Ibid., 485.

132. Ibid., 137.

133. Ibid., 485.

134. Sorensen, *Kennedy*, 484.

135. Giglio, *The Presidency of John F. Kennedy*, 131.

136. It was around this time that Kennedy's remark about businessmen made its way into *Newsweek*.

137. Giglio, *The Presidency of John F. Kennedy*, 133–34.

138. Two-thirds of these reductions were by 50 percent or more, while the rest were between 25 and 50 percent. On balance, average tariff rates on dutiable goods fell by 36 percent, to 39 percent in the United States and other developed countries.

139. Giglio, *The Presidency of John F. Kennedy*, 150–53.

140. Ibid., 153.

141. John F. Kennedy, "Address at Rice University on Nation's Space Effort," 12 September 1962, http://www.jfklibrary.org.

142. Giglio, *The Presidency of John F. Kennedy*, 154.

143. Ibid., 153.

144. Tom Wicker, *One of Us: Richard Nixon and the American Dream* (New York: Random House, 1999), 542.

145. Melvin Small, *The Presidency of Richard Nixon* (Lawrence: University Press of Kansas, 1999), 185.

146. Ibid., 205.

147. Ibid.

148. Ibid., 188.

149. The impetus for the dramatic increases in Social Security came from the chairman of the House Ways and Means Committee, Wilbur Mills, a Democrat from Alabama. As a means of adding momentum to the Democratic presidential nomination in 1972, Mills abandoned his trademark pay-as-you-go approach to spending in the hope of emerging as the champion of the elderly. With the polls showing Nixon running even with or behind the presumptive 1972 nominee, Ed Muskie, for the majority of his first term, Nixon did not wish to antagonize this important constituency. The Tax Reform Act of 1969 that Nixon signed on December 30, 1969, contained a 15 percent increase in Social Security benefits effective January 1, 1970. In the next two years, Congress used bills increasing the federal public debt ceiling to boost benefits. Nixon signed the Social Security Amendments Act of 1971 on March 17, 1971, which contained another 15 percent increase in benefits, retroactive to January 1, 1971; increased the taxable wage base from $7,800 to $9,000 effective January 1, 1972; and increased the Old Age, Survivors, and Disability Insurance payroll tax rates on employers and employees to 5.15 percent each beginning in 1976. Nixon signed the Social Security Amendments Act of 1972 on July 1, mandating an immediate 20 percent increase in benefits and benefits to inflation beginning in 1975 and that increased taxable wage base from $9,000 to $10,800 in 1973 and to $12,000 in 1974, with automatic adjustment thereafter. President Nixon signed the Social Security Benefits Increase Act in 1973, which increased benefits by 7 percent in March 1974 and by another 4 percent in June 1974.

150. Small, *The Presidency of Richard Nixon*, 192.

151. Ibid., 208.

152. Ibid., 207, 209.

153. Ibid., 209.

154. Ibid., 206.

155. Ibid., 210–11.

156. This is known as the Smithsonian Agreement.

157. Herbert Stein, *Presidential Economics: The Making of Economic Policy from Roosevelt to Reagan and Beyond* (New York: Simon & Schuster, 1985), 190.

158. Richard Nixon, "State of the Union Address," 22 January 1970, http://www.infoplease.com/t/hist/state-of-the-union/183.html.

159. Wicker, *One of Us*, 507–16.

160. These laws consisted of (1) the Endangered Species Act; (2) the National Environment Policy Act; (3) the Clean Air Amendments Act of 1970; (4) the Coastal Zone Management Act of 1972 (protecting estuaries); (5) the Marine Mammal Protection Act of 1972; (6) the Noise Control Act of 1972; (7) the Safe Drinking Water Act of 1974 (authorizing the EPA to establish and enforce health-related standards for water purity and requiring all water systems to comply with them); and (8) the Extension of the Solid Waste

Disposal Act of 1965 (addressing solid waste problems and requiring a series of research and demonstration projects) (Small, *The Presidency of Richard Nixon*, 196–201).

161. Small, *The Presidency of Richard Nixon*, 200–201.

162. Ibid.

163. Ibid., 211–12.

164. Ibid., 213.

165. Ibid., 202.

166. Ibid., 203.

167. "Poll Approval Ratings Compared: Bush's Low Job Approval Is Far Below Some Two-Term Predecessors," 2 November 2005, http://www.cbsnews.com/stories/2005/11/02/opinion polls/main/1005327.shtml. This poll was taken weeks after Nixon dismissed Watergate special prosecutor Archibald Cox in what became known as the "Saturday Night Massacre."

168. Ibid.

169. Burton I. Kaufman and Scott Kaufman, *The Presidency of James Earl Carter, Jr.*, 2nd rev. ed, (Lawrence: University Press of Kansas, 2006), 35–36.

170. Ibid., 71–72, 91–92.

171. Ibid, 122, 131.

172. Under existing federal regulations, the price of natural gas shipped across state lines was capped at $1.44 per 1,000 cubic feet, while the unregulated price of natural gas shipped within one state had increased to $1.90 per 1,000 cubic feet. This price differential caused pipeline companies to reduce interstate shipments of natural gas.

173. Jimmy Carter, speech delivered 18 April 1977, http://www.pbs.org/wgbh/amex/carter/filmmore/ps_energy.html.

174. Kaufman and Kaufman, *The Presidency of James Earl Carter, Jr.*, 70–71.

175. Ibid., 85–87.

176. Ibid., 173–86.

177. Kaufman and Kaufman, *The Presidency of James Earl Carter, Jr.*, 95–96.

178. Ibid., 136.

179. Timberlake, *Monetary Policy in the United States*, 348–56.

180. Kaufman and Kaufman, *The Presidency of James Earl Carter, Jr.*, 203–5.

181. Ibid., 207–8.

182. Ibid., 168.

183. Lou Cannon, *President Reagan: The Role of a Lifetime* (New York: Simon & Schuster, 1991), 275.

184. Thomas Laubach, New Evidence on the Interest Rate Effects of Budget Deficits and Debt (Washington, D.C.: Board of Governors of the Federal Reserve System, May 2003), http://www.federalreserve.gov/pubs/feds/2003/200312/200312pap.pdf.

185. From 1980 to 1988, real household income rose by 5.8 percent at the 20th percentile, 7.1 percent at the 40th percentile, 9.0 percent at the 60th percentile, and 12.5 percent at the 80th percentile.

186. Robert P. O'Quinn, "Information Technology Increases Earnings Differential and Drives Need for Education," Research Report 110–16, prepared for the Joint Economic Committee, 110th Congress, 1st session (May 3, 2007).

187. David H. Autor, Frank Levy, and Richard J. Murnane, "The Skill Content of Recent Technological Change: An Empirical Exploration," *Quarterly Journal of Economics*, 118, no. 4 (November 2003).

188. "The Globalization of Labor," in *World Economic Outlook* (Washington, D.C.: International Monetary Fund, April 2007).

189. Sylvia Nasar, "Economists' Advice for Clinton," *New York Times*, 19 July 1993, 81.

190. Gwen Ifill, "Clinton's Blunt Reminder of the Moood that Elected Him," *New York Times*, 24 January 1993, 1.

191. Alan Greenspan, *The Age of Turbulence: Adventures in a New World* (New York: Penguin Press, 2007), chap. 7.

192. The congresswoman who cast it, Margery Margolis Medvinsky, a Democrat from Pennsylvania, lost her seat in the next election.

193. Such was the headline that adorned the cover of the New York *Daily News* along with a cartoon depicting the speaker as a child throwing a tantrum (17 November 1995).

194. See Jason De Parle, "The Clinton Welfare Bill; A Long, Stormy Journey," *New York Times*, 15 July 1994, 1.

195. "Welfare: Moynihan's Counsel of Despair," *First Things* (March 1996): http://www.firstthings.com/article.php3?id_articles=3836. For a discussion of Moynihan's falling out with Clinton over welfare, see John F. Harris, *The Survivor: Bill Clinton in the White House* (New York: Random House, 2005, 233–34. See also Daniel Patrick Moyniham, "When Principle Is at Issue," *Washington Post*, 4 August 1996, C7.

196. Bill Clinton, "How We Ended Welfare, Together," *New York Times*, 22 August 2006, A-19.

CHAPTER 6

1. Thomas Jefferson, letter to John Taylor, 4 June 1798, http://odur.let.rug.nl/~usa/P/tj3/writings/brf/jefl122.htm.

2. Abraham Lincoln, letter to Henry L. Pierce and others, 16 April 1859, http://teachingamericanhistory.org/library/index.asp?document=101.

3. Richard C. Hofstadter, *The American Political Tradition and the Men Who Made It* (New York: Vintage, 1989), 65.

4. Saul K. Padover, *Thomas Jefferson on Democracy* (New York: Mentor Books, 1939), 177.

5. Because this account of Jefferson's view of Jackson came from Jackson critic Daniel Webster, Sean Wilentz doubts its authenticy in *Andrew Jackson* (New York: Times Books, 2005).

6. Andrew Jackson, "Farewell Address," 1837, http://www.nationalcenter.org/Jackson's Farewell.html.

7. James Thomas Flexner, *Washington, the Indispensable Man* (Boston: Little, Brown, 1974).

8. Harry L. Watson, "Andrew Jackson," in *The Reader's Companion to the American Presidency*, ed. Alan Brinkley and Davis Dyer (New York: Houghton Mifflin, 2000), 103.

9. Ibid., 141. In this instance, the interested party was an evangelical missionary who, in defiance of state law, took up residence among the Cherokee.

10. Robert V. Remini, *The Revolutionary Age of Andrew Jackson* (New York: Harper & Row, 1976), 115–18.

11. See Remini, *The Revolutionary Age of Andrew Jackson*, and John Ehle, *Trail of Tears: The Rise and Fall of the Cherokee Nation* (New York: Anchor Books, 1988).

12. Remini, *The Revolutionary Age of Andrew Jackson*, 108.

13. Wilentz, *Andrew Jackson*, 67, 68, 140.

14. Buddy Levy, *American Legend: The Real Life Adventures of David Crockett* (New York: Penguin, 2006), 169.

15. Abraham Lincoln, letter to Alexander Stephens, 22 December 1860, http://teachingamericanhistory.org/library/index.asp?document=1073.

16. Catherine Clinton, "Zachary Taylor," in *The Reader's Companion to the American Presidency*, ed. Alan Brinkley and Davis Dyer (New York: Houghton Mifflin, 2000), 155.

17. http://www.whitehouse.gov/history/presidents/2+12/html.

18. Clinton, "Zachary Taylor," 153.

19. Ibid.

20. Robert E. Lee may well have fought for the North. Ulysses S. Grant, who served under Taylor's command in Mexico, presumably would have done so again.

21. William A. DeGregorio, *The Complete Book of U.S. Presidents*, 3rd ed. (New York: Barricade Books, 1991), 184.

22. James M. McPherson, *Battle Cry of Freedom: The Civil War Era* (New York: Oxford University Press, 1988), 68.

23. Ibid., 75.

24. Ibid., 76.

25. http://members.tripod.com/~mbphish/chapter13.html.

26. DeGregorio, *The Complete Book of U.S. Presidents*, 194.

27. Arthur M. Schlesinger Sr., "Historians Rate U.S. Presidents," *Life*, 1 November 1948, and "Our Presidents: A Rating by 75 Historians," *New York Times Magazine*, 29 July 1962.

28. See William A. Dunning's *Essays on the Civil War and Reconstruction* (New York: Harper & Row, 1965 [1898]) and *Reconstruction, Political and Economic, 1865–1877* (New York: Harper 1962 [1909]). Dunning's interpretation dominated academic and popular interpretations of Reconstruction until the 1960s.

29. For this positive view of Johnson, see Claude Bowers, *The Tragic Era* (1929), George Fort Milton, *The Age of Hate: Andrew Johnson and the Radicals* (1930), Lloyd P. Stryker, *Andrew Johnson: A Study in Courage* (1929), and Robert W. Winston, *Andrew Johnson: Plebian and Patriot* (1928).

30. John F. Kennedy, *Profiles in Courage: Decisive Moments in the Lives of Celebrated Americans* (New York: Harper and Brothers, 1956), 123.

31. Kennedy consulted Dunning's essays, Stryker's *Andrew Johnson* and Bowers's arguably racist *The Tragic Era*, published in 1929. See Kennedy, *Profiles in Courage*, 257–59.

32. Eric Foner, "Andrew Johnson," in *The Reader's Companion to the American Presidency*, ed. Alan Brinkley and Davis Dyer (New York: Houghton Mifflin, 2000), 204.

33. James K. Polk, *Polk: The Diary of a President 1845–1849*, ed. Allan Nevins (Capricorn Books, 1968), 362.

34. Foner, "Andrew Johnson," 204.

35. Ibid., 205.

36. John Alexander Carroll and Odie B. Falk, *Home of the Brave: A Patriot's Guide to American History* (New Rochelle, N.Y.: Arlington House, 1976), 212.

37. Brooks D. Simpson, *The Reconstruction Presidents* (Lawrence: University Press of Kansas, 1998), 68.

38. Ibid., 67.

39. Ibid., 80.

40. Ibid., 140.

41. Ibid., 77–78.

42. Ibid., 77.

43. Foner, "Andrew Johnson," 206.

44. Carroll and Falk, *Home of the Brave*, 214.

45. This was very much a replay of the displeasure Congress voiced when Jackson asserted his right to dismiss officials within the executive branch who had obtained Senate confirmation. In this instance, Congress, as evidenced by its ability to pass this measure, had become the stronger of the two parties, and the president, the weaker.

46. Jean Edward Smith, "Abraham Lincoln and U.S. Grant," in *Lincoln Revisited*, ed. John Y. Simon, Harold Holzer, and Dawn Vogel (New York: Fordham University Press, 2007), 176.

47. Ibid., 172.

48. See Eric Foner, *Reconstruction: America's Unfinished Revolution, 1863–1877* (New York: Harper & Row, 1988), 488–99.

49. Carroll and Falk, *Home of the Brave*, 217.

50. Henry Adams, *The Education of Henry Adams* (New York: Mariner Books, 2000), 266.

51. Josiah Bunting III, *Ulysses S. Grant* (New York: Times Books, 2004), 136–37.

52. Ibid.

53. Simpson, *The Reconstruction Presidents*, 155–56.

54. Foner, *Reconstruction*, 158.

55. William McFeeley, "Ulysses S. Grant," in *The Reader's Companion to the American Presidency*, ed. Alan Brinkley and Davis Dyer (New York: Houghton Mifflin, 2000).

56. Ibid.

57. Frank Scaturro, *President Grant Reconsidered* (New York: Madison Books, 1999), chap. 5.

58. Simpson, *The Reconstruction Presidents*, 145.

59. Foner, *Reconstruction*, 494.

60. Simpson, *The Reconstruction Presidents*, 145–48, and Foner, *Reconstruction*, 494–97.

61. Foner, *Reconstruction*, 496.

62. Simpson, *The Reconstruction Presidents*, 177.

63. Ibid., 175.

64. Ibid.

65. Ibid.

66. Ibid., 188.

67. Ibid., 190.

68. In *US v. Cruitshank*, 1876, The Supreme Court reasoned that the Fourteenth Amendment regulated the behavior of states, not of individuals and businesses.

69. Rayford W. Logan, *The Betrayal of the Negro* (New York: Collier Books, 1968), 25.

70. Ibid.

71. Scaturro, *President Grant Reconsidered*, 101.

72. Foner, *Reconstruction*, 582.

73. Ibid.

74. As he did Ross, John F. Kennedy devoted substantial attention to Lamar, whom the author praised for his support of the gold standard when his constituents were demanding increased silver coinage (see Kennedy, *Profiles in Courage*, chap. 6 and 7). For an assessment of Lamar's role in bringing down the elected government of Mississippi, see Nicholas Lemann, *Redemption: The Last Battle of the Civil War* (New York: Farrar, Straus and Giroux, 2006).

75. Logan, *The Betrayal of the Negro*, 28.

76. Michael Vorenberg, Rutherford B. Hayes, 232.

77. Logan, *The Betrayal of the Negro*, 31.

78. Ibid., 45.

79. Charles Calhoun, *Benjamin Harrison* (New York: Times Books, 2005), 33.

80. Ibid., 56.

81. Ibid., 48

82. Calhoun, *Benjamin Harrison*, 117.

83. Albert Bushnell Hart and Herbert Ronald Ferleger, *Theodore Roosevelt Cyclopedia* (New York: Roosevelt Memorial Association, 1941), 381.

84. Ibid., 322.

85. Edmund Morris, *Theodore Rex* (New York: Random House, 2001), 55.

86. Ibid.

87. Ibid., 56.

88. Willard B. Gatewood Jr., *Theodore Roosevelt and the Art of Controversy: Episodes of the White House Years* (Baton Rouge: Louisiana State University Press, 1970), 112.

89. Ibid., 125.

90. Hart and Ferleger, *Theodore Roosevelt Cyclopedia*, 381.

91. Morris, *Theodore Rex*, 200.

92. Ibid., 471–72, 474, 478–79.

93. Lewis L. Gould, *The Presidency of Theodore Roosevelt* (Lawrence: University Press of Kansas, 1991), 243.

94. Ibid., 239.

95. Morris, *Theodore Rex*, 475.

96. Ibid., 58.

97. "Woodrow Wilson Great Man Says Lloyd-George, Praises Work at Conference, His Ideals and Purposes," *New York Times*, 4 February 1924, 11.

98. William Allen White, *Woodrow Wilson* (Cambridge, Mass.: Riverside, 1924), 43.

99. John Morton Blum, *Woodrow Wilson and the Politics of Morality* (Boston: Little, Brown, 1956), 6.

100. See Woodrow Wilson, *Division and Reunion, 1829–1889* (New York: Collier Books, 1961), and *A History of the American People*, vol. 5 (New York: Harper and Brothers, 1901). Wilson would denounce the second Ku Klux Klan, founded in 1915, which became a major instigator of violence against blacks in the 1920s.

101. Nicholas Patler, *Jim Crow and the Wilson Administration: Protesting Segregation in the Early Twentieth Century* (Boulder: University Press of Colorado, 2004), 77.

102. M. E. Hennessy, "Wit and Humor of Woodrow Wilson . . . He told Darkey Stories as Only a Southerner Could," *Boston Globe*, 4 February 1924, 7.

103. "Race Policy Problem," *Washington Post*, 30 September 1913.

104. Arthur S. Link, *Wilson: The New Freedom* (Princeton: Princeton University Press, 1956), 251.

105. Bruce Bartlett, *Wrong on Race: The Democratic Party's Buried Past* (New York: Palgrave Macmillan, 2008), 103.

106. Stephen R. Fox, *The Guardian of Boston: William Monroe Trotter* (New York: Atheneum, 1971), 172.

107. Link, *Wilson: The New Freedom*, 251.

108. Ibid., 245.

109. "President Resents Negro's Criticism: Refuses to Be Questioned about Racial Segregation in Government Offices," *New York Times*, 13 November 1914.

110. Patler, *Jim Crow and the Wilson Administration*, 40.

111. Link, *Wilson: The New Freedom*, 253.

112. David M. Kennedy, *Over Here: The First World War in American Society* (New York: Oxford University Press, 1980), 281.

113. "Roosevelt Takes Up I.W.W. Outbreaks: Declares Government Should Suppress Lawlessness and Counter-Lawlessness Also, 'Must Hold Scales Even,'" *New York Times*, 17 June 1917.

114. Dyer related to a congressional committee that a U.S. Army Reserve Corps Lieutenant had told him of state militias and local police joining the rioters, of mobs nailing boards over the doors of homes of blacks before setting them afire, and of children being tossed into flames.

115. "Negroes in Protest, March in Fifth Av. 8000 Men, Women, Children Demand That Discrimination and Oppression End," *New York Times*, 29 July 1917, 12.

116. Kendrick A. Clements, *The Presidency of Woodrow Wilson* (Lawrence: University Press of Kansas, 1992), 160.

117. Ibid.

118. Hofstadter, *The American Political Tradition and the Men Who Made It*, 350.

119. D. Kennedy, *Over Here*, 77.

120. Meirion Harries and Susie Harries, *The Last Days of Innocence: America at War, 1917–1918* (New York: Random House, 1997), 363.

121. Fox, *The Guardian of Boston*, chap. 7.

122. See Margaret Macmillan, *Paris 1918* (New York: Random House, 2001), 306–21.

123. Fox, *The Guardian of Boston*, 233–35.

124. Wilson had alienated Irish Americans by not pressing the case for Eire's independence in Paris. Some of their Italian American counterparts took offense when he became embroiled in a tiff with Italian Prime Minister Vittorio Orlando over the latter's demand that Italy be granted the port city of Trieste.

125. John Morton Blum, *Joe Tumulty and the Wilson Era* (New York: Houghton Mifflin, 1951), 51.

126. Link, *Wilson*, 21.

127. Alpheus Thomas Mason, *Brandeis: A Free Man's Life* (Princeton, N.J.: Princeton University Press, 1956), 505.

128. When he won the 1920 Republican presidential nomination, Harding was having a surreptitious affair with the wife of his best friend. Harding's handlers made certain that she and her husband left the country when the campaign got under way. As president, Harding continued his dalliance with Nan Britten, a former campaign aide who claimed to have given birth to his child. In addition to the Teapot Dome scandal, mentioned in chapter 2, a series of others involving graft and featherbedding have taken their toll on Harding's reputation. For additional information, see John W. Dean, *Warren G. Harding* (New York: Times Books, 2004), Frances Russell, *The Shadow of Blooming Grove: Warren G. Harding and His Times* (New York: McGraw-Hill, 1968), and Laton McCartney, *The Teapot Dome Scandal: How Big Oil Bought the Harding White House and Tried to Steal the Country* (New York: Random House, 2008).

129. "Wilson Great Man Says Lloyd-George," 11. See also Dean, *Warren G. Harding*, 70.

130. Fox, *The Guardian of Boston*, 237.

131. Dean, *Warren G. Harding*, 123–25.

132. Ibid., 124.

133. Nathan Miller, *Star Spangled Men: America's Ten Worst Presidents* (New York: Scribner's 1998), 205.

134. Dean, *Warren G. Harding*, 125.

135. "Harding Says Negro Must Have Equality in Political Life," *New York Times*, 27 October 1921, 1.

136. Fox, *The Guardian of Boston*, 249.

137. James Chance, *1912: Roosevelt, Taft, and Debs* (New York: Simon & Schuster, 2004), 275.

138. Ibid., 275.

139. What he actually said to the American Society of Newspaper Editors on January 17, 1925, was, "After all, the chief business of the American people is business. They are profoundly concerned with producing, buying, selling, investing and prospering in the world." See Calvin Coolidge, *Foundations of the Republic* (New York: Scribner's, 1926), 187–88.

140. Calvin Coolidge, *Have Faith in Massachusetts* (New York: Houghton Mifflin, 1919), 9.

141. Robert Sobel, *Coolidge: An American Enigma* (Washington, D.C.: Regenery, 1998), 144.

142. "Opponents of 'Birth of Nation' Win: Amendment to Censor Bill is Passed by Senate," *Boston Post*, 18 May 1915, 1.

143. "Censors Bill Near Bad Snag: Coolidge Vote Stops Reconsideration by Senate: Coolidge Vote Stops Reconsideration by Senate," *Boston Post*, 19 May 1915, 1.

144. Donald R. McCoy, *Calvin Coolidge: The Quite President* (Lawrence: University Press of Kansas, 1988), 125.

145. Calvin Coolidge, "Sixth Annual Message," 4 December 1928, http://www.presidency.ucsb.edu/ws/index.php?pid=29569.

146. David Greenberg, *Calvin Coolidge* (New York: Times Books, 2006), 87.

147. William Monroe Trotter, telegram to Coolidge, 1 August 1927, and Edward Everett Sanders to Winfield Scott, Commissioner of Pensions, U.S. Department of the Interior, 2 August 1927. Both in the Papers of Calvin Coolidge, Library of Congress, Reel 64, item 93.

148. Thomas Sugrue, *Starling of the White House: The Story of the Man Whose Secret Service Detail Guarded Five Presidents from Woodrow Wilson to Franklin D. Roosevelt* (New York: Simon & Schuster, 1946), 39.

149. Calvin Coolidge, speech delivered at the dedication of a government hospital for Colored Veterans of the World War, Tuskegee, Alabama, 12 February 1923, in Calvin Coolidge, *The Price of Freedom* (New York: Charles Scribner's Sons, 1924), 279.

150. Walter White to Calvin Coolidge, 22 August 1923. Papers of Calvin Coolidge, Library of Congress, Reel 63, item 93. (Correspondence on this topic continues on reels 63 and 64.)

151. William Henry Lewis to C. Bascom Slemp, 14 November 1923, Papers of Calvin Coolidge, Library of Congress, Reel 139, item 661.

152. See McCoy, *Calvin Coolidge*, and Greenberg, *Calvin Coolidge*.

153. Robert H. Ferrell, *The Presidency of Calvin Coolidge* (Lawrence: University Press of Kansas, 1998).

154. Calvin Coolidge, "Authority and Religious Liberty," speech delivered 21 September 1924, printed in Coolidge, *Foundations of the Republic*, 103.

155. Coolidge, *Foundations of the Republic*, 71–72.

156. *Tulsa World*, 26 September 1923, 1.

157. Calvin Coolidge, "Tolerance and Liberalism," speech delivered 6 October 1925, printed in *Foundations of the Republic*, 300.

158. John M. Barry, *Rising Tide: The Great Mississippi Flood of 1927 and How It Changed America* (New York: Simon & Schuster, 1997), 261, and Amity Shlaes, *The Forgotten Man: A New History of the Great Depression* (New York: HarperCollins, 2007).

159. Barry, *Rising Tide*, 266.

160. Donald J. Lisio, *Hoover, Blacks, and Lily-Whites: A Study in Southern Strategies* (Chapel Hill: University of North Carolina Press, 1985), 30.

161. Henry Gantt, quoted in Barry, *Rising Tide*, 266.

162. Ibid., 262.

163. For a fuller account of these atrocities, see Barry, *Rising Tide*.

164. Gilbert Jones, *Freedom's Sword: The NAACP and the Struggle against Racism in America, 1909 to 1969* (New York: Routledge, 2005), 120.

165. Shlaes, *The Forgotten Man.*

166. John F. Kennedy, "Inaugural Address," 20 January 1961. http://www.american rhetoric.com/speeches/jfkinaugural.htm.

167. For a recapitulation of how federal funds were used to perpetuate racial discrimination, see Ira Katznelson, *When Affirmative Action Was White: An Untold History of Racial Inequality in Twentieth-Century America* (New York: W. W. Norton, 2005).

168. Greg Robinson, *By Order of the President: FDR and the Internment of Japanese Americans* (Cambridge: Harvard University Press, 2001).

169. For a fuller discussion of this debate, see Michael Beschloss, *The Conquerors: Roosevelt, Truman and the Destruction of Hitler's Germany, 1941–1945* (New York: Simon & Schuster, 2002).

170. For critical appraisals of how Roosevelt's administration performed in this regard, see Arthur D. Morse, *While Six Million Died: A Chronicle of American Apathy* (New York: Overlook Press, 1998), and David S. Wyman, *The Abandonment of the Jews: America and the Holocaust, 1941–1945* (New York: The New Press, 1998). For more positive appraisals, see Robert N. Rosen, *Saving the Jews: Franklin D. Roosevelt and the Holocaust* (New York: Thunder's Mouth Press, 2006), and William J. Vanden Heuvel, "FDR and the Holocaust," *American Heritage* (July–August 1999). For a summary of debates that ensued among FDR's advisers, see Beschloss, *The Conquerors.*

171. See Raphael Medoff and Cindy Bittinger "How Anne Frank Almost Got to America," *Jewish Tribune*, 29 March 2006, 6.

172. John McCain with Mark Salter, *Hard Call: Great Decisions and the Extraordinary People Who Made Them* (New York: Twelve, 2007), 309.

173. For a fuller account of Truman's civil rights record, see Michael R. Gardner, *Harry Truman and Civil Rights: Moral Courage and Political Risks* (Carbondale: Southern Illinois University Press, 2002).

174. For a sampling of these, see Michael Beschloss, *Presidential Courage: Brave Leaders and How They Changed America, 1789–1989* (New York: Simon & Schuster, 2007), chap. 25–28.

175. James David Barber, *The Presidential Character: Predicting Performance in the White House* (Englewood Cliffs, N.J.: Prentice Hall, 1972), 258.

176. McCain and Salter, *Hard Call*, 314.

177. Harry S Truman, *Years of Trial and Hope* (New York: Doubleday, 1956), 183.

178. McCain and Salter, *Hard Call*, 313.

179. For an account of the Truman-Jacobson friendship, see Beschloss, *Presidential Courage*, chap. 25–28.

180. Dwight D. Eisenhower, *Waging Peace* (New York: Doubleday, 1965), 175.

181. Ibid., 250.

182. For a fuller account, see David Nichols, *A Matter of Justice: Eisenhower and the Beginnings of the Civil Rights Revolution* (New York: Simon & Schuster, 2007.)

183. David L. Stebenne, "Harry S Truman," *The Reader's Companion to the American Presidency*, ed. Alan Brinkley and Davis Dyer (New York: Houghton Mifflin, 2000), 414.

184. See Rowland Evans and Robert Novak, *Lyndon B. Johnson and the Exercise of Power: A Political Biography* (New York: New American Library, 1966), chap. 7, and

Robert A. Caro, *The Years of Lyndon Johnson: Master of the Senate* (New York: Knopf, 2002).

185. This may be changing. See Nichols, *A Matter of Justice.*

186. Eisenhower, *Waging Peace*, 156.

187. Nichols, *A Matter of Peace*, 161.

188. Ibid., 159. Among those he singled out were Albert Gore Sr., John F. Kennedy, Frank Church, Mike Mansfield, and Wayne Morse. Johnson had pulled them into his orbit through previous measures he had guided through that assisted them politically in their states. See Evans and Novak, *Lyndon Johnson and the Exercise of Power*, chap. 7.

189. Taylor Branch, *Parting the Waters: America in the King Years, 1954–63* (New York: Simon & Schuster, 1989), 220–22. For an assessment of Johnson's role in passing the civil rights bill of 1957, see Evans and Novak, *Lyndon B. Johnson and the Exercise of Power*, chap. 7, and Caro, *The Years of Lyndon Johnson.*

190. Theodore C. Sorensen, *Kennedy* (New York: Harper & Row, 1965), 471.

191. James N. Giglio, *The Presidency of John F. Kennedy* (Lawrence: University Press of Kansas, 1991), 160.

192. Ibid., chap. 7.

193. John F. Kennedy, "Report to the American People on Civil Rights," 11 June 1963, http://www.jfklibrary.org/.

194. Giglio, *The Presidency of John F. Kennedy*, 184.

195. Kenneth W. Starr, "Richard Milhaus Nixon," in *Presidential Leadership: Rating the Best and the Worst in the White House*, ed. James Taranto and Leonard Leo (New York: Wall Street Journal Books, 2004), 178–82.

196. Elizabeth Drew, *Richard M. Nixon* (New York: Times Books, 2007), 43.

197. Lou Cannon, "Reagan's Southern Stumble," *New York Times*, 18 November 2007.

198. Lou Cannon, *President Reagan: The Role of a Lifetime* (New York: Simon & Schuster, 1991,) 208. Cannon points out that Reagan was only four years old when the film was released. It made, however, several subsequent reappearances at local theaters throughout the 1910s, 1920s, and 1930s.

199. Ronald Reagan, *Ronald Reagan: An American Life, the Autobiography* (New York: Simon & Schuster, 1990), 52.

200. Cannon, *President Reagan*, 520.

201. June Masuto Goto, letter to President Ronald Reagan with enclosures, 19 December 1997, ID544222, Ronald Reagan Presidential Library. See also, *Pacific Citizen*, 15 December 1945.

202. See Alvin S. Felzenberg, *Governor Tom Kean: From the New Jersey Statehouse to the 9-11 Commission* (New Brunswick: Rutgers University Press, 2005), 309–11.

203. Remarks of President Ronald Reagan on signing the bill providing restitution for the wartime internment of Japanese-American citizens, 10 August 1988, and Julie Johnson, "President Signs Law to Redress Wartime Wrong: Former Internees to Get Payment and Apology," *New York Times*, 11 August 1988, A16.

204. Sheila Graham, *Confessions of a Hollywood Columnist* (New York: Bantam Books, 1970), 263. The club in question was the Lakeside Country Club in Northern Hollywood. Reagan subsequently joined the Hillside Club in West Los Angeles.

205. In these states, the federal government owned at least 30 percent of the land, a considerably larger share than in other regions. For decades, westerners had been able to use federal multiple-use lands under the jurisdiction of the Bureau of Land Management for grazing animals or for mining minerals. Westerners were concerned that new federal environmental regulations were unfairly restricting their access to these lands. They began the Sagebrush Rebellion to press their concerns on Congress and the media.

206. Cannon, *President Reagan*, 520.

207. Cannon, "Reagan's Southern Stumble."

208. Cannon, *President Reagan*, 521–23.

209. Lou Cannon, *Reagan* (New York: Putnam, 1982), 270.

210. Ronald Reagan, remarks at a commemorative ceremony at Bergen-Belsen concentration camp in the Federal Republic of Germany, 5 May 1985, http://www.reagan.utexas.edu/archives/speeches/1985/50585a.htm.

CHAPTER 7

1. Richard Brookhiser, *Founding Father: Rediscovering George Washington* (New York: The Free Press, 1996), 101.

2. R. B. Bernstein, *Thomas Jefferson* (New York: Oxford University Press, 2003), 103.

3. Michael Beschloss, *Presidential Courage: Brave Leaders and How They Changed America, 1789–1989* (New York: Simon & Schuster, 2007), 7.

4. Brookhiser, *Founding Father*, 100.

5. Richard Brookhiser, *Alexander Hamilton: American* (New York: Touchstone, 1999), 3.

6. Ibid., 43.

7. Ibid., 62.

8. Ronald P. Formisano, "James Monroe," in *The Reader's Companion to the American Presidency*, ed. Alan Brinkley and Davis Dyer (New York: Houghton Mifflin, 2000), 74.

9. Most of the 1812 hawks saw war with Britain as a means of acquiring Canada. The impressments issue, however, was the rationale on the minds of most of the public and perhaps Madison.

10. The United States claimed that the northern boundary of the Oregon Territory west of the Continental Divide was the 54°40' north parallel. The United Kingdom claimed that the southern boundary of its Columbia Territory was the Columbia River. The Anglo-American Convention of 1818 had settled on the 49° north parallel as the boundary between the United States and what would become Canada east of the Continental Divide. The Oregon Treaty, which the Senate ratified on June 18, 1848, extended the boundary along this parallel to the Strait of Juan de Fuca.

11. David Herbert Donald, *Lincoln* (New York: Simon & Schuster), 302–3.

12. Roy Jenkins, *Truman* (New York: Harper & Row, 1986), 61.

13. Ibid., 62.

14. Ibid., 49.

15. Richard E. Neustadt, *Presidential Power* (New York: The Free Press, 1990), 146–47.

16. Ibid.

17. Jenkins, *Truman*, 67.

18. Conservative estimates put the number of expected American casualties during such an invasion at 500,000. The extent of the resistance the Japanese displayed at Okinawa, the Japanese government's call for resistance to the last individual should foreign troops set foot on the home islands, and its relentless opposition to unconditional surrender have led most who have studied Truman's action to share his assessment of the situation he faced as he made his momentous decision.

19. Jenkins, *Truman*, 72.

20. Ibid., 101.

21. Late in the Second World War, tensions arose between Roosevelt and Churchill over Britain's determination to retain its Asian colonies. The president expressed support for an independent India, but he also seemed to support allowing China, then under the control of Chiang Kai-shek, to exercise control of Hong Kong.

22. David M. Oshinsky, "Harry S Truman," in *The Reader's Companion to the American Presidency*, ed. Alan Brinkley and Davis Dyer (New York: Houghton Mifflin, 2000), 394.

23. James David Barber, *The Presidential Character* (Englewood Cliffs, N.J.: Prentice Hall, 1972), 280–81.

24. Neustadt, *Presidential Power*, 43.

25. Greg Behrman, *The Most Noble Adventure: The Marshall Plan and the Time When America Helped Save Europe* (New York: The Free Press, 2007), 252.

26. Truman was following a precedent himself, one that James K. Polk set in 1846 when he asked Congress to acknowledge that a state of war between the United States and Mexico already existed. Lyndon Johnson did likewise when he asked Congress to approve the Gulf of Tonkin Resolution, granting him the power to repel supposed North Vietnamese attacks on American military personnel with force. The two presidents Bush, reminiscent of Truman's actions in 1950, asked Congress for the power to enforce United Nations decrees.

27. The U.N. Security Council resolution Truman went to war to enforce had passed primarily because Stalin had ordered Soviet diplomats to boycott the session at which the resolution was considered. He took this action to protest the United Nations' refusal to admit as a member the People's Republic of China, the communist government Mao Zedong established on the Chinese mainland after his forces defeated those of Chiang Kai-shek in a civil war in 1949. While in control of the island of Formosa, Chiang's government continued to fill China's seat on the Security Council.

28. See John Lewis Gaddis, *Strategies of Containment: A Critical Appraisal of American National Security Policy During the Cold War*, rev. ed. (New York: Oxford University Press, 2005).

29. Neustadt, *Presidential Power*, 103–22.

30. Oshinsky, "Harry S Truman," 401.

31. Ironically, Truman's preoccupation with Europe may have set the United States on a course toward future conflicts in Asia. For instance, he was less willing than was Roosevelt to press European powers to grant independence to their Asian colonies. Then again, Roosevelt had not had to deal with a world perceived to be dividing into two spheres of influence.

32. James MacGregor Burns, *John Kennedy: A Political Profile* (New York: Harcourt, Brace, 1960), 55–56.

33. "What our young had saved, our diplomats and our President had frittered away," he said. See Hugh Brogan, *Kennedy* (Harlow, U.K.: Longman, 1996), 9.

34. John F. Kennedy, *The Strategy of Peace*, ed. Allan Nevins, (New York: Harper & Row, 1960), 65–81.

35. Brogan, *Kennedy*, 58–59.

36. Giglio, *The Presidency of John F. Kennedy*, 49.

37. Ibid., 58.

38. Theodore C. Sorenson, *Kennedy* (New York: Bantam, 1965), 346.

39. Arthur M. Schlesinger Jr., *A Thousand Days: John F. Kennedy in the White House* (Boston: Houghton Mifflin, 1965), 359.

40. Herbert S. Parmet, *JFK: The Presidency of John F. Kennedy* (New York: Dial, 1983), 176–77.

41. Ibid., 78.

42. Michael Beschloss, *The Crisis Years: Kennedy and Khruschev, 1960–1963* (New York: Edward Burlingame Books, 1991), 278.

43. Kennedy cut off relations with one reported mistress after the FBI director told him that the woman was simultaneously involved with Giancana. Robert Kennedy, upon learning that another of Kennedy's amorous interests, Ellen Romesch, had ties to the KGB, ordered the woman deported to her native East Germany. For additional details on these episodes, see Giglio, 148–49, 267–70; and Michael Beschloss, *Crisis Years*.

44. Giglio, *The Presidency of John F. Kennedy*, 197.

45. Brogan, *Kennedy*, 137.

46. Giglio, *The Presidency of John F. Kennedy*, 198.

47. See John F. Kennedy, "Cuban Missile Crisis Address to the Nation," 22 October 1962, http://www.americanrhetoric.com/speeches/jfkcubanmissilecrisis.html.

48. John F. Kennedy, commencement address at American University, 10 June 1963, http://www.american.edu/media/speeches/Kennedy.htm.

CHAPTER 8

1. Theodore C. Sorensen, *Kennedy* (New York: Harper & Row, 1965), 442–43, 487.

2. In the words of Clinton's second chief of staff, Leon Pannetta, "Bill Clinton was very smart and not very organized." See Mark Leibovich, "A No-Nonsense Style Honed as Advocate and First Lady," *New York Times*, 26 October 2007, 1.

3. He used those words when articulating how his brand of conservatism differed from that of other Republicans, who, in his view, sought to submerge the differences between the two parties. In the 1990s, the latter process became known as "triangulation."

4. Hugh Brogan, *Kennedy* (Harlow, U.K.: Longman, 1996).

5. Reagan's first chief of staff, James Baker, managed Gerald R. Ford's primary campaign against Reagan in 1976 and George H. W. Bush's in 1980. His third chief of staff, Howard Baker, had competed against him for the 1980 presidential nomination; while Senate majority leader Baker had criticized Reagan at a time when he appeared the most vulnerable politically. After Reagan appeared inattentive and not in command in his first

debate with Walter Mondale, Baker, then in the Senate, said that "what you saw in the debate was what you see in Cabinet meetings." See Chris Matthews, *Hardball* (New York: The Free Press, 1988), 157. But when the time came to demonstrate that Reagan was both in command and innocent of charges that he had willingly diverted arms for hostages and authorized the transfer of funds to Nicaraguan "Contras" ("freedom fighters"), Reagan retained Baker to do precisely that.

6. Had Wilson been a lifelong politician, Lloyd-George argued, the professor-turned-president might have been better able to overlook attacks and more able to give up personal animosity. See "Europe Is Stirred by Wilson's Death: Lloyd-George Calls Him 'Glorious Failure Who Sacrificed His Life for His Ideal,'" *New York Times*, 4 February 1924, 1, and "Wilson Great Man Says Lloyd-George . . . Calls Animosities Tragedy of His Life," *Boston Globe*, 4 February 1924, 11.

AFTERWORD

1. Jacob Weisberg, *The Bush Tragedy* (New York: Random House, 2008), 236.

2. See Benjamin Wittes and Jack Goldsmith, "Will Obama Follow Bush or FDR?" *Washington Post*, 29 June 2009.

3. Bush would have no quarrel with Obama's insistence that he would resort to signing statements only when it was "appropriate" to discharging his constitutional duties. See Michael D. Shear, "Obama Pledges to Limit Use of Signing Statements," *Washington Post*, 10 March 2009; and Charles Savage, "Obama Says He Can Ignore Some Parts of Spending Bills," *New York Times*, 12 March 2009.

4. Weisberg, *The Bush Tragedy*, 38.

5. Ibid., 39.

6. Bill Minutaglio, *First Son: George W. Bush and the Bush Family Dynasty* (New York: Three Rivers Press, 1999), 110.

7. Weisberg, *The Bush Tragedy*, 45.

8. Ibid., 47.

9. Ibid., 50.

10. Ibid., 60. With Bush at its helm, the Rangers traded Sammy Sosa to the Chicago White Sox in exchange for Harold Baines.

11. Barton Gellman, *Angler: The Cheney Vice Presidency* (New York: Penguin, 2008), 263.

12. Ibid., 79.

13. Ibid.

14. Ibid., 63.

15. Sister Helen Prejean, "Death in Texas," *New York Review of Books*, 13 January 2005.

16. George Lardner Jr., "Begging Bush's Pardon Power," *New York Times*, 4 February 2008.

17. Ibid., 96.

18. Ibid., 87.

19. Ibid., 97.

20. Ibid., 107.

21. Ibid., 67.

22. John F. Harris, "Bush's Hispanic Vote Dissected," *Washington Post*, 26 December 2004.

23. George W. Bush, second inaugural address, 20 January 2005.

24. See Charles Krauthammer, "Charlie Gibson's Gaffe," *Washington Post*, 13 September 2008; and Weisberg, *The Bush Tragedy*, chap. 6.

25. President George W. Bush, speech to the American Enterprise Institute, 27 February 2003.

26. Found at http://uselectionatlas.org/RESULTS/index.html.

27. She returned during his second term as deputy secretary of state for public diplomacy.

28. See Shirley Ann Warshaw, *The Co-presidency of Bush and Cheney* (Stanford: Stanford University Press, 2009).

29. Gellman, *Angler*, 33.

30. Forty years earlier, Vice President Lyndon B. Johnson, who was also the outgoing Senate Democratic majority leader, hoped to preside over the Democratic Senate caucus. Picking up on colleagues' distaste for allowing a member of the executive branch to oversee or observe their deliberations, Johnson absented himself, abandoning hopes he once had of serving as JFK's "point man" on Capitol Hill. Robert Dallek, *Flawed Giant*, 8.

31. Gellman, *Angler*, 99.

32. For a fuller discussion of the "unitary executive" principle, see ibid., 97–100; and Jack Goldsmith, *The Terror Presidency: Law and Judgment Inside the Bush Administration* (New York: Norton, 2007).

33. In Federalist Paper No. 70, Hamilton had made the case against a plural executive, not against legislative or judicial oversight of a single executive.

34. It granted the president the final authority to determine whether standards for the humane treatment of detainees had been violated and prohibited prosecution of government personnel's actions committed in advance of the statute's passage.

35. See Lincoln's message to Congress, 4 July 1861.

36. Interview of the vice president with Martha Raddatz, ABC News, 19 March 2008.

37. Gellman, *Angler*, 145.

38. Ibid., chap. 12.

39. Ibid., 338.

40. At the intervention of Senator Edward Kennedy, more than $1 billion would be tacked on to Pentagon budgets for this purpose between 2003 and 2005.

41. Weisberg, *The Bush Tragedy*, 211.

42. The last publicly available projections of future federal budget surpluses issued by the Congressional Budget Office and the Office of Management and Budget before President Bush took office were $5.6 trillion over fiscal years 2002–2011 and $2.9 trillion over fiscal years 2001–2010, respectively. U.S. Congress, Congressional Budget Office, *The Budget and Economic Outlook: Fiscal Years 2002–2011* (January 2001), 2, found at http://www.cbo.gov/ftpdocs/27xx/doc2727/entire-report.pdf; Executive Office of the

President, Office of Management and Budget, *Mid-Session Review: Budget of the United States Government, Fiscal Year 2001* (26 June 2000), 4, found at http://www.gpo access.gov/usbudget/fy01/pdf/msr.pdf.

43. Gellman, *Angler*. Chapters 3 and 10.

44. Boards of Trustees of the Federal Hospital Insurance and Federal Supplementary Medical Insurance Trust Funds, *2009 Annual Report of the Boards of Trustees of the Federal Hospital Insurance and Federal Supplementary Medical Insurance Trust Funds* (12 May 2009), 3, found at http://www.cms.hhs.gov/reportstrustfunds/downloads/tr2009.pdf; U.S. Congress, Congressional Budget Office, *The Long-Term Budget Outlook* (June 2009), 1, found at http://www.cbo.gov/ftpdocs/102xx/doc10297/06-25-LT BO.pdf.

45. John B. Taylor, "Housing and Monetary Policy," presentation to Jackson Hole Conference (September 2007), found at http://www.stanford.edu/~johntayl/Housing %20and%20Monetary%20Policy-Taylor-Jackson%20Hole%202007.pdf.

46. Gellman, *Angler*, 272.

47. Ibid., 272–74.

48. U.S. Department of Housing and Urban Development, *Urban Policy Brief* (August 1995), 1, found at http://www.huduser.org/publications/txt/hdbrf2.txt.

49. See, generally, Robert P. O'Quinn, "The U.S. Housing Bubble and the Global Financial Crisis: Housing and Housing-Related Finance," prepared for the U.S. Congress, Joint Economic Committee (May 2008), 13–14, found at http://www.house.gov/jec/news/Housing%20Bubble%20study.pdf; and HUD Regulations found at http://www.novoco.com/low_income_housing/resource_files/hud_data/GSEs.pdf.

50. Jo Becker, Sheryl Bay Stolberg, and Stephen Labaton, "Bush Drive for Home Ownership Fueled Housing Bubble," *Washington Post*, 21 December 2008.

51. Ibid.

52. Eli Lake, "Clinton Spars with Petraeus on Credibility," *New York Sun*, 12 September 2007.

INDEX